PUTTING IT ON

PUTTING IT ON

THE WEST END THEATRE OF MICHAEL CODRON

Michael Codron
and
Alan Strachan

Duckworth Overlook

First published in the UK and in the US in 2010 by
Duckworth Overlook

LONDON
90-93 Cowcross Street
London EC1M 6BF
info@duckworth-publishers.co.uk
www.ducknet.co.uk

NEW YORK
141 Wooster Street
New York, NY 10012
for bulk or special sales contact sales@overlookny.com

A catalogue record for this book is available
from the British Library

ISBN 978 0 7156 3944 3 (UK)
ISBN 978 1 59020 483 2 (US)

Typeset by Ray Davies
Printed and bound in the UK by
the MPG Books Group

CONTENTS

To The Memory of David.
Of course.

FOREWORD

As good a point as any to begin an account of years spent in and around theatres would be to recount my last visit to what is in effect my local neighbourhood theatre, the Ellen Terry Theatre in Smallhythe, Kent, the county where I have lived blissfully for over forty years.

The theatre is adjacent to the timber, thatched cottage, now a museum, where Ellen Terry lived and from which she was briefly brought out of retirement by Henry Irving to bolster a failing London Season. It is a converted barn, cosy and exquisitely uncomfortable but attracts a loyal following. The museum itself is preserved with great love and in addition to the possessions and costumes worn by Ellen Terry, and some bequests from her kin John Gielgud, surprisingly has a distressed wall map of the London Underground of the 1930s with each West End theatre marked. Some have gone, others renamed or re-sited but most remain. In that medieval setting it is a pleasing anachronism to which I'm always drawn on any visit. But back to that visit and its springboard.

Two lunch guests had wondered what to do to spend a hot Sunday afternoon and I suggested to Jenny Topper and Wendy Wasserstein that we visit the Ellen Terry Theatre. Jenny cannot fail to appear in later entries; she ran Hampstead Theatre on which Board I had been a member for years and has been my friend for all those years; Wendy Wasserstein had written a New York success, *The Sisters Rosensweig*, the English version of which I was currently producing. They wandered round the house but I stayed at the entrance where I was greeted by the Curator and his wife; a charming couple who bring with them a whiff of the boards in their speech and manner.

'This isn't your first visit is it?' I was asked.

'No, many many times.'

'Haven't you a theatrical connection?'

Before I could reply, he had remembered.

'You're Michael Codron, aren't you? What are you putting on?'

'He's putting on weight,' his wife volunteered, again before I could reply. 'That's why I didn't recognise him.'

Those extra pounds, as well as plays every year since 1956 are, indeed what I have been putting on. Here goes.

MICHAEL CODRON

I gratefully add my thanks to Alan Strachan without whose patience and scholarly research I wouldn't have remembered many of the things he has unearthed, and to my girls Sandi and Ali, who have typed every darn word of them.

NOTE

This book was first suggested two years ago. Previously Michael Codron had been approached more than once to write his autobiography – many friends and colleagues had also suggested he do so in order to record an extraordinary theatrical career – but he did not feel able to do this. Nor did he want a 'ghost-written' book. Having seen so many of his productions, and also having had a strong personal tie as a director for him over various productions since the 1970s, it seemed an intriguing further collaboration for me to work with him on the story of his career. Over eighteen months subsequently there were many meetings over a tape-recorder and I was also helped by access to the Michael Codron Ltd Archives in the Aldwych Theatre. These cover in some detail his productions since his offices moved to the Aldwych in 1981. The Theatre Museum, still scandalously under funded and with a much scaled-down operation now based at the Victoria and Albert Museum, has records of box-office receipts and some photographic material, also useful. Sadly archives for the years 1956-81, covering a busy period including his collaborations with Harold Pinter, Joe Orton, John Mortimer and others, have disappeared, possibly during the move. No amount of investigation to date has managed to trace them, disappointingly for future researchers too.

The narrative is mine but I have attempted to keep Michael's voice to the fore as much as possible.

A list of acknowledgements appears later in the book, but prominent acknowledgement of – and thanks to – Sandi Pescod and Alison Tucker at the Codron office, for always-willing help and, especially, final preparation of the text, is especially necessary.

Thanks are also due for the patience of partners Peter Hulstrom and Jennifer Piercey.

ALAN STRACHAN

AT RISE ...

The *ne plus ultra* of the theatrical producer of popular imagination must be Max Bialystock, the venal, finagling figure created by Mel Brooks in *The Producers* on film and on stage, whose protégé-convert Leo Bloom proclaims:

> I wanna be a producer,
> Sport a top hat and a cane,
> I wanna be a producer,
> And drive those chorus girls insane!

The conventional notion of the producer has a seductive Bialystock aura – a somewhat large-scale, flamboyant figure definitely, cigar smoking possibly, sitting behind an impressive desk with banks of telephones and piles of scripts, often Jewish, tough but sentimental, located ideally in premises inside a theatre or at least in the theatre districts of Broadway or Shaftesbury Avenue in London's West End, with office walls crowded with framed posters of past productions and glossy, lovingly signed photographs of glamorous stars.

Some of the great producers of the past have lived up to most of this image – Florenz Ziegfeld, David Belasco, Jed Harris, Charles Frohman or David Merrick on Broadway, or Charles B. Cochran, Harold Fielding (a showman-producer who went under with a lavish tribute musical to his idol Ziegfeld) and Henry Sherek in London's West End – often cultivating their own myths (Merrick, a genuine *monstre sacré* – 'The Abominable Showman' – working from an office painted in his trademark bright red, the 'Merrick Red' featured on his shows' posters, in New York's Imperial Theatre, or Hugh Beaumont of the H.M. Tennent firm, which dominated the West End for decades, wreathed in cigarette smoke and mystery up in his eyrie in the dome of Shaftesbury Avenue's Globe – now Gielgud – Theatre).

Today the reality is very different and decidedly less colourful, with even fedoras and astrakhan coats endangered species, let alone top hats and canes. Whereas for years a redoubtable figure like Broadway's Cheryl Crawford was an exception, producers – sometimes still called impresarios or theatrical managers – are now often female; one of the most successful, certainly in financial terms, of recent times has been Judy Craymer who steered the Abba musical *Mamma Mia!* from the West End to international success. Moreover, with ever-rising production costs for musicals and plays alike, fewer producers can afford the luxury of working solo.

For decades from the late 1950s, the posters for a high percentage of the most adventurous plays in the commercial sector of London's West End have carried the simple billing (in much smaller typeface) above the names of stars, author and the title of the play: 'Michael Codron presents'. Later in his career there would be separate billing as 'Associate Producer' for his long-time personal and business partner David Sutton, after whose retirement in 1996 the billing occasionally carried the Codron name in alliance with a co-producer or producers.

The firm of Michael Codron Ltd has been responsible for the London – and occasionally New York – commercial original productions of plays by most of the leading British playwrights of the era since 1956 (only rarely did the company present revivals or American or European plays). They are remarkable for both their quality and their range; the authors most associated with the Codron name include Alan Ayckbourn, Alan Bennett, Michael Frayn, Simon Gray, Christopher Hampton, David Hare, Frank Marcus, John Mortimer, Joe Orton, Harold Pinter, Willy Russell and Tom Stoppard. The productions' range covers revue and popular comedy – work from Peter Cook, Rowan Atkinson, Joyce Grenfell, Victoria Wood, Philip King, Ray Cooney and Terry Johnson – alongside the penetrating work from his major dramatists and through to a younger generation of writers including Patrick Marber, Joe Penhall and Moira Buffini. These have used virtually every major director of the period, from Peter Hall, William Gaskill, John Dexter, Peter Wood, Lindsay Anderson and Michael Blakemore through to the generation of Richard Eyre and Trevor Nunn and then to Sam Mendes, Roger Michell or Fiona Buffini. Similarly the designers and lighting designers attached to Codron productions – the name soon became a benchmark for a consistently high and often innovative standard of physical production values – represent the outstanding talent of the time, often spotted early in their careers (Tony Walton, Timothy O'Brien, Alan Tagg, Mark Thompson included). Few major acting names are missing from Codron's posters. From the knights and senior greats of John Gielgud, Alec Guinness, Michael Redgrave, Ralph Richardson, Paul Scofield, Robert Stephens and Donald Sinden, to a later generation (Michael Gambon, Alan Bates, Tom Courtenay, Ian McKellen,

1. 'The wall of shame' part of the Aldwych Office Staircase.

Antony Sher) with a similarly distinguished list of Dames (Eileen Atkins, Judi Dench, Wendy Hiller, Celia Johnson, Diana Rigg, Helen Mirren, Maggie Smith, Joan Plowright) and major names including Glenda Jackson, Margaret Leighton, Penelope Keith, Felicity Kendal, Patricia Routledge, Penelope Wilton, Maureen Lipman and Alison Steadman, the cream of British acting talent featured regularly in Michael Codron productions.

If being a producer involved simply shopping for top talent then anyone with the money could do it, but the reality is infinitely more complex. The process of putting together a commercial theatre production involves, at base, its financing – raising the capital to launch the production and budgeting for its continuing run. A very few producers might use their own money exclusively while others rely partly or entirely on investors (backers or sometimes 'angels') – finding them, and then keeping them, is one of the toughest aspects of the job. Over the years Codron productions attracted a core of loyal, long-term investors; unusually, the firm's system involved its backers in all productions without the option to pick and choose (the box office record was such that backers were mostly happy with this arrangement). The usual agreement is that the producer's only financial reward for putting all the elements of a production together, until such time after opening when the capital or launch cost of the production has been recouped from box office takings each week over an agreed 'break figure' (costs of weekly theatre rental, salaries, royalties, advertising, etc.), remains only a weekly management fee covering contracting creative personnel, casting, rehearsal arrangements, the continuing administration of the production, handling wages, insurance, publicity, etc. This fee usually begins to be paid during the immediate run-up to rehearsals and through to the opening and earlier run until recoupment, after which the production's profit is divided between producer and backers (usually 50/50, occasionally 40/60). When the Codron office opened in 1956 a medium-sized cast, one-set play might be capitalised at around £2-2,500 with the management fee around £20 per week. If successful it might recoup within a few weeks of opening, especially if it had already enjoyed a successful pre-London tour, usually the system in those pre-preview days. Today even a play on a modest scale launched directly into the commercial sector would be budgeted at a minimum £400,000 (correspondingly the management fee would be around £2,500-£3,000), one reason why so few plays now open straight into the West End, with many instead originating in the subsidised London or regional houses, with most physical production costs already paid for an often critically approved play prior to re-opening in London. Even a medium-sized play – unless an immediate capacity hit – might be lucky today to recoup significantly before six months of the run. In the glory days for the straight play in the West End in the 1970s and 1980s it was still possible to make major financial killings from a success – Frayn's *Noises Off* was the Codron office's prime example – coining significant profits for producer and backers alike, with residual profits rolling in from movie sales, Broadway and overseas productions and repertory and amateur rights. With rare exceptions such as producer David Pugh's handling of Yasmina Reza's three-hander *Art* with constant attractive cast changes, each for limited runs, helping establish it as an epic runner, there have been far fewer such instances in recent times.

Financial acumen and an eagle eye for the fine print when negotiating deals with agents for dramatists, actors and designers or with theatre owners, go only so far to define a good producer. The real, priceless gift is more unquantifiable, an almost alchemical sense of gauging a script (good relationships with literary agents help here) and then of how to put together the right ingredients, how to 'matchmake' the play with the right director and designer and then collaboratively to select the best combination of actors, finally negotiating the most suitable theatre for the project (some middle-sized West End theatres – the Apollo, Wyndham's, the Criterion – seem perfect for comedy in particular). Casting a play is much more difficult today when the virtual demise of the repertory theatre system has created a generation of younger actors for whom the theatre is often decidedly a secondary preference to a television or screen career, while established actors, including those few with genuine box office 'muscle', are now more reluctant to commit to anything other than limited-season West End runs, which still generally prohibit the ability to take on other work that is possible within the subsidised theatre's repertoire system. Actors' agents, similarly keen on the usually greater percentage of income for their businesses from clients' screen work, tend to be less interested, at times even positively discouraging stage work, compared with a previous era of agents mostly with a theatre-based background (many of them ex-actors) in developing clients' longer-term careers.

Putting together a production also involves collaboration on vital related areas such as publicity strategies and the selection of advertising images and poster designs. In the immediate post-war years this involved predominantly a typographical approach; for most of its long reign through the 1940s into the 1960s as London's leading commercial management, the H.M. Tennent firm under Hugh Beaumont rarely deviated from posters in its standard black and red lettering on a white background without any graphic imagery (not essentially much different from Victorian playbills) but gradually, as advertising and later marketing became increasingly crucial to the commercial theatre, the whole question of a production's defining image gathered momentum. The Codron office was in the vanguard of this – one of the most delightful theatre posters of the 1950s was that for his production of Sandy Wilson's musical adapted from Ronald Firbank's *Valmouth*, created by the show's designer Tony Walton at Michael's suggestion, evoking all the hothouse mischief of the Firbank/Wilson style. Later, in the 1960s and 1970s the Codron posters mostly were the work of a stylish, clever designer, Yves Simard – his early Ayckbourn posters, the Christmas-themed *Absurd Person Singular* and Bayeux-inspired *Norman Conquests* included, were especially witty – before bringing on board Michael Mayhew (also responsible for many memorable National Theatre poster designs) and then the large advertising and marketing firm of Dewynters (responsible for early iconic images such as those haunting eyes for *Cats* or the urchin-child of *Les Miserables* for Cameron Mackintosh). The Codron office was also in the vanguard of change in production photography, moving from the posed and air-brushed Angus McBean style adored by H.M. Tennent and most established managements in the 1950s, towards a more vibrant immediacy.

For many years John Haynes, who also regularly took the photographs for the Royal Court, produced invariably striking work for Codron productions, arrestingly displayed outside the theatre; gradually from the 1990s onwards colour photography came to predominate.

Theatre press publicity was also barely understood when Michael Codron Ltd began. A doyenne such as Vivienne Byerley, Press Representative of H.M. Tennent for years, seemingly almost went out of her way to avoid a show gathering too much coverage beyond sending out an all-purpose press release announcing a production's details, casting and opening date and then sitting back until the first night and the distribution of critics' press night tickets, all very *de haut en bas*. The actor–dramatist Emlyn Williams said that all the 1950s fuss about the arrest of John Gielgud (H.M. Tennent's regular leading star) for importuning in a Westminster lavatory could easily have been avoided: 'If he'd told Vivienne Byerley right away nobody would ever have known a thing about it.'

There were a few respected independent freelance Press Representatives around at the time – Frank Rainbow or the splendidly named Torrington Douglas among them – but the 1960s saw the birth of a new approach, much more press friendly (especially with the emergence of newspapers' colour supplements) and often finding publicity opportunities in new areas such as fashion shoots or guest newspaper columns. The Codron office for many years used Genista Streeten and then Lynne Kirwin, both informed and inventive, regularly thinking up pre-opening original angles for publicising a production, a writer or an actor. This area would become just as vital for producers in the post-production period when a play might be struggling to build an audience after opening to mixed reviews or without the insurance of a major box office name. The days have long gone when a producer could simply open a play and then, given some positive reviews and a fair box office wind, just take out a few newspaper ads with some tempting critical quotes and then sit back and count the money. As much effort – in publicity and marketing – has to go into a production after the opening night as in the preparation and rehearsal period. Just as important as the initial capitalisation and budgeting is a producer's continuing 'good housekeeping' ability – the estimation of that point during a run when an extra advertising push might be necessary or when to renegotiate rental terms with the theatre owner or royalty arrangements with authors and directors during a box office downturn – all of which demands constant vigilance. Tom Stoppard, amongst others, has pointed out that on a Codron production there would rarely if ever be disagreement about budgeting a production's initial costs and that no corners would be cut on the physical production, on sets and costumes, but that during even a capacity-house run there could be long discussions over the necessity of a replacement £50 sweater for Felicity Kendal, all part of a production's housekeeping.

The Codron management has successfully weathered the changes in a career spanning more than half a century, a time which has seen the landscape of London's commercial theatre irrevocably altered. Where other producers have tended to specialise – Cameron Mackintosh and Andrew Lloyd Webber both focusing essentially on musicals, Duncan C. Weldon on glossy star revivals, John Gale on boulevard comedy, Thelma Holt on boldly cast revivals (including the rarity of Coward's *Semi Monde*), Bill Kenwright on musicals and popular star vehicles, Robert Fox on impeccably mounted productions of such regular playwrights as Edward Albee or David Hare, with Maggie Smith a regular star – the Codron range has been unrivalled (Michael White has had a similar eclecticism but is much less prolific), stamped always by the sense of what amounts to the closest he has come to a philosophy of producing: 'I don't see why commercial can't be good.' He clearly proved his point; many of the plays he originally presented have had London revivals by other producers – indeed, it could be said that the repertoire of the Donmar Theatre in particular would have been somewhat impoverished under both Sam Mendes and Michael Grandage had it not been for the Codron back catalogue.

There are only a few features in his personality characteristic of the Max Bialystock-style producer. He is Jewish certainly, his offices are in a theatre and he is a cigar smoker (his office chair has a needlepoint cushion worked with Mark Twain's defiance: 'If I Cannot Smoke Cigars in Heaven Then I Shall Not Go.'), but he is unlikely to chase chorus girls and he is dapper and usually quietly-spoken, famous – notorious, even – for his pause technique, on the telephone particularly, rivalling that of the legendary late literary agent, Pat Kavanagh. Even in the modern world of the digital revolution, faxes and e-mails, this can still be a devastating negotiating ploy. He pretends innocence, claiming that it is only an aspect of a fundamental shyness, but undoubtedly over the years more than a few dramatists' or actors' agents have been so thrown by the Codron pause that they have been flustered into agreeing terms more favourable to him than to their clients. Fellow producers especially envy his deal-making ability when negotiating one of the most vital elements on any production, the theatre rental. Perhaps having been a theatre owner for a period himself (for a time in the 1980s Michael Codron Ltd also owned and operated the Vaudeville Theatre in the Strand) as well as having managed the Aldwych Theatre for its American owner for over twenty years has helped him here, but only very rarely has a theatre owner bested him in negotiations (the consistent quality of Codron productions and his track record, of course, are pluses for prospective landlords too). In personal negotiations he also can assume a daunting impassivity; the dramatist Peter Nichols once described him as 'giving his well-known impersonation of an Easter Island statue'.

Originally he worked out of a tiny office-cum-bedsit in Chelsea and then in Regent Street premises, but since the early 1980s he has been ensconced in a suite of offices in the Aldwych Theatre off the eastern end of the Strand. One of the West End's most attractive and best-maintained medium-sized houses (suitable for musicals and plays alike), it opened in 1905 as a companion theatre to the Strand (now Novello) Theatre on the other corner of the block with the Waldorf Hotel in between, originally run by the Edwardian actor manager Sir Seymour Hicks in partnership with the Anglophile American producer Charles Frohman (now again the theatre is linked with America, owned by the New York producer–theatre proprietor James M. Nederlander and managed by the Codron firm). Over the years the theatre has been home to the Aldwych farces, mostly by Ben Travers, in the 1920s and 1930s and to the Royal Shakespeare Company as its London base between the 1960s and early 1980s. Currently it houses the musical *Dirty Dancing,* which has established itself as a mega-runner – 'I hope it will see me out,' according to Codron at 80.

The firm's offices are up some flights of chilly stone stairs (no elevator), reached from a discreet pass-door near the Aldwych box office. There is a cheerful front office, high-tech computers rubbing shoulders with anti-quated Roladexes, with burnt-sienna carpeting and pale apple-green walls, covered in a higgledy-piggledy arrangement of framed posters from art exhibitions (Otto Dix, the legendary Diaghilev Exhibition, the National Portrait Gallery's British Raj exhibition), caricatures of various Codron London productions by the masterly William Hewison, which so often illuminated the pages of *Punch* and later *The Times* as tellingly as the reviews they accompanied (sadly, now a lost art), and a watercolour of trees by Michael's partner Peter Hulstrom. One corner near the water cooler (kept from the set of Joe Penhall's *blue/orange*) is devoted to some New York productions – his Tony Awards as co-producer of Stoppard's *The Real Thing* and Frayn's *Benefactors* (together with an enlarged version of the classified advertisement in the London newspaper theatre listings

that for a time carried the wonderfully misspelt puff for *The Real Thing* –
not entirely inappropriate for a play of sexual passion and romantic agony
– as 'Best Lay of the Year') and the star-studded posters (Glenn Close,
Jeremy Irons, Sam Waterson) for those productions.

On a wall near the door is a framed tribute, in exquisitely worked
illuminated lettering by fellow producer Kim Poster, presented to Michael
by the producers' organisation SOLT (Society of London Theatre) on the
occasion of his 50th Anniversary as a West End producer in 2006 (his 25th
was marked in 1981 by an *Evening Standard* Personal Award of a silver
cigarette box at a National Theatre ceremony attended by his parents), the
words contributed by one of his most frequently produced dramatists,
Michael Frayn:

> MICHAEL CODRON
> Prince of Producers,
> Emperor of Impresarios,
> King of Comedy,
> Dreamer of Drama,
> Employer of Players,
> Author of Angels,
> Angel of Authors,
> Foremost of Friends.

Beyond the outer office is a corridor with a staircase leading to a few
upstairs offices, its whole wall area literally covered in framed posters for
past Codron productions, almost 200 altogether – that arch-Roundhead
Lindsay Anderson (although not averse himself occasionally to taking the
Cavalier commercial theatre's shilling) used to refer to it as Michael's 'wall
of shame' – and the door to the producer's inner sanctum is at the foot of
the stairs across the passage from the outer office.

This inner office is generously sized and high ceilinged – the sienna
carpet runs through into the bright, airy room that has windows on the left
overlooking the lower end of Drury Lane, while at the far end a series of
curved windows forming an elegant semi-circle provides a commanding
view up and down Aldwych. In here the walls are a different shade – a kind
of dark terracotta (once described as 'the colour of the blood of pantomime
directors'). There are no theatre posters in this room but instead a series –
mostly painted in the 1970s and 1980s – of brightly DayGlo acrylics by
Philip Le Bas of theatre exteriors housing Michael Codron productions,
themselves a vibrant, vivid testament to a time of real innovation and

excitement in London's commercial theatre sector. Low bookshelves – largely filled by printed editions of plays originally produced out of the office – run along one corner's lower walls, the surfaces crowded with memorabilia and photographs, including one of Michael's parents and more books with a large framed photograph, prominently placed, of a handsome, blue-eyed man with corn-coloured hair, a strong jaw and an engaging broad smile (Michael's one-time partner, in life and business, David Sutton). The desk is a sleek slab of dark polished wood on steel legs, crowded less by telephones than by scripts, jars of pens and a huge bowl for postcards received. On the floor is a large green ceramic crocodile – further testaments to this idiosyncratic absorption are all over the room in the shape of literally dozens of china, wooden, furry, metal or plastic crocs, of all sizes. There is little evidence, however, of his other passions for lions' heads (curiously, also one of Hugh Beaumont's quirks), which are mostly housed in his London apartment, or, most consumingly, his interest in memorabilia and art connected with Queen Caroline (unhappy wife of George IV), of which he has a world-class collection, displayed in his country house in Kent.

In this office the putting together of all the nuts and bolts involved in assembling major West End productions takes place. In his heyday Michael would regularly produce up to ten plays in a year, always with a remarkably small and loyal permanent staff; although in more recent years his output has diminished – no single commercial producer could produce ten London productions in one year today – there he can sit alone, contemplating that crucial alchemical aspect of building up a production or talk on the telephone to dramatists, directors or designers. At times they will come to the office for further discussions and on occasion actors might join, and depending on status, either talk over a role or audition for one (the office, comfortable but not opulent, crowded but not oppressive makes a much friendlier audition space than some bleak, hired rehearsal room or empty theatre).

I have spent fair amounts of time in that office, often surprised to spot something – usually a crocodile – previously unnoticed. Since 1975 – most recently in 2009 – I have directed regularly for Michael Codron Ltd; only part jokingly, I have at times described Michael as my help in ages past, my hope for years to come (although he threatens imminent retirement, nobody associated with him can quite believe it).

This book is, of course, designed essentially as a survey of a phenomenal theatrical career and of Michael Codron's crucial part in the British theatre since 1956, but to an extent this scrutiny is possible only because of my own

2. Michael's Aldwych office, with some of Philip Le Bas' acrylics.

crowded – some would say misguided or misspent – theatre-going youth. Rather like the late director, Frith Banbury, as a boy in Scotland I 'got' theatre the way other children get religion or music or sport and then, luckily based in London during later school holidays and doing student jobs in university vacations, I could indulge in constant theatre-going. In those late 1950s and early 1960s days it was possible to see three productions on a Saturday alone – one had sometimes to be nippy and learn the quickest routes through the West End's side streets to get to and from various theatres – usually with one at 2.30, another at 5.00 or 5.30 and an evening show at 8.30. Cost was fairly minimal – the Gallery then cost only 2/6d or 3/- (25p or 30p – although top-price tickets have mostly kept generally in pace with inflation, the lowest price theatre seats are now, comparatively, considerably more expensive). Entry from the warmly lit theatre foyers was usually taboo; Gallery queue stools had largely vanished by 1960 and entrance was usually through a side door, safely away from the more affluent patrons for Stalls and Circle (where evening dress for opening nights was still prevalent), up uncarpeted stone stairs reeking of Jeyes Fluid, tickets bought from a usually ill-tempered old biddy, barely glimpsed through a small iron-grilled window near the bottom of the stairs, dispensing entry from a numbered roll of cloakroom-style tickets. Generally it was a first come, first seated system up in 'the gods' and so it helped to be young and fleet; if one wasn't fast enough up the flights of stairs, most of the first rows of benches (no luxury then of individual seats for the 'paupers' referred to by Dame Edna Everage) would be taken and then it was like being up the North Face of the Eiger looking down on actors' bald spots (only extremely rarely, however, was there any audibility problem).

Over the years I graduated to better seats although still, as a director, I make a point in the West End of watching a dress rehearsal and at least one preview from high up in what used to be galleries, now dignified as 'Upper Balconies' or whatever, but which still for me carry such potent associations that I can almost smell the Jeyes Fluid once again.

Somewhat indiscriminating, to say the least, in the earlier days – I would catch everything from the cheesiest thriller to the visiting Moscow Arts Theatre, or the revelatory 1960s World Theatre Seasons of foreign companies presented by Peter Daubeny (a Marco Polo of impresarios) at the Aldwych – slowly I came to comprehend from the theatre programmes (6d and fastened then with a gummed label – 'Please return if seal broken' – usually merely a cast list with advertising and lengthy credits acknowledging 'Stockings by Kayser Bondser', 'Cigarettes by Abdullah' and 'Wardrobe care by Lux': another age) that the majority of the new plays to which I seemed to respond most were presented by an outfit called 'Michael Codron Limited'. My regular attendances meant that the friendlier Gallery box office ladies would occasionally scribble me a 'Pass' on a scrap of paper allowing me into a lower level if there were empty seats, even, very rarely, on first nights; by such means I was able to be really in amongst the drama at such electric opening nights as *The Killing of Sister George* or *Ride A Cock Horse*. Notes, of course, were written up afterwards.

I have worked out that over the years I have missed only twelve productions presented out of the Codron office. In those earlier years I would even often catch plays at then still flourishing touring venues such as Golders Green Hippodrome, Wimbledon Theatre or Brighton's Theatre Royal, and so occasionally was able to see plays (the first production of Joe Orton's *Loot* included) which, for whatever reason, never made it into London. This 'education' was, I would claim, of infinitely more value to me as a director subsequently than any university drama course could have been. And so, to no small degree, the writing of this book also goes some way towards repayment of my debt to 'Michael Codron Ltd', a powerful influence on me even before I met the man behind the billing. It also, I realise, represents my thanks which, as I hope he knows, are heartfelt.

CHAPTER 1

FIRST ENTRANCES

As a teenager at St Paul's School in London, Michael Codron occasionally performed, sometimes as a double act with his classmate and friend Michael Oliver, self-penned sketches in school concerts ('I did not hide myself under any bushel.'). He was especially pleased with one performance in which he and Oliver had impersonated Samuel Pepys (an old boy of the school) and Sir Christopher Wren, strongly linked to St Paul's: 'Two Jewish boys from North London pretending to be Old Paulines, but it got quite a few laughs.' They were followed on the programme by 'a younger boy from Junior School with a large nose and freckles who did a kind of stream-of-consciousness monologue, simply hurling himself into this wild kind of Danny Kaye act. He was so funny that I thought at once: he's got it and I haven't. Maybe I shouldn't perform again?'

Whether Michael's first glimpse of Jonathan Miller in performance in the later 1940s planted some seed of the urge to become a producer rather than a performer is moot, although gradually throughout the rest of his time at St Paul's and then at Oxford he appeared less and wrote and produced more. Miller's and Michael's paths rarely crossed but still they had more than St Paul's in common. Some years later, in the early 1960s, with Michael beginning to establish himself as a major player among West End managements, his productions including several successful revues (two written principally by Peter Cook), Miller joined up with Cook, Alan Bennett and Dudley Moore in *Beyond the Fringe*, the production that in 1961 began the decline of the old style Shaftesbury Avenue revue.

It was in that show that Miller, in one of his most striking numbers, declared, 'I'm not a Jew. I'm Jew*ish*,' a stance that Michael might well have adopted. His religion was and remains not unimportant to him; also homosexual, he is conscious of belonging to two minorities in England (actually three – the Sephardi Jews from which his lineage sprang make up only twenty per cent of Jewry as against the Ashkenazis' eighty per cent). Although he ceased regularly to attend synagogue as a young man, still until his parents' deaths in 1981 he would, whenever in London, go home

1

every Friday night for the ritual family meal complete with candles and Cholla bread, the sole exception to the customs of Kiddish being that 'instead of being served the usual sickly Palwyn wine there was always by my plate half a bottle of Beaujolais, a parental concession to the three years at Oxford which, it was held, had refined my palate.'

Years later, echoing Miller's *Fringe* sketch, Michael would define his stance as, 'I *feel* Jewish, but I don't observe the rituals.' It was only several years after his father's death that he finally travelled to his family's ancestral home of Rhodes. His father, Isaac (Haco) Codron, was born there in 1898, the only boy – consequently much spoiled – among seven sisters. Originally from Spain, the family (who never changed its name) had been in Rhodes since the days of the Inquisition, part of the great medieval Diaspora of Sephardi Jews from the Iberian Peninsula (themselves likely descendants of Arab, Berber and European converts to Judaism in between the emergence of the earliest Jewish communities in Asia, North Africa and Southern Europe and the twelfth century) and, indeed, Haco's mother tongue was Spanish. Gradually in the twentieth century the whole family began to move away from the island, leaving only one of Haco's sisters still in Rhodes; when the Nazis invaded she was sent to Auschwitz where she died.

On Michael's sole visit to Rhodes in 1988 he was not at his best ('It was a miserable time'), following the break-up of his personal partnership in the most enduring relationship of his adult life with David Sutton (also his business partner for over three decades). He was still both troubled and shaken by the acute awareness that the split had been very much his own fault ('There's no fool like a middle-aged fool,' a friend who worked at Asprey's had reminded him). Although he was with a new partner (a comparatively short-lived relationship) it was an uneasy time, not least because this new lover, Mark Brough (known as Mark 1 later, distinguishing him from Mark Rayment, a subsequent and longer attachment, known as Mark 2), disliked Rhodes intensely.

Nevertheless Michael was considerably moved to see his aunt's name inscribed on the memorial to the Wartime Dead of Rhodes in the Square of the Hebrew Martyrs and to be shown his family's old house in the medina by an old woman who had survived Auschwitz and had known his aunt and his family. He also visited the little synagogue in which his father had been barmitzvahed.

Haco himself, both loved and also immensely respected by Michael, always remained something of an enigma, rarely elaborating in much detail on his earlier life; like many who adopt a new country, he tended somewhat to airbrush a previous existence. Some tantalising hints were offered: 'He spoke occasionally round family dinners about a time he had spent in the Belgian Congo – there was a photograph of him with a large dog and a mandolin, which he would still sometimes play on Friday nights. But exactly what he was doing there was never explained.' Nor was a period spent in France prior to his arrival in London: 'After his death a nephew of mine met a Codron in France who asked him if he knew that his grandfather had been married once previously, before leaving for England. It was, according to this other Codron, an arranged marriage from which he freed himself to come to London to work in the carpet and textile import-export business.'

Whatever the truth of that, Haco by the later 1920s was established in London working for the Landau family, a large Sephardi dynasty specialising in textiles imported from Hong Kong and sold widely in outlets ranging from upmarket department stores to Woolworths. The Landaus were both kind and supportive to Haco, even when he left to set up his own textile business, initially in Dagenham and then expanding – largely on the advice of his most important member of staff, the astute and long-serving accountant, Mr Viney – into a subsidiary chalk-mining business near Oxford. Eventually the company's head offices moved into the City – at 11-12 Moorgate – as the business prospered ('My father worked very, very hard for us.').

In 1928 his father met an attractive, quiet young woman six years his junior, Lily Morgenstern, from a large Ashkenazi family in Stepney in London's East End, who was then finishing a course at Pitman's Secretarial College. After a short courtship they became engaged and they were married in a Paris Registry Office in 1929. No explanation for the venue was forthcoming. Is it remotely possible that if Haco *had* been previously married he may not have been properly divorced from his first wife in a supposedly arranged marriage and wanted to marry Lily quietly, away from English legal eyes? There seemed to be no tensions between him and the Morgenstern family – quite the reverse – and so it does seem initially odd that a big Jewish family wedding was not arranged. But then neither Haco nor Lily was in any way flamboyant; Haco was punctilious in business, indeed in every department of his life. A more likely reason for marrying in Paris is that it was a romantic gesture on Haco's part to show Lily something of Paris before settling down to the life of an ultra-respectable London businessman.

3. Michael's parents, Haco and Lily Codron; Haco with
his ever-present pipe on a cruise.

The Codrons set up home first in a flat in a mansion block, Harvard Court, in Honeybourne Road off Finchley Road, a spacious apartment with big, light rooms and high ceilings. It was a part of London evocative of the area explored by John Mortimer in his 1959 play *The Wrong Side of the Park*, later produced by Michael. It was in Harvard Court that Michael was born (8 June 1930) – home births were much more frequent then – to be joined by a brother, David, eighteen months later.

Three years later, the Codrons moved to Farm Avenue in Cricklewood, then and still a prosperous North London area. Their nearest neighbours were the bandleader, famous for his radio broadcasts, Henry Hall and his family; often the Codron boys would go to bed 'listening to our neighbour on the radiogram, lulling us to sleep with numbers like "The Very Thought Of You"' (one of Michael's most regularly cast actors later, Richard Briers, also spent some of his childhood in Farm Avenue, although the two never met then).

The Codrons were regular attendees at the Spanish/Portuguese syna-gogue in Lauderdale Road 'where the big cheeses were the grand families such as the Nabarros, the Moccattas and the Sebag-Montefiores', survivors of the great 'Cousinhood' of nineteenth-century Jewish grandees, but who from the first Michael considered 'very stuffy – I found it very hard to take, the airless atmosphere there. And besides, it seemed to me that all the good tunes were with the Ashkenazis.' The Chief Rabbi, or Haham, originally from Gibraltar, befriended the Codron family and gradually they became key members of the synagogue. Essentially, in London then 'we moved in an exclusively Sephardi circle'.

Michael's education began in Cricklewood where 'two very sweet, very kindly ladies with time on their hands – the Misses Challen and Biggs – had opened a kindergarten called Westcroft'. Apart from his tables and 'penmanship' (Michael's handwriting, initially elegant, degenerated over years of hasty notes and signatures) he learned comparatively little there but he did make two friends – Michael Halse ('My best chum at Westcroft') whose father had a butcher's shop on the Finchley Road, and Michael Oliver 'whom we used to bully rather because he came to school in shantung shirts with elastic at the wrists'. Oliver, later a schoolmate of Michael's at St Paul's and then a successful lawyer, would become Michael's legal adviser and an enduring friend for over seventy years.

Also at Westcroft, 'Misses Clifford and Biggs gave me my first show business break by casting me as Rumpelstiltskin in a school play – and he's rather a bossy personality, isn't he? – which must surely have had an effect on me.'

Another upwardly mobile move during the Blitz – this time to a flat in Willesden in 'quite an elegant block' with the somewhat incongruous Morningside name of 'Tarranbrae', which Michael and his mother hated – coincided with a change of school when he was sent off to Brighton to board at 'a rather posh Jewish boys' school with an extremely pompous headmaster, Mr Lyon Maris'. Michael was not best pleased – 'I was so happy and so content in London, being lovingly looked after by devoted parents' – and even less pleased in September 1939 'when we were on holiday at Shanklin on the Isle of Wight watching Arthur Askey in a Concert Party when it was announced that war had been declared. I always held it against Hitler, apart of course from obvious other things, that he had interrupted Arthur Askey.'

The Brighton school moved at an early stage of the war 'when Lyon Maris suddenly took it into his head to evacuate us all to a big, sprawling house in Betws-y-Coed, but we'd been there barely ten minutes before it burnt, in a gratifyingly spectacular manner for all the boys, right down to the ground.' Michael's parents came to fetch him 'although from the train we could see the still-burning school'. There was a brief family holiday in

Brighton, coinciding with the dreadful news of the fall of France to the Nazis: 'I remember standing by myself on the front and thinking, "We're going to be invaded," and that this was the end of all that I knew.'

With the start of the Blitz on London, Willesdon seemed suddenly vulnerable; crouching under the table in Tarranbrae's dining room was less than adequate protection against the increasingly frequent German raids – and his father decided, largely because of his connections in the hosiery business, on Leicester as a suitable centre to which to evacuate the boys and Lily, while he would visit whenever possible with a wartime rail service at weekends. Initially they stayed at The Bell Hotel; the inconvenience of having to give up the bedroom he shared with his brother David whenever an important actor visited the local theatre was tempered for Michael by the reflected glamour of rubbing shoulders with personalities such as Diana Churchill and her husband Barry K. Barnes, a popular star couple of the time.

Eventually they moved into a rented flat in Leicester's Stonygate district, with Haco visiting more regularly after moving a section of his business to Leicester. It transpired that he had chosen well geographically – Leicester suffered only one Luftwaffe raid throughout the entire war, when a plane making for Coventry dropped a bomb. In Leicester his father joined the Home Guard: 'A kind of apotheosis for him, with his pipe clenched in his mouth, the émigré become the typical English gent.' Still he talked little of the past, never dwelling even on previous troubles such as Italy's invasion of Rhodes in 1911 and his enforced Italianisation (he had become naturalised shortly after Michael's birth): 'Never once did he speak any of the languages he knew and could have taught us. He knew Spanish, Italian, Greek, French and Hebrew.'

Lily enthusiastically joined the WVS, becoming quite an important figure, so before long the Codrons were 'mixing with the *gratin* of Leicester'. They attended synagogue – Michael's barmitzvah was held there – but in Leicester 'that was a non-Sephardi synagogue'. Michael and his brother attended a top Leicester school, Wyggeston Grammar School, which he described as 'a kind of fiefdom of the Attenborough family at that time'; Richard Attenborough had recently left the school,

David was the popular Head Boy – 'A figure of extreme glamour – we all had a crush on him, especially when he played the Chocolate Soldier in *Arms and the Man*' – and the youngest brother John, 'was my chum in the same form, while Attenborough *père* was Dean of the University, which abutted on to the school.'

Wyggeston's sister school for girls provided the female leads in school plays – 'I fell hopelessly in love with the girl who played Beatrice in *Much Ado about Nothing*, blonde and unattainable, definitely my type. I used to say to myself, "A star danced, and under that was I born."' The urge towards theatre, crystallised previously by that early exhilarating Rumpelstiltskin and occasional visits to the West End with Lily, now began to grow. Leicester had a flourishing amateur dramatic scene even in wartime, the most lively and adventurous group being The Little Theatre Club based in the town centre under the energetic leadership of the Christopheron family, 'which did rather interesting, often unappreciated work'. Michael became a regular visitor to The Little Theatre, especially if a production involved the Christopherons' son: 'Martindale Christopheron was very beautiful, cherubic-looking and fair-haired – also unattainable – I immediately transferred all my feelings for "Beatrice" to him, the first inklings I had that perhaps I was not as other men.'

Michael also started regularly visiting the city's still-active Repertory Theatre. 'This was run by a very strange, rather cynical ex-actor called Jack Endell and I was soon very much under his influence theatrically. He may have had feelings towards me and perhaps there were occasional pats on the knee suggestive of something more than avuncular, but nothing sexual ever happened.' Endell had been a minor actor in the West End and now was running the Leicester venture for J. Baxter Somerville, an active theatre manager of the period who would later be a crucial figure in Michael's early career. Although Endell cultivated an acid, world-weary, cynical exterior, he knew good theatre and good actors. Amidst the fluffy escapist light comedies he would as often as possible programme more adventurous, probing contemporary work; Michael was especially struck by Robert Ardrey's Pirandellian *Thunder Rock*, a scrutiny of isolationism in wartime, and by the psychodrama of Thomas Job's *Uncle Harry* (both had been big West End successes for Michael Redgrave) as well as by visiting actors doing 'special weeks', including Donald Sinden. Most impressive was a uniquely gifted actress who died too young, Maureen Pryor ('Pook'), a Leicester favourite who gave an electrifying performance in Sutton Vane's spectral drama set on board a liner in mid-ocean, *Outward Bound*: 'This had a profound effect on me. I felt that this was what death was going to be like.' Even as a boy, clearly he was especially drawn to plays that functioned on more than one level.

Simultaneously other artistic leanings were nurtured too: 'I was being taught piano by a woman called Marjorie Moss, who lived in an elegant house in the same road as the synagogue and I always preferred going to her house than to the synagogue.' Miss Moss trailed clouds of reflected glamour too: 'She was great friends with the popular pianist Eileen Joyce who stayed with her whenever she played Leicester's de Montfort Hall, always featuring her show-stoppers of Richard Adinsell's "Warsaw Concerto" from the film *Dangerous Moonlight*, or the Grieg Piano Concerto – I can never hear the latter without thinking of Eileen Joyce. She had real charisma – she would enter to tumultuous applause, trailing a chiffon handkerchief matching her gown, setting it meticulously on the piano. I felt very proud that it was my piano teacher's friend's fingers, not Ann Todd's, that were crushed so cruelly on screen by James Mason in *The Seventh Veil*.'

At the end of the war, with Michael now a teenager of fourteen, all the family were still in Leicester, although there was now a new shadow, just perceptible at this stage, over the family: 'I seem to remember that this was the first time my mother had not been well,' Michael recalled. Lily had always been very close to her family and to her mother especially, all based in Stepney, in St Peter's road near the Watney's Brewery, the hops from which scented the whole area. As a boy Michael would travel on the District Line out to Stepney Green Station (he was both fascinated by and fearful of the huge, 'terribly sinister' poster of the shadowy, caped man advertising Sandemann's Port in the underground passageway). Lily had been the fourth of five sisters and there were also two brothers – Harold ('the stalwart of the family') and the slow, somewhat autistic Sidney. Michael's Aunt Sophie, who worked as a secretary to the film and flour magnate J. Arthur Rank, outlived them all: 'She was the most civilised of all my aunts. She never married although my parents tried to fix her up with a Canadian soldier. My parents put up the money for the wedding but he did a bunk with it.'

This very different, colourful, tribal East End world was exotic and alluring to a boy who knew so little of the paternal side of his family, but the Morgenstern connections became less close with the death of Lily's mother towards the end of the war while Lily was in Leicester. She felt always 'a deep sense of guilt – something primal – that she had not been there. She became slightly vacant and troubled, almost without us noticing at first, but then slowly deepening.'

Once again it was left to his father to fix where the family should live on coming back to London. They ended up in Haslemere Gardens – 'It wasn't located anywhere, really. Sort of vaguely Hampstead Garden Suburb. There was a statue on the North Circular Road nearby called "La Deliver-

4. The Codron family at Haselmere Gardens.

ance", which was considered rather chic but that was about it. Our house was brand new – we were the first in it – and our opposite neighbours were the parents of a director I would work with later, Braham Murray (né Goldstein) although I never knew him then.'

Much more interesting to Michael was his move to a new school. St Paul's School in West London had been a leading London establishment since its foundation in 1509 by John Colet. Idiosyncratically divided not into houses but into clubs (A, B, C, etc.) it had a formidable reputation for sport (principally rugger) although its academic standing was also extremely high. Its old boys – Paulines – included such varied luminaries as Pepys, John Milton, Judge Jeffreys, G.K. Chesterton, Compton MacKenzie and Isaiah Berlin.

Although nominally a Christian foundation, Jewish boys attended; along with Oliver Sacks and Jonathan Miller, the Shaffer twins and future playwrights Peter and Anthony were in the form above Michael while his old chum from kindergarten, Michael Oliver, was in his form. Colet had laid down that there should be 153 scholarships available, the same as the number of fish in the New Testament fable, and after an interview with the headmaster (High Master in Paulinese) Walter Oakeshott, Michael was granted one of them and he began his three years at St Paul's in 1945; his time there would stamp him enduringly.

9

Oakeshott was an impressive personality, outwardly somewhat acerbic, even dry, but a man of immense humanity, respected – even revered – by masters and pupils alike. He had had the tricky task of supervising the school's wholesale evacuation to join with Wellington at Crowthorne while St Paul's was requisitioned by Old Pauline General Montgomery (a large painting of whom was hung prominently in the school after the war) and then in 1945 overseeing the return to badly bomb-damaged buildings. He made the transition surprisingly smooth; St Paul's was soon running at full strength again, with a first-rate staff under Oakeshott balancing the classroom and sports field with unerring skill.

Michael adapted quickly to life at St Paul's, sensing at once 'an incredible atmosphere, a hub of culture like nothing I'd known. The sporting side was strong but there was a strong artistic and intellectual bent too, including the G.K. Chesterton Society (the writer was an old Pauline, although neither I nor my classmates then had any idea of his almost rabid anti-Semitism). The Society's debates, modelled on the Oxbridge Unions, seemed to me very sophisticated, with motions such as "Woolworths has done more for humanity than Shakespeare." Altogether St Paul's was a tremendous crucible for encouraging us to think for ourselves.'

The school had some outstanding teachers at that time, not all of them cut from conventional cloth; Michael was highly impressed by 'a very sophisticated form master, Mr Langland, a great Francophile who told us in some detail of his favourite practice – eating runny, oozing French cheeses smelly enough to lift a manhole. That, too, in its way may have influenced my life!' Michael himself was even more captivated by Mr Whitting, 'a truly wonderful history master who really enthused me – it became my favourite subject. His approach was so unusual, not remotely dry or dictated by dates and facts. He used a bigger brush, and he made the past so vivid and real.'

He found himself in 'something of a hothouse form', his classmates including Chris Barber, later a great name in British Trad Jazz ('We all thought he was a bit of a weed and weren't very kind to him on the bus to school – the Number 28 from Temple Fortune Lane – all tricked out in our black blazers.'), Emmanuel Rubinstein and Antony Lejeune, son of the *Observer*'s movie critic C.A. Lejeune ('As a result we were able to get her to the school to talk on modern cinema.'). Also in his form was the ebullient Gino Bertuzzi, son of the respected Maitre d' at the Savoy Hotel: 'Gino was the apple of his father's eye. He would ask Gino to bring his friends to dinner in one of the Savoy's Gilbert and Sullivan rooms, so there would be these snotty little schoolboys being waited on in the Iolanthe Suite or wherever, being treated as adults. The precocity must have been revolting. What must the waiters have thought?'

Sport – rugger was fiercely championed – Michael cleverly dodged out of by pretending a great interest in fencing; his brother David (Codron minor) made up for any lack of application on Michael's part by being brilliant at all games. There was no question, however, about his real inclinations; before long he was helping to organise school concerts and 'writing little skits' for them, often performing too until the precocious talent of Jonathan Miller burst into the spotlight. One of the masters, Major Harbord, was in charge of school plays and entertainments; he had a brother, Gordon Harbord, who had acted before becoming a respected theatrical agent (Michael would later negotiate for clients of Harbord, who lived in some style in St Martin's Lane), and he would supervise the boys' make-up ('bringing a whiff of professional theatre with him').

Regularly Michael would write several sketches for the termly revue, usually directing too, although on occasion they would be supervised by the Head Boy, Alan Cooke: 'A truly charismatic figure, tall, good at games as well as intellectually bright, in control and worshipped generally from afar.' Michael was amongst the adoring ones; only subsequently at Oxford did Michael realise that Cooke too was gay.

Inevitably at St Paul's and with adolescence Michael found his feelings about his sexual nature confirmed: 'I fell in love with the captain of swimming, Alan Spiro, who was very kind, well-built and Jewish (unusual for me), from a very cultivated family in Fitzjohns Avenue. We went off together for a weekend in Stratford-Upon-Avon staying in a little bed and breakfast place and we saw Peter Brook's romantic, Watteau-style production of *Love's Labour's Lost* with Paul Scofield as Don Armado looking like Don Quixote. After we got back Alan's parents asked me to come and see them at home – and although they were polite enough they asked me firmly not to be so friendly with Alan, saying, "We know what your feelings are for our son and we would rather that you didn't pursue it."'

Michael was then just eighteen, precocious – even sophisticated – in some ways but also emotionally inexperienced and vulnerable, and the Spiros' meeting 'came as a horrible shock', shattering what was his first real love affair rather than a romantic crush. He realised later that 'there must have been a little gay set at school' while at least he had Michael Oliver as a confidant. Oliver, too, was gay – he and Michael were never lovers, however, which is perhaps one reason why their friendship so steadfastly

11

endured – and they 'compared notes, as it were, on each other's emotional dramas'. It must be remembered that they were at a school which, for all its liberal virtues, was fused with that strong English public school tradition of muscular Christianity and that, moreover, homosexual activity in the UK was then against the law (it would remain so for another two decades) while the late 1940s and the 1950s were stamped in England by a curiously prurient and often vicious homophobia. Both Michaels were also fearful of any parental discovery.

Inevitably an air of the clandestine or furtive – bringing mixed feelings of shame and excitement – marked many young men's early sexual explorations at that time. Michael Oliver 'fell heavily for a good-looking boy who was a boyfriend of the pop music mogul Larry Parnes – a dangerous world'. For both boys there was a sense of, in Oscar Wilde's phrase, 'feasting with panthers' as Michael was well aware: 'I was beginning to find out about bars and clubs – not that I much enjoyed doing it. There was the "A & B", a louche little bar off Wardour Street – they all seemed to be up poorly lit alleys – and a tiny bar up from the Palace Theatre stage door. It was there that I met Denis Heymer, a cockney boy, the prototype (fair, tall, seemingly unattainable). This was just a fling, not a serious thing. Afterwards Denis lived with Frankie Howerd and I got in touch with him on the phone many years later after Frankie died. He asked: "Are you that pretty little Jewish kid?" to which I had to reply, "No – I'm a corpulent, white-haired Jewish businessman."'

More serious was his affair with a darker character, a bisexual charmer called Kenneth Hume: 'I met him in a bar. He was wicked, a really bad boy, living in a tiny house in Spring Street and he fell heavily for me – I'd find him waiting for me at the school gates. Later he married Shirley Bassey and it was quite stormy. He obviously did like living dangerously; after they divorced he married her a second time.'

Although clearly extremely bright with an agile, quick brain, Michael was less than assiduous when it came to studying subjects he had little enthusiasm for, which boded ill for his School Certificate examinations, vital should he want to try for a university place. History had become something of a passion; Mr Whitting sensed that fascination and generously offered to help cram Michael for Oxford – he had a useful connection with Worcester College – and his influence on Michael was such that he pulled his socks up enough on other subjects to scrape through those for his Higher School Certificate. After the usual Oxford grilling at Worcester College he was offered a place there to read history. He would receive no scholarship and no grant but his parents were so proud of his achievement that his father was happy to pay for Michael's further education (although even then the thought – barely voiced – floated in the air that he might subsequently join the family business).

Michael put such thoughts aside and celebrated his Oxford place with an orgy of theatre-going. At St Paul's he had become a precociously voracious galleryite, usually queuing for hours perched on tiny stools in line for cheap gallery seats, often for productions at the Lyric, Hammersmith (later the Lyric would be a crucial venue in Michael's early career). There he saw such memorable productions as *The Brothers Karamazov* with John Gielgud and Edith Evans as well as Donald Wolfit in *King Lear* at the King's, Hammersmith, which was then bang opposite the school.

There was more queuing for gallery seats in the West End, 'waiting assiduously on our little stools with friends from school' in the courtyard between the Ambassador's and St Martin's theatres for more sophisticated revue material at the Ambassador's, where Hermione Gingold held virtually unbroken court throughout the war and immediately post-war years in the *Sweet and Low* series of revues. Much theatrical gossip was exchanged by more seasoned galleryites in the queue, swapping insider information on Hermione (and her namesake rival Hermione Baddeley), Ivor Novello, 'Binkie' Beaumont, Noël, Gertie *et al*, much to the boys' eavesdropping fascination. Even more 'in' theatrical scuttlebutt came from the stage as Gingold and company gleefully skewered other West End shows and stars: 'They were often wildly camp but we loved it all, even though there must have been times when we weren't really sure what we were laughing at. I especially remember Gingold doing a wicked Margaret Lockwood skit moaning about the shackles of her movie contract – "While working for Gaumont/ *Je n'ai pas un moment*," – and, I suppose, at root these shows must have influenced me when I started to write proper revue at Oxford and then later when I put on my early revues.'

All the excitement of finishing at St Paul's and the anticipation of going up to Oxford were doused in an icy shower when Michael received his call-up papers in the summer of 1948, threatening to postpone his longed-for university days for another two years while he did his National Service. Conscripted into the army he abruptly found himself plunged in misery, in the unwelcome and unwelcoming world of Basic Training at Catterick. Luckily very slim in those days, he rapidly lost even more weight in his first dismal Catterick days and after a medical he was declared 'not fighting material'. 'It was judged that I was underweight, undernourished and overstressed and they let me go. I did learn to peel potatoes – the one thing that has stayed with me from that time.'

His brief and inglorious time in His Majesty's Forces meant that Michael missed what would have been his first term at Worcester. As it was he was avid for Oxford life by the time he went up finally, in January 1949.

CHAPTER 2

ET IN ARCADIA ...

His path to Worcester College had been considerably smoothed – as Michael was well aware – by St Paul's Mr Whitting, who knew Worcester's highly regarded Provost, J.C. Masterman. Michael had won a state scholarship to Durham University and he had also applied for a scholarship place at Christ Church, Oxford; that college had strong links with Westminster School and after a viva with the forbidding historian Hugh Trevor Roper, Michael lost out on the scholarship to Westminster's Oleg Kerensky. 'Rather miffed', he announced that he would take himself off to Durham, although he unruffled his feathers when Whitting sagely advised him to persist with Worcester. His interview with Masterman had gone well, the Provost stressing that the college hoped that although Michael was absorbed by the theatre he would 'become a serious historian and not prance around running the ETC' (the University's Experimental Theatre Club, recently set up to present more radical work than the long-established Oxford University Dramatic Society, the OUDS).

Oxford's charms have seduced many stronger young wills than Michael's however. There was in his time something of the careless, even reckless hedonism of another post-war generation, as captured in Evelyn Waugh's novel set partly in 1920s Oxford, *Brideshead Revisited*. Michael's year saw the first recent intake of non-combatant undergraduates; Britain may have been still in the grip of the Age of Austerity with rationing restrictions and an infrastructure largely awaiting post-war reconstruction but in privileged, serene Oxford many of the Class of 1948 were set on having as good a time as possible in their student years.

Worcester, too, was a beguiling college. Mellow-stoned with leaded windows and graced by one of Oxford's most beautiful gardens, complete with lake, it was most conveniently situated not far from the railway station at the opposite end of Beaumont Street from the Randolph Hotel, with the Oxford Playhouse equidistant between the two. It was also just down Walton Street from the area known as Jericho where more Bohemian and independent undergraduates could find digs or rent bijou cottages. In his first year Michael had 'a rather pokey room in the medieval part of Worcester, the bit above the Buttery', moving the following year to the ground floor and 'a glorious, large panelled room with a marvellous view of Worcester's gardens' (he moved into digs in his final year).

Initially his tutor at Worcester was De Vere Somerset, a languid don with an aloofly mandarin manner 'who seemed as uninterested in teaching me as I became in being taught by him'. He was then 'farmed out' to another don, who was no more inspiring.

There were no other Paulines at Worcester in his first year, although the college had some artistic bent. Michael soon became and remained good friends with Anthony Besch (a successful opera director subsequently) 'who was part of the cultivated side of Worcester (it was pretty sporty at that time) and a leading light in the college's De Quincey Society'. He was tactfully helpful to the still somewhat gauche Michael ('Perhaps better not to wear a clip-on bow tie' was one of his hints) as was Godfrey Smith, also at Worcester.

It was Alan Cooke, the one-time glamorously godlike Head Boy from St Paul's, and now 'a big noise in the OUDS', who first gave Michael a proper 'entrée' to a whole group of new friends. Cooke was then the lover of John Schlesinger, another magnetic Oxford figure (he had already made his first film, *The Black Horse*) and also active in undergraduate theatre. Through them Michael was soon closely linked with 'a crowd from New, a very posh college, with what seemed to be a large gay population' including 'a very charismatic young don, Merlin Thomas, who had a lovely, lilting Welsh accent'.

Thomas took greatly to Michael, becoming an early mentor, even inviting him to dine at New's formidable High Table (daunting for even the most self-assured student), when Grace was said by the philosopher Isaiah Berlin, one of Oxford's most brilliant leading lights: 'At dinner he seemed older than God to me. Quite recently I was looking up some dates and realised he would have been only just forty!' Thomas also took Michael off to Paris for a brief holiday during one university vacation.

Dons such as Thomas then played a vital role in Oxford's theatrical hierarchy; they included Merton's Robert Levens (whose redoubtable wife Daphne occasionally would take on roles in OUDS productions), John Bryson at Balliol and, top of the heap, Exeter College's Nevill Coghill, who had worked on a West End H.M. Tennent production of *A Midsummer Night's Dream* with Gielgud, as well as directing some noted Oxford Shakespeare productions (including a famous *The Tempest* in Worcester College's garden) and later collaborating on a musical of Chaucer's *Canterbury Tales* based on his translation.

Coghill had been very influential too in the launching of the ETC, although Michael and most of his friends found him somewhat old fashioned and prissy. A story went round Oxford at that time of a rich American student, 'according to scandalous rumour eventually married by the Pope to another man, who visited a smart antique shop near Queen's College and fell in love with an exquisite Madame Recamier-style chaise-lounge. He was told that it was already sold, which only increased his determination to have it: "I'll pay you more than you've been offered. I must have it. Please, please tell me who it is." On being told that it had already gone to Professor Nevill Coghill he paused only briefly before replying, "I see. In which case I'll be on it sooner than I'd imagined."'

Something of this orchid-house camp, almost defiantly snook-cocking and sybaritic, coloured much of Oxford during this time. Through Alan Cooke and John Schlesinger, Michael was cast in Cooke's production of Pinero's Victorian farce *The Magistrate*, playing the small part of an Italian waiter. Michael also directed Henry Fielding's burlesque tragedy of *Tom Thumb* ('Oh Huncamunca, Huncamunca, Oh!') and this led to his principal role in the OUDS, the supervision of the Society's Smokers. Cooke had remembered Michael's skits from St Paul's, and it was a clever move to bring his organising skills to the Smokers. They were, like those of the Cambridge Footlights, regular evenings of sketches and songs, mostly original. Crowded, boisterous and well-wined affairs (all male in those days), they were held in the OUDS Club Room, equipped with a small stage and some basic lighting, just opposite the New Theatre.

The Smokers became Michael's fiefdom – 'I wasn't above appearing in and directing my own shows' – and under him the evenings became markedly more professional, smoothly programmed and exploiting what was then almost an embarrassment of riches of writing and composing undergraduate talent. Sometimes he wrote in partnership with a razor-sharp Wykehamist from New College, John Mayer, whose colourful, later varied career included a spell behind the counter at Tiffany's in New York.

He especially enjoyed collaborating with an astonishingly versatile music student, Stanley Myers, so precociously brilliant that he won a Music Scholarship to Balliol, which he was told he was too young to take up immediately, whereupon he went at once to Queen's College, which had no such reservations. Michael had met Myers briefly before Oxford: both had spent time some years previously at a Jewish boys' holiday camp ('he usefully told me what masturbation and menstruation meant'). At first he was still somewhat in awe of the seemingly worldly wise Myers: 'He led an even more louche life at Oxford than I came to do. He always had a copy of *Sporting Life* under his arm and lots of ladies around him, among them a very vivacious dark-haired girl who was a dancer, Eleanor Fazan.'

Together Myers and Michael came up with a huge amount of material for Smokers and they also wrote an annual OUDS pantomime together – 'They were rather like extended Smokers, with lots of Oxford and topical jokes' – which Michael directed. The best of their three was a version of *Cinderella*, subtitled because of its strong element of Gilbert and Sullivan pastiche *Trial by Jewry*. In those days the national press regularly covered Oxbridge productions; *The Times* found the show, set in Ochsford, a village in the Ruritanian Alps with its own university, 'a smart, smart pantomime' and the *Daily Mail*, after noting the presence of 'Chips' Channon and Terence Rattigan in the audience, praised 'snappy dialogue and highly original songs' in this 'sparkling excursion into pantomime' by the OUDS. In the little village that academic Oxford essentially then was, it soon spread around that Michael's lyrics had deeply offended the decidedly humourless Daphne Levens with a crack about her appearance as Aase, the old mother to the star undergraduate actor David William's Peer in an OUDS *Peer Gynt*: 'Why are your shoulders so hunched?' 'Because I'm carrying the whole show.'

Perhaps the very best work from the team of Codron and Myers was in a Smoker of March 1951 under Michael's supervision (his billing now was 'devised and directed by'), which also had material from John Mayer and one number from Sandy Wilson who had been recently at Oriel College (this was quite a catch – Wilson had already contributed material to London shows including Hermione Gingold's Ambassador's revues). The pervasive influence of West End intimate revue still lingered; Mayer's song 'Don't Let's be Beastly to the OUDS' had at least the honesty to add 'with apologies to Noël Coward', the number being a blatant rip-off of 'Don't Let's be Beastly to the Germans', while the closing item, virtually a mini-musical with Michael's book and lyrics to Myers' music, a clever spoof fusion of Lewis Carroll and Websterian Jacobean drama called *Malice in Wonderland or Honi Soit Qui Malfi Ponce*, had all the arch, knowingly 'in' characteristics of the Gingold series. The cast included future dance critic Clement Crisp (a lifelong friend) and director Colin George.

All this hectic extra-curricular activity inevitably attracted Worcester's notice and Michael was called in for a chat with J.C. Masterman who expressed 'in sorrowful tones' the college's feelings: 'We know what you're up to and it's a disappointment to the college. We thought you were going to be a true history scholar.' Michael's guilt spurred him briefly to apply himself but his social and theatrical activities soon swamped even his best intentions. He organised for the ETC a Festival of New Plays, including work by undergraduates, greatly taking to the role of what he described as 'a mini-impresario – I did all the packaging', with some help from the Playhouse's formidably efficient administrator, Elizabeth Sweeting. The productions included a much-praised Christopher Fry play, *The Boy with a Cart*, mounted at Mansfield College where Michael had been impressed by a production of undergraduate Michael Meyer's play *The Ortolan*, featuring a local girl called Margaret Smith, a student at the Playhouse who also shone in some of Ned Sherrin's Oxford revues,.

Luring eminent theatre people from London to talk to undergraduates also became one of Michael's tasks (willingly taken on) and he managed to bring down the likes of Peter Ustinov and the eminent West End producer of T.S. Eliot's plays and light comedy alike, the portly *bon viveur*, son of a variety booker, Henry Sherek ('almost single-handedly responsible for my *not* going into the theatre immediately after Oxford. When I told him I'd like to produce he gave me a withering look and said, "You have to be born to it."'). His big coup – 'this brought me great *réclame*' – was to coax down Hermione Gingold for whom he organised a party in Worcester's gardens: 'There was the usual frivolous crowd, in all senses camp followers of hers, and so we were all distinctly startled when Bill Gaskill (later a Royal Court director, famous for his austerity) whom we all revered for the purity and deep seriousness of his ETC productions, arrived at this garden party for Gingold dressed in very tight trousers and a lace jabot. He pranced – no other word will do – up to Gingold, practically doing a *jetée*, saying, "How wonderful to meet you," and then waltzed off. Gingold simply looked after him before turning back to me with a raised eyebrow to drawl, "You see a lot of that in the industrial North."'

Altogether for Michael all of this added up to 'an absolutely charmed existence'. He had gone up still comparatively unworldly while now he was finding a genuine niche in an exotic, hothouse world. The New College crowd with which he had fallen in had introduced him to people such as Antony Blond, another Jewish boy – later an enterprising publisher – who also came across little overt anti-Semitism at Oxford then, Leslie Walford who had an open Rolls Royce ('We all used to hang casually around the Randolph Hotel on Sundays at lunchtime hoping he'd say, "Come on –

we're off to the Bear at Woodstock.'"), Toby Roe ('He owned White's Bar, was known to be definitely louche and left Oxford under a bit of a cloud') and, resulting in another of his most lasting friendships, Edward Montagu, soon to be Lord Montagu of Beaulieu.

Tall and disarmingly charming, Montagu was also rather shy: 'He was keen to get into our set, the theatrical world. He was something of an amateur photographer and later took the pictures of Smokers for us. He once gave a memorable summer party in New College Gardens – a strawberry party with the fruit sent from Beaulieu. Later he gave a party at his impressive digs in Wellington Square with Terence Rattigan among the guests to celebrate a Smoker. Also there was the rather pompous Martin Stevens – he became a Tory MP – who was mad keen to be in with both the Toffs and the Aesthetes. We were leaving the party when we saw marching towards us the entire and rather drunken Bullingdon Club who were clearly very puzzled by Stevens's choice of company. "Ask them up! Before they turn nasty!" hissed Stevens, so I did and then back at the party I found myself at the centre of a human tug of war with a plaintive cry from Montagu: "Mind the Canalettos!"'

All of this Sebastian Flyte and Antony Blanche side of Oxford co-existed alongside Michael's continuing sexual confusions. Oxford was further advanced than Cambridge in its attitude to women then, but women were still vastly outnumbered in the undergraduate population and the rules about mixing were medievally draconian. Not surprisingly, in an atmosphere not unlike an extension of public school in some ways, many young men, barely out of adolescence, were sexually ambivalent or perplexed. On Michael's part: 'During my first term I remember thinking that I knew I was gay but I was having no sex.'

Then, in the heady aftermath of the successful opening of *The Magistrate* in his first summer term, he became lovers ('My first Oxford sex – although it wasn't a serious thing') with Andrew Porter, who had supervised the music for the production (Porter established a career as a leading music critic. Years later, when Edward Montagu gave a party for the Class of 1948, Porter made a speech in which he said that he had slept with everyone at the table bar one: 'Nobody wanted to ask the identity of the odd man out').

There were, inevitably, several of his 'crushes', not least that over John Ellison ('A prototype of my English rose type – blond, blue-eyed, tall, sporty. And unattainable.'), later Governor of the Bahamas. By contrast he was plunged into emotional turmoil, genuinely perturbed by the depth of his feelings when he fell helplessly in love with an Exeter College under-graduate, Paddy Malone: 'I was ill with love. He was a great combination of looks and charm but rather pure, much sought after by others besides me. I remember sitting alone in Worcester's gardens on my nineteenth birthday, thinking, "I am never ever again going to be as happy as I am at this moment." So when I am happy, as I am from time to time, I measure it against that moment.'

The happiness was short-lived ('Although Paddy reciprocated to an extent, it was all rather chaste'). Malone did invite Michael to his home in the Potteries: 'A rather chilly house where his parents took me aside to make it clear, very politely, that this friendship was not what they would want for their Paddy.' It recalled his conversation with the equally polite and civilised Drs Spiro when he was at St Paul's – and it was as lacerating.

Sometimes these bruises to the heart made him question his religion: 'I even seriously contemplated becoming a Catholic and went to talk to David March at St Bennett's but he was awfully austere and didn't seem quite to understand. It was a friend, James Roose-Evans, later a director, then trying to decide whether he had a real calling for the priesthood, who advised against, gently but rightly telling me I'd be doing it for all the wrong reasons.'

At other times he could forget the emotional *sturm und drang*, as when he enjoyed an Italian summer holiday in the company of two friends, Fred Beattie and John Sainsbury, also at Worcester (it had not escaped Michael's notice that the 'Toffs' set would often refer to Sainsbury as 'the Grocer'). In Sainsbury's Riley, they travelled to Rome (where they met up with Andrew Porter and his mother to celebrate Porter's twenty-first birthday), Florence and Venice, staying in *pensiones* and enjoying endless sun and alfresco meals.

In Venice there was one chill reminder of the real world's pressures when, sitting one day with his friends in St Mark's Square, Michael spotted his Oxford friend Jonathan Guinness walking through the square. He was about to go over to him but was stopped by Sainsbury: 'Remember who his mother is.' She was Diana Mitford; she had left Jonathan's father Bryan Guinness to marry Sir Oswald Mosley, the anti-Semitic leader of the British Union of Fascists.

It was something of an understatement when Michael admitted back in Oxford that 'history was taking something of a back seat'. He added, 'I did hardly any work at all and there were periods about which I knew next to nothing, so much so that in my Finals there were two papers that I could

21

5. An 'Isis Idol' at Oxford – 'the era of the brocade waistcoat'.

barely even attempt.' He managed, just, to scrape a Third Class Honours degree, not what had been expected of 'a serious historian' but not disastrous enough to upset his parents.

Because he had been unwillingly detained in Catterick during what should have been his first Oxford term, Michael was allowed to stay on for an extra term, a real bonus for him. He had fallen in love with Oxford – 'I simply could not get enough of the place' – and indeed had even spent chunks of his vacations there rather than in London. The future – increasingly now suggesting some parental employment – he would put to one side to enjoy a final few months in Oxford.

In his final year he had lodged 'in a rather gloomy room in Wellington Square with a landlady whose full English breakfasts were always afloat on a tide of fat, but who was most understanding'. In his extra term he lived in the High Street, usefully near the Taj Indian restaurant and Hall's the Tailor where he had an account and which now provided most of an increasingly elegant wardrobe including his brocade waistcoats ('It was the era of the elaborate waistcoat particularly'). He made sure he looked at his smartest in one of them for a photograph in the Student *Isis* magazine when he was given the accolade of an 'Isis Idol' profile piece. There were rebels against the prevailing peacockery, including the aspirant journalist Alan Brien who looked 'rather vulpine in hairy tweed jackets', some of whom cultivated a rough machismo. Michael remained defiantly among the peacocks (previously it had been Kenneth Tynan in his gold lame suit), describing himself as 'looking somewhat Levantine in those days, with a lot of black hair, and I was very, very thin. One of my encounters in those days – "a squeeze" we'd say now – once told me, "You look like an El Greco gone wrong."'

That carefree last term was filled by avid theatregoing – often in quick day trips to London – and continued involvement with the Smokers. There was still a good deal of congenial company around even if, with so many of the New College crowd and most of his best friends having gone, some of that Arcadian, latter-day *Brideshead* atmosphere had evaporated too. The later 1950s would be a harder-working undergraduate era. And in the spring of 1952 Michael too had to face leaving what had been his pre-lapsarian cocoon for three years to face up to the hard facts of making a living in the real world.

CHAPTER 3

APPRENTICESHIPS

Wantage is not so very far from Oxford but to Michael, who found himself based in the town for nearly a year after his extra term in paradise, it could well have been initially in outer Siberia. It certainly seemed like exile to him.

His father had decided his immediate future for him. To give Michael the job of overseeing business at the agricultural chalk quarry in Childrey near Wantage, which Haco had bought on his accountant's advice and was doing well, would he thought be precisely the kind of occupation 'to make a man of you' as he put it to his son. Based first in a stuffy Wantage hotel and then in a poky little flat above a dress shop, it was hardly how Michael had envisaged his ideal postgraduate existence. The work was drearily routine, the quarry staff – as he was well aware – knew that he was the boss's boy and so rather mollycoddled him. His only compensation was that the proximity to Oxford meant that he could, in his first small car, drive quickly to The Bear at Woodstock for convivial drinks with friends or on to Oxford for meals (Wantage, like most small English towns in the 1950s, was no gastronomic centre) or to see the latest OUDS or ETC shows.

One new friendship he formed in Wantage was with John Betjeman; he had plucked up the courage to knock on his door and introduce himself and Betjeman had asked him in, subsequently inviting him to the occasional meal. When he became aware that the theatre was Michael's consuming interest the poet introduced him to the artist John Piper and his wife Myfanwy (Benjamin Britten's occasional librettist) who lived in Henley, where Myfanwy was involved with running the Kenton Theatre, a delightful, intimate theatre near the bridge.

Michael, who always enjoyed women's friendship, as well as enjoying Myfanwy's personality, found himself drawn to the congenial company of a local girl, the lively and funny Molly Norridge, whose father ran a successful sanitaryware business. Molly drove a dashing little MG sports car and sometimes brought him to her home; her parents took a shine to him, Mrs Norridge possibly nurturing hopes in a matrimonial direction. However, once when he was driving Molly's MG to the White Horse in

Uffington he reversed somewhat cavalierly into a bollard, sending Molly towards the windscreen. There was no lasting damage but when he took Molly home, her face dramatically bloodied, her mother's reaction was an unexpected: 'Well, now you've *got* to marry her.'

There was to be no future there. Nor was there in the quarry business, although Michael did his work with abstracted efficiency. Then Haco proposed another move, back to London – a plus in itself – but with the proviso that Michael should now enter the family business. Without a private income and with a degree that would make little impression on any potential employer, Michael realised this was, and always had been, the expectation. It would also mean the added restriction of returning to live at home.

So in early 1953 Michael began the daily commute, bowler-hatted with his father, to the Moorgate offices. He was miserable – 'I had no feel or flair for that business. All the time I kept thinking I was going to make a total hash of it' – although dutifully he went through the motions, mindful too that his brother had worked in the business for a period before being called up into the RAF and had made a success of it. His life was pressured further by his double existence; at home and at Moorgate a seemingly compliant embryo-businessman son, while in the evenings often his 'feasting with panthers' drew him into London's homosexual worlds.

One aspect of his other life followed the familiar pattern of attractive young man being taken up by sophisticated older man – as, say, Terence Rattigan, a rising playwright, had been by 'Chips' Channon. In his final year at Oxford, Michael had met at a post-Smoker party the interior designer David Hicks who had come to the party with Rattigan. Hicks was confidently debonair, well connected and bisexual (later he married Lady Pamela Mountbatten) and was then building up his fashionable interior design and consultancy service – the business was called Marble and Lemon – catering to London's rich and to high-class companies. After the party he took Michael back to the Randolph Hotel where their affair began. As he was leaving next morning he told Michael: 'When you come to London I want to see a lot more of you.'

Now Michael was meeting Hicks regularly and being introduced to the world of discreetly sophisticated gay life in the capital; monied, articulate and stylish. Often at his exquisite house in Chester Place Hicks hosted 'exclusively all-male dinner party affairs – David's adoring mother sent the food up from the basement in the dumb waiter with excellent wines; a world headily intoxicating for a young man only recently out of the cocoon of Oxford. At the other end of the scale Michael would occasionally resume his patronage of London's semi-secret haunts, sometimes at the Rockingham Club in Soho's Archer Street, all striped Regency-style wallpaper, rose-tinted wall sconces and soft music, presided over by the familiar sardonic personality of Toby Roe, previously of the louche White's Club in Oxford. The Calabash in Fulham, run by photographer Leon Maybank and the A & B in Soho (standing for Arts and Battledress, having been set up during the war when so many patrons were in uniform) were other private, discreet gay clubs of the era.

There was also the SF Grill in Denman Street near the Piccadilly Theatre stage door, (SF stood for its owner Stan Freeman, not Stage and Film as popularly supposed) frequented by a more show business, mixed crowd – Lionel and Joyce Blair, Diana Dors, Pete Murray the disc jockey, chorus girls – and where Michael at times would meet up with Michael Oliver, now carving out his legal career. When it closed, much of the clientele moved on to the late-night nearby White Room, still as popular as in wartime, a dimly lit piano bar where either John Bannerberg or the dapper, improbably named Marc Anthony tinkled the keys.

The tensions within Michael came to a head with his anxieties over Edward Montagu – now Lord Montagu of Beaulieu – and what became known as 'The Montagu Case', a widely publicised 1954 'scandal', which showed the British, particularly the popular press, seized by one of their least attractive fits of pruriently self-righteous morality. Montagu and two friends, Michael Pitt-Rivers and the *Daily Mail* journalist Peter Wildeblood, were arrested on charges of 'gross indecency' involving two airmen at a small private party held in a beach house on Montagu's estate overlooking the Solent. The 1950s made for what Michael recalls as 'a genuine climate of fear for homosexuals'; prominent instances of prosecutions for homosexual offences included those of actors Max Adrian (imprisoned for six months) and John Gielgud (who was only fined – to much publicity), as well as theatrical photographer Angus McBean. But under the almost rabidly homophobic David Maxwell-Fyffe as Home Secretary in Winston Churchill's last cabinet, for every high profile case there were dozens of ordinary men caught, often by police entrapment in cruising areas or lavatories, whose lives and careers were destroyed. In the Montagu case there was some disquieting doubt about the consistency of the airmen's evidence and the trial was presided over by a clearly prejudiced judge; nevertheless, all three men were sent down, Montagu for fifteen months.

It was at this time that Michael wrote a letter to a friend 'discussing

6. Young man about town in the country – a photograph
taken by John Schlesinger.

Edward's case and making it very clear what my point of view was', a letter
that his father found on Michael's desk and with which he confronted him,
saying quietly, 'I have read this letter and I think you must be a pederast.
Do you realise that you are committing yourself to a life on street corners?'

The language may have been somewhat out of melodrama but Haco's

27

fears were real. The stigma of homosexuality in that period's climate was heavy, much of it based on ignorance; it was still widely believed that homosexuality was a disease or even a mental illness that could be cured, often by aversion therapy. It would be more than another decade before the Wolfenden Report began the path to decriminalisation and, as importantly, to wider understanding.

In the shame of being ashamed – he was bitterly conscious of the degree to which the discovery must have devastated his father – Michael agreed to visit a Wimpole Street psychiatrist, arranged by Haco. Michael attended several sessions – it must in some ways have been a relief to be able to unload some of his confusions and hopes to an impartial listener – before the remarkably sensible psychiatrist wrote to his father:

'… whether or not I can cure your son is academic. But one thing is clear – you must let him try what he wants to do.'

Haco, also remarkably, agreed. He released Michael from his Moorgate shackles and set him free: 'Never again, not even once, right up to when he and my mother died years later was the subject of my sexuality ever mentioned.' The only problem was the question of how Michael might find some entrée into the world he so longed to inhabit. The sole family contact with the theatre was a tenuous one; Lily's cousin Sophie had a husband – Sam Burns – who was second in command to the boxing and sporting promoter Jack Solomon and had met the impresario Jack Hylton through charity and sporting events. Sam offered to write a letter of introduction to Hylton for Michael (at the time Sam did not tell him that he had added to the request that Hylton see his relative 'but discourage him. He's part of a good family business').

Jack Hylton had been one of the most popular dance-band leaders in Britain before he branched out, building up what by the early 1950s had become something of a show-business empire. As well as having leases on theatres in the provinces and in the West End (the Victoria Palace, where he produced all the Crazy Gang shows, the Vaudeville and the Adelphi), he presented summer variety seasons and pantomime throughout the country and big musicals – *Wonderful Town*, *Pal Joey* – and plays in London.

Michael was nervous when meeting him in his Pall Mall office but found him 'benign, as he usually was'. Down-to-earth, short, podgy and rather round-shouldered with a still-strong Lancashire accent, Hylton ran a tight ship in his London office and at first it seemed that no job was available before Hylton mentioned that he was preparing a major production for the cavernous Stoll Theatre in Kingsway. This was Arthur Honneger's dra-

matic oratorio *Saint Joan at the Stake* with Ingrid Bergman, who had appeared previously in the piece for Milan's San Carlo Opera House
directed by her then husband, Roberto Rossellini. The costumes from
the San Carlo version were coming from Italy and Hylton needed someone to co-ordinate them, 'preferably somebody who spoke Italian'.
Michael took a breath, crossed his fingers and said that he did (in truth
he had picked up a smattering on his Italian holiday) and would be
delighted to tackle the job.

Hylton took him on 'for free – I didn't get a salary. I was put in this tiny
room with all these medieval costumes around me', working under Bryan
Michie ('a giant of a man'), Hylton's main talent person who looked after
all the firm's big shows. Discreetly gay, Michie got on well with Michael on
realising his willingness to work hard and his unquenchable passion for
the theatre. Michael also rose in the organisation's eyes when it was
belatedly realised that *Saint Joan at the Stake* had a running time of barely
ninety minutes and nobody had any idea of what might partner it at what
was now extremely short notice. It was Michael who piped up that he had
heard that the Ballet Rambert's *Giselle*, particularly the second act that
could stand by itself, was very fine. He was promptly sent off in the little
Sunbeam Talbot, which he so prized, to the old Marlowe Theatre, Canterbury where the Rambert Company was appearing and to open
negotiations with the *grand dame* Marie Rambert.

Before finalising the deal Hylton deputed Michael to bring Marie Rambert together with Ingrid Bergman ('She was a goddess to me. I was totally
overawed at the thought of meeting her'). Bergman was installed in a suite
at the Savoy, protected by Rossellini and her tough European manager
Gino Arbib. Michael arrived as scheduled with Rambert and knocked on
the suite door only to hear his goddess command, 'Ring the office. I'm not
letting you in.' So, in those days before mobiles, Michael had to abandon
the distinguished choreographer in the corridor while he found a public
telephone, to discover that the Hylton office had bungled by forgetting to
budget for Bergman's *per diem* payments. A Hylton emissary was sent
racing along the Strand with a hefty wad of £5 notes (big pieces of paper at
the time) which Arbib then ordered Michael to slip, one by one, under the
door with a surprised Rambert looking on. Finally, Bergman opened the
door, 'clutching a stonkingly large gin but with a broad smile, her eyes
sparkling', a goddess restored. The two women got on and negotiations
were eventually happily concluded.

Gradually he was earning if not money then at least a good number of

Brownie points in the Hylton office. Another of his tasks became to back up Bryan Michie in covering variety acts or plays at one or other of the try-out theatres off the West End beat on behalf of the management. After office hours Michael would often take himself off to one of the various London Empires – Chelsea, Streatham, Chiswick, Shepherd's Bush – or drive out to Kew to cover the offerings at the 'Q' theatre where productions were seen before occasionally being picked up for subsequent West End production.

The 'Q' operation was run by a benign despot, Beatrice de Leon, from a show business family (her cousin, the established agent Herbert de Leon, became one of Michael's regular backers). She was known as a notorious penny pincher on salaries; she was once heard firing off instructions to an assistant about how many pounds a week to pay one actor – 'She'll ask for five, she's worth two, offer her three, settle for four' – and Max Adrian was less than pleased when he went to discuss a new play with her (reluctantly, his agent having told him that the salary would only be £7) to read upside down on her desk a list of possible casting for the role with a note against his name: 'If Max Adrian, £6.'

Some of these expeditions would inevitably be a waste of an evening but still everything was grist to Michael's mill. He was gaining invaluable knowledge of artists – he began to realise what fine actors rather than just personalities some variety or revue performers could be (Beryl Reid and Jimmy Jewel among them) – and of production values and, occasionally, something interesting might turn up. A 'Q' play that impressed him as having further commercial possibilities was *Ring For Catty*, 'a funny and sometimes touching piece' by the actor Patrick Cargill and his partner Jack Beale, based on their meeting in a TB ward. On Michael's recommendation Hylton took out an option on the play and before long seemed to have brought off the coup of casting Richard Attenborough (a big name from British movies and recently from the first cast of Agatha Christie's *The Mousetrap*) in the leading role.

Another project that Michael brought to Hylton turned out to be extremely profitable. Michael received a letter from Julian Slade, who had written revues when an undergraduate at Cambridge – he had met Michael when catching Oxford shows – about a just-opened musical, which he had written with the actress Dorothy Reynolds for the Bristol Old Vic where he was a junior member of the company, saying that it was going very well and that although it had on it 'the thumbprint of Linnit and Dunfee' (a leading West End management company), nothing was definitely fixed and that 'it might be the sort of thing to appeal to your boss'.

Hylton agreed to Michael's suggestion of a rail trip to cover the production at Bristol, unaware that there was an ulterior motive; Michael Meacham, 'an extremely good-looking, fair-haired actor' on whom he had had a major 'crush' at Oxford, was in the cast. But it was an uncomfortable journey; Julian Slade was represented by the mighty MCA organisation, then the most powerful agency in London, and for the performance that Michael caught there was a formidable fellow-travelling posse of sleekly tailored 'gentlemen-agents' – Terence Plunket-Greene, Kenneth Carten and Philip Pearman – 'all these queeny agents from MCA, all obviously thinking why is this snotty little creature from Jack Hylton travelling with us?'

Michael thought that the musical – called *Salad Days* – was 'fresh and entertaining' with some, for him, nostalgia-inducing scenes set in an idyllic Oxford (Michael Meacham's presence reinforced the feeling). He reported positively back to Hylton, warning him 'not to star it up', which he knew would compromise its special charm, and which was agreed. Hylton then did a deal with Linnit and Dunfee, speedily closed his long-running American import *The Moon is Blue* at the Vaudeville even although it was doing still strong business, and moved *Salad Days* into its ideal intimate auditorium; it would be in residence there on the Strand for four years.

The *Salad Days* notices were ecstatic and the morning after opening Hylton added to Michael's euphoria: 'This one will run. You're now going to be put on salary.' He moved to another room tucked away in the 'warren of offices' in Pall Mall at the foot of the Haymarket (Hylton's own office was sumptuous, with a dramatic view right up the Haymarket); Michael, again invaluably for his later career, found himself doing artists' contracts, checking every detail ('I would do a précis of every single contract, building up a kind of Roladex system') although he continued to monitor productions in the evenings. It was at this point, working such long hours, although willingly, that he felt he could no longer go on living at home. Moreover David Hicks had been pressing ('We can't have you living way out in Hampstead Garden Suburb any more') and was suggesting that Michael move into a mews flat at No. 8 Egerton Garden Mews. This belonged to Hicks's secretary, Heather Dickson Wright, but she was living clandestinely (her parents would not have approved) with 'a bit of a villain' and her empty flat was conveniently close to Chester Terrace. Michael was delighted to be 'living in a Knightsbridge Mews in a very chic flat – later the premises became a restaurant, called No. 8, run by the trail-blazing transsexual April Ashley – opposite a vile-tempered agent called Joan Rees'. He quickly took to life in what was then quite a ritzy but

31

still pleasingly slightly raffish area – the rackety pub, The Bunch of Grapes, was on the corner of his mews.

The Hylton office had now plunged into preparations for one of the firm's most spectacular productions, *Kismet* for the vast Stoll Theatre. The George Wright/Edwin Forrest musical, loosely based on episodes from *The Arabian Nights* with music borrowed from Borodin, had been a Broadway hit – the big numbers 'And This is My Beloved' and 'Stranger in Paradise' were popular in the UK too – and Hylton was set on making the London production equally eye-popping. For added box office insurance he imported all three of the New York stars: Alfred Drake (in his first London appearance – he had not repeated his Broadway successes in *Oklahoma!* and *Kiss Me, Kate* in the West End), Joan Diener and Doretta Morrow.

Michael was in a well-placed position to observe and grasp something of the mechanics of putting together a large-scale project: 'My little office was right next door to the bookkeeper Mrs Cohen who handed out the *per diems* in cash. The choreographer, Jack Cole, would be in regularly for his. He was a difficult personality but his contribution to that show was incredible.' He would also encounter the diva figure of Joan Diener, wife of *Kismet*'s director Albert Marre (her two successes in a career otherwise consisting of famous flops were in *Kismet* and *Man of La Mancha*, also directed by Marre), swathed in sables and usually 'with a tiny Chihuahua peeking out from her awesome embonpoint'.

Handily placed between the Stoll and the Pall Mall office was another favourite – and much more respectable – watering hole of Michael's where he often stopped off during *Kismet* preparations. He had become a regular at the first-floor restaurant, The Grill and Cheese, in the enormous Coventry Street branch of Lyon's Corner House. Before the war it had been a well-known gay pick-up venue (known to regulars as the Lily Pond), but its post-war makeover had transformed it and now it was even more popular than the grander ground floor Brasserie with its marble floor and Palm Court trio. It was always jam-packed with many actors and a West End crowd who liked its informal smoky atmosphere and unpretentious, affordable menu featuring Welsh Rarebit or poached eggs on toast. A loyal regular was Kenneth Williams whose career in London, following his Dauphin to Siobhan McKenna's heroine in *Saint Joan* and his radio appearances with Tony Hancock, was beginning to take off. He loved The Grill and Cheese: 'Everybody goes there – O, just everyone, and you get people going round tables waving at everyone. It is a riot.'

Williams would hold court there, often telling outrageously embroidered anecdotes of his family life in his uniquely malleable voice, sliding from nasal whinny to plummy condescension in an instant, surrounded by theatrical acquaintances, some of them – John Schlesinger included – already known to Michael, and others such as Rachel Roberts, Anna Massey and John Perry from the H.M. Tennent office. Michael, too, became an habitué, entranced by ('even slightly under the spell of') Williams and his ability to take a subject and spiral it into delirious comedy. Their close friendship – one of the very few that he formed with an actor – was important to Michael, his 'Grill and Cheese relationship'.

Kismet, keenly awaited in London where the critics were slightly ambivalent about an invasion of American musicals – *plus ça change* – was also to give Michael an eye-opening insight into how even the seemingly craftiest and most experienced producers can go wrong. During rehearsals Hylton decided that Alfred Drake should see a proper English pantomime and so booked a box at the Palladium for Drake, himself and Michael to see Max Bygraves lead the current extravaganza. The lights dimmed, the overture struck up, the curtain rose on the perennial Village Green scene with the chorus displaying unusually dazzling dentistry for local peasantry, Hylton waved expansively towards the stage – 'This, Alfred – this is real English pantomime' – and promptly fell into a deep sleep, leaving Michael to cope with an increasingly bemused Drake for the rest of the long evening. The word 'pantomime' was to echo after *Kismet*'s first night. Its ersatz Turkish Delight gaudy exoticism had delighted an escapism-hungry crowd, with Diener's huge if hardly subtle voice practically shattering the Stoll's chandeliers in 'Not Since Nineveh', but the next morning Michael found Hylton in his office, surrounded by unanimously positive notices, moaning, 'What have I done? Oh, what have I done?' Michael asked him what on earth was wrong and Hylton looked up almost tearfully to explain, 'I thought they'd dismiss it as just a pantomime so I sold half the show to Prince Littler.' (Another major theatre-owner and producer. And *Kismet* was soon established as a profitable hit.)

Hylton was relying increasingly on Michael, often asking him to accompany him when he visited out of town venues such as The Grand Theatre, Blackpool. Once, when taking notes there at a post-production meeting in Hylton's hotel suite, his boss asked 'out of the blue if I wanted to see his appendicitis scar. Before I could answer he had dropped his trousers and lifted up his shirt so I could see not only an impressive scar but this enormous member, which went some way to explain his priapism.'

One of Michael's unofficial duties was regularly to look after one or other of Hylton's 'nieces' while they waited for him to turn up at the theatre or a restaurant. Although married with a son and a daughter, living in 'a sweet *rus in urbe* mews house in Mayfair', there was also a little house tucked away behind the Dorchester Hotel for the 'nieces', of whom there seemed a never-ending supply.

Hylton was extremely discreet but he was still surprised when the Moral Re-Armament organisation began to court him, mainly through its member Doctor Dyce who had a magnificent Berkeley Square house. He invited Hylton, who insisted that Michael accompany him, to a specially organised concert at MRA's Westminster Theatre base where they were 'ushered into rather throne-like seats in the front row while a girls' choir sang at us for quite a time'. Hylton did not respond further to MRA overtures; his verdict to Michael at the end of the singing had been terse: 'Forty fookin' virgins!'

The wily agent-cum-fixer Gino Arbib turned up in Michael's life once more when he alerted Hylton to the possibilities for London in a hit Paris revue created by Robert Dhery, *La Plume de ma Tante*. Discovering that Michael had a passport, Hylton summoned him at once to Croydon Airport to join him on the trip to vet the production of what Michael thought was 'an elegantly staged and very funny revue' (there was a good deal of mime – the show's highlight was an hilarious wordless scene involving monks on bell ropes – reducing the translation problem). Hylton seemed keen too but was even keener to visit a nightclub he had been recommended, a little *boîte* where Stephane Grapelli played the violin. There he picked up a girl who both Michael and Arbib thought promised to be 'a bit of a disaster'. It transpired that she was indeed a disaster for Hylton – she refused to sleep with him. He and Michael made their way home, Hylton disconsolately muttering, 'Fookin' Paris. You can have more fun in London on a rainy Monday night.' 'When I explained to Hylton that last Monday night had been the first-year anniversary party of *Salad Days* held in the Wedgewood Room at the Vaudeville, with all the actors present, Hylton confided that after we had left, he and the co-owner of the Vaudeville, Jack Gatti, had invited a couple of ladies of the night to perform together in front of them. Part of my education! Hylton had also asked me to provide a lady for him and one for myself from the concierge of the Claridge where we were staying in Paris. I was able to say that this was forbidden by the hotel management. Phew!' There was some consolation; *La Plume de ma Tante* enjoyed a very big West End success at the Garrick.

By 1955 Hylton's astute business sense had alerted him to the possibili-

7. Jack Hylton, with modest billing.

ties of television. A major change in British life in the mid-fifties was the introduction to rival the BBC's monopoly of a new, commercial station. Instead of one giant company, the Conservative government set up the commercial enterprise on a regional basis, franchises being awarded to companies for different areas of the country. Companies included ATV for London weekend programmes and ABC for the Midlands, with tycoons like Val Parnell of the Moss Empires Group and Lew Grade on their boards. The London weekday franchise was Associated Rediffusion (the press baron Lord Rothermere was its big cheese), which could hardly deal with Moss Empires or the Grade agencies for light entertainment programmes, instead approaching Hylton who formed, extremely cannily, Jack Hylton Television Productions Ltd to provide Rediffusion's television light entertainment product, unique in television then. Rediffusion was not alone in contracting out areas of programming (ATV for a time initially contracted H.M. Tennent for its drama – fondly known in the industry as 'Binkievision') but it had no significant jurisdiction over what Hylton's company provided, which tended to focus on old Hylton favourites, most notably The Crazy Gang, Elsie and Doris Waters ('Gert and Daisy'), Arthur Askey or Robert Dhery and the *La Plume de ma Tante* team. Associated Rediffusion wanted him to create a series of light entertainment shows and had wooed him heavily, looking to him and Bryan Michie to help them. Michael vetted Hylton's contract to produce a series of shows to be televised from the old

35

Wood Green Empire, for which he was, it read, to receive £30,000 for a first series, a genuinely mind-boggling fee for the time. Michael assumed that there had been an error and went to see his boss to point out that Rediffusion had mistakenly added an extra nought, to which Hylton looked up to say only, 'No, £30,000. That's what they're paying me.'

Television began to take first place with the workaholic Hylton. His shows were sadly routine, however, mostly trotting out familiar acts and just sometimes showcasing young singers such as Shirley Bassey, but rarely surrounding them with production values of any imagination. They were, as Michael said, 'essentially photographed versions of stage variety shows'. Hylton's libido came to blind his judgement somewhat also. He fell extremely heavily for an Italian singer, Rosalina Neri, 'a workaday Sophia Loren' of modest talent at best but whose bottle-blonde voluptuousness ensnared Hylton. 'Mistakenly – or, just possibly, deviously – he asked Bud Flanagan of The Crazy Gang to help her with her barely existent English but all she ever came up with was "Jack likes my pussy", so that was stopped pretty quickly.' Despite massive public indifference and dreadful press comments Hylton continued determinedly to programme Neri, paying sizeable sums for her exotic gowns, in show after show. He even headlined her in *The Rosalina Neri Show*, programmes that became notorious for their wobbly sets and the star's propensity for mangling or forgetting her lyrics. Hylton, of course, could not have foreseen that television would sound the death knell of the variety theatre on the stars and material from which he drew for his television output.

Then it transpired that because of a film offer Richard Attenborough was not after all going to star in *Ring For Catty*: 'So I went to Jack and in my arrogance I said, "Well, if you're going to concentrate on television can I take up your option on *Ring for Catty*?" And he said "Yes" and let me go.' It was time. His years with Hylton – in many ways a good mentor for him however different in temperament – had given him invaluable and appreciated experience but, as he expressed, 'All the decisions you take when you're working for someone else are very different from doing it on your own.' He had done next to no direct negotiations with agents for the services of writers, actors, directors or designers, and had no experience in the crucial area of working from scratch closely with a creative team when preparing and budgeting a production. But he had been a very rapid learner and by now had a fairly comprehensive knowledge of West End theatre politics (as Byzantine then as they are now) and of the basic nuts and bolts of theatre production.

With no hard feelings on either side Michael left the Hylton office, his place taken by another mustard-keen young man who would similarly go on to produce: Bob Swash ('much more intellectual than me'). It was late 1955 and having scraped together the £100 needed to take out a year's option on *Catty* – his sole asset as a producer apart from his wits – he now prepared to set himself up as an independent impresario in the West End.

CHAPTER 4

FIRST FIRST NIGHTS

The landscape of the London stage in early 1956 against which the firm of Michael Codron Ltd was established was very different from that of today.

Then there was no National Theatre and no Royal Shakespeare Company, although The Old Vic, in less than glorious repair, still gave the capital regular Shakespeare productions. In effect London theatre meant the Shaftesbury Avenue-dominated West End. There were a few off-West End ventures such as 'Q' and the Lyric, Hammersmith where the H.M. Tennent management had based the Company of Four, its non-profit operation, for some years after the war into the early 1950s. The little Arts Theatre just off the Charing Cross Road presented some adventurous work and under Peter Hall's regime there London had recently seen Samuel Beckett's much discussed and controversial *Waiting for Godot*. There would be, too, from April 1956, the newly formed English Stage Company based at the Royal Court in Sloane Square under George Devine, whose commitment was to new work and who had announced a first season to include a play by actor John Osborne titled *Look Back in Anger*, and the British premiere of Arthur Miller's *The Crucible*.

It was Miller who had famously remarked on a visit to London at this time: 'The London theatre is hermetically sealed off from life.' There was an abundance of superb, technically polished acting, stylishly impeccable, but hardly any of it was yoked to contemporary plays of any relevance or resonance. English acting then was essentially informed by the theatre rather than by life.

There were many busy producers – Donald Albery, Henry Sherek, Linnit and Dunfee, Stephen Mitchell, Robin Fox, Peter Saunders, Emile Littler and Peter Daubeny included, very different personalities with their own tastes and styles, if mostly very much of the urbane Garrick Clubbing 'gentleman producer' school – although easily the most powerful was the H.M. Tennent Ltd firm, which had risen to prominence before the war and was now controlled by its late founder Harry Tennent's protégé Hugh Beaumont, known by the not always affectionate diminutive of 'Binkie'. A classic instance of an iron fist sheathed in an exquisitely tooled glove of the softest velvet, Beaumont favoured reassuringly illusionist theatre, co-cooned behind the proscenium arch, his productions regularly using the grandmasters of decorative design (Oliver Messel and Cecil Beaton) and headed by stars loyal to the firm including John Gielgud, Rex Harrison, Michael Redgrave, Ralph Richardson, Anton Walbrook, Edith Evans, Vivien Leigh, Margaret Leighton, Margaret Rutherford, Diana Wynyard, *et al.*

In the immediate post-war period the Tennent domination of London's commercial theatre was the source of some jealousy from fellow producers while some directors and actors felt that heterosexuality was a bar to employment (not fundamentally true – certainly the Inner Circle of Ten-nentry was gay but the often alleged Beaumont 'casting couch' was a myth). Questions were even asked in the House of Commons about the justice of a near-monopoly situation and the validity of Tennent's non-profit wing. Beaumont had certainly been wily over the latter, but stayed always within the letter of the law.

Beaumont's taste – which often coincided with but never anticipated that of the public – dictated the Tennent house style. Revivals of Oscar Wilde, sumptuously presented, were a speciality while Noël Coward and Terence Rattigan were virtually house authors. In 1956 he was at his zenith. From the Tennent offices high up in the Globe (now Gielgud) Theatre, giving him a symbolically commanding vista of Shaftesbury Avenue, he oversaw that year no less than a dozen productions. Revivals dominated – two Shavian reappraisals included – alongside a brace of new Cowards: *South Sea Bubble* with Vivien Leigh, and *Nude with Violin* starring and directed by Gielgud. The firm's new play for 1956 was Enid Bagnold's *The Chalk Garden* with Edith Evans and Peggy Ashcroft, directed by Gielgud, its orchidaceously mandarin dialogue echoing the last defiant trumpet notes of the post-war poetic drama movement led by Eliot and Christopher Fry, which proved to be a false dawn.

Elsewhere there were thrillers galore, a speciality of producer Peter Saunders, with Agatha Christie's *The Mousetrap* in its infancy and *Spider's Web* at the Savoy. Broad English farcical comedies, often rooted in a Forces setting or in a domestic world, curiously preserved alike in the amber of a previous era, could be phenomenally popular – the Whitehall farce *Dry Rot* with Brian Rix and the comedy *Sailor Beware!* both clocked up over 1,200 performances. Musicals then, as now, proliferated although to nothing like the extent of today; alongside the smaller-scale English *Salad Days* and Sandy Wilson's artful pastiche *The Boy Friend*, big Broadway imports (*Kismet, South Pacific, The Pajama Game*) also thrived, together with large-scale American plays with a military or a wartime background (*No Time for Sergeants, Teahouse of the August Moon*).

At that time work from Europe often seemed to prosper in London; Ugo Betti's *Summertime* and Jean Giraudoux's *Tiger at the Gates* had been successful and 1956 saw another, Jean Anouilh's *The Waltz of the Toreadors* do well, as his work often did then. The most significant director of his era, Peter Brook, directed virtually no new English work then; he spent the first decade of his career staging mainly European work – usually French, from Anouilh and Sartre to the musical *Irma la Douce*.

It has become almost a critical commonplace – a lazy one – to portray the post-war British stage as a time of inky darkness before the new dawn launched by *Look Back in Anger* in 1956. The immediate post-war decade had in fact seen work as varied as *The Cocktail Party*, *The Lady's Not For Burning*, and plays by N.C. Hunter or Wynyard Browne of more than middling interest, not to mention two masterpieces *maudits* – John Whiting's *Saint's Day* and Rodney Ackland's extraordinary *Absolute Hell* (originally *The Pink Room*) set on the eve of Labour's 1945 election victory, reviled at the time (Beaumont was aghast at its canvas and subversion and most critics totally failed to grasp the thrust of Ackland's satire), but subsequently reclaimed by Richmond's Orange Tree Theatre under Sam Walters and then at the National Theatre.

Undoubtedly, however, there was a good deal of meretricious work around in 1956. Revue, Michael's pet genre, was flourishing and often commercially very profitable (*For Amusement Only* by the established Peter Myers/Ronald Cass team ran for some 700 Apollo performances). But in its self-regarding parochial perspective, revue was beginning to display signs of atrophy. Like so much London theatre it was mostly thriving at the box office but it also illustrated the core of truth in Arthur Miller's verdict on the British stage at that time.

There was another crucial difference between then and now. Production costs were still low. An average-size-cast play with a single set could be mounted in Shaftesbury Avenue for around £2,000 (today it would be nearer £400,000). Raising the capitalisation was not the complex process it has become, leading often these days to several producers grouping together to present a play (not infrequently now there are more producers than cast names on a play's poster), considerably reducing the number of solo producers with a distinctive, individual voice.

It was still difficult to come from nowhere however. Even with his Hylton background, Michael still had to address various key issues, not least that of finding office space. That question was to a degree answered for him when David Hicks had to tell him that Heather Dickson Wright's father – an awesome figure, vividly evoked by Heather's sister, 'Fat Lady' Clarissa, in her autobiography – had rumbled her affair and had ordered her to end it and return to living at Egerton Mews. This coincided with Michael's relationship with Hicks running its course; neither had assumed that it was to be an enduring partnership and they remained friends.

On the grapevine Michael heard about the possibility of a flat in Paultons Street in Chelsea being available. An Oxford friend, Robert David Macdonald, had left without taking his degree (later he would form one of the triumvirate that transformed Glasgow's Citizen's Theatre) and was now 'running around town with a very racy crowd – he was a chum of Bill Gaskill's – and he told me that his mother had just bought a house in Paultons Street, which had a flatlet intended for him but he wanted to be independent and live on his own, so I should go and see her'.

Jane Macdonald, an eminent dermatologist at the Skin Hospital in Lisle Street, had just got home when Michael called and she somewhat disconcerted him after introductions with: 'I've been staring at a pimply Polish arse all afternoon – God, I need a gin!' She cross-questioned him candidly, asking outright, 'I assume you have the same proclivities as my son?' and when Michael nodded, went on, 'That's fine by me, but the flat is on the top floor and I do not want the clump, clump of guardsmen's boots outside my door all night.' Michael assured her 'that guardsmen were not my bag', which seemed to decide Mrs Macdonald. So Michael was soon installed upstairs at No. 3 Paultons Street (a fashionable enough address for company notepaper and telephone number – the theatre world was, and remains, even in the digital era, peculiarly snobbish about such details) in a large bed/sitting room, which he could convert into an office during the day (there was no way he could afford separate premises).

Another stroke of luck came his way when Richard Eastham agreed to work for him as general manager. Respected in the theatre world, Eastham had run a repertory company at Amersham and then worked for H.M. Tennent but, robustly heterosexual, he did not happily fit in with the atmosphere there under Beaumont and his associate John Perry, and so the firm 'lost him'. Also at this time Michael's personal life altered when he and a new lover, the fair-haired and affably handsome Michael Charlesworth – he had nothing to do with the theatre, much as he enjoyed it, and worked in the personnel department of Quaker Oats – began a serious relationship that would last for the time that he lived in Paultons Street.

41

Altogether his luck seemed to be holding, confirmed when he encountered unusual kindness and co-operation from the agency representing the authors of *Ring for Catty*. The firm of Eric Glass Ltd (Michael called it 'The Glass Menagerie') was based in handsome Berkeley Square offices, where in a vast room overlooking the square Eric Glass and his wife Blanche sat at massive desks. Eric was gently spoken (he – and Blanche – tended to call everyone from managing director to office boy 'sweetie' or 'my dear' on the telephone), sallow and rather sluggish-looking (his brain however was monkey-quick), while the diminutive Blanche, despite being plagued by arthritis and skin trouble, was always impeccably dressed and coiffed and invariably cheerful ('You'd always be greeted with "Hello, sweetie!"'). Michael later reflected: 'They probably saw me as wonderful pickings, someone inexperienced who could bend to their will. They kind of took me over for a while. Perhaps also I was a surrogate son figure – there was a son but he was apparently disinherited and was never discussed. But they were genuinely very kind to me then and when I later did plays by some of their other clients.'

The Glasses were indeed of enormous help in the setting up of Michael's first West End venture, although they too of course would be doing well from their percentages of clients' earnings should *Ring For Catty* succeed. They helped Michael cast the play – their client Patrick McGoohan (still some years away from stardom in the cult TV series *The Prisoner*) played the lead – and it was directed by actor/director Henry Kendall, also a Glass client, while 'through their finagling they steered me towards the Lyric Theatre, Shaftesbury Avenue, where they'd heard there could be an imminent closure leaving the theatre available for a limited season prior to *South Sea Bubble* opening there'.

The capitalisation was simple. Michael had left Hylton without having had access to his list of backers (producers tend to guard their 'angels' closely) but he was able to obtain an overdraft from his bank ('secured in my father's name – he was happy to do this'), the Glasses invested some money and Michael contributed the small amount he had managed to save. It cost 'just over' £2,000 to launch his first venture.

'At that age you don't worry,' said Michael, who was still only twenty-five at the time. He knew that *Ring For Catty* was no masterpiece but with its well-observed sanatorium setting (Jack Beale had spent time in a TB hospital) and adept interweaving of laughter and sentiment, it was by no means a bad example of the well-made West End play and with McGoohan, the popular William Hartnell (long before the first *Dr Who*) and

Andrew Ray in the cast he had put together a strong package. Rehearsals went well – Michael from the start was not one of those producers who hover over proceedings like a nervous nanny, preferring rather to attend the first day of rehearsal, returning for a later run-through, although naturally always available in the event of any crisis – before the company played one try-out week in a freezing Harrow and then opened directly (no previews then) on Shaftesbury Avenue in February 1956; Haco and Lily – along with several other family members – were at Michael's first West End first night. The top price – in line with most plays in the West End then – was £1/6s (£1.30); programmes of the period regularly advertised Soho and central restaurants with pre- or post-theatre meals at 7/6d for three courses.

The press endorsed Michael's own feelings about his production; *Ring For Catty*'s scrutiny of the pathos and the fun of life in a hospital ward was judged enjoyably skilful if occasionally too manipulatively sentimental. His cast was treated well; the nurse, Catty, is not a lead role but McGoohan and Hartnell, confined to bed for much of the evening, and Andrew Ray as an introverted boy were all widely praised.

'It was doing solid business at the Lyric when I had to close it to make way for Coward's play. Then, with even more arrogance I transferred it to the Lyric, Hammersmith. Absolutely the wrong way round. It didn't make money overall, although it just about washed its face. Two years later I was stuck in Brighton having a dismal time with a new play, *Fool's Paradise*, en route for London. I sneaked off one afternoon to the cinema and saw *Carry on Nurse*, very surprised to see among the opening credits: "Based on a play by Patrick Cargill and Jack Beale"! So later I rang Eric Glass who said, "Oh, sweetie, I forgot to tell you. We sold the play to Peter Rogers and Gerald Thomas but they never got the film together. They sold on the rights as a tax dodge and we get one percent of the gross." So, as the film was quite successful, *Ring For Catty* did eventually pay off.'

With his bank manager still sympathetic, Michael was confident enough to set up his next production, reassured that it would be backed to a significant extent by Heather Dickson Wright's lover (the affair continued despite her parents' despair) John Taylor who was 'in property' in Curzon Street offices. The agent Derek Glynne had sent Michael a new play – *A Month of Sundays* – by his client Gerald Savory about which H.M. Tennent were dithering, and Glynne was unable to push Beaumont into a decision. Savory, an ex-actor and much-married *boulevardier*, had written the long-running, pre-war hit *George and Margaret* and was still something of a name dramatist.

8. The first 'Michael Codron Presents' – *Ring for Catty*, 1956.

Michael took out an option, although as with *Ring For Catty* he was open-eyed about *A Month of Sundays*; while not in the first rank, it was another skilfully handled, well-made play with the bonus of touching on a central subject, which could well strike a chord in a grey 1950s London.

Well before *The Good Life* or the Green movement, Savory dramatised the urge to get out of cities and back to the land with his story of a couple and their three very contrasted daughters leaving London to experiment with self-sufficiency in Cornwall, using traditional farming methods and

9. William Hartnell, Patrick McGoohan, Terence Alexander (L-R) in
the sanatorium of *Ring For Catty*, 1956.

shunning chemicals, like pioneer settlers in America. A love-interest subplot involved a strapping farmhand bemused by the townees' ineptitude
and a comic plus was the character of Major Twomely-Bickford, a gentle-
man-hobo with a handy habit of fainting whenever he is asked to move on,
gloriously played by the incomparable veteran A.E. Matthews, who rarely
stuck precisely to any script but whose ad-libs provided often better lines.

Again the notices on the play's opening in the spring of 1957 confirmed
Michael's opinion; it was generally described as amiable if undemanding,
but Matthews was universally adored (he celebrated seventy years on the
stage during the run, an event that was much publicised. Characteristically, to the backstage party organised by Michael and the company,
he invited the youngest actress in every show in London) and both Ian
Hunter and Jane Baxter (she had appeared in *George and Margaret*) as the
parents were popular West End actors, if not major box office names.

A Month of Sundays settled down to a respectable run at the Cambridge,
a larger house than Michael ideally would have liked, but then a new kid

on the block without a really 'hot' or starry property was not going to see a prime theatre fall into his lap unless a theatre owner was desperate. Similarly Michael understood that exciting scripts hot off the typewriters of major writers were not going to come his way yet awhile. But even his earliest productions, while unlikely to be ever considered great plays, were marked by an ability to sniff out something in a script – the hospital background and the men's back-stories in *Catty*, the rural dream backbone of *A Month of Sundays* – with which audiences could identify, a strain at least to a degree plugged into some contemporary reality.

Savory's play had been a close-run thing however, exposing Michael to a producer's worst nightmare. After an enjoyable rehearsal period – the play was directed by Wallace Douglas, a comedy specialist and Jack Hylton regular – the brief pre-London tour opened at Nottingham where Michael received a bombshell: 'John Taylor came to me and admitted that he couldn't come up with his share of the money. It was quite terrifying. I was already committed to the Cambridge, of course. I had to throw myself on the mercy of Derek Glynne.'

Glynne was less sunny a personality than either Glass, telling Michael, 'You have jeopardised my client,' and giving him a very hard time. Eventually Glynne did help arrange the remaining capitalisation 'but he insisted on stringent financial conditions, which did me no favours at all'.

This nerve-testing episode reinforced Michael's feeling that it might be unwise to launch his next production directly into the mainstream West End, and instead he set it up to be launched at the Arts Theatre. He was very drawn to the offbeat quality of Mervyn Peake's *The Wit to Woo*; Peake, as devotees of his in fiction novels like the *Gormenghast* sequence knew, was a magical verbal stylist and Michael often was drawn to dramatists with an individual tone of voice in their dialogue (Pinter, Orton, Stoppard *et al*). *The Wit to Woo* in some ways recalled Peter Ustinov's more fanciful work such as *No Sign of the Dove*, a similarly fantastical comedy with an underlying serious strain, although Peake's exuberant dialogue is his uniquely. Its central character is a young man, Percy Trellis, so tongue-tied when with his beloved Sally that with the help of his resourceful servant Kite he stages his own death (shades of Priam Farll in Arnold Bennett's *Buried Alive*), watching his coffin (filled with his books) go off for burial. Since Sally aches for excitement he returns in the guise of his more assertive cousin October Trellis, a Bohemian artist, and seems to be doing well until Sally begins to miss the gentler cousin, forcing him to return again as Percy, facing a difficult time persuading everyone he is not a ghost. Woven into this plot were four comic undertakers (later transformed into bailiffs) and Sally's father, periodically descending from an upstairs room in a bed suspended on ropes.

Peake's writing demanded imaginative casting and a production of distinctive flair. Michael opted for the young director Peter Wood who had been prominent in undergraduate Cambridge theatre and had recently been responsible for some admired Arts Theatre work, including Eugene Ionesco's absurdist *The Bald Prima Donna*. The droll and inventive Colin Gordon was cast as Percy/October while Michael was thrilled when Kenneth Williams agreed to take on the crucial Jonsonian role of Kite.

Williams responded positively to the play at once: 'It is always the words that interest me and Peake's dialogue was full of verbal conceits and wonderful imagery and, above all, theatrically effective,' he wrote to a friend, adding that the part of Kite 'glittered with malevolence and vituperative wit'. He and Peake developed an immediate rapport during rehearsals: 'I always remember talking to Mervyn Peake in the stalls in rehearsals and saying to him, "You love the word PLUM, don't you?!" And being shocked and delighted when he replied, "Yes, and BUM and COME – lovely sounds!"'

His actor's instincts and intelligence told Williams, rightly, that *The Wit to Woo* would wither on the vine without a knife-edge production of wholehearted theatrical bravura. Later in his career he often battled from the outset with directors when he sensed that his own opinions (by no means always right) were being ignored; he and Wood had no clash of egos on Peake's play but he always felt that it was ill-served at the Arts. He had a point in this instance; Peake's style called for a heightened, zestful relish while it was mainly played in a modern high-comedy style with a good deal of 'throwaway' technique, so compromising the play.

Michael had responded to the piece's 'experimental quality and its rich, textured dialogue' but although it was greeted as undeniably an original, most critics had the same cavil, that after the wit and power of the first act the play sank into absurdity. The one element to emerge as an unqualified success was Williams's Mosca-like Kite, a hypnotic study in the grotesque, perfectly pitched to Peake's Gothic style amid too many performances that missed the authentic tone. There was enough of a Peake fan club to keep the Art's box office moderately busy but there was absolutely no chance of a subsequent profitable West End transfer.

Financially Michael was just about still afloat, although there had been little profit over his three productions to date to supplement the office's weekly management fee (usually £20 per week then for a play's preparation period, rehearsals and run). Haco had allowed Michael at least to try in his ideal profession and indeed he and Lily were quietly proud of what he had achieved in less than two years. But Haco worried about Michael and money and had, ominously, recently voiced hints of the possibility of a return to Moorgate.

There was by this time in 1957 the sense of a palpable shift, just finding its impetus – the suggestion of a Kraken wakening – in the theatre. After a decidedly shaky start with 'literary' theatre including plays from Angus Wilson and Nigel Dennis, the English Stage Company had begun to find its voice with *Look Back in Anger* (from which Beaumont departed at the interval), initiating the groundswell that would gradually transform the Royal Court into a powerhouse of urgent British contemporary writing. Plays by such new voices as John Arden and Arnold Wesker were in the pipeline, while no less an Establishment star than Laurence Olivier was preparing to appear at the Court in Osborne's play *The Entertainer*. And over in East London the Theatre Workshop Company under Joan Littlewood, which had taken over the old Theatre Royal, Stratford E15, was beginning to make waves with radical reappraisals of major English classics and several plays by Bertolt Brecht (whose Berliner Ensemble had made an influential London visit in 1956), also introducing a rumbustious new Irish writer, Brendan Behan, with *The Quare Fellow*. Britain was still under Tory rule, despite Anthony Eden's Suez debacle – for a period managing to turn both the USA and the USSR against the UK – with a last grandee, Harold Macmillan, now presiding over a government that saw Etonian privilege exert its most exclusive-ever cabinet stranglehold. There were signs, however – increasingly so as that government gradually became further frayed and then mired in scandal – of a Labour revival, even if Harold Wilson did not lead the Party to victory until 1963.

It was looking just possible that the cracks in the carapace or 'hermetic seal' that Arthur Miller had described as encasing the English stage might widen, breaking open the shell to reveal the body of a theatre hungry for the new air beginning to pump into it. But in that event could the commercial theatre capitalise on the stimulus to revitalisation?

And would Michael, still financially underpowered and still struggling to establish the Codron firm on a solid footing, be able to carve out a niche for himself within it?

REVUE REVIEWED

Two minor Shaftesbury Avenue plays and the off-West End brief run of an oddball play – 'My spectacular initial unsuccess' according to Michael – made little impression on either the West End Establishment or Mr Codron senior. Himself frustrated – 'I was looking for something in my own handwriting, as it were' – Michael was well aware that as a tyro producer with no significant track record, he was unlikely to receive virgin scripts from leading literary agents and that top actors' agents would not always return the calls of a young newcomer. He would have to strike out for himself.

The turning point came in 1957 with a show from the area of his old love – intimate revue. Although soon to be more or less killed off – as it transpired Michael would be partly responsible, albeit unwittingly, for the genre's demise – revue in the 1950s was still flourishing and often extremely profitable. The days of the sumptuous, vast-cast, C.B. Cochran-produced Noël Coward revues – *London Calling!*, *On with the Dance*, *This Year of Grace* – were over and the smaller-scale productions of Cochran's rival André Charlot provided the template for the shows of the vintage intimate revue years from the mid-1930s through a wartime and immediately post-war boom to the 1960s. Coward, launching his post-war revue, *Sigh No More*, in lavish Gladys Calthrop designs tried to recapture some of the scale of his golden days of big production numbers such as 'Dance, Little Lady' but taste had changed from that period of large chorus lines of 'Mr Cochran's Young Ladies' (the West End's answer to Ziegfeld Girls) and the public failed to respond.

Much more successful were those productions using the Charlot sketch-song-dance formula but on a more modest scale. The 1930s had seen strings of popular intimate revues – the Herbert Farjeon series at the Little Theatre or Norman Marshall's Gate revues at the Gate Theatre off the Strand – with a large pool of brilliantly versatile performers. 'The Two Hermiones' – Gingold and Baddeley – Joyce Grenfell (who first appeared in a Farjeon revue), Henry Kendall, Beatrice Lillie, Leslie Henson, Binnie and Sonnie

Hale, Walter Crisham, Stanley Holloway, Cyril Ritchard and Hedley Briggs were all regular and highly popular revue performers who became prominent before the Second World War.

The wartime years saw an abundance of revue – the format suited a public hungry for diverting fun – with leading commercial managements including H.M. Tennent, Linnit and Dunfee and Frith Shephard (inevitably one of his shows was called *Shephard's Pie*) taking up the genre. Farjeon continued to entertain during the war, most notably with 1940s *Diversion* (initially only for matinees in the early blackout days) at Wyndham's, with an extraordinary cast that saw Edith Evans make her revue debut (scoring a big success with a monologue of a hop picker bombed out of her home in the East End). Joyce Grenfell, Dorothy Dickson (illustrating revue's somewhat incestuous kind of parody performing Farjeon's 'Nightingales in Berkeley Square', which spoofed the original Eric Maschwitz 'A Nightingale Sang in Berkeley Square', from another contemporary show, *New Faces*), Bernard Miles and Peter Ustinov all joined Evans on the same stage.

The productions on which Michael cut his adolescent teeth were, by and large, preserved in the aspic of wartime and immediately post-war revue. The director Laurier Lister was the guiding spirit of a clever series – *Tuppence Coloured* and *Penny Plain* included – which often featured his partner Max Adrian, a master of the genre, along with Elisabeth Welch and Joyce Grenfell before her solo career. By far the most influential – and Michael's favourites – were the Ambassador Theatre's revues, the *Sweet and Low*, *Sweeter and Lower*, and *Sweetest and Lowest* series mostly written by Alan Melville with music predominantly from Charles Zwar, which all starred Hermione Gingold with her unmistakable voice of black velvet laced with prussic acid and mouth caught permanently it seemed between sneer and leer. Gingold, who could be an inspired clown, was the acme of high camp, scoring especially heavily in monologues such as 'Blanchisseuse Heureuse', about a laundress so prosperous she lives in the Savoy Hotel; she was always supported by a team of individual drolls such as Walter Crisham (also a nifty dancer) and Gretchen Franklin. These revues were extremely well-produced affairs and wittily designed but the content was parochial not to say parish pumpery, often archer than the Admiralty (a good deal of cross-dressing was involved as a rule) with coy 'in' references to a tightly exclusive West End world of theatreland's The Ivy restaurant (a bitchy sketch set therein was, naturally, titled 'Poison Ivy'), 'Binkie' and 'Noël and Gertie'. Parodies of other West End shows were a regular feature; most lethal, in a later revue from the same Ambassador's stable, *Slings and Arrows* (1949), was Gingold's merciless send-up of Eileen Herlie's tragic excesses in a *Medea* revival, brusquely dismissing into the wings an extra usurping her space against a pillar – 'This is my personal column'.

Revue in the 1950s still had a rich pool of writing and performing talent and quite a few of Michael's old Oxford friends – Sandy Wilson and Stanley Myers included – were making their early marks while Eleanor ('Fizz') Fazan, now married to Myers, had established herself as a coming chore-ographer and director. Occasionally the familiar, formulaic revue mould would be broken. *Cranks* (1956) was a trail-blazing show, which made a big impact on many younger revue talents; originating at another enterprising, small off-West End theatre, which gave fresh young writers and perform-ers early breaks – The New Watergate – it was devised and directed by a remarkable ballet talent, John Cranko. With a cast of only four – including Annie Ross and Anthony Newley – it had a surreal quality, heightened by striking, often eerie minimal designs by Michael's old Wantage friend, the painter John Piper, the bright sophisticated music from John Addison, and by Cranko's ceaselessly inventive use of mime and movement. Even the production photographs – by a young Anthony Armstrong-Jones – had a new kind of grainy, unposed informality. It successfully transferred to the West End, although Cranko could not follow up this theatrical success; both *New Cranks* and a dismal 1958 musical *Keep Your Hair On* were short-lived flops.

A much more representative revue of the same period would be a show like *For Amusement Only* (1956) by the prolific team of Peter Myers and Ronald Cass. This had the familiar show business central (almost sole) focus – a burlesque of Ruritanian Rudolf Friml/Sigmund Romberg *Student Prince*-style musicals, a Liberace skit and a spoof of the Laurence Olivier/Marilyn Monroe movie partnership on *The Prince and the Showgirl*. Michael was less interested in this style of self-referential show than in something original like *Cranks*.

He found it at The Other Place – Cambridge. Michael knew Bamber Gascoigne – then an undergraduate – slightly, and got wind of something unusual in the pipeline in the shape of the 1956 Cambridge Footlights revue, written single-handedly by Gascoigne. He made sure that he caught an early performance of the show, *Share My Lettuce*. It hit him immediately that this was 'a distinctive and, vitally, young voice and moreover I at once judged Kenneth Williams perfect to be the lynchpin of the show … and then later I thought he showed great courage in agreeing to be in what was after all only an undergraduate revue'. It looked as if *Lettuce* might have the makings of a production with the stamp of his own handwriting. He made sure that it would look good – Disley Jones came up with stylish, simple but boldly effective sets and costumes – while he also made an inspired choice of director/choreographer. The format of *Lettuce* – sketch, dance and song – may have been conventional enough (although it relied less on punch lines or song 'buttons' than most revues) but Michael had responded to 'an intriguing vein of the surreal running through it' and judged, rightly, that 'Fizz' Fazan could tease out that quality in the material. For him 'she had a quirky quality' compatible with the material's often insouciant, impudent wit and she was, remarkably in the hothouse theatrical world, ego-free and vitally adaptable.

She had beautifully staged a company number, 'Wallflower Waltz', a plangent, elegiac song (a departure from the mainly percussion-heavy syncopated Keith Statham score), with the girls ruefully lamenting their lack of dancing partners while the boys waltzed between them dancing with lengths of different-coloured chiffon (the eight-strong cast were colour coded throughout). On the first night of the Brighton try-out, Kenneth Williams's chiffon band failed to descend from the flies and he had to improvise, darting between the dancers trying to grab the chiffon 'partners' of the other men. The growing laughter told him he was on to something and, not entirely to the delight of the other men he pranced about increasingly dementedly ('Give me a bit! I ain't got a bit!'), while the girls drifted around dreamily warbling, 'Wallflower Waltz where we sit around the walls.' Michael loved it too – 'I knew a good thing when I saw it' – as did Fizz and he insisted that the number remained in its 'accidental' form throughout the run.

Another who appreciated the show's mix of tradition and innovation was Maggie Smith, gleefully joining in the subversion of 'Wallflower Waltz'. Once he had cast Williams, Michael recalled the sharpness of Smith's comedic touch (as Margaret Smith) in Oxford productions: 'It might be taking something of a risk but I felt that she and Ken might have an affinity.' He was right; Smith and Williams struck up an immediate and enduring friendship. Despite his huffs and fusses Williams often could be shrewdly perceptive, spotting in Smith 'a fundamental hysteria ... we share a quiet desperation which isn't always quiet!'

There were some who insisted that Smith's vocal mannerisms owed a great deal to Williams at his most nasal, although in fact her comedic stance – that wary scepticism when faced with a recalcitrant universe – which shared, too, something of her great revue predecessor Beatrice Lillie's drollery, was more than in embryo before she even met Williams. She was the only female co-star about whom he never said or wrote a disparaging word. Formidably gifted, Smith had been absent in America since her success in Oxford theatre and in a Watergate show, most significantly in Leonard Sillman's 1956 version of his *New Faces* revue on Broadway. She had a considerable impact, her stand-out numbers including 'Darts', as a wife dissatisfied with her marital lot playing dangerous darts with her husband and, memorably, portraying an insecure showgirl in a Ziegfeld-style turn, clad in nothing but strategically placed bunches of oranges (coincidentally she was coloured orange in *Lettuce*), trepidatiously descending a precipitous staircase as 'Miss Bowls of Sunshine'.

Michael found her irreverent zest refreshing; meeting him to discuss the show with Fizz at the Cambridge Theatre where his production of the conventional *A Month of Sundays* was running, Smith glanced casually at the stage before remarking, 'Gosh, I didn't think they designed sets like that anymore!' ('You've got chutzpah, but that won't stop you being cast,' thought Michael). Her wit and youthful energy – that of the whole cast in fact – appealed to him and those qualities informed the enterprise: 'It was a very *young* show. The cast were young, the author virtually only just out of adolescence and its whole attitude in the sketches and songs – about dating, mating, jilting and jiving – was quirky and fun.' Michael himself was twenty-six.

Michael decided not to open *Lettuce* directly on Shaftesbury Avenue but to give it a limited run initially at the Lyric, Hammersmith. It was, for him, 'always a congenial, intimate house' and it had, moreover, an established revue tradition from shows under Nigel Playfair and Laurier Lister. A plus was its manager, the endearingly Falstaffian J. Baxter Somerville; as the name suggests he had been something of an 'actor-laddie' prior to going into theatrical administration, and at that time he also managed the Theatre Royal, Brighton where *Lettuce* had its first try-out. Somerville, a life enhancer, took a shine to Michael as a potential, up-coming new producer and did a favourable deal for *Lettuce*.

However *Share My Lettuce* – billed as 'A Diversion with Music' – was not all fun in its progress to the Lyric, Hammersmith in 1957. Williams, prickly and prone to fits of insecurity as always, could be extremely difficult and in rehearsal could often be cutting, especially at the expense of fellow actor Philip Gilbert, confiding to his *Diaries* (one of the most angst-packed books ever published): 'This cruel streak must be controlled – it's something venomous that comes popping out ... I think it's all bound up with sexual frustration.' He would predictably veer from euphoria to despair (he was writing very soon after the first 'very enjoyable' *Lettuce* rehearsals: 'This stuff has no intrinsic worth') and his moods added to the Brighton try-out nerves after he objected to some changes in one of his numbers, upsetting even the usually calm Fizz: 'At rehearsals Fazan had hysterics and left the stage. Codron burst on and shouted at us we weren't co-operating. Then Disley Jones charged B. Gascoigne with subversion and ordered him out of the theatre.'

All of this – fairly par for the course on the Richter scale of tension on out of town try-outs then – exemplified how much was riding on the production for those involved. Michael, in order to capitalise the show sufficiently to give it the high production values he wanted to bring to it, had taken on a somewhat dubious Denmark Street music publisher, Edward Kassner, as an 'angel', one of his backers. But because of the size of his investment Kassner, after learning that Michael's management fee was £20 per week (the fee is a producer's sole reward on any production until production costs are recouped and the venture goes into profit) demanded half, leaving Michael earning a princely £10 per week. With cast member Roderick Cook, always waspish, predicting disaster, the perky singer Barbara Evans saying to him just before the first Brighton performance: 'You are prepared for some booing, aren't you? They've booed John Gielgud here,' the battles over the script, on one occasion leading to Michael locking Bamber Gascoigne in his room at the Royal Crescent Hotel to finish rewrites (eventually the finished *Lettuce* script for London also incorporated some revisions to lyrics by Gascoigne's Cambridge contemporary Michael Frayn) not surprisingly Michael remembered Brighton as 'rather a traumatic time'.

Despite the wobbles *Lettuce* opened to a delighted and unbooed reception in Brighton (Roderick Cook cried copiously afterwards, 'Oh, please, please forgive me!') and then met with a terrific welcome from its first-night audience at the Lyric, Hammersmith (more than one critic noted that there seemed few present over thirty). It transferred to the West End, first to the Comedy, then the Garrick ('This is the longest tour in town,' moaned Maggie Smith as she moved out of another dressing room). Its notices were mixed – 'A nibble is enough of this *Lettuce*' grouched the *Daily Express*'s John Barber, rarely joyous – but the *Evening Standard* was particularly enthusiastic, praising its 'freshness' and hip, throwaway nonchalance. For Michael 'this was the turning point. I decided I *would* have a go and see what I could do. I told my father, "I'm going to carry on." *Lettuce* gave me the courage to think, "This is my voice."'

Audiences adored the material, not least Smith's lament as a love-starved, railway-buffet tea lady in 'One Train He'll Come' and Williams and Smith leading the company in 'Party Games', a polished sketch on social behaviour during which Smith, à la Lillie, manoeuvred a rope of beads all down her body and up again. And despite his volatility, Williams was moved enough on the final night of the run to make 'a wee speech at the end and I felt very serious and sentimental and sad' (the next week saw him dismiss the project as, for him, 'a waste of time').

Lettuce established Michael as a young producer with an attitude of his own. It also fixed Williams and Smith as new revue stars. But while Williams was not averse to continuing in the genre – and to working with Michael again – Smith, never one to stand still for long (agreeing with Noël Coward's adage: 'Never boil your cabbage twice'), wanted to extend her range and took herself off to the Old Vic, where she began to dazzle London in Restoration Comedy and to appear in Shakespeare and J.M. Barrie before becoming part of the first National Theatre company at the Old Vic under Laurence Olivier.

Michael was spreading his net to find new material for Williams, in the meantime producing two bill-paying but anodyne plays. Peter Coke's comedy *Fool's Paradise* (Apollo, 1959) was even lighter than his successful *Breath of Spring*; the central premise was the impoverished state in which the ex-wife and the widow of a rich man find themselves thanks to that gentleman's quirky will. Set in a vast Westminster mansion, the complications of the plot included an eccentric woman wearing a sought-after emerald necklace and swathed from head to foot in silk to ward off the atmosphere's radioactive dust (a somewhat bleakly unrewarding 'joke' in a nuclear world). The financial risk was cushioned by Michael co-producing with the play's wealthy director, Australian-born Allan Davis ('a terrible director, but nobody had told me that'), but even all the indefatigable vitality of the star, Cicely Courtneidge (the pleasure of getting to know her and Jack Hulbert, her husband, was Michael's single happy memory of the production), could not save a rickety plot. Michael also brought in from Windsor Theatre Royal (in association with Windsor's managing director John Counsell, who also directed the play) a comedy by Harold Brooke and Kay Bannerman, *How Say You?* (Aldwych, 1959). The authors had had a major success with *All For Mary* and their new play saw its star, the much loved Kathleen Harrison, give another of her cockney stalwarts, the feisty

Gladys Pudney who is petitioning for the restitution of conjugal rights, stoutly defended by Sidney Pudney on the grounds that he has never set eyes on the woman in his life. The case of Pudney v Pudney involves two young opposing barristers whose antagonism of course eventually leads to true love. The early scenes in Chambers dragged but once in the court-room, the play was divertingly enlivened by Harrison's chirpy forthrightness and by a show-stealing later scene again involving the great light comedian A.E. Matthews – Michael loved watching 'Matty' at work – as an important but finally unhelpful witness in the case. Neither venture was a financial bonanza although both were impeccably and most stylishly produced (Tony Walton's lavish design for the mansion of *Fool's Paradise* was stunning). But neither could genuinely be described as 'stamped by Michael's handwriting'.

Cambridge once again was where he would find gold. Michael had got to know the sometimes mad, usually bad and often dangerous to know William (Willie) Donaldson, a Cambridge contemporary and friend of Bamber Gascoigne. An uncategorisable fusion of erudition (while success-fully posing as supremely indolent, he and friends such as the future dramatist Julian Mitchell produced an impressive Cambridge literary magazine), politesse and often flagrantly blatant misrule, Donaldson – prior to his metropolitan descent into drugs, prostitutes and the inspired creation of Henry Root – had, on coming into family money, bought the Jack Waller production company and, overnight, become a theatrical pro-ducer. His first production – J.P. Donleavy's version of his own novel *The Ginger Man* – was a major *cause célèbre* in London and, notoriously in Dublin, and he was eager to continue to make his mark (later Michael would note: 'It was Willie's misfortune that his first production was a success. Also he never had good, restraining business associates, as I had').

At the suggestion of a savvy young London agent, the sleekly camel-hair-coated Donald Langdon, Willie Donaldson and Michael went to Cambridge together to see what Langdon vowed would be a watershed in Footlights work and in revue alike, a new show, *The Last Laugh*, the 1959 Footlights revue written by undergraduates Peter Cook and John Bird, both already snapped up as Langdon clients. Cook – whose pervasive influence over Oxbridge comedy would continue into the Monty Python era and beyond – was something of an established Cambridge legend while Bird, permanently clad entirely in black, stood out even in an unusu-ally gifted undergraduate theatrical era including Derek Jacobi, Corin Redgrave, Trevor Nunn and Eleanor Bron. Bird had recently directed Cook and Bron in N.F. Simpson's Absurdist comedy *One Way Pendulum* (some like to claim Simpson as a major influence on Cook's style but in truth Cook emerged from the womb with that comic perspective already largely formed – a stronger influence was probably Spike Milligan, whose work he adored) and all three were heavily involved in *The Last Laugh*.

The revue took place throughout in a nuclear bunker with the end of the world imminent; it had a complex physical production including an elaborate sound plot and ambitious use of back projections, with a ten-piece jazz band. Each sketch or episode ended with a death, there were no chorus lines or drag turns – Eleanor Bron at last broke the old Footlights all-male tradition – and the musical numbers were integrated into the action. It was an angry, even at times strident show, written and performed by young people instinctively reacting against a world of what they regarded as ossified tradition, genuinely believing that their generation in a nuclear era had a voice and a role to play. Bird was by nature more of a political animal than Cook whose satire almost always involved mockery, and their different perspectives made for an evening decidedly bifurcated in tone. Bird said himself later, 'Peter provided the only material that was actually funny'; Cook's nine contributions – out of a total of twenty-eight – were easily the stand-outs and included elaborations of his famous Arthur Boylett (later Mr Grole) creation and of his sketch involving a religious eccentric claiming to be carrying the Holy Bee of Ephesus in a cardboard box (the piece now had Grole with a viper – categorically 'not an asp' – in a box).

The Last Laugh died something of a protracted death on its opening; it was much too long (the theatre manager, after four hours, simply went backstage and commanded the cast to stop) and Murphy's Law sailed into overdrive with malevolently malfunctioning lighting and sound cues. After the predictably terrible reviews Bird and Cook reshaped the show, which received an unexpected boost from Alistair Cooke who caught the revised version about which he then raved ('never a fumbling line or gear') in *The Manchester Guardian*.

Willie Donaldson decided on the spot that John Bird was a genius of twentieth-century theatre, taking him on board at once to rework his material into a new show for the West End, *Here is the News*, with additional material from N.F. Simpson and (reputedly) Eugene Ionesco, the cast headed by Cleo Laine and Sheila Hancock. Donaldson genuinely aimed to bring something different to the British stage. He sensed, as did Michael, an established order changing as the monochrome pall of the Age of

Austerity began to lift and as the rigid hierarchies of public school, Oxbridge and St James's clubs were dissolving but, as Donaldson was usually the first to admit, his organisation was hopeless. He allowed the show to be rewritten to accommodate the talents (modest, as it transpired) of a busty ex-stripper whose boyfriend, no stranger to London's underworld, would significantly back the venture in return. Murphy's Law returned with a vengeance on its first night on the road, on a sodden Bank Holiday Monday in Coventry, with spectacular technical disarray; Sheila Hancock recalled subsequently that it was the most hostile audience reception she had ever experienced (she and Cleo Laine, spotted outside the stage door by irate patrons, were chased in the rain up the road). Donaldson brought in Fizz Fazan to attempt a rescue job and she did manage to effect cuts and some improvements (not, however, enough to satisfy the Broadway producer Willie brought to see the show in Oxford hoping for more investment, whose verdict at the interval was: 'You call this a fuckin' revue? There's no fuckin' girls, there's no fuckin' dancing. I'm fuckin' off back to London'). *Here is the News* was doomed and closed its tour three weeks before its scheduled West End opening.

Michael was wiser. And luckier. He had admired the aims if not the execution of *The Last Laugh* but only Cook's sketches really grabbed him ('they were simply hilarious') and he moved quickly. He talked first to Kenneth Williams, who wrote in his *Diaries* in June 1959: 'To Michael Codron. Lunched with him. He has found good material from a boy called Peter Cook from Cambridge. It sounds excellent.'

By now, on top of the success of *Share My Lettuce*, Williams's star was in the ascendant. Famous from *Hancock's Half Hour* on radio (Tony Hancock was, if anything, even more complex-ridden than Williams, and later on television had Williams dropped after only one series) with his nasal catchphrases of "Allo' and 'Stop messing about', he was equally popular in *Beyond Our Ken* and *Round The Horne* with Kenneth Horne, also on radio, building up a repertoire of characters as striking as Cook's Boylett or E.L. Wisty, with his ruminative rustic Arthur Fallowfield ('The answer lies in the soil'), and his imperishable partnerships with Hugh Paddick as the Hoorays Rodney and Charles, and the camp 'Polare'-spouting dual of Julian and Sandy.

Michael arranged a lunch with Cook and Williams – of whom Cook was an admirer – after which he immediately commissioned an entire West End show from Cook, a remarkable step and gesture of belief from a producer towards an undergraduate writer, someone even younger than him (he had showed a similar trust in Bamber Gascoigne). The vein of the surreal to which Michael had responded in Gascoigne's material was something he particularly encouraged Cook to extend also. It would be contained within the song-sketch-dance format but without elaborate set changes (Michael went again to Tony Walton, skilled with shows requiring fleet-ness of movement) and with a significant musical element. He wanted to break from the gentility so prevalent in intimate revue with archly sexless choreography (what Bernard Shaw used to describe as 'skirt dancing') and chose Paddy Stone as director/choreographer, another calculated gamble. Stone, a Canadian, had worked with the Winnipeg Ballet and danced memorably in the London production of *Annie Get Your Gun* and he, like Michael, wanted an altogether leaner, athletic approach (Stone's work had an affinity with that of a Broadway contemporary, Bob Fosse, in its angular sexiness).

With Maggie Smith gone 'legit' Michael co-starred Williams with Fenella Fielding who had first become known to him from North London amateur dramatics before appearing for him in *Valmouth*. This was a 'calculated risk', much as he had appreciated her contribution to his production of Sandy Wilson's musical; her swoopingly dipping vocal cadenzas and ability (shared with Williams) to switch on the turn of a sixpence from gutter to Grosvenor Square, marked her out as a high-camp performer and two Baroque artistes in the same show might possibly present problems.

Initially all seemed set fair with *Pieces of Eight* – eight performers in a show with an 8 p.m. curtain – and Williams seemed happy with his material and with Paddy Stone ('an excellent director'), noting only of Fielding after the first company get-together: 'She'll be OK.' There were the usual company tensions over who had potentially the best material and Fielding occasionally sobbed to Paddy Stone that so little had been tailored specifically for her and that so many songs were given to the singer Myra de Groot (she had a point – eight numbers rather stretched Ms de Groot's vocal resources). Michael has a particular memory of the vivacious performer: 'I have addressed many companies on stage out of town either before or after a performance to give them news about a show's future, sometimes very good sometimes not so good; invariably there is no marked reaction en bloc, the preference being to return to their various dressing rooms to consider how what I have relayed to them affects their livelihoods, careers and general well-being. Except on one occasion: *Pieces of Eight* was touring with no West End theatre booked. We were coming to the end of our tour and playing the vast Royal Court Theatre, Liverpool when suddenly the Apollo on Shaftesbury Avenue – the ideal home for the revue – became available and we were offered it. I travelled to Liverpool, told the cast and received the usual non-committal response from all the company except Myra de Groot, a volatile and gifted Jewish torch singer. She at once enthusiastically embraced me and said, "Oh, Michael, darling, thank you! Thank you – we're all going to make a fortune!" A few weeks later she left the show with absolutely no warning. She'd fallen in love with an American and was following him there. Or was he Australian? She became a regular on *Neighbours* and in his last letter to me Kenneth Williams referred to her having recently died in Australia.'

Cook had written *Pieces of Eight* with Williams foremost in his mind, giving him the chance to show off his range of personae and accents in a splendid gallery of grotesques and drolls – an increasingly desperate salesman of luminous leprechauns; a pinched, thin man cursing a cruel fate that prohibits him from filling the job of a fairground fat man; a sulkily discontented secret agent or, as the descendant of Cook's Boylett, the man in the railway carriage with a viper ('not an asp') in his box.

Oddly enough, although very popular and widely quoted (Williams was, for once, lost for words when he was introduced to Judy Garland who then recited most of the sketch to him), the spies sketch was one not entirely suited to Williams. In his personality, combining boyish sprite with a kind of aloof detachment (Peter Shaffer used the word 'Carthusian' to define Williams's private life of autodidactic austerity), there was a strain of ferocious rage (Richard Williams was 'on' to this aspect of his namesake, inspiredly inviting him to narrate his animated movie of Gogol's *Diary of a Madman*), a subterranean cockney savagery, which did not quite suit some of Cook's more contemplative material, tailored for his own obsessives and bores. They were perhaps conveyed more truthfully by performers less mercurial than Williams. The very best of Williams in *Pieces of Eight* was revealed in a sketch not by Cook but by Harold Pinter, to whom Michael went 'when it seemed that Cook, overextended as usual, might not come up with enough material in time'. Set in a late-night coffee stall, 'Time to Go' was a miniature masterpiece of an old newspaper vendor chatting to the more laconic figure of the stall's owner; Williams inhabited every nuance and pause in the dialogue with masterly control and the utmost respect (Pinter occasionally contributed further outstanding revue material – for a Lyric, Hammersmith show of 1959, *One to Another*, he came up with another splendid duologue for Boss and Foreman faced with an industrial crisis).

10. Kenneth Williams and Fenella Fielding in 'If Only'
from *Pieces of Eight*, 1959.

Michael remembers a 'comparatively trouble-free tour' although there was a good deal of tweaking on the road; 'I enjoyed the impresario's role in shaping the running order, trying to bring the show's mixture of elements into the best possible alignment' (hardly surprising perhaps, that he later became a great jigsaw fan). In revue a good sketch can lose its impact cushioned by the wrong material, and a nifty song must have the right

11. 'Revue Reviewed'

amount of air before and subsequently, any rearrangements involving revision and re-rehearsal of scene and costume changes (backstage during the pre-London tour of any revue could resemble the frantic second act of Michael Frayn's *Noises Off*).

The only sign of stormy weather was what Michael would describe as 'the violent love-hate relationship that developed gradually between Kenneth and Fenella'. She respected his talent but noted, with some perceptiveness: 'He wanted me to be good, but not too good.' Offstage, initially, she could keep on an even keel with him by joining in animated and often hilarious discussion of the subject of most consuming interest to Williams, namely 'the bum' or the state and constant torture of his bowels. She realised that he was possibly more self-centred than evil ('He was a genius in his field and geniuses tend to be kind of childlike') but found on stage his upstaging tricks and frequent improvisations tricky to cope with.

The big drama came during the West End run at the Apollo in the 'Espionage' sketch; with Fielding in glittering sequins and Williams in unrelieved black, both complaining of the inadequacy of their spies' out-fits, each equipped with a cyanide pill. Fielding was scheduled to kill herself before crawling into the winds to croak her last while Williams was left to die a showy solo onstage death. One night, malevolently, Williams simply refused to give Fielding the cue line for her exit. Eventually clocking what he was up to Fielding retaliated by simply stopping, refusing to compete, and said, 'Last one dead is a cissy,' and walked off in a rather jerky blackout. Williams 'went ballistic', alleging that Fielding had publicly impugned his sexuality (about which he was always prickly) and refused to speak to her offstage (she had already been reduced to 'Madam' or 'La Fielding' in his *Diaries*). Michael and David Sutton appeared the following night, Michael having had morning calls from both stars giving their respective versions of events, and managerial soothing resulted in a 'kind of rapprochement'. But the atmosphere had become subtly poisoned; Wil-liams was constantly writing to or telephoning Michael to complain about Fielding ('her pauses are becoming a joke') and in his *Diaries* he was referring to *Pieces of Eight* as 'this dreary, boring revue' and to the depres-sion caused by 'the futility of my lonely existence – desperately trying to keep my little life clean and ready for inspection'.

The trouble, always, was that no inspector ever called. Even if one had, it is most unlikely that Williams, incapable of sharing his privacy, would have let him in.

Despite the constant carping, Michael still liked and admired Williams and wanted to maintain his relationship with him. *Pieces of Eight* ran profitably for over a year and he was anxious to keep the series going and to continue the mission to pump new blood into the intimate revue format, although he knew that with Smith *hors de concours* and Fielding *persona non grata* with his star, he would have to find him another stage partner. His choice of Sheila Hancock was astute; she had successfully appeared for Michael when taking over from Joan Sims the smallish but rewarding maid's role in the comedy *Breath of Spring* (1957) and he had been 'much impressed by her versatility' in the Fizz Fazan-directed revue *One to Another*, most notably in a touching Pinter sketch with Beryl Reid in which they played two down-and-out bag ladies in a late-night milk bar (echoes of 'Time to Go'). She had also worked for Joan Littlewood in the Wolf Mankowitz musical *Make Me An Offer*, learning how to improvise with confidence, potentially a useful tool when working on stage with Williams.

Even Williams was keen on her, at least initially ('She's a lovely girl!') and she had the guts to stand up to him although she was well aware of how frightening he could be to women: 'He would try to break you. The break came on tour one night when I answered him back with an ad-lib. I took him on and we did a massive improvisation on the spot and he began to respect me.' Nevertheless within a few weeks he would enter in his *Diaries*: 'I could take Fielding for eighteen months so I'm sure I can take her'(just as Paddy Stone, once so favoured, was included in his savage denunciation of every aspect of this new show in May 1961).

The real problem on *One Over the Eight* (it had a cast of nine), which opened at the Duke of York's, was that Peter Cook, by no means for the first or last time, was more than slightly overstretched. He was preoccupied with ambitious plans for a night club (The Establishment in Soho), with a good deal of radio and television work, not to mention his commitments as main writer of and performer in a new revue for the Edinburgh Festival, *Beyond the Fringe*, which – produced by Willie Donaldson (effected very much by the intriguing from and the connivance of Donald Langdon and with Donald Albery as Donaldson's main investor and co-producer) – opened at the Fortune shortly after *One Over The Eight*.

Cook's contributions were on this occasion often not up to his usual standard. Sadly his outstanding sketch, 'One Leg Too Few', an enduringly brilliant piece of comedy writing, did not survive the try-out tour. It famously involved a one-legged actor auditioning for the role of Tarzan to a theatrical agent given the immortal lines: 'Your right leg I like. I like your right leg. A lovely leg for the role. That's what I said when I saw you come in. I said, "A lovely leg for the role." I've nothing against your right leg. The trouble is – neither have you.'

Unaccountably Williams turned against the sketch, fearing it might cause offence (he was not always so politically correct). There remained a handful of bright spots from Cook – Williams as a bird watcher, or in 'Hand Up Your Sticks' ingeniously capitalising on his talent for rapid-fire word-play as a bank robber ineptly rehearsing his hold-up, and in a lethal send-up of David Frost (never a favourite of Cook's) as the author of a

12. Kenneth Williams goes 'Birdwatching' in *One Over the Eight*, 1961.

universally panned play cheerfully rising above the derision ('"effete" was the nearest I got to a compliment in a critical reaction ranging all the way from "dire" all the way up to "abysmal"') to pick out distortedly selective advertising quotes (this sketch remained a favourite of Michael's – he had it played to a delighted response from a younger generation at a 2007 SOLT [Society of London Theatre] Dinner held for him celebrating his 50 years as a producer).

There was on this occasion a good deal of 'additional material'; Michael called in John Mortimer who provided 'Night Life' with Williams in his element as one of his pompous egoists, a provincial business man ('I am in string – I am up in town for the String Show') and Hancock in hilarious form as a jaded club hostess, while N.F. Simpson, Lionel Bart and the promising young director Steven Vinaver contributed other songs and sketches. The physical production was even more polished than *Pieces of Eight*: with Paddy Stone at the helm again, Tony Walton once more de-signed, this time considerably aided by the superb back projections supervised by the *wunderkind* lighting designer Richard Pilbrow (it was one of the first West End shows extensively to capitalise on the fluidity of back projections, now technically less cumbersome). However, some of the remaining material was well below par – 'Interesting Facts' with Williams holding forth about the remarkable lengths of intestines ('four miles of tubing' – he managed to extend the word 'tubing' inordinately) in the human body was simply an old Cook sketch from a Pembroke College Smoker, while other pieces literally petered out as if Cook had lost interest. Moreover the songs in *One Over the Eight* wasted good performers such as Hancock, Lynda Baron and the agile dancer/singer Sheila O'Neill.

The reviews were disappointing, some of them depressingly so – but they seemed to have absolutely no effect on either a booming box office or Williams's popularity. The star was nonetheless virtually always miserable, although if Hancock was 'off' when ill he very rapidly revised his opinion ('Sheila Hancocks don't grow on trees'). His *Diaries* record regular moans at Michael, once involving 'a great set-to with Michael about not having one decent actor in the company. It's disgraceful' (a bit rich considering his previous praise for Hancock and for Lance Percival, also in the company and an excellent foil). He also took against Paddy Stone in a major way; now he was 'a director with no idea of what sort of show he was to create on the stage'.

A good deal of Williams's bile then was possibly to do with the runaway success of *Beyond the Fringe* in London. He wrote that Hancock 'is absolutely speechless with rage at those lovely notices for Cook, when this was the man that practically brought our show to disaster' but he might well have been speaking for himself. And indeed it must have hurt when Jonathan Miller of *Beyond the Fringe* seemed to disparage their work in an *Observer* piece, writing that in the *Eight* shows Cook's sharp wit was blunted by its gay commercial setting: 'Tinselly dance routines a-fidget with glow paint and fishnet would follow one of his dour, screwy little numbers and promptly erase it from the mind of the audience.'

This was not strictly accurate, even allowing for the inferior musical element in *One Over the Eight*. Stone's choreography never was 'tinselly' while sketches such as 'Not an Asp' and 'Birdwatching' were widely quoted by a whole younger generation, and Miller's piece also overlooked the underrated (and scandalously underpaid) contribution to *Beyond the Fringe* of Fizz Fazan who took over the direction of what in Edinburgh was a loosely sprawling show, helped mould it into a cohesive whole and who also could soothe the not infrequent internecine tensions. But it is still undeniably true that *Beyond the Fringe* – even if it spawned few imitations – with its permanent set, no costume changes and no choreography, sounded if not quite the death-knell of intimate revue then at the very least a strong warning chord.

The *Fringe* boys did capture something of a shift in Anglo-Saxon attitudes after more than a decade of Tory rule, a period which until the aftermath of Suez in 1956 had not seen that authority seriously challenged, certainly never with such devastating irreverence, not least in Cook's depiction of Harold Macmillan. Without directly asking for it the *Fringe* creators became credited with the 'Satire Boom'; against this Michael's *Eight* revues could seem less substantial (although a number like *Pieces of Eight*'s 'Don't Let Labour Ruin It', sung by a couple of upper-class twits, is more subversive than it initially seems) but it would be unfair to overlook their scenic innovations or the cunning way they could introduce into a familiar format some work by Cook, Pinter, Mortimer, Simpson *et al*, which was bracing, original and often wildly, surreally funny. And, as Michael said of Williams: 'He was the best revue star we ever had. And it's a great pity that intimate revue died – although it certainly went out in style.'

Michael was not ready to give up, even if he well knew that 'the success of *Beyond the Fringe* made it impossible for us to continue with the Apollo series'. Other producers – a new name, Charles Ross, particularly – tried to keep the traditional revue flag flying, while for a brief time television stars such as Stanley Baxter and Betty Marsden could find a public with shows including *On the Brighter Side*. When *Beyond the Fringe* finally vacated the Fortune, soon afterwards it had another long-running hit with the South African-inspired *Wait a Minim!*, which had a vein of political satire running through it. Steven Vinaver directed an offbeat show, *Twists,* and the mime expert Julian Chagrin led a clever diversion, *Chaganog* (the 'og' came from another performer, George Ogilvie) featuring a talented young dancer/choreographer David Toguri; both shows recalled the style of *Cranks*. A gallant effort to evoke revue's glory days took the stage with the defiantly titled *All Square* (1963), mainly the work of Alan Melville still parodying other shows (a sketch called *Blast!* spoofed Lionel Bart's *Blitz!*), its cast led by experienced revue names such as the great Beryl Reid, Naunton Wayne and Joyce Blair. The latter neatly impersonated Millicent Martin in a spoof of television's *That Was the Week That Was*, ironically the very weekly programme that was strangling shows represented by *All Square,* which tried to turn the clock back in a finale that saw the entire company changed into evening dress, hallmark of the audience of a vanished era.

Michael was astute enough to avoid that kind of approach, but he 'always had a kind of mission to keep the cause of revue alive and throughout the rest of my career I have had several little forays, although sometimes they have been more oddball, difficult to categorise shows or entertainments, into the genre'. Traditional intimate revue may have practically vanished but any genre is capable of renewal or reinvention. And revue was given a massive boot up the bottom with one of those 'difficult to categorise shows' when Michael and Willie Donaldson co-produced *An Evening of British Rubbish* at the Comedy Theatre in 1962. This *sui de generics* piece – there are some hardcore old fans who rate it still the funniest evening of a theatre-going lifetime – had its origins somewhere in Donaldson's vague desire to do a show with Spike Milligan ('a large, vulgar, slapstick revue with nudes and peacocks') ideally involving the band of the Coldstream Guards (the projected title was *The Royal Commission Revue* – there was a revue with that title written by John Antrobus 'with additional material by Spike Milligan' later at the Mermaid Theatre but with no nudes, peacocks or band, and with no Donaldson input). He came close to this kind of anarchic show with a revue written by another of his favourites, the bug-eyed comedian/author Marty Feldman, combining wild slapstick comedy and jazz. This costly venture, titled *Wham, Bang, Thank You Ma'am* had a bizarrely mixed cast including the monocled old music hall star Fred Emney, jazz singer Annie Ross and a chorus line of pulchritudinous dancers (one of them Willie's current dalliance) and a large orchestra. Its production period was disorganised even by Donaldson standards and it closed almost immediately on the road.

Michael also had a penchant – fortunately less impulsive than Willie's – for anarchic comedy (he has always, for instance, been drawn to the sense of incipient danger in ventriloquists' acts) and, 'albeit with some trepidation' (like most of Donaldson's partners or collaborators), agreed to co-produce a new revue for the West End. There were no nudes or peacocks; *An Evening of British Rubbish* was structured – the word is used loosely – around The Alberts, a surreal act involving brothers Douglas and Tony Gray and the incomparable 'Professor' Bruce Lacey (also a painter and sculptor), who looked in their dark velvet jackets like a fairly conservative trad-jazz band but whose act would spiral into the deliriously, surreally subversive. They were great favourites of those such as George Melly and the Bonzo Dog Doo Dah Band; they had recorded with Spike Milligan with the revered George Martin producing and had appeared with great success at Peter Cook's Establishment Club where their act included an unforgettable Dadaist quiz show. Custard pies, exploding cellos, fart jokes and exotic props – a large pantomime horse included – featured strongly in their act. Sometimes in *British Rubbish* the lugubriously eccentric Joycean poet Ivor Cutler – billed as 'The Scottish Surrealist' and later Buster Bloodvessel in the Beatles' film *Magical Mystery Tour* – would

13. Revue with a difference. 'Professor' Bruce Lacey with two machine operated 'actors' in *An Evening of British Rubbish*, 1963.

disrupt proceedings; at other times the saucer-eyed Joyce Grant would divert with an hilariously genteel striptease or a piercing coloratura burst of 'Pale Hands I Loved'. There were some echoes of The Goons, but more potently the later world of *Monty Python* and, in particular, Terry Gilliam, was never far away, not least in the way *British Rubbish* comedy created a kind of anarchic collage of British imperialist history (The Alberts were especially drawn to the Boer War), giving it a very 1960s demystification and subversion.

No two performances were ever the same. The Alberts delighted in confusion; one night, as described by Donaldson's biographer, Terence Blacker, a group of attendant varied 'celebrities' – David Frost, Lynn Redgrave, the boxer Henry Cooper and director Joan Littlewood (a great Alberts fan) included – were invited up to be served a full three course and coffee dinner on stage while the show carried on in front of them.

Perhaps not unexpectedly the reviews for *British Rubbish* were polarised, the majority betraying varying degrees of bemusement although Bernard Levin, then at the peak of his *Daily Mail* power, waxed ecstatic. British audiences then were rarely comfortable with 'spontaneous' shows (the largely improvisatory Second City revue group from Chicago failed to find much favour in 1960s London) and The Alberts were essentially a minority cult. The show managed a healthy run but Michael politely declined when Willie invited him a few years later to join him in presenting The Alberts once more, this time in their own unique take on *The Three Musketeers* directed by Fizz Fazan. He was wise – this ramshackle show ran for only two weeks. There was a distinct recollection of The Alberts when Michael presented the equally unpredictable Ken Campbell in his *Jamais Vu* (Vaudeville, 1993) – he greatly admired Campbell's phenomenal comedic energy and at times inspired invention.

Also unconventional but more disciplined was a production in 1964 from Michael's *alma mater*. University revue – virtually always meaning Oxbridge – still popped up occasionally in the capital. Two future stars of television's *The Goodies* – Bill Oddie and Tim Brooke-Taylor – featured in *Cambridge Circus*, produced by Michael White at the Lyric, Shaftesbury Avenue in 1962 (that year's Footlights Revue, *Double Take*, directed by an undergraduate, Trevor Nunn, did not make it to the West End). Michael's choice was characteristically idiosyncratic; originating at Oxford for the Experimental Theatre Club, it was a revue – almost a mini-musical in scale – called *Hang Down Your Head and Die*.

Directed by Braham Murray, one of contemporary Oxford theatre's *wunderkinder* (a laid-back Texan, Michael Rudman, was another in a fierce rivalry), this had a large cast – seventeen – plus musicians. As president of the ETC Murray was determined that it would live up to its experimental tag: 'What could a group of university students do that professionals couldn't? The commodity we had was time, time to create a show and produce it. We decided to take a theme, research it and, through improvisation, develop it into a rough script.' The theme chosen – capital punishment (still practised in Britain in 1963 although Labour's Sidney Silverman was driving hard for an anti-hanging Bill) – had obvious theatrical possibilities, from Punch and Judy to folklore. Workshop sessions produced a chief researcher – David Wright – who worked the material into an initial scenario with two contrasted composers, Greg Stephens and David Wood, the former skilled in the tradition of American folk music while Wood could write Gilbert and Sullivan or music-hall pastiche equally adeptly. The research covered investigation into Royal Commissions, victims' stories and public opinion, all to be contained within a circus format with two Ringmasters, the strongman as Hangman, the traditional white-faced clown as the Condemned, the carpet clowns as the vox pop and the sequinned female assistants leading the applause and covering up the grisly reality of executions.

It could have been an inchoate mess but somehow the mixture of docudrama and the particularly effective music produced a vigorously exciting show, even if the debt Murray owed to Joan Littlewood and Theatre Workshop (he had already directed *The Hostage* for the ETC and had seen the more recent *Oh What a Lovely War* six times) was unmistakable. It was fuelled by a white-hot sense of injustice that quite literally came searing across from stage to auditorium. Rehearsals were volatile – opinionated undergraduates were never going to be completely compliant – throughout an unusually long period while the show took shape, hitting a major crisis when the working script submitted to the Lord Chamberlain's office (still a requirement for any new work before a licence for public performance – only club theatres escaped its jurisdiction – could be issued) was returned with over half the material blue-pencilled. Justifiably the creators felt that this was a clear case of political censorship with the State protecting its own legal interests.

It was Murray – by now, of course, something of an expert on capital punishment – who had the bright idea of consulting the QC Gerald Gardiner, a leading anti-hanging spokesman, after the ETC had been given the right to appeal against the Lord Chamberlain's office. Gardiner made it icily clear at a meeting with the assistant controller of the Chamberlain's office that he regarded the script's censorship as political, hinting equally coolly that as the likely next Lord Chancellor under a Labour government, he would abolish the office (Labour returned to power later that year and, after a drive much motivated by George Strauss MP, the Lord Chamberlain's office was abolished in 1968). Murray also cannily made sure that the press – always keen to photograph the pretty girls in the show – splashed the story of the threat to a controversial piece of theatre.

Virtually all the excisions were restored. Ironically, one cut that the Chamberlain's office refused to revoke produced one of the most piercingly memorable highlights of the evening. The creators of *Hang Down Your Head and Die* were refused permission to act out the electric-chair executions of Julius and Ethel Rosenberg. The Lord Chamberlain would allow only the reading of a newspaper eyewitness account, detailing the stark fact that 'it took three jolts of electricity, each lasting roughly fifty-seven seconds, to kill them'. What Murray's production did instead – a masterstroke – was to have the carpet clowns sit in a semicircle around a single bentwood chair while the account was read out, pausing for fifty-seven seconds when the first mention of the electric jolt was mentioned. It had an effect on the audience more devastating than any re-enactment could have produced.

The production was a major success in Oxford. Richard Eastham caught it early in the run and advised Michael to take a look; he in turn was much impressed, 'moved and enthused by both the material and by the quality of the performance'. The general manager of the Oxford Playhouse, Elizabeth Sweeting (also a co-founder of the Prospect Company), was a wise old bird, skilled in the ways of theatrical negotiation. When she heard of Michael's interest she advised Murray not to say much, warning him that 'Codron was famous for his silences, which usually led to his prey begging him to produce his play with the result that Codron was able to extort a very favourable deal'. As Murray remembered it, he and Michael sat in silence for what seemed like an eternity before a brief exchange:

Codron: What would you like to do with this?
Murray: I don't know.
A VERY LONG PAUSE
Codron: Would you like to take it to London?
Murray: Yes.

It was like a dream to Murray and all involved but very quickly Michael had dealt with Equity and nervous theatre owners presented with an amateur show (it eventually played a limited season at the Comedy Theatre over the 1963 Easter vacation). Its cast contained some remarkable future talent – two Monty Pythons (Michael Palin and, as the Condemned, Terry Jones), David Wood (who became a leading writer for children's theatre), a critic (*The Sunday Times*'s Robert Hewison) and actors Michael Elwyn and Richard Durden. Michael, moved by the show's content, was equally affected by the cast's commitment and by the burning passion communicated by Braham Murray; he felt an affinity with Murray, slightly confused at this crucial stage of his life, born into a Jewish family and struggling also against parental expectations that he should follow them into a world of commerce. When *Hang Down Your Head* was bought for Broadway Michael did what he could to protect Murray's interests and to prevent major alterations but there was little he could do without direct involvement in what turned out to be a botched New York production to shield Murray from managerial ineptitude on an awesome scale. The disaster of the show in New York did have one legacy however; two members of its young cast, Gerome Ragni and James Rado, decided to collaborate with the composer Galt MacDermot, resulting in the 'Tribal Love-Rock' musical *Hair*, its anti-Establishment stance and mixture of song and sketch owing not a little to the style of *Hang Down Your Head*. Disappointing for the director although the Broadway experience must have been, before long he was working successfully back in the UK, brushing aside American offers for the 'new Orson Welles' and then beginning his long association with The Royal Exchange operation in Manchester.

Another Oxford show, strikingly contrasted to *Hang Down Your Head*, was the revue *Four Degrees Over* (1966), which Michael produced at the tiny Fortune Theatre. David Wood – with some inspired clowning – very much took the limelight in this daedal, diverting song/sketch show. Also featured were more *Hang Down Your Head* alumni, including Bob Scott (latterly a Knighted Voice of Manchester) and the often delirious musical feats of John Gould at the piano.

Amongst his other 'excursions' into the world of post *Eight* and *Fringe* revues or entertainments, Michael was saddened by the failure to find a public for *The Golden Pathway Annual* (Mayfair, 1974) by John Burrows and John Harding, a sharp-eyed but beguiling exploration of English childhood and the eccentricities of a class system both intricate and seemingly indestructible, going from post-war babyhood to Start-rite shoes and through school and adolescence. In the same year, dazzled by what he had seen of the unique Scottish-born, dancer/mime-choreographer Lindsay Kemp's work, he presented Kemp's company in *Flowers* (Regent, 1974), an evocative version of Jean Genet every bit (and more) as exotically perfumed as the original, fused with iconic gay imagery glimpsed through quantities of smoke and dry ice. Again – this time more or less as he anticipated – this could only reach a limited audience.

A new kind of revue had been launched at the riverside Mermaid Theatre in Blackfriars (under its founder and director Bernard Miles, himself a veteran of Herbert Farjeon revues and of the music halls) with musical compilation shows, beginning in 1972 with *Cowardy Custard*, which had Patricia Routledge and John Moffatt leading a celebration of Noël Coward's songs, interspersed with material from his sketches and plays. Its Cole Porter-based successor, *Cole* (1974), which included Julia McKenzie, Una Stubbs and Kenneth Nelson in its equally lustrous cast, was similarly successful. Michael became involved as a co-producer with a follow-up to *Cole*, structured around a script from Benny Green and directed by Wendy Toye, the cast including Stubbs and a young Su Pollard. Unfortunately *Cole* had used most of the truly vintage Porter material and although it had some exhilarating choreography, *Oh Mr Porter* (1977) was never varied or rich enough in musical texture to enjoy

14. Jean Genet meets Lindsay Kemp in *Flowers*, 1974.

similar success; it did not move, as had been expected, from the Mermaid (nor did another of Miles's notions – a compilation of Farjeon material titled *Farjeon Reviewed,* which sadly revealed how time can sometimes curdle once-rich material).

Another original act that Michael had appreciated from his early Fringe sighting of them was the eccentric duo of Hinge and Bracket. Much, much more than a drag act, Patrick Fyffe and George Logan created in Dame

Hilda Bracket and Dr Evadne Hinge two authentic *monstres sacrées*, English Eccentrics with a razor-sharp sense of malice and rivalry under the cosy chat of church services and Am. Dram Gilbert and Sullivan, when the soprano (occasionally prone to wobble) of the Dame would have to match the ruthless timekeeping of the doctor at the keyboard. Sometimes their use of the double entendre could be so subtle (and on occasion so spectacularly filthy) that they had to plot pauses several beats later for the audience to catch up. They appeared successfully for Michael in *Hinge and Bracket at the Globe* (1980), by far the best of their various London appearances.

He had an even bigger success at the same theatre the following year when he presented a new star, *Rowan Atkinson In Revue* (Globe, 1981). Michael had been tipped the wink about Atkinson's prodigious talent by his friend and Atkinson's astute agent Richard Armitage of the Noel Gay Organisation (he was Gay's son and the principal begetter of the smash-hit revival of his father's musical *Me And My Girl*), who had snapped up the young Atkinson (along with Stephen Fry, Hugh Laurie and Emma Thompson) while he was still an Oxford undergraduate. Atkinson had appeared in a Hampstead Theatre revue, which first introduced London audiences to such classics as his pedantic schoolmaster's 'Roll Call' sketch. Michael's timing was astute; Atkinson had made a major breakthrough on television's *Not The Nine O'Clock News* and audiences were hungry for more of him. At Michael's insistence, the show, with Richard Curtis's considerable writing contribution, was meticulously produced; he brought in Mel Smith to direct and gave him a strong design team to provide much more than the ubiquitous black drapes and follow-spots of limited season revue. Once again he was conscious, as he had been with Kenneth Williams two decades previously, of bringing a new and unique comedic talent to the fore: 'It was a success beyond all my imaginings at the Globe.'

The timing – so vital – was just right with Atkinson (although America was not ready for his pre-*Mr Bean* persona when soon afterwards he took his show – Michael was not involved – to Broadway, where it flopped quickly). And, mysteriously, the timing was somehow just wrong when Michael presented Victoria Wood the following year. He and David Sutton had been entranced by her work in her own play, the award-winning *Talent*, at the King's Head Theatre, on television with Julie Walters, and her appearances on Russell Harty's chat show. Early in 1981 she had a big success back at Islington's King's Head appearing in tandem with her then husband Geoffrey Durham, aka 'The Great Soprendo', a magician with a distinctive Tommy Cooper-ish giggle (but whose tricks actually worked) and the magic passwords of 'Olé, Torremolinos!'. Clad in lurid pink, this 'slick spick with Spanish varnish' spoke in English less broken than fractured, a kind of mangled Spanglais ('I am very large in the Canaries') and Durham made a splendid counterpart to Wood in *Funny Turns* (1982), which Michael brought into the 500-seat Duchess following its sold out Islington run. Wood, equally strikingly attired in a yellow trouser suit and navy shirt (one critic likened her to 'a startled canary which had collided with an inkwell') was characteristically self-deprecating – she compared her pores to a doily – and wry on the problems of being a Lancashire girl in London ('You won't get mugged but you might get an Arts Council Grant'), mining rich and perceptive comedy out of quotidian material based on adolescent angst, dieting, cystitis and cellulite ('like finding razor blades in the Weetabix' was LBC's Sue Jameson's description of this material). Best of all in this show were her songs, rueful and touchingly funny; she was still to write her most popular numbers such as that rousing hymn to middle-aged lust 'Let's Do It' ('Beat me on the bottom with the *Woman's Weekly*') but in her musical pieces here she used traditional lyric formulae to create a kind of genuine urban poetry (Michael Coveney, in *The Financial Times*, rightly asserted that *Funny Turns* offered the best lyrics on the London stage at the time apart from the National Theatre's revival of Frank Loesser's *Guys and Dolls*).

There was one voice of quite violently bilious dissent; Tom Sutcliffe in *The Guardian* dismissed the show that the paper's first string, Michael Billington, had praised at the King's Head. Perhaps Wood had not yet quite moved on from the cusp of real fame on which she had been hovering, perhaps the pairing of comedienne/singer and magician perplexed the wider public, but for whatever reasons audiences simply did not come to Catherine Street; even a two-hander with no huge running costs in a small theatre was stubbornly refusing to reach its weekly break figure, despite predominantly glowing reviews. Wood and Durham had been contracted for twenty weeks, but *Funny Turns* was forced to close after only seven. However, this was one of those rare shows on which investors did not seem to mind losing their money. Replying to Michael's letter announcing the closure and financial loss, the veteran producer and investor Emile Littler said, 'You have nothing to apologise about,' while another regular 'angel', Eric Kilner, wrote: 'It makes a loss much more acceptable if it helps to encourage such a splendid talent!'

With *Funny Turns* and another small-scale, intimate musical revue, *Who Plays Wins* (Vaudeville, 1985), – pairing the two pianos and voices of

Richard Stilgoe and Peter Skellern (whose 'She's A Lady' was very popular then) sleekly staged by Mike Ockrent – both failing commercially, Michael was in some distress faced with what looked like another looming flop when a pet project, a revue based on the career and material of Joyce Grenfell, tried out at Farnham's Redgrave Theatre in early 1988.

Re:Joyce!, as the 'entertainment' was titled, coincided with a particularly difficult and emotional time in Michael's private life – the break-up, awkward and even agonising for both men, of his long personal partnership with David Sutton, and he was often perceptibly edgy, distracted and occasionally even tearful during its preparation period. It reunited him with the production's original co-deviser and director, James Roose-Evans, a friend since Oxford, founder and first director of London's Hampstead Theatre, which Michael had done a considerable amount to help launch and equip and later on the board of which he sat for a lengthy period. Roose-Evans had also directed for him, with 1963's *Private Lives* revival, which Michael took from Hampstead into the West End and his own version of Laurie Lee's *Cider With Rosie* (Garrick, 1963). But in its first incarnation *Re:Joyce!* was beset by problems.

Roose-Evans, who would go on to edit Joyce Grenfell's *Letters* and had established good relations with her estate and delightful widower Reggie, was partnered in the show's original shaping with Maureen Lipman, scheduled to play Grenfell, and whose talent Michael greatly admired (to date he had presented her only in her husband Jack Rosenthal's 1981 backstage comedy *Smash!*, very much based on Rosenthal's nightmare but often hilarious experiences when working with some big Broadway names on the West End musical expansion of his modest but poignant television play, *Bar Mitzvah Boy* – the play closed on the road, despite Lipman and Nigel Hawthorne heading the cast). Michael had loved Grenfell's work since boyhood, catching her in Laurier Lister's revues as well as in her solo shows and he wanted to distil something of the essence of a special performer as well as to showcase some less-familiar material alongside much-loved classics.

The script was still in somewhat fluid shape when rehearsals began for Farnham in early 1988. Michael was 'very, very enthusiastic', having heard Lipman try some of the projected material, about the prospects for what he felt could be 'much more than an impersonation of an adored performer'. But the project soon hit various rocks: 'The main canker in the bud was that Jimmy Roose-Evans was directing Hugh Whitemore's play, *The Best Of Friends*, more or less simultaneously. He would do most of a morning with

77

15. 'George, don't do that!' – Maureen Lipman as
Joyce Grenfell in *Re:Joyce!*, 1988.

Maureen and then vanish, instructing her somewhat gnomically: "I have to go. There's a chair. Imagine that it's a tree."' Understandably nervous – she had never been alone (pianist excepted) on a stage for a whole evening previously – 'Maureen got impatient'. Little had been finally decided about any setting while the director was so regularly unavailable, and what turned up on the Redgrave Theatre stage for 'a nightmare technical rehearsal' seemed suited more to a show about Beatrix Potter than one centred round Joyce Grenfell. The stage was backed with a vast semi-circle of ruched, white muslin drapes looking like a washing line of outsize knickers, against which stood prominently a Welsh dresser of stripped pine, shelves crowded with knick-knacks, while from time to time a hologram of Grenfell would arbitrarily light up the stage floor.

Lipman was clearly plugged into the material when it came to most of the monologues but she was hamstrung by an unresolved script, the physical production and a palpable lack of chemistry between her and the pianist/occasional narrator John Gould. As dismayed as Michael by Roose-Evans's seeming inability to put things right, finally she insisted, 'This can't go on,' while rejecting Michael's suggestion of Paul Kerryson (director of 70, Girls, 70) as a replacement after Michael had the producer's unpleasant task of firing the director, also a friend. Faced with the distinct prospect of abandoning a cherished enterprise almost as soon as begun, after a little uncertainty as to how to proceed Michael swung into action, asking a few colleagues to see it and advise. No one seemed hugely hopeful, least of all Louis Benjamin of the Stoll Moss Theatre group who advised him: 'It's no good. Don't bring it in,' adding – mindful of Lipman's current success as Beatie with the first of a series of memorable BT commercials, delighting in a grandson's sole O-Level in biology ('He's got an 'ology') – 'You should get her to do something with an "'Ology" in it.'

But then, 'Once again, I was rescued. This time partly by Paul Gane who owned the Fortune Theatre where *Joyce Grenfell Requests the Pleasure* had run, saying he would house the show for a limited season over Christmas 1988. But I still had to get the show right.' At this point the biographer has to enter the narrative. I was among the colleagues asked to go to Farnham before it closed; I had directed various productions for Michael, he knew of my involvement with the creation of both *Cowardy Custard* and *Cole* at the Mermaid, and I was about to leave Greenwich Theatre, which I had run for over a decade to return to freelance work. I caught the final Farnham Saturday matinee when it seemed to me that although the set was hideous and the script lopsided in its equilibrium between the sketches/songs/

monologues and the material on Grenfell's life and career, there were more than occasional flashes in Lipman's performance to make me want to work on the project with her.

Michael had another stroke of luck after Paul Gane's offer when Peter Rice turned out to be available as designer. Rice, with whom I had worked on occasion at Greenwich and in the West End, was also a veteran of revue design – he designed *Joyce Grenfell Requests the Pleasure* – and came up with a seductive and adaptable dove-grey surround with steps up to an oval centre frame, behind which a screen could take various lighting states and occasional back projections (Ben Frow's costumes – Grenfell's dresses based on Victor Stiebel's originals – were a plus, even at Farnham) using a few simple trucked pieces such as a church pew or an airline seat for specifically set items. Michael also struck lucky with Denis King, once of the King Brothers group and now a prolific composer of musicals and television scores, who agreed to be the Pianist/Narrator; he knew Lipman socially and a warm stage rapport was also quickly established.

Over the summer of 1988 I worked extensively on script revisions with Lipman, keeping a cornerstone of the most meaty original songs and sketches but extensively reworking, including shaping a completely new opening – a biographical piece with a spot-lit Grenfell moving gently to music, recalling a childhood performance on an ocean liner – that bookended the evening with its moving close as Grenfell lived out her dream of perpetual motion in dance. Also much extended was a virtuoso turn of several Grenfell creations at a sophisticated cocktail party, with Lipman in exhilarating comedic form rapidly switching voices and body languages, particularly hilarious as a gushing literary groupie fazed only momentarily by an unfortunately swallowed olive stone. This exploited her talent for physical comedy just as much as the more familiar 'Lumpy Latimer' or the nervy nursery schoolteacher of 'George, Don't Do That'. She could also reinvent Grenfell's more serious material, especially in the second act opener 'First Flight', as an anxious middle-aged mother travelling to the USA to meet her son's black wife for the first time.

Michael seemed pleased with the changes but hardly ever appeared at rehearsals even though they were held in a church hall close to his office. He watched a final run-through – 'which I saw through a haze of tears and which made me burst into tears totally at the end. At that point, of course, I'd split up with David and was on edge but also the beauty of it and the transformation of what it had been at Farnham were simply too much for me'.

80

Of all his subsequent shows after the *Eight* ventures *Re:Joyce!* was per-haps the closest to the spirit of old-style intimate revue and the genre still seemed to have life. Grenfell's material still delighted and beguiled, of course, albeit much of its comedy was of a gentler era, but it was also a true triumph for Lipman who managed to inhabit the material with the utmost respect while going into a dimension beyond a technically impeccable impersonation, although she suggested Grenfell's mixture of gaucherie and a particular kind of sexiness (this was a woman wooed by Aly Khan) and slightly sibilant voice with artful skill. What she found in addition was the *essence* of Joyce Grenfell – an unusual kind of moral gravitas, elegance of mind and unfashionable goodness below the gawky comedic persona – climaxing in that extraordinary close with Grenfell dancing in a circle on and on until the curtain fell.

Despite packed and well-received Fortune previews, Michael was vis-ibly highly jittery about the show; his nerves were most manifest after a late preview when, hearing we wanted to try an alternative (and rehearsed) opening, he used words that he admitted were 'unusual coming from a Jewish producer' to beseech us 'in the bowels of Christ' not to change anything (we rehearsed it again, tried it out before an audience and re-turned to the stronger original). Briefly, the atmosphere was clouded although everyone involved was aware of how much seemed to depend on this production for Michael.

The first night was initially stickier partly because in such a small-capac-ity house as the Fortune critics have to be placed in the Circle as well as in the Stalls and it took the audience time to attune to such an unfamiliar (so much so that to some it was new) format as intimate revue. Gradually the sheer amperage of Lipman's performance and of the often unfamiliar material took over and the curtain fell to what seemed genuinely apprecia-tive prolonged applause. Michael remained anxious however until the next day's notices – 'the first review I saw was Irving Wardle's in *The Times*, which was very enthusiastic. I was very relieved'. Most of the reviews were similar and the Fortune Theatre's first season sold out almost immediately. Eventually *Re:Joyce!* returned to play four London seasons (the latter two at the Vaudeville, which Michael then owned), tour the UK twice, play in America at New Haven's Long Wharf Theatre and finally it was televised. It was one of the most profitable Michael Codron productions.

Still, to most producers revue's days were virtually over – few younger ones were interested in the form, time-consuming, unpredictable and often expensively involving re-rehearsals to replace outdated or poor material.

One enterprising younger impresario, Robert Fox, took a punt with a single-theme show, exploiting a contemporary social phenomenon and bestselling book, with *The Sloane Ranger Revue* (Duchess, 1986) but he burned his fingers, even with the experienced Ned Sherrin at the controls, and has not returned to the format.

Michael's last – to date – involvements with his first love among theatrical forms also included a single-theme show, a joyous enterprise that went through various incarnations before its final shaping as *The Shakespeare Revue* (Vaudeville, 1995). The production, devised from the outset by two bright young RSC actors, Christopher Luscombe and Malcolm McKee, had its origins in the 1993 celebrations in Stratford-Upon-Avon's Holy Trinity Church for Shakespeare's birthday, when some light relief was required to leaven the readings. Gradually the pieces led to more discoveries and into a complete stage show based on the vast body of work from comic writers using Shakespeare as raw material (illustrating Falstaff's vaunt: 'I am not only witty in myself but the cause of that wit in other men'). With material drawing from plays, musicals, comic novels and previous revues, the devisers also included some straight material (*Cymbeline*'s 'Fear no more the heat o' the sun', albeit in a Stephen Sondheim setting from *The Frogs*) to bring the balance of light and shade essential to a good revue, that vital fusion crucial to a form with no underpinning storyline.

The writers ranged from music-hall composers, Cole Porter, Noël Coward, Herbert Farjeon, Alan Melville (an old Gingold number 'Which Witch?' stood up well) and Sandy Wilson with later material from Dillie Keane, Stephen Fry, Maureen Lipman and Victoria Wood. Some of the material was side-splitting – not least Wood's enthusiastic Am-Dram director giving her cast 'notes' after a *Hamlet* rehearsal ('Polonius, try and show the age of the man in your voice and in your bearing, rather than waving the bus pass') and a superb piece of wordplay in Perry Pontac's parody 'Othello in Earnest' pairing Lady Bracknell with an Othello sounding remarkably like Jack Worthing but born in Africa, cradled in whatever came to hand, giving rise to Lady Bracknell's aghast reaction with 'A sandbag?').

Michael caught *The Shakespeare Revue* in its first run of performances at the RSC's Barbican Centre in The Pit. It had two further brief Pit seasons before he brought it to the Vaudeville with the authors in the cast alongside two versatile performers, both with good singing voices, Janie Dee and Susie Blake. The infectious zest and wit of the show, combined with the sense the material's diversity provided of revue's progress in his lifetime,

16. 'Revue Revivified' – Martin Connor, Janie Dee, Christopher Luscombe, Susie Blake, Malcolm McKee (L-R) in *The Shakespeare Revue*, 1996.

gave him a special involvement with the evening; its devisers in the published version thanked him for 'his constant care and attention and the wisdom he had brought to bear'.

The Shakespeare Revue had a successful post-West End tour after the Vaudeville season. *Alarms & Excursions* (1998, Michael Frayn's 'entertainment' of eight pieces all centred around the perils of modern technology, was also for Michael something of a pleasing return to the delights of shaping and structuring revue, these days (while television sketch shows continue to thrive with performers such as Alexander Armstrong and Ben Miller, Catherine Tate, etc.) on stage mostly confined to somewhat exclusive or 'in' parodic showbiz entertainments such as the *Forbidden Broadway* or *Jest End* format. Nobody, certainly, could have worked harder than Michael to keep the revue flag intermittently still flying.

CHAPTER 6

THE NEARLY MAN

Returning to the early days of the Codron operation, if *Share My Lettuce* and *The Wit to Woo* had given Michael a reputation as a new London impresario with a taste for the unexpected, his following West End production was by contrast almost defiantly retrograde. *Breath of Spring* (1957), an artfully contrived frivol centred around a group of gallant old broads defying the dreariness of old age by taking to crime – they engineer thefts from furriers – was by Peter Coke, one of a handful of reliable contemporary confectioners (William Douglas Home, Arthur Watkyn, Jack Popplewell, Kenneth Horne, Hugh and Margaret Williams included) of the kind of undemanding light comedy, vanished now, but which used to satisfy a mainstream Shaftesbury Avenue audience. Often, in the quaint ad-speak of the time, before the arrival of more aggressive PR in the theatre world, these would be puffed as 'suitable for the tired businessman', ideal for the public then to fill an evening after cocktails and before dinner or a supper club.

Peter Coke was something of an oddball character, an elegant *flaneur*. Stowe-educated and from a conventional naval background, he had a flourishing early acting career (he played Lord Pym in William Douglas Home's long-running 1947 comedy *The Chiltern Hundreds* and became widely known in the title role of *Paul Temple* on BBC Radio). Later, retiring to Norfolk, Coke became a successful antiques dealer with his partner Fred Webb and was known too as the creator of extraordinary, sometimes extremely elaborate (and pricey) shell sculptures. Wryly amused by the theatre world's antics, he never took it very seriously.

Breath of Spring was larky enough and had excellent dialogue – plays by actors often do – and Michael was able to attract a first-rate cast of accomplished character actors, none more adroit than the much-loved Athene Seyler. She never had an agent – highly unusual for a star – and Michael had formally to call on her in Chelsea 'to discuss terms', which, as it transpired, required little negotiation. Her status gave her automatic top billing and, regarding payment, she said only in tones brooking no denial: 'It'll have to be eighty' (£80 per week was then by no means outrageous for an established star). With Seyler's gift for effervescent comedy (she wrote, with the actor Stephen Haggard, a shrewd book on *The Craft of Comedy*) *Breath of Spring* had a decent run at the Cambridge before a transfer to the more suitably intimate Duke of York's, but in no area did it greatly build on the Codron outfit's reputation.

Years later, no doubt with some affectionate nostalgia and also admiration for the performances of a cast including Dora Bryan (doing the splits at an age ungallant to mention) but perhaps not entirely wisely, he transferred the Chichester Festival production of the Broadway musical based on Coke's play, *70, Girls 70* (Vaudeville, 1991) – one of the few New York failures from the John Kander/Fred Ebb team – to London. The characters in this version were mainly old musical or vaudeville performers living in retirement in a faded New York hotel but the show, with a somewhat below-par score, followed the fate of so many backstage stories on stage and managed only a modest West End run.

All the Codron productions of 1958 – five in total – originated at the intimate and charmingly designed Lyric Theatre, Hammersmith in West London, which Michael described as 'comparable to the Almeida Theatre subsequently'. Although for him in the later 1950s 'it still had the air of The Company of Four about it' (this had been H.M. Tennent's 'off-West End' operation, a non-profit outfit based at the Lyric), 'it undoubtedly still possessed a certain cachet'. He liked the personnel there, friends from *Share My Lettuce* days – J. Baxter Somerville, that key figure in his earlier career, was manager with the somewhat dicier personality of Reg Cornish as day-to-day manager – 'naughty Reg Cornish wasn't above a little cheating on me – handing out cloakroom tickets for the gallery, pocketing the cash and later saying it had been empty' – with, as the usual designer, the affable Disley Jones, Cornish's partner, who, like quite a few of Michael's collaborators during his career, also ran an antiques shop; tucked away behind Selfridges, the shop sold slightly over-priced bibelots and Michael was an occasional customer.

As he acknowledges, the 1958 Codron Hammersmith season could not have happened without David Hall, his partner at the Lyric, a contemporary with private means who was responsible for introducing him to John Mortimer, who would become the first significant dramatist of 'Codron's authors' – he would nurture seven Mortimer projects over the next twenty years. David Hall had heard Mortimer's radio play *The Dock Brief*, an hour-long two-hander first broadcast in 1957, produced by a radio doyenne, Nesta Pain, to considerable acclaim and which went on to win the

Prix Italia. It is easy to overlook the importance of radio in shaping some of post-war British theatre's major playwrights. Today, with so much of the BBC's drama output bought in from outside independent companies, the Corporation has nothing like the vibrancy that existed when BBC Radio Drama had a legendary team of Drama producers – alongside Pain, outstanding talents included R.D. Smith, Hallam Tennyson, Douglas Cleverdon, John Tydeman and Donald McWhinnie – constantly seeking out and encouraging new radio writers, with a resident large drama repertory company. The output was awesome. Not only Mortimer but also other dramatists who became part of the Codron stable – Harold Pinter, Joe Orton, Giles Cooper, Tom Stoppard and Alan Ayckbourn – all had crucial early radio experience (in Ayckbourn's case as a producer), vital in developing that individual tone of dialogue which has always been a touchstone of Michael's in his response to a new play.

Mortimer was then a client of the long-established A.D. Peters Literary Agency (later he moved to the redoubtable Peggy Ramsay when she left that outfit to go solo – Michael recalls her always referring to him, somewhat mock-respectfully, as 'Mortim-aire') and was establishing himself in the legal world (his father, Clifford Mortimer, of whom he would go on to write in *Voyage Round My Father*, had been a legal *eminence gris*). He had already published a few novels, usually well received, mostly – like his work for the stage too – drawing on his own life and experience and often recalling the war years and that euphoric 1945 feeling of optimism after Clement Attlee's landslide victory. Quality reviewers had often predicted great things for Mortimer's fictional career; on more than one occasion favourable comparisons were made with the novels of Henry Green, another distinctive stylist. Married to the glamorous but troubled Penelope, also a novelist, his lifestyle (very Habitat then) was already fixing him in the media's eyes as one of the key figures among London's fashionable literati, trendy dressers and regulars at the new *trattoriae* – Mario and Franco's, La Terazza, etc. – beginning to sprout in Soho as the dreary London of the Age of Austerity began to be transformed.

When Michael read the original one-act script of *The Dock Brief* he was 'immediately struck by the freshness of the writing' and said, 'Yes I'll do it and did John have another play with which to pair it?'

There was, briefly, talk of putting it together with a one-acter by Eugene Ionesco, *The Bald Prima Donna* (Mortimer always claimed that at the time he was ignorant of the émigré Romanian Ionesco's work, thinking people meant Unesco – many years later he adapted the play as *The Hairless Diva* for Watford's Palace Theatre), understandable in light of *The Dock Brief*'s touches of the surreal, which made it a distant cousin of plays classified as Theatre of the Absurd. However, Mortimer came up with *What Shall We Tell Caroline?*, another quirky one-act piece, set in a boy's school with an eccentric headmaster (not the last such character in the Mortimer canon), his scatty wife, a spivvy, banjo-strumming master (unforgettably played by Michael Hordern, lecherously smouldering) and the daughter of the central couple, the eponymous 'heroine', virtually silent throughout the play, until her near-curtain assertion of independence. Directed by Stuart Burge and impeccably cast – Maurice Denham and Brenda Bruce joining Hordern – it made, with *The Dock Brief*, a classily diverting evening.

Michael certainly needed a box office success after the opening production of the 1958 Lyric season, an excursion into deepest Ibsen territory with one of the most intractable of his plays, *Little Eyolf*, a great play but never an easy one to handle at the box office. An unsparing illumination of a marriage and of haunting guilt – the Allmers's lame son is drowned in an accident (an imperishable line – 'The crutch! The crutch is floating!' – conveys the offstage disaster) – mingles with scenes going beyond the bounds of naturalism, mostly featuring the powerfully unsettling symbolic figure of The Rat Wife, in a piece that Michael included mainly because it involved minimal financial risk: 'In effect I was employed by David William, who had been a huge star for the OUDS at Oxford where he had played Prospero, Peer Gynt, Richard II and others. When he came down from Oxford he inherited some money but decided "I'm not going into theatre until it becomes a little nicer". Well, I don't think it had become that much nicer a few years later but he was anxious to make his name as a director as well as an actor and he came to me asking me to produce *Eyolf* for him, saying, "You're someone who can come up with the goods."' Despite some favourable reviews comparing Ibsen's scrutiny of a guilt-stalked marriage with that in Tennessee Wiliams's *Cat on a Hot Tin Roof*, also seen at that time in London, the Allmers' anguish failed to draw Hammersmith, let alone the town; Michael's only abiding memories of it are the depressing box office returns and 'Robert Eddison, as Allmers, moving about the stage very, very slowly in open-toed sandals'.

The Mortimer double bill that followed was widely praised when it opened at the Lyric in April 1958 with some comparisons – to Mortimer's chagrin – with the absurd world of Ionesco. Photographs of the Mortimers and their five children (two by Penelope's first brief marriage) were splashed across the *Daily Express* whose critic had hailed Mortimer as 'a brilliant new comic playwright'. The then crucially influential Harold Hobson – his *Sunday Times* column could make or break a play's fortunes, on occasion salvaging a piece disdained in the daily press – was also enthusiastic while his equally important *Observer* counterpart, Kenneth Tynan, although admiring *The Dock Brief*, cannily rumbled the repetition of its verbal tropes in the less tautly written *Caroline*.

The Lyric's box office was healthy enough to warrant a West End transfer with the same cast to the Garrick Theatre where John Hallett, another influential figure in Michael's career, was manager, for a strong and popular run. *The Dock Brief* was also immensely successful overseas, especially in Eastern Europe (the Mortimers were often jaunting off to various Eastern bloc countries to spend the zlotys and other exotic currencies of the royalties never sent to the UK) where the play's prison-cell setting also carried extra layers of metaphor. It was also filmed (1962), less than brilliantly, with Richard Attenborough miscast as the murderer Fowle and a tricksy Peter Sellers almost sabotaging the movie as the barrister Morgenhall. It had a tepid revival in 2007 at the Savoy Theatre with Edward Fox as Morgenhall, uneasily paired with Mortimer's over-extended reworking of a previous television play, also with a legal background, *Edwin*.

The Dock Brief still stands as one of Mortimer's best pieces for the theatre. The growing symbiotic relationship between prisoner and legal representative – Michael Hordern mesmerising again as the failed shabby barrister, almost unable to credit his luck when, after years of waiting, his first case comes his way, with Maurice Denham matching him as the South London pigeon fancier accused of murdering his wife – as they rehearse the roles of judge, jury and witnesses is beautifully charted. While the second scene, touching and ruefully funny when it transpires that Morgenhall has failed to rise to the occasion only for his client to be pardoned because of his lawyer's ineptitude, manages to maintain the play's fine equipoise, leading to the oddly exhilarating ending seeing both men dance their way out of a just-opened prison-cell door. Some aspects of Morgenhall undoubtedly drew on Mortimer's father and his legal cronies – and some of his dialogue would recur, almost verbatim, in later plays as well as in *Rumpole of the Bailey* in fiction and on television – but the play retains its spry originality and a unique kind of Dickensian zest.

Michael could have wished for another Mortimer play more quickly – but had to wait until 1959 – when his Lyric venture had further trials. Immediately after *The Dock Brief* he had 'the bitter disappointment' of

Harold Pinter's *The Birthday Party*, a swift London flop after encouraging weeks in Cambridge and Oxford. Then the following production, Donald Ogden Stewart's *Honour Bright*, was also a failure despite its searingly urgent theme; with a boy genius at the heart of the plot, it was the first mainstream play in London to tackle the nuclear threat. It was possibly just ahead of its time; a few years later Robert Bolt's *The Tiger and the Horse*, very much exploring the same themes but with the lure of both Michael and Vanessa Redgrave, was a major West End success. Donald Ogden Stewart, who had been a regular at the Algonquin's Round Table in New York before a screenwriting career (including *The Philadelphia Story*) in Hollywood, was a refugee from Senator McCarthy's HUAC hearings and the black list, 'an urbane and witty man living in great style in Hampstead where he and his wife ran a kind of salon, which impressed me no end'. His play was well constructed, articulate and lucid but it failed to find a large audience. Only the final production of the Hammersmith season, the riotous triumph of Sandy Wilson's *Valmouth*, matched *The Dock Brief*'s success.

When Michael received the script of Mortimer's *The Wrong Side of the Park* in 1959 he was 'enthused at once ... I saw Mortimer as a major coming new dramatist. And I didn't think I was wrong then. I felt this play was a real confirmation of his talent for scrutinising new territory.' He now knew Mortimer and 'the redoubtable Penny' much better, occasionally visiting their lively, colourful North London home near John Barnes department store. With the Mortimers 'now established as real movers and shakers on the London social scene', Michael also enjoyed occasional lunches with Mortimer, always a beguiling raconteur of legal and theatrical anecdotes.

What especially appealed to Michael about *The Wrong Side of the Park* – he did not care for Mortimer's original title, *North-West Passage* – was that 'it was much more than a tale of metropolitan adultery'. Within the framework of the well-made West End play, Mortimer suggested a partial departure from naturalism with elements of its setting, a faded old North West London house 'on the cold, windy, unsunny side of the park', made of transparent walls, glossed by an unusually detailed list of atmospheric sound effects. Mortimer created a very palpable sense of a world in flux, a London subtly changing as old certainties crumble and as relationships undergo sea changes against a background of inner-city, post-war redevelopment and gentrification. He also created the best role he ever wrote for a woman in the central figure of Elaine Lee, a 'beautiful but tired' woman in her late thirties, married to a kindly but dull civil servant (Richard

Johnson) and sharing the house with his parents and her unmarried pregnant sister, played by the rising young Wendy Craig (whose clandestine
affair at the time with Mortimer – leading to her pregnancy – was later
much publicised). Michael presented the play once again in partnership
with David Hall and also with its director Peter Hall (the last play he
directed originally in the commercial sector for twenty years), and
shrewdly cast Margaret Leighton as the insecure Elaine, full of a yearning
that she cannot quite articulate. She was magnificent in the role of a
character who only too easily could have been a tiresome solipsist. A
genuine golden girl with a salty wit, lack of pretension and a matchless gift
– demonstrated in her playing of Terence Rattigan's or Tennessee Williams's women – of combining a tensile strength with moving
vulnerability, Leighton captured most affectingly the dilemma of a woman
caught between two worlds, unable to free herself totally from her youthful
wartime ideals and memories of her first husband, killed in the war. This
was especially potent at the close of the first act as Elaine, evoking that
curious sense of time suspended in wartime, recalls: 'All those coloured
bottles and the headscarves covered with De Gaulle, Roosevelt and Chiang
Kai-Shek ... and the great, sad noise of your friends bumping away against
the clouds.'

Leighton's scenes with the play's catalyst – one of those enigmatic or
ambivalent strangers who intrude into the ménages of so many plays of the
period – a charming, slightly spivvy chancer, Miller, who comes to lodge
in the house, had a mesmerising, erotic edge which could magnetise the
house, decidedly and unusually adult for a British play of the period
touching on sexual frustrations. The scenes undoubtedly gained some of
that edge from the fact that Leighton and Robert Stephens – playing Miller
– had a torrid backstage affair during the run (Mortimer's plays at this time
seemed to have as much backstage activity as on), finished only when
Leighton left the play.

There was a good deal of socialising during the pre-rehearsal period –
Michael recalls meetings with Peter Hall 'who was then living with Leslie
Caron in extreme splendour in a grand house in Montpelier Square in
Chelsea' – and rehearsals were smooth, although there was 'a decidedly
tricky out of town start when the play did a week, with much fanfare for
the golden boy Hall returning to the home of his classical triumphs, in the
cavernous barn of the Royal Memorial Theatre, Stratford-Upon-Avon'.

The Wrong Side of the Park opened in London – at another barn for a play,
the Cambridge Theatre – to strong notices and settled down after a first

night party at the Mortimers' ('a case of life imitating art because their house in NW6 *was* on the wrong side of the park. Although there would soon be an upwardly mobile move to Belgravia'), to business lively enough for a transfer to the more suitable, smaller St Martin's. Even with such a cast and mostly enthusiastic notices it never quite became a copper-bottomed, smash hit and it closed when Leighton left the cast in a vain attempt to patch up her volatile marriage to Laurence Harvey.

Michael also had to deal with box office troubles beyond the ordinary at this time. Worried by slipping returns for Mortimer's play, he dropped in to the St Martin's foyer one afternoon to find every single box office telephone off the hook: 'I was livid and said to the box office woman, "What on earth are you doing?" to which she replied, "I'm doing the advance. I can't do both." I made my displeasure known and, back at the office, at once rang the owner of the St Martin's, Bertie Meyer, to insist: "Unless that woman is sacked, the curtain will not go up tonight" – I couldn't do that these days, when she'd need at least three written warnings and a tribunal. Anyway, Meyer got the message and she did not reappear at the St Martin's. A few years later – proving my theory that they never get sacked, just moved on – I went into the Globe when I had a play on and there she was – the same woman – in charge of the box office. As soon as she saw me she burst out: "Oh, Mr Codron, I don't know what you must have thought of me – that business at the St Martin's. I don't know what came over me. And I've got such respect for you. And for all you've done." I thanked her before she continued. "And I'm so glad you're doing so well here at the Globe." At which point the phone rang. She picked it up with: "Hello, Palladium!"'

It was during the run of *The Wrong Side of the Park* that Peter Hall made Michael an offer that could have irrevocably altered the pattern of his career. Hall, who had taken over and recharged the Memorial Theatre in Stratford – his production of *Coriolanus* with Olivier was a particular personal highlight – was soon to launch a permanent ensemble, the Royal Shakespeare Company, combining Stratford with a new London base, housed in the West End's Aldwych Theatre, and he invited Michael 'over a convivial dinner' to run this London RSC arm. Michael respected Hall's flair as much as Hall admired Michael's entrepreneurial skills and Michael was 'hugely flattered, although there was just a tiny afterthought that it might be a way of silencing part of the competition' (Hugh Beaumont, a Stratford Governor, was distinctly alarmed by this spearhead of subsidised rivalry in the West End's heartland). However, despite the temptations –

to which a year or so previously he may well have capitulated – Michael now felt 'sure enough of my path as an independent producer' to turn Hall down ('David Jones took that role initially – and he was, I think, much better at it than I could have been').

Mortimer and the Codron office rejoined forces shortly afterwards on a cleverly balanced triple bill with Mortimer contributing *Lunch Hour* along-side Pinter's masterly *A Slight Ache* and N.F. Simpson's office-set *The Form*, presented under the less than imaginative umbrella title *Three* (1961) at the Arts Theatre, later moving – the New Wave proving that it had 'legs' now – to the Criterion. Mortimer was a decade older than his fellow dramatists, as the star, playwright/actor Emlyn Williams ('always rather *de haut en bas*' recalled Michael) bitchily reminded him when he met all three writers: 'Well, you got into the New Wave just as the Tube doors were closing!'

Lunch Hour, also originally a radio play, was a gently ironic small-scale tragi-comedy, set in a shabby King's Cross hotel bedroom where a middle-aged businessman has planned the seduction of a young female colleague, only to be interrupted at key moments by the establishment's refined manageress. The businessman has concocted an unnecessarily compli-cated reason for the hiring of the room by the hour – the girl is his wife who has travelled down from Scarborough for an important family discussion. But his scheme backfires when the girl gradually enters into the scenario so convincingly that she finally comes to take the 'wife's' side against her 'husband's' selfishness. Consummation remains to be wished with the fall of the curtain. Wendy Craig, still involved with Mortimer although now married herself, was delightfully feisty as the girl and Alison Leggatt, an unusually versatile character actress, nailed down the manageress to the last disapproving sniff. She was equally fine as the wife in Pinter's *A Slight Ache*, easily the best of a trio described by one critic as by 'three of the most brilliant playwrights working today', in which Richard Briers as the muf-fled and mute figure of The Matchseller made an early West End impression.

During this most prolific period of his playwriting career Mortimer wrote *Two Stars for Comfort* (Garrick, 1962) for which Michael, producing solo, was able to lure Trevor Howard, still a major star, for a rare stage appearance. He was aware of the risks – Howard was a formidable toper – not least that 'this play presented an added worry in that it was set in a kind of converted boat with uneven floors and low ceilings. Not perhaps the ideal set for a bibulous star.' But he knew too that on form the actor could shake hands with greatness, especially when portraying flawed or self-deluded men such as Sam, the genial publican at the centre of Mortimer's play.

Two Stars for Comfort was in some measure drawn from an early (unpublished) novel set near Mortimer's childhood (and later-life) home, 'in a timbered riverside inn near the Thames at Henley, in the gin and lime belt' as Mortimer describes it. Sam enjoys his flirtations with and attempted seductions of local Regatta beauty queens while, in parallel, a group of brashly iconoclastic undergraduates rehearse a play, which mercilessly sends up and exposes the shop-soiled realities behind Sam's casual philandering. Sam is trapped, like a fly in amber, in a happier prelapsarian past; on his best nights Howard was incomparable, deeply moving in his subtle delineation of a character on the rack of his moral despair.

Bernard Levin in the *Daily Mail* led the critical praise ('Two stars? Make it five!') and Howard received hats-in-the-air notices, although rehearsals had at times been touch and go, despite Michael Elliott's simpatico directorial hand and the presence in the cast of several fine and supportive fellow actors such as Peter Sallis. So Michael was 'more than slightly trepidatious' when he went to wish his cast good luck on opening night, passing a long queue sitting on stools, waiting for the Gallery door to open, all down the alleyway alongside the Garrick leading to the stage door. He found Howard in expansive mood in the star dressing room: 'He asked me: "Would you like a drink? I've nothing in here yet but we could nip out." I thought, "I mustn't be managerial and stuffy," so I said "OK" and we went out past what must have been a somewhat bemused Gallery queue seeing their star leave the theatre half an hour before the show, past the crowd outside the front of the theatre and into a sort of gin palace on the corner of Irving Street just across the road. He was clearly relishing my obvious anxiety. He sank his Scotch in one, clapped me on the shoulder cheerfully and said, "You shouldn't worry, Michael – the demons are with me tonight!" And indeed they were – he gave a magnificent performance.'

Sadly it was not always so and the Garrick run was on occasion more than a trifle bumpy. But never so much as on the very last performance of the production when it finished a brief post-West End tour at the Golders Green Hippodrome 'with a packed and largely Jewish audience, many of whom would have known my family and who were subjected to the sad, sad spectacle of Trevor Howard totally out of it – he really didn't know where he was. I was tempted to get up and say, "Would you all like your money back?" but forced myself to sit through it.'

Despite Michael's regard for the play, Mortimer's agent Peggy Ramsay,

PROGRAMME
ONE SHILLING

✳ *Two stars for comfort*
✳   *by John Mortimer*

GARRICK THEATRE

17. 'The demons are with me' – Trevor Howard in
Two Stars for Comfort, 1962.

although she continued to represent 'Mortim-aire', felt that the dramatist had not fully realised his central creation, Sam. She was disillusioned: 'Mortimer's big weakness is a passion for success and the trappings of success … success, when indulged in, saps people's character and drains their true talent away. He could be a superb artist, not merely a successful one, and it's this which makes me sad.'

A tippling star also added to the various problems – 'quite a saga' – on Mortimer's next play, *The Judge* (Cambridge Theatre, 1967) an unusually flat title from Mortimer, so adept normally at naming his work. The play was rather flat too, with some clumsily worked flashback scenes, and Mortimer's legal commitments prevented him from significantly addressing the problems in rehearsal or during the pre-London tour. The play had been already produced in Hamburg, to a chilly reaction ('What's the German for "Boo"?' a somewhat disoriented Mortimer had asked his hosts during a noisy curtain call. 'Boo' they had told him) but the author seemed disinclined to do much work on the piece subsequently. Peter Hall had politely passed on Michael's offer to direct (Stuart Burge from *The Dock Brief* took it on), 'the set was quite hideous' and it proved 'stubbornly difficult to cast'.

So the omens were hardly propitious for this ambitious play, tackling – somewhat self-consciously – big themes of Guilt, Revenge and Duty. The eponymous Judge (Patrick Wymark, then a familiar television face) is facing the close of his career, coincidentally presiding over what will be his last assizes in his native cathedral city, still haunted by guilt from his adolescent indiscretion with an Archdeacon's daughter. Now also aged, Serena has become a louche dowager, presiding over a rackety establishment above her antiques shop, wreathed in a Gauloises fug, name-dropping Bloomsberries and quoting Cocteau, one of her cronies from a spell in Paris.

Serena was played finally by Patience Collier, herself something of a *grande dame* in theatrical circles; some actors revered her and treasured her trenchant 'notes' on their performances whilst others reached for the garlic and crucifix at her approach backstage. Michael could never quite forget Noël Coward speaking of Collier to him: 'She is a charming woman often. But unless you are very careful she will build a nest in your hair.' She made Michael's life difficult with constant carps and moans: 'I was summoned regularly to the Albion Hotel in Brighton on tour before London to hear her complaints, largely about Patrick Wymark as the Judge. And it was, of course, true that he was not averse to a tipple. Altogether it was not a happy experience.'

It was on this production that 'the seeds of doubt were planted in my mind that John Mortimer might after all not make the absolutely first-class dramatist that I had thought he might possibly become. *The Judge* had well-observed characters and mostly good dialogue, but it always seemed rather laboured. And it was never got quite right.'

Michael also observed on *The Judge* how vital the choice of theatre – given the vagaries of the commercial theatre system often necessarily left to luck and settling for whatever is available – can be for a production. He felt that the wide single-circled Cambridge Theatre was quite wrong to house *The Judge* ('it is certainly not a happy theatre to be in when you're not filling it'). He elaborated by pointing out that 'theatres are divided into clever audience-friendly Edwardian theatres in which you enter from the front of the stalls and unless you're very early, you see people. And then there are houses built later like the Cambridge and the Queen's, where you come in from the back of the auditorium and see rows of empty seats usually. It was very clever of the designers of those Edwardian buildings.'

No such worry about choice of theatre clouded the production of Mortimer's most popular and longest-running play, *Voyage Round My Father* (1971) which opened at what is widely considered the crown jewel of West End theatres, the Theatre Royal, Haymarket. Since *The Judge* Mortimer had written a varied quartet of short plays, *Come As You Are* (1970), which did not come Michael's way, a troubled venture with a volatile star (Glynis Johns) produced in London by Broadway's Alexander Cohen (it contained one miniature gem in *Bermondsey*, a vignette of sexual juggling in a South London pub) and a sketchy, unsatisfactory adaptation of Robert Graves's *I, Claudius* (1972) presented by Michael White.

Michael indeed was not originally involved with the stage version of *Voyage Round My Father*. Once again radio – 'the gentlest and least noticed of all media' in Mortimer's words – was the origin of the piece, first with *The Education of an Englishman* (broadcast in 1964), a memoir play plotlessly but cunningly making a kind of mosaic of scenes from Mortimer's youth, which had Roger Livesey as Mortimer *père*, the still fiercely independent, blind Clifford Mortimer. Then Mortimer wrote a kind of sequel in *Personality Split* (1964), tracing the experiences of "Henry Winter" (a regular name for Mortimer's various autobiographical creations in fiction and on stage) in his wartime job with the Crown Film Unit before his formidable parent steers him towards the law ('you'll find it can exercise a certain medieval charm'). Later still (1969) there was a well-received television play of *Voyage Round My Father*, using elements of both radio pieces, with Mark Dignam playing the senior Mortimer figure.

Much of the material from radio and television was retained or slightly reworked in what became *Voyage Round My Father* on stage. It still remained less a play, more of a collage, a sequence of vignettes (the short burst was usually more Mortimer's forte than the longer haul), some of them rather too obviously set pieces, such as the scene with the eccentric headmaster from the schooldays section of *The Education of an Englishman* and the Crown Films Unit sequence involving a callow young Mortimer. These were retained more or less intact, while some roles, such as the son's candid girlfriend, later wife (very much based on Penelope Mortimer), the only character to question the way the family avoid any reference to the father's blindness, were significantly expanded.

The play was first presented at South London's Greenwich Theatre in 1970, directed by Claude Watham, better known for his television and film work, with Mark Dignam again as the father. It was Peggy Ramsay who urged – 'even nagged' – Michael into going to Greenwich: 'Peggy said it was in danger of going badly awry. I liked the play, although the Greenwich set was poor and I could see what Peggy meant. Everybody beforehand thought it would be almost automatically wonderful with all those ingredients. And Mark Dignam was very good. But – and this isn't all that unusual with projects which seem perfect on paper – it just hadn't come together. There seemed quite a lot of unhappiness around the venture. I didn't own the rights and at that time the thought was that it might transfer with Anthony Pye-Jeary, then Greenwich's Press Officer (later a key figure in the mighty Dewynter's advertising agency), producing it with the theatre's publicist Peter Wright. But Peggy was worried that they had no real producing experience and doubted their ability to capitalise the production sufficiently. So when I said I should be interested – although when I saw the play I immediately thought, "This is a wonderful part for Alec Guinness" and I honestly thought that commercially the play demanded a star – of course I became this monster from the West End swooping down on South London and scooping up Greenwich's hit. But really it wasn't like that.'

Guinness was at once attracted to both part and play – he was fascinated by the challenge of playing a blind character, denying the actor use of his eloquent eyes (later he used what he had discovered when playing the blind butler Bensonmum in the Neil Simon-scripted film *Murder by Death*) – and Michael invited Ronald Eyre, a quiet but meticulously focused ex-schoolteacher who had given the RSC a major hit with his joyous rediscovery of Dion Boucicault's *London Assurance*, to direct. Guinness had some say in the casting; he was especially keen that his friend Leueen MacGrath, whose busy love life had included a marriage to Broadway's George S. Kaufman, should play his wife. He brushed aside the worries of both producer and director that her distinctively plummy voice might sound peculiar: 'Well, if you'd had in your mouth what she's had in hers over the years, you'd sound peculiar too.' Rehearsals were comparatively peaceful although Mortimer, only an occasional presence in the rehearsal room these days – by now he was a legal superstar, regularly appearing, always for the defence, in high-profile and landmark cases such as the prosecution for obscenity of Hubert Selby Jr's novel, *Last Exit to Brooklyn* – remained concerned that Guinness, undeniably charismatic and deftly finessing the father's diktats ('Nothing narrows the mind as much as foreign travel'), was missing a crucial aspect of the role. For Mortimer there was a vital substrain of frustrated rage to be exposed (nowhere more potently than in the deathbed scene with the father's outburst: 'I'm always angry when I'm dying') and he persuaded Michael to set up a lunch with him and Guinness also present ('Can't we coax more fire out of him?' he asked Michael). Michael was well aware that it was difficult to pin the star down over anything major to do with a role he was determined to play his own way, and so he was not entirely surprised when 'late in the lunch – only towards dessert – did the subject arise when John suggested delicately that there could be more fire in the father's belly, only for Guinness, after a brief and heavily charged pause, to respond, in clearly hurt tones: "But haven't you noticed? I do tap my boiled egg quite crossly in the breakfast scene."' The subject was not pursued.

Voyage was a commercial producer's dream play, cunningly mixing nostalgia with an occasional 'daring' touch (a scene involving two lesbians) pitched perfectly to its mainstream audience, housed in London's most elegant playhouse with an international star supported by a strong cast. Jeremy Brett played the son and Nicola Pagett the strong-willed Elizabeth, with the splendidly orotund Jack May – once an OUDS colleague of Michael's – as the headmaster ('Noah' to the boys – his 'litter of runts' – with his wife as 'Mrs Noah' and his son 'Shem') warning his charges of unnatural affections, a signal of which is the offer of cake by predatory boys ('Remember the only real drawback to our great public school system is unsolicited cake').

Business was capacity from the start, although Guinness – who tended to look for grit in his oysters – grew distinctly tetchy with those seated in the front row of the stalls who would regularly leave programmes distractingly on the front of the stage. He would make his first entrance from the wings and, should he spot any offending programme, simply change the set move across the stage, somewhat shattering the illusion of the character's blindness, to descend upon the offending object, speaking the while, and flick it with his Malacca cane into the lap of the startled culprit.

His was a meticulously shaded study, funny, rueful and touching, although for some there was a prevalent nimbus of sanctity around his father, somewhat at variance with the character's inner turbulence. Mortimer had been right – more fire was needed. Guinness's successor, Michael Redgrave, caused some considerable anxiety when taking over the role. He was suffering from Parkinson's disease (then undiagnosed), which had caused an invidious deterioration in his memory. On his previous theatrical outing, William Trevor's *The Old Boys*, he had finally to resort to a hearing aid through which to receive his prompts and it had to be sent for during rehearsals for *Voyage*, although, as in *The Old Boys*, once launched into the run it became much less required (sadly, the hoary old Ned Sherrin anecdote of a performance when Redgrave, supposedly picking up a radio cab firm's calls through his earpiece, turned to a startled Jane Baxter as his wife to announce: "I am to proceed at once to Flask Walk, Hampstead" is apocryphal). Redgrave presented an initially jauntier figure, with something of the Edwardian *boulevardier* in his performance of music-hall songs ('Pretty Little Polly Perkins of Paddington Green') but he also found and fascinatingly mined an area of darkness in the role (taking his cue from a line of the son's: 'My father had a great capacity for rage, but never against the universe'); in Redgrave's performance, which was not widely reviewed (although *The Observer* described it as 'one of the most quietly astonishing performances on the London stage'), this was a man patently staving off terror at the spectre of death.

Altogether *Voyage* enjoyed a run of nearly two years at the Haymarket. Michael always had happy memories of the production although his response to the play was more limited. He particularly realised how much of the production's success was due to the director; Ronald Eyre handled the play with a musician's attention to scoring in Voytek's simple but adaptable and effective dappled design. Over thirty years later he saw it revived, remarking subsequently: 'Ron Eyre managed to make it seem a much better play than it seemed when it was revived (in 2006) at the Donmar.'

In the years following *Voyage* (it had yet another incarnation, as a television film, with Olivier as the father) Mortimer's public image, even after divorce from Penelope, remarriage and more children, not to mention the revelation of his fathering Wendy Craig's son, gradually grew into that of National Treasure, part G.K. Chesterton, part John Betjeman, a kind of fondly indulged, avuncular and raffish court jester, especially after the success of his much-loved legal creation of Rumpole of the Bailey on television and in novel form. His plays took second place; he and Michael worked together only twice more.

Collaborators (Duchess, 1973) was written after his divorce, recycling a good deal of the material covered also by Penelope in her fiction, most specifically in her brutally clear-eyed dissection of their marriage in *The Pumpkin Eater*. The play was to a degree inspired by the suggestion of Peggy Ramsay, who was always fascinated by the elements of public performance and competition in her client's first marriage, that he write 'a funny savage play about the marriage of two writers'. Michael realised *Collaborators'* potential at once and such was the combined standing of Mortimer and the Codron firm at that time that it was cast with unusual speed, to include Glenda Jackson (at the peak of her film fame then), John Wood and the Mortimers' friend Joss Ackland in the leading roles.

Wood played Henry Winter (yet another outing for Mortimer's favourite alter-ego name) a barrister and radio dramatist living with his wife Katherine in North West London amidst the domestic mayhem involved with several small children and copious drying nappies. A brash American movie producer – none too subtly named Sam Brown – promises to transform their lives by persuading Henry to work on a film script, to Katherine's sardonic disapproval ('You'll become someone ghastly … who drives a white Jag, with cashmere polo necks and an identity bracelet and a house in Weybridge'). Initially the Winters baffle Sam, bemused by Henry's Anglo-Saxon irony and flip insouciance (Katherine tells Henry, 'You don't ever talk, you tell jokes') and made apprehensive by Katherine's brusque candour ('Is she the sort that likes to cut ball occasionally?' he asks Henry, to whom she is 'The Lady Macbeth of Belsize Park').

To sophisticated London theatregoers *Collaborators* offered a fishbowl view of a much-publicised marriage, yoked to a reworking of Noël Coward's *Private Lives* (Henry and Katherine are definitely kin to Coward's Amanda and Elyot) updated to the world of the Stringalongs and company from the sharp-eyed comic-strip 'Life and Times in NW1' illustrated by 'Marc' (Mark Boxer) whose cartoons of trendy contemporary metropolitan life had already immortalised Mortimer, highlighting – as he did with Pinter – the trademark heavy-rimmed spectacles. This retread of the John and Penelope Mortimer marriage was often acrid, biliously funny and at times bruisingly tender; like Coward's 'two violent acids bubbling away in the same matrimonial bottle' they find it equally impossible to live together as apart. The dialogue had authentic sting – Joss Ackland and his wife once were part of a summer Italian villa party with the Mortimers and he recalled the atmosphere as 'like Albee's *Who's Afraid of Virginia Woolf?* on ice' – with some inspired riffs such as the Winters' song-and-dance routine to various standards with 'Dance' in the title ('I Won't Dance', 'Dancing on the Ceiling' *et al*) and substituting 'fuck' for every mention of 'dance'. This caused Michael 'no little trouble with Mr Irving Berlin and his representatives'.

Collaborators was a major success at the box office but 'its first production was not altogether happy'. Jackson was bang on target with all Katherine's vitriolic scorn but the character's inner landscape of despair eluded her totally while Wood was a fussily mannered Henry. Joss Ackland did his best with Brown, although the production overemphasised his stereotypical American crudeness. When the time came to recast, Michael pressed hard on behalf of Michael Gambon, then just on the verge of great things, 'but he did not appeal enough to Mortimer's conception and John Thaw took over – more than creditably, it must be said'. But the play itself obstinately never quite took off; it could be intriguing to see it revived.

The final Mortimer/Codron union was a disappointing conclusion to their partnership. Once again the project originated on radio, with the 1976 broadcasts of first, *The Fear of Heaven*, with both John Gielgud and Denholm Elliott in vintage form, a duologue between two ailing elderly men lying in hospital beds beneath the magnificently painted ceiling in an historic building now housing the Hospital for Transients and the Urban Poor in Sienna, while *The Prince of Darkness* involved a modern miracle that takes place in an achingly with-it South London rectory. The broadcast coincided with the noisy publicity surrounding two high-profile Mortimer legal *causes célèbres* at a time of rapidly shifting Anglo-Saxon sexual boundaries, the *Gay News* and the Linda Lovelace (*Deep Throat*) trials, underlying Mortimer's assertion that the plays had a quasi-religious message: 'If you abolish the idea of sin you take a lot of the fun out of sex.'

The double bill's stage premiere as *Heaven and Hell* saw Mortimer and Michael return to Greenwich where the first play, without the virtuoso playing of its radio duo, seemed somewhat recondite as well as static, for all its slyly subversive wit. Finally it was dropped altogether for the West End and Mortimer extended his second piece, reworking it as *The Bells of Hell*.

When a bishop suddenly announces a visit to South London where the trendy vicar, Gavin Faber, holds regular meetings and Bondage Nights for his gay and transvestite parishioners, his wife reports that only a curling kipper and some sliced bread are available in the fridge for supper. Much to Gavin's eloquent scepticism his curate prays for food, giving rise to the play's best joke, the visual coup when Mrs Faber opens the fridge to find it vomiting forth an unending stream of loaves and fishes. The original play had been an amusing, if slender, satirical comedy while its extension transformed it into a sniggering overextended *New Statesman* competition entry. John Tydeman, who had directed both plays on radio and at Greenwich, did what he could but even his experience with Peter Woodthorpe (as Gavin), who by now had to be kept on something of a firm leash, could not prevent the actor from sailing way over the top to become as camp as several serried rows of tents.

Heaven and Hell was a short-lived flop at the Garrick Theatre. Mortimer kept writing occasionally for the theatre – most notably with the RSC version of *A Christmas Carol*, and another legal drama that had a juicy role for Leslie Phillips even if it recycled rather too many old anecdotes, *Naked Justice* (West Yorkshire Playhouse, 2001) but that was under the banner of producer Duncan C. Weldon. He never appeared again on a Michael Codron poster. They had enjoyed 'many happy times' over their various outings, particularly earlier in Mortimer's career, but for Michael the sense always subsequently remained that of all his prime stable of front-running playwrights, Mortimer was 'the one that got away'.

CHAPTER 7

TRIUMPH AND A DISASTER

The establishment of Michael Codron Ltd as a power in London's commercial theatre had a great deal to do – as Michael always acknowledged – with the off-West End world, initially at the Lyric, Hammersmith and subsequently at the smaller Arts Theatre. The experience of *Share My Lettuce* had reinforced his regard for the Lyric as a congenial venue where the jocund Shakespearean presence, always encouraging, of J. Baxter Somerville and an efficient stage crew were compensations enough for 'naughty Reg Cornish' and his occasional fiddles. Also the theatre's public reputation was still high, the legacy of The Company of Four. Beaumont, to whom Hammersmith was 'Here Be Dragons' territory – although he knew perfectly well the Lyric's usefulness financially to the Tennent empire in launching less- immediately commercial ventures – used to refer to it, slightingly and inaccurately, as 'The Audience of Four'. Similarly at the Arts, Peter Hall's regime, although comparatively brief, had confirmed the theatre's reputation as a venue for less-conventional productions, often from the modern European theatre.

At Hammersmith during the 1957-8 season that launched John Mortimer, Michael had not been able to programme quite as boldly as he might have wished. David William's money had cushioned *Little Eyolf* ('I was really only the man doing the contracts on that one') and, of course, he was not entirely his own man, with David Hall joining him in producing the season, albeit as 'a kind of sleeping partner'. Bright – an Oxford Double First – and with private wealth, Hall lived in considerable style in St Leonard's Terrace with a *soignée* and extremely social wife who was never quite sure of the theatre world or of Michael ('Come in, you stinker' was her usual greeting at home). Hall had no office and rarely visited Michael's but he was crucial to that season and not only financially – after all he had been shrewd enough to option Mortimer's *The Dock Brief*: 'David Hall was a kind of bulwark for the enterprise. I couldn't have done that season without him.'

Michael was still able to include in that season two projects to which he had responded immediately and passionately. One would be the smash hit of the Hammersmith project. The other was to develop an initial reputation as one of the post-war British theatre's most notorious flops.

Sandy Wilson, after his forays into revue, where his path had crossed Michael's (they also had Michael Oliver as a solicitor in common), had become extremely rich from the international success of his artful and loving pastiche of the 1920s musical, *The Boy Friend*. Originally a short piece for the Player's Theatre, in its fuller revised version it ran for five years in the West End and also went to Broadway (with a fresh young talent – Julie Andrews – as ingénue Polly Browne). The New York production was handled by the famously pugnacious duo of Ernie Martin and Cy Feuer, seriously major players after the runaway success of *Guys and Dolls*; having professed to love the show's intimate, small-scale charm and vowing to preserve that quality in New York, they proceeded to want to 'beef it up' in rehearsal, exaggerating the performances, altering the delicate orchestrations for a big, brassy Broadway sound and finally firing the director, Vida Hope (Feuer took over), with Feuer banning Wilson from rehearsals ('I kicked him out of the theatre and hired a Pinkerton detective to stand at the stage door and bar his entry'). The production was a success but nothing like the epic runner it was in London.

Not surprisingly, Wilson was now extremely wary of the theatre world's chicanery: 'He really did not trust anybody, certainly not anyone connected with the coarsening of *The Boy Friend*, but he brought his next show, *Valmouth*, to me.' There were certain conditions – Vida Hope must direct, for instance – but Wilson would then help out with the production's capitalisation. A large-cast musical with an orchestra, several settings and period costumes would have been well beyond Michael's Lyric budget.

Valmouth was adapted from the 1919 novel (more novella – it is just over 100 pages long) by Ronald Firbank, although Wilson cunningly introduced characters from other Firbank fiction, not least the unusually worldly prelate Cardinal Pirelli ('I stayed at the Ritz in Paris / And my comfort was quite complete / When I stay at the Ritz in New York / I am given the Bridal Suite').

Set in the south-west spa town of Valmouth where the air is so invigorating that centenarians and a remarkable longevity of the sexual impulse are common, it involves several grandes dames, all still larky (although Mrs Hurstpierpoint may try to mortify the flesh – 'it was rumoured she wore a bag of holly leaves pinned to the lining of her every gown'), naughty sailors, a local wench left pregnant by her naval lover Dick, about to return with his shipboard chum Jack Whorhound ('That little lad is, to me, what Patroclus was to Achilles, and even more so'), a nun allowed on one day in the year to break her vow of silence, and Mrs Yajnavalka, a black masseuse ('I've got magic digits / I can ease your aches and fidgets') and all-round fixer.

On the page the piece seems an unlikely candidate for musicalisation. If its descriptive style is Impressionist, its dialogue is more Pointillist and the dread trap of Highest Camp is omnipresent. Wilson, however, somehow managed to capture all the fantastical filigree atmosphere of Firbank, whose interiors are stuffed with *lapis lazuli* chaises longues covered in jaguar skin and dimly lit Ingres portraits, the exteriors perfumed with orchids and pierced by peacocks' cries on lawns studded with erotic statuary. The prose exudes a scent of tuberoses mixed with the heady incense of his Catholic trappings; in the wrong hands it could easily have degenerated into a cloying potpourri but Wilson's book and lyrics evoke all of Firbank's eccentrically potent sorcery.

He had originally written *Valmouth* for – unlikely venue – the Royal Court when the ESC were looking for a vehicle for the outsize talent of Bertice Reading, who had impressed London in Errol John's *Moon on a Rainbow Shawl* and in Carson McCullers's *The Member of the Wedding* in Sloane Square. The ESC felt unable to take on such a buoyant period piece, dripping with aristocratic high jinks, but when Michael heard Wilson play and sing through his score he became committed at once: 'I loved it from the start and although Sandy said he'd help with the capitalisation only if it was done the way he wanted, I agreed with that way in any case.'

Wilson's score, ranging from lilting ballads to company chorales, served Reading especially well; she made a superb centre to *Valmouth* as Mrs Yaj, swathed in exotic turbans and shawls, an expansive, life-enhancing presence whether in a gentle lullaby or togging herself up in her finery in the show-stopping 'Big Best Shoes'. He also wrote witty lyrics, studded with some internal rhymes worthy of Cole Porter, in the numbers for Fenella Fielding as Lady Parvula de Panzoust; neither he nor Michael considered anyone else for the part, that of an ageing but still game nymphomaniac set on one last fling. With Mrs Yaj's connivance she sets out to ensnare a handsome farm lad, with only minor scruples ('After four honeymoons in Valmouth's hotel – to be forced to take to the fields!'), while explaining in song to the shade of her favourite husband that each of her many flings ('One of our footmen, as they oft do / Looked so handsome with his livery on – and off, too') really was only 'A Passing Phase'.

It was quite a cast – Doris Hare played old Granny Tooke and Patsy Rowlands her dreamy granddaughter Thetis – and *Valmouth* gained another trump card when Michael asked Tony Walton to design, a decision which definitely went some way towards Michael's realisation of the designer's importance to a production (the firm would go on to use the cream of British designers – some of them at the start of their careers – and the standard of the physical productions would become a Codron hallmark).

Walton was then only twenty-three. He had studied at the Oxford School of Technology prior to the Slade, working regularly at Wimbledon Theatre during his training. Newly married to Julie Andrews he accompanied her to New York for *The Boy Friend*, working as a book illustrator and designing a much admired off-Broadway revival of Coward's Regency musical *Conversation Piece*. Always brilliant at the evocation of unusual, imaginative landscapes (*Pippin* for Bob Fosse or John Guare's *Six Degrees of Separation*), he was an inspired choice for *Valmouth*. He once said, 'My main instincts are those of a painter' and he gave the show a gauzy, slightly decadent look with a sly nod to Aubrey Beardsley, his costumes likewise suggesting the evanescence of Firbank in filmy, plumed creations across a palette of colours with the subtlest brush, a touch which he even gave to *Valmouth*'s poster.

18. A Tony Walton design for *Valmouth*, 1958.

Vida Hope's rehearsals were enjoyable but disciplined, although off-stage there were occasional dramas. Bertice Reading led, to say the least, a colourful life; she was then renting an apartment in Jermyn Street above the Turkish Baths (now Floris) but her extravagant lifestyle meant regular bailiffs' visits and Michael often had to race over to Jermyn Street to bail her out. In her gratitude Reading then fell madly in love with Michael: 'Bertice saw life as a kind of extravaganza. When she fell in love with me, as she claimed – although she'd previously fallen for Oscar Lewenstein at the Royal Court – she began to wear this massive Star of David in her remarkable décolletage. The story goes that while Bertice and Fenella were sharing a railway carriage on their way to opening on tour, Bertice confided, "I have this problem – I've fallen in love with Michael Codron. Tell me what to do." To which Fenella, who knew well which way the wind blew (her parents once had harboured hopes for her and me) responded: "You'd be better employed learning your lines."'

Michael had chosen to open *Valmouth* in Liverpool at the New Shakespeare Theatre ('a rather dingy barn') mainly because of the reputation recently created there for adventurous work under Sam Wanamaker and Anna Deere Wiman, but they opted to forget to tell him that the theatre would not be paying the going union rates for the stage crew. Local dockers had to be brought in to help with the scene changes; the production manager, Jack Hanson, found himself desperately and sweatily having to shift scenery himself to keep the show moving. The company 'somehow managed to finish a dress rehearsal of sorts, but we were very edgy on opening and widely compared, to our disadvantage, to another new British musical, *Chrysanthemum* with Pat Kirkwood trying out at Liverpool's Royal Court'.

At Hammersmith it was a critical and public hit, playing to packed and cheering houses throughout its limited run. It looked as if Firbank, whose books sold poorly in his lifetime, might enjoy posthumous popularity and that his special blend of subtlety and exuberance could prove more than caviar to the general. However, its commercial transfer was jinxed; there was a perilous shortage of available West End theatres and Michael was forced into another unlovely barn, the Savile (now a cinema) at the upper end of Shaftesbury Avenue, although he was grateful for the support of Geoffrey Russell, his landlord. More crucial was the loss of Bertice Reading, booked for a Broadway version of William Faulkner's *Requiem for a Nun*. Her replacement Cleo Laine was perhaps technically the better singer but she utterly lacked the voluptuousness, physical and vocal, for Mrs Yaj and, fatally, coupled with her insistence on new arrangements for her numbers from her husband John Dankworth, *Valmouth* lost a vital amount of its amperage. Reading could unify an audience and fill even an unfriendly auditorium with communal joy. The reduced impact of the Savile version definitely contributed to the unexpected brevity of its West End run; it closed after 102 performances.

Surprisingly, even allowing for its challenges, only one major revival of *Valmouth* has been seen, when the Chichester Festival mounted it in 1982 with Reading, Fielding and Hare all in their original roles with the novelty of a spectral-thin Robert Helpmann, like an apprehensive chamois goat, titupping his way through Cardinal Pirelli. But John Dexter, a superb director who never understood musicals, coarsened the show, allowing far too much cheap campery and some alarmingly unsubtle performances. When Michael saw it he was probably right in saying: 'I think *Valmouth* was before its time when I did it but then when it was at Chichester the timing – over which one never has total control – wasn't quite right either.'

At least *Valmouth*'s Hammersmith success ('it was a happy show, and audiences at the Lyric just adored it') compensated to some extent for the mind-numbing failure there of a previous production when a new play about which Michael had been publicly and privately enthusiastic failed so cataclysmically critically and at the box office.

The Birthday Party, now an established modern classic of English drama, was Harold Pinter's first full-length play, written while he was still an actor. Michael had heard of *The Room*, Pinter's one-act play produced at Bristol in May 1957, and later that year at the National Student Drama Festival when it was favourably reviewed by the *Sunday Times*'s wayward but influential drama critic, Harold Hobson (those who saw both productions infinitely preferred the original, directed by Pinter's old friend from Hackney schooldays, Henry Woolf, which was much more alert to the play's comedic vein). Michael contacted Pinter's recently acquired agent Emmanuel (known to most who knew him as Jimmy) Wax, an impressive character with an Oxford First (he read law) and once a judge with the British Army of Occupation in Europe: 'Rather a Buddha-like figure who operated his ACTAC agency from an elegant mews house off Cadogan Square. It was always a pleasure to go there – he was a "gent". He arranged for me to meet Harold in the cocktail bar of the Regent Palace Hotel.'

Recently Michael had moved his office from Paultons Street to premises in Regent Street near Austin Read – he had been alerted to the possibility of this space by the canny and camp Scottish agent Jimmy Fraser – he called most of his clients 'hen', irrespective of sex – of the Fraser & Dunlop agency, also operating (in considerably grander offices) at No. 91 Regent Street.

Michael was somewhat abashed about his workaday office, hardly likely to impress as the premises of a leading London management. By the same token Pinter, always guarded about his privacy, was then living in unglamorous Chiswick digs (Michael never entered a Pinter home until success took him to Regent's Park stuccoed splendour) and so for both men the hotel bar provided suitably Pinteresque neutral territory.

The Regent Palace just off Piccadilly Circus was then a classy hotel, all stylish Art Deco with blond wood, glass and shining chrome in the cocktail bar; Michael always wondered, after hearing of Pinter – reluctant usually to analyse his work in interview – describing what his plays were 'about' as 'the weasel under the cocktail cabinet', if the remark was somehow suggested by that Regent Palace bar.

Their meeting went well – especially given that both could be reticent men (while Pinter's pauses in his plays became famous, Michael's taciturnity, real or usefully feigned, as a negotiating ploy with agents, became equally legendary) – and at the end of their first meeting Pinter gave Michael a copy of *The Birthday Party* to take away.

There was no way Michael could have known that he would be reading an early work by a writer who would become internationally produced as a major twentieth-century dramatist, one with whom he would have a happy partnership for over thirty years, with Pinter as dramatist and then later director, and who would go on to win the Nobel Prize for Literature. His reaction on reading the play, however, was immediate: 'I took it home, read it and then said to Jimmy Wax, "I'll do it." I responded to it at once and I knew that this was a new, really special voice – I think, because of the menace and the fear, but also, maybe because of our mutual Jewishness, some of the writing, a lot of Goldberg's incantatory speech, spoke very strongly to me.'

Interestingly in the light of the initial critical tendency to find Pinter obscure, gnomic, earnest and driven by menace, Michael – like many in the theatre world – seemed to grasp instinctively what Pinter essentially was about even if he could not analytically define it: 'I don't in any way want to denigrate the play or seem brighter than I was, but the *framework* of it, the kind of "repertory play" structure – I'm not talking about its content – was sort of familiar. And a lot of it was, I thought, very funny.'

Michael here was latching on to something crucial about Pinter. As

David Baron in his years as an actor in provincial rep and during his time in Ireland with the great if erratic actor/manager Anew McMaster, Pinter had played in countless rep war horses from most of the Agatha Christie thrillers through Coward, Rattigan and Priestley to seaside-set farces (he had also appeared in *Ring for Catty* in Torquay). This experience not only taught him all about the structure of the well made play (and *The Birthday Party*, with its tight construction and three beautifully crafted curtains, is nothing if not theatrically effective) but must too have seeped into his memory bank; Pinter seemed always to be a writer with a kind of hotline to his own subconscious, even if that material was transmuted in the writing.

Of course there are universal, mythic and symbolic layers in *The Birthday Party* and of course it dramatises one of the key themes of twentieth-century writing, the individual or non-conformist (the lodger, Stanley) against society or the state (the invasive Goldberg and McCann) pressuring him to conform and so 'reclaim' him – as Pinter's astute biographer, Michael Billington, has stressed even Pinter's early work stamps him as a political writer – and of course Pinter's attachment to the work of Kafka and Beckett, both of whom had powerful impacts on him, colours the writing of the play. But what Michael and others responded to was, at the square root, that quality described by the German director Peter Zadek who succinctly described Pinter's writing as 'like a mixture of Beckett and Agatha Christie'. This potent fusion was what drew Michael to Pinter's writing – its poetic rather than its prosaic quality, whereby the events taking place in a room can take on the elements of, in all senses, a mystery play. The comedy, too, was a strong draw; a good deal of the double act between Goldberg and McCann must have recalled many of those evenings Michael has spent at London's Empires monitoring variety for Jack Hylton, seeing such acts as Jimmy Jewel and Ben Warris or Sid Field and Jerry Desmonde.

Michael took great care in casting the play and he was able to attract actors who mostly, like himself, grasped the individual quality of the play, responding to its tone and its special music rather than worrying about 'meaning' – it is no accident that so many post-war dramatists (Ayckbourn, Bennett, Frisby, Harwood, Howarth, Livings, Orton, Osborne, Pinter, Nichols) began as actors or performers who wrote dialogue to which actors could attune themselves. Beatrix Lehmann, a sharply intelligent woman (and herself a writer) played the doting landlady Meg, the slightly chubby, jowly Richard Pearson, subtly tracing Stanley's body language from slothful slouching to broken-backed abject submission, was ideal for Pinter's tenant (this Stanley clearly was guilty of *something*) and John Slater, gimlet-eyed and bulkily bodied, made a formidable presence as Goldberg.

As director, Michael's first choice was Peter Hall – ironic in the light of later events – but he was unavailable and so Peter Wood, who had recently had a major success with a scrupulous production of O'Neill's *The Iceman Cometh*, was offered the production, which he accepted 'but only after his Cambridge chum, John Barton, nodded in our direction on reading Peter's script'. It was, as it transpired, for all Wood's intelligence, not the ideal marriage of dramatist and director: 'Harold was even then quietly but definitely a forceful personality and that jarred with Peter Wood, also a forceful personality, although I always thought he directed the actors very well.' What was definitely an error was the set design; *The Birthday Party* works best with a realistic or quasi-realistic, rather seedy, seaside boarding-house parlour, ideally suggesting something out of a rep standby such as *A Basinful of the Briny* (Tom Piper's design for Sam Mendes' National Theatre revival caught this quality perfectly). The distinguished West End designer J. Hutchinson Scott, master of the Colefax and Fowlered Belgravia drawing room, came up with a spacious conservatory setting, which naturally rather perplexed the author who had in mind something more akin to the shabby south-coast digs he had often stayed in as an actor when on tour. When he tackled Wood about the design he was countered with: 'They have conservatories like this all the way along the south coast' and despite Pinter's continued demurrals the set went ahead.

As Pinter allowed, when reflecting years later on that first production: 'It was the first time the play had been done. It wasn't quite like anything else … It mixed what appeared to be naturalistic with highly stylised structures.' Many productions of *The Birthday Party* opt visually for either the naturalistic or for the imaginatively heightened whereas in fact ideally it requires a cunning blend of both. But what would eventually become comprehensible was not easily perceptible in 1958 and Wood's basic approach, possibly inevitably given his F.R. Leavis-biased Cambridge education, was – as it had been with Peake and would be with Orton too, although he was a perfect match with Stoppard – over-cerebral: 'Temperamentally Harold and Peter were completely at odds. Peter was very Oxbridge in his attitude. Harold would write studious notes and Peter would read them and say things like, "This is the Preface to the published edition, is it?" This was very daunting for a man like Harold who had not been published, had not been to university and was a working actor.'

Although the atmosphere remained mostly polite, 'gradually a kind of *froideur* developed between Harold and Peter.'

On its brief pre-Hammersmith tour *The Birthday Party* seemed to take on the hallmarks of success, despite the set and the substrain of tension between author and director. The performances were fine, particularly those of Lehmann and Pearson, her Meg smothering Stanley with a love clearly more than maternal (nobody could accuse the first production of short-changing the Oedipal element in the play), very funny but piercingly affecting at times too, the laughter often catching in the throat as it does often in Pinter. In Cambridge it was extremely popular with a mainly student audience who seemed to cotton on to the play's style quickly – the *Cambridge Daily News* reported 'a great ovation' – and the response in Wolverhampton, an unlikely venue (indeed the Grand's manager, reassured by John Slater's name in the cast, only booked it because he assumed it must be a broad comedy), was also encouraging, while the final week in Oxford put what seemed the seal on a success with local critics even spotting the resemblance of Goldberg and McCann to Hemingways' thugs in *The Killers* or T.S. Eliot's Eumenides figures in *The Family Reunion* ('Kafka, spiced with humour' wrote the *Oxford Mail*, whose critic could not have known of Pinter's admiration for Kafka's work).

It was only natural, then that 'we all thought we had something both fascinating and innovative. They really took to it on tour'. What seemed at first a minor blow was that Harold Hobson would not be attending the Hammersmith Monday opening but he would come to the midweek matinee and of course all the other major London critics would be present on Monday. The first night on that 19 May, 1958 went well enough – many of Pinter's Hackney friends were in the house – and so nobody was quite prepared for the 'uniformly scathing reviews' the next day. Some of them – Milton Shulman (rarely a champion of the unfamiliar or experimental) in *The Evening Standard,* and the *Daily Telegraph*'s dinosaur W.A. Darlington (author of that classic, *Alf's Button*, and in his notice bidding fair to rival his Victorian predecessor Clement Scott who had so reviled Ibsen and *Ghosts*) – seemed almost defiantly philistine, while the majority berated Pinter for what they saw as wilful obscurity. The magazine *Theatre World* spoke for most of the London critics – 'Most of the characters appear to be mentally defective' – accusing Michael of 'trying to follow Beckett, Ionesco and Mortimer with a play by a writer not in the same category'.

Where provincial critics had had no difficulty in piercing to the heart of the play, the metropolitan press – much of it blind previously to any merit in *Waiting for Godot* and *Look Back in Anger* – were unperceptive to the point of myopia. They also had tin ears; even allowing for the fact that Pinter's was a new voice, virtually no mention was made of his matchless, spiky, adrenaline-powered dialogue. The comedy passed them by too. Only some of this reaction can be explained by Wood's production, which Pinter always felt overstressed the grotesque. The fact is that the majority of daily drama reviewers at that time – things have at least somewhat improved – were hacks who treated the theatre as just a branch of show business and who were happiest with the familiar pap of the light comedies and thrillers still dominating Shaftesbury Avenue. There were some notable exceptions – J.C. Trewin in particular alongside Hobson and Tynan – but very few had any notion of production values let alone of the actor's craft or the director's contribution.

The box office at Hammersmith simply collapsed – there had been no great advance booking – and Michael very quickly was forced to consider his options. In those days the Sunday notices on occasion could rescue a play after poor daily reviews and Hobson had been kind to *The Room*. But he could (or would) not come until the Thursday matinee – even although in the future they lunched occasionally together at Prunier's, Michael never found out why Hobson had not attended the opening night – and the more popular Sundays were unlikely to buck the trend of the dailies (they did not). In the meantime, 'Baxter Somerville, who was genuinely trying to help me, said I could close on the Saturday and until my own next production, *Honour Bright*, was ready he would bring in a thriller that was looking for a theatre, and this would considerably cut my losses'. The takings were dire; the whole week took £260.11s.5d – Pinter always kept a framed copy of the week's receipts, which included the midweek matinee figure of £2.9s, that performance's audience supplemented by the unpaid presences of Harolds Hobson and Pinter. It would take a miracle; it seemed, to turn the box office round enough to make up the opening losses, with only a limited run.

When Harold Hobson's notice appeared at the weekend in *The Sunday Times* it was highly enthusiastic (although he concentrated on the play's atmosphere of terror – 'It cannot be seen but it enters the room every time the door is opened' – to the exclusion of virtually all its other elements) but it was too late. The notice had gone up (on the Friday) at the end of that one Lyric week that the play would close on the Saturday. Michael blames himself for closing *The Birthday Party* so quickly: 'I really made a major mistake, although I wrote, rather pompously, a note to Hobson saying the takings had been cauterised by these notices. But a wiser man would have kept it on until the Sundays.'

In fact, he would have had to rely on *The Sunday Times* alone. The *Observer* did not echo its enthusiasm, the popular Sundays were dismal and even Hobson's power might not have been sufficient to create the kind of massive box office surge required. Ironically, the production's replacement, *The Key of the Door* by Philip Mackie, was a flashback-structured thriller so complex in plot that it baffled even more than *The Birthday Party* and closed almost as abruptly.

Worst of all for Michael was 'the misery of having to go and tell the cast we would be closing early – an awful experience always but somehow more so in this case. Even worse, of course, was reading Hobson's review when it was too late to retrench. I was very bruised, more than I could show, by the whole experience – I'd describe it as definitely one of my lowest periods in management'.

Pinter too must have been bruised by the collapse of a play on which he had set such hopes and in which he still believed (as did Michael) but he did not hold the closure against his producer. He moved on, continuing to mine an impressive vein of radio drama, writing *The Hothouse* (which he did not show to Michael or any management then – it remained unproduced until 1980), contributing his unusual voice to several revues (including his piece for Kenneth Williams and Peter Reeves, 'Time to Go' in *Pieces of Eight,* which Michael rated as one of the great revue sketches, echoing Billington's comparisons with the Shallow and Silence scenes in *Henry IV, Part 2*), seeing some consolatory rehabilitation for *The Birthday Party* in a top-flight and widely seen television production and beginning another full-length play.

In the meantime, with the success of *Valmouth* partly salving the bruises of *The Birthday Party*, Michael produced *Fool's Paradise, How Say You?, Pieces of Eight* and Mortimer's *The Wrong Side of the Park*. The Codron firm was now, if not quite yet among London's elite, definitely transformed in reputation. Even though he was a shrewd and sometimes tough negotiator (his telephonic technique could panic those on the other end into hasty deals) he was gradually becoming respected by agents and by the actors who worked for him.

His personal life had undergone a more seismic sea change. The relationship with Michael Charlesworth petered out, without acrimony, basically because of the age-old problem in the theatre, whether among gay or straight: 'Michael Charlesworth felt, increasingly, that the theatre, involving all that working in the evenings too, was simply too demanding a mistress and he didn't want to take second place.' Charlesworth was soon living with Roger Stock, a passionate equestrian: 'They were taken up by the H.M. Tennent set, especially Binkie and John Perry, and when Roger and Michael Charlesworth parted ("Well," Roger said to me, "Michael Charlesworth has left me, so we're sisters in sorrow") Binkie pounced on Stock, set him up in a stables business and provided for him in his will.'

Actually by that time Michael was not at all sorrowful. He had decided to move from Paultons Street: 'Through Tom Hearn, a Worcester friend, I found a cosy flat in Tite Street, Chelsea – in a block called Chelsea Lodge – the rent was £8 a week, which I could just about afford as well as the office in 91 Regent Street. It overlooked the windows of the flat Ned Sherrin had at the time and we could wave across to each other. I'd been to see the flat and agreed to take it and I was driving off in my little Sunbeam Talbot when I saw a good-looking, fair-haired young man walking along. I thought it was Peter Sutton who'd been an assistant stage manager for me on *Ring For Catty* and *A Month of Sundays* – he met his partner, the actor Anthony Oliver on the latter play and they lived in Pimlico where they also had an antiques shop. I stopped the car and leant out to say, "Hello Peter" but he replied, "No, I'm not Peter, I'm David."'

David Sutton was Peter's twin brother. An actor, he had worked for Richard Eastham at Amersham and also extensively in regional repertory. In Scarborough his work had included the first British production since Hammersmith of *The Birthday Party*, instigated by Scarborough's Library Theatre director and great enabler Stephen Joseph (rather surprisingly – he trailed few traces of show business – he was Hermione Gingold's son) who had also invited Pinter to direct. The cast included Alan Ayckbourn (another of Joseph's protégés) then barely out of his teens, as Stanley; it was on that production, famously, that Ayckbourn asked his director/author about his character's background, to be told simply: 'Mind your own fucking business. Concentrate on what's there' (as Ayckbourn would acknowledge this was not rudeness, just Pinter's way of reinforcing the ability of the text to work for the actor, a lesson he did not forget).

Charming, funny, slightly freckled and tall, with a broad smile that could captivate men, women and children (the playwright Terence Frisby said that David's open expression and snub nose reminded him of Terry in *Terry and the Pirates*, a 1940s American comic strip), David Sutton was then twenty-four, five years younger than Michael: 'He was exactly my type. In fact I'd met him before through Jimmy Fraser but no spark was struck then

19. David with Michael's dog Golda.

because I was with Michael Charlesworth.' A definite spark – mutually – was struck that evening in Chelsea, however: 'David had previously lodged with Ronnie Barker and his wife who used to warn him about the need to avoid getting in with what they euphemistically called "the Noël Coward set" but that didn't seem to put him off me. Now he was in digs across the river in Battersea. I offered him a lift home – and that is how it all began.' It was the start of a personal – also later a business – partnership that would last for over a quarter of a century, by far the most significant relationship in each man's life.

When Michael was moving into Tite Street the next day he invited David to move in with him and drove over to Battersea to collect his belongings: 'David came downstairs with his clothes packed and a tin of pilchards – I asked him if it was his trousseau.' David always would claim that the biggest advantage of moving in with Michael was that he no longer had to catch the late-night bus home, which stopped in Chelsea at Oakley Street – 'Oakley Street for those that dare!' the conductor would call – and then walk over the bridge to Battersea. But Michael was more romantic: 'I must have been really, really in love. He moved in with me the morning after the night before, as it were.'

David had a strong irreverent streak, useful for puncturing Michael's occasional more self-important or pompous moments and he was no respecter of persons. As twins do, he and Peter confided everything to each other; when David told Peter that he and Michael were now 'an item' Peter's response carried no disapproval but did have a caveat: 'That's all very well. But just to warn you, he's the type that will run to fat', a comment gleefully reported back to Michael. He found David 'much more sophisticated than I was in many respects – "I only have brown sugar" or "I only drink Earl Grey tea" – and that early period with him rather reformed me in so many ways'.

Life could at times be difficult in those first days of careless rapture when David's career could take him away from London. He had been taken on as a client by Jimmy Fraser while a powerful casting director, Miriam Brickman, also began to try to help boost his career, about which he could be somewhat diffident. When David was working at the old Guildford rep Michael was regularly there: 'I used to drive down – I was just so in love, more than ever before – nearly every night to drive him home after the show.' Then Miriam Brickman, who cast the ESC's productions, smoothed David's casting as the nervy radio operator 'Sparks' (he was at his best in sensitive or highly strung roles) in the Royal Court's touring production of Willis Hall's *The Long and the Short and the Tall,* which would mean a longer separation: 'The production opened in Glasgow and I flew up secretly to surprise him on his first night. He was very good in it, alongside some strong new talent – Frank Finlay, Peter Gill before he turned to directing – and I remember going into the Glasgow dressing room he and Gill shared. They were laughing like mad about some incident onstage and I felt a bit excluded for a bit in that world. Maybe it was partly because I was, at that stage, not doing really good work with plays like *How Say You?,* which paid the rent but I *knew* was not that great. I used to get quite tough lectures by this young firebrand that David could be about the state of the West End!'

The Codron business was indeed seesawing at this time, not helped by his frustration at being unable to find more writing of the calibre of *The Birthday Party.* He had become friendly with Lionel Bart ('although his parties at Reece Mews were too wild for me'), hyperactive and with a very low boredom threshold, then rolling in the royalties from *Lock Up Your Daughters,* finishing *Oliver!* and looking for ways to spend some of his money, his latest resolution being to become involved in new writing, preferably in the West End. He had come across a new play, for a young cast, *Why the Chicken?* by John McGrath (later of the 7:84 Company), which he had asked John Dexter, then riding high in the wake of Arnold Wesker's trilogy of Royal Court plays, to direct. Michael agreed to co-produce; he had reservations about the play's structure but 'it was rather an adventurous play, a very young play' and he liked its abrasive dialogue. It was strongly cast with Terence Stamp, Michael Caine, Elizabeth McLennan (married to the play's author, a situation that caused some friction) and David Sutton in major roles. Somehow even with – or perhaps because of – such ingredients, it all went very wrong from the outset. Dexter, whose fuse was always short, clashed violently with the volatile and often drunk or high Bart, who 'disastrously' decided he would take over (he owned the rights to the play) after Dexter walked out. On the road audiences were thin and unresponsive – nobody outside some of the London theatre world had heard of Stamp or Caine then – and the whole miserable enterprise fizzled out (Bart had lost interest well before) in the vast and thinly attended Golder's Green Hippodrome.

Michael collected David after the final nail in *Why the Chicken?*'s coffin: 'During the drive home to Chelsea I heard – again – all that was wrong with the West End. I slightly lost patience and said, "In that case why do you keep on acting? You could come and join me in management." And he did. So one morning soon afterwards we left Chelsea Lodge together for the office – now in 117 Regent Street opposite Garrard the jewellers (now Zara), parking behind Berkeley Square – in David's Mini – it was the nearest place to park near the West End then without getting a parking ticket.' Remarkably Richard Eastham showed no resentment. 'He took the whole thing in good part. There was no "Oh, I see, now the boyfriend is muscling in."' Eastham had, of course, known David as an actor and they got on very well together.

David joined Michael Codron Ltd just before a very busy time. The office had two productions in preparation – a large-scale new British musical, *The Golden Touch*, and finally, the new full-length play by Harold Pinter, which Michael had recently received from Jimmy Wax. It was called *The Caretaker*.

CHAPTER 8

ART FOR THE ARTS' SAKE

The new Codron offices at 117 Regent Street had an unassuming entrance off a little arcade next to a long-established coin-specialist shop. A spacious elevator, very different from the notoriously cramped lifts – to take two people one had to know or want to know the other rather well – leading to the Tennent offices in the Globe or, later, to Duncan Weldon's Triumph Theatre setup in The Strand Theatre, took one up to the third floor and the outer office. There were only two others – a long, narrow room with a fine view of Regent Street, which was Michael's office and another space divided up for Richard Eastham and David Sutton.

In the early days the furnishings were modest although gradually Michael acquired a polished desk, some very 1960s pearly table lamps and a sleek black leather sofa facing the desk. Soon in the outer office – which always had fresh flowers – Sheila Devo was installed as general assistant and secretary. Trim, her dark hair always immaculate, and ultra-efficient she would remain with the firm for twenty years. And when Richard Eastham retired his place was taken by a remarkable production manager, Joe Scott-Parkinson, tall, courteous, gentle of manner and speech but with a steel core when it came to keeping directors and designers within budget. Joe tended to use 'heart' as an endearment (both Michael and David often, in the manner of the era, used 'dear') but it could carry a multiplicity of meaning ('A very good design, heart, but do you not think it might maybe be better without the rake and the backcloth?' conveyed to a designer that it was back to the drawing board). That quartet – there was no in-house accountant then – of Michael, David, Scott-Parkinson and Sheila Devo comprised the entire permanent staff of Michael Codron Ltd until 1982; quite often in a given year that office would oversee anything up to a dozen productions.

David took well to office life. As an actor he had lacked, as he acknowledged, any tough core of ambition and he became as absorbed as Michael by the alchemy of the business, that aspect of a production's preparation that is the most fulfilling – for Michael at least, more satisfying than raising the capitalisation – the matching of authors to actors, directors, designers and lighting designers. When Michael started up, not much attention was paid to stage lighting – some directors still supervised their own – but by the early 1960s a whole new industry with its generation of young talent to follow trail-blazers like Tennent's Joe Davis or Michael Northen was emerging. The traditional footlights and front-of-house style gave way to a very different approach, often using visible lighting rigs and top lighting, all making greasepaint redundant and so forcing actors to reconsider stage make-up. Michael realised this very quickly and was in the vanguard of the lighting revolution, fascinated in particular by the work of Tony Walton and the lighting genius Richard Pilbrow (of the theatre projects firm) with projections, subsequently using such creative lighting designers as Mark Henderson, Mick Hughes, Leonard Tucker and Jason Taylor.

David made a good professional counterpart to Michael too, although it was a long time before he would finally accept 'Associate Producer' billing. While as positive as Michael when enthused by a project his head was cooler and he was altogether more pragmatic, on more than one occasion stopping Michael from rushing into expensive mistakes (Willie Donaldson, always trying to involve Michael in his dottier schemes, used to call David 'Stonebum' for this capacity to block a project). Some in the theatre world greatly underestimated him at first, assuming his job was a sinecure from a doting lover keen to be with him at work as well as at home. Most soon realised their mistake; David, always refusing any suggestion of sharing an office with Michael, soon became wise to dealing with agents and handling contracts while his actor's mental file of other actors or of stage management personnel was often very useful to the firm.

Particularly pleasing to David was the fact that he would be involved in *The Caretaker*; he had happy memories of his Scarborough experience of *The Birthday Party*. Michael had been touched that Pinter wanted him to produce it in London despite one major proviso, made clear by Jimmy Wax from the outset. With so little money coming in for his client from *The Birthday Party* and subsequently – even though his stock had risen somewhat with its television production and some further radio plays – Wax had negotiated a deal with the American millionaire producer Roger L. Stevens (at one time he had owned The Empire State Building) to whom word had filtered of Pinter's reputation as a rising writer, giving Stevens the option on Pinter's next three full-length plays (he got quite a bargain – it cost him £1,000, a lifeline for Pinter but probably about a fortnight's worth of tips to Stevens). A very savvy operator, Stevens would much prefer to see *The Caretaker* given a London production, ideally a success, before launching an unknown writer in New York. This meant that Michael would not own the US or subsidiary rights to the play; nevertheless he was prepared to live with that.

He had known 'with absolute certainty' on first reading the script that '*The Caretaker* was something special, even better than *The Birthday Party*'. At once he connected with its distilled, burning-glass focus on the power struggles between two brothers and a bedraggled old tramp in a seedy room packed to the rafters with worthless furniture, detritus and a stove (dominated by a plaster Buddha), responding again to Pinter's unerring mastery of stage space, his suggestion of panic and dread and – again crucially for Michael – to his comedic gift, the laughs this time sometimes devastating in their often unexpected rightness of timing.

David agreed with him: 'My resolve to do it was strengthened by David who was as much under the spell of this new voice as me. He said: "It will be to your eternal regret if you don't do it."' Feeling a debt to David Hall who had supported *The Birthday Party* and Hammersmith, Michael invited him to join him in the venture, which, first aimed for production directly into the West End, was to be launched at the intimate Arts Theatre instead.

He was determined to assemble the personnel for Pinter's play with care: 'Harold and Peter Wood hadn't finished on the best of terms and in any case Jimmy Wax told me that Harold wanted to use the director of his radio work, Donald McWhinnie.'

This would involve a considerable risk on Michael's part. McWhinnie, a somewhat reserved Yorkshireman, was on the staff at Broadcasting House but his background was almost entirely in radio with only one professional London stage production (Beckett's *Krapp's Last Tape*, a necessarily static play, at the Royal Court) to his credit. But Michael respected Pinter's judgement and he also liked McWhinnie when they met (both tended to be taciturn – it must have been a meeting pregnant with Pinteresque pauses). Together they chose a young designer, Brian Currah, who had done some inventive work at the Arts for Caryl Jenner's children's theatre company and so had the advantage of knowing the awkward Arts stage well.

Casting began fairly smoothly. McWhinnie knew Donald Pleasence from radio; he was then not yet forty but McWhinnie strongly urged the case for him to play Davies the tramp, sensing that the flexible Pleasence voice with its distinctive cawing note could be perfect for the character's volatility, swinging from querulousness to ingratiating mateyness. Pleasence's response was immediate: 'I read it and instantly felt it was

122

wonderful and I had to do it.' With his radio-director's ear always sensitive to Pinter's rhythms, McWhinnie also suggested Peter Woodthorpe for the withdrawn, damaged Aston. He could be a tricky actor to control – he became more so over the years – but had already, in his first professional job, proved his special quality in *Waiting for Godot*, and both Michael and Pinter agreed to the casting. The third role – the watchful, seemingly razor-sharp, manipulative Mick, Aston's protective brother – proved trickier. Quite a few possibles were unavailable, while others were reluctant to take a risk on a comparatively unknown writer at a salary much less than West End money.

Not long before rehearsals were due to begin in March 1960 Pinter caught a television play, *Incident*, involving a ruthless neighbour conniving at the harrying of a renegade soldier. The unscrupulous character was played by the young Alan Bates who had made an impact at the Royal Court as Jimmy Porter's friend Cliff in *Look Back in Anger*, and in the London premiere of O'Neill's *Long Day's Journey into Night*. Pinter said, 'I watched Alan leaning against a wall, smoking a cigarette and at once called the director and said, "We've found our Mick."' It was less simple to land him; Bates's then agent was the languid Philip Pearman at MCA who was advising his client to take the rival and much better paid offer of Hotspur in a television *Henry IV, Part 1* – he thought little of Pinter's play, which at the Arts would pay only £50 per week. On this occasion Bates, often procrastinatory about offers, overruled him, explaining later: 'I didn't immediately understand the play but I just knew emotionally that it was wonderful. However mystifying or alarming it may be, it haunts and resonates in a hugely dramatic way.'

This haunting resonance was what that original *Caretaker* unforgettably captured. The universality of the play – it has been given all-female productions, all-black productions (one at the National Theatre) and has connected to audiences in virtually every world language – seemed to speak to audiences (and, on this occasion, to most critics) with little of 1958s accusations of perverse obscurity or 'Theatre of the Absurd and/or Menace' labelling.

McWhinnie was a gentle, unassuming personality with a rare knack of directing without appearing to be doing very much at all, creating his productions more, it seemed, by osmosis. He could also make actors feel secure (surprisingly not all directors realise the importance of this). Bates felt confident enough about the essence of Mick – 'He's got a fantasy of this life he wants to live ... His brother is disturbed and Mick is instinctively,

123

20. Space Invader – Donald Pleasence (Davies) and
Alan Bates (Mick) in *The Caretaker*, 1960.

hugely protective of his brother. And because he's a protector he's jealous
of the tramp. I understood all that intuitively. I didn't need to have anything more specific' – but as they began to put the play together at the end
of a rehearsal period during which McWhinnie had said little to him, he spoke
to the director: 'Now this is a bit of a journey into the unknown. Please, please
give me notes.' At the next run-through Michael was present: 'After it Donald

said everything was fine and gave only a few notes about some moves. Alan then came right downstage, looking enquiringly at his director, who looked back at him for a while and then gave him the thumbs-up sign. That was his note. Donald was an unusual director – his talent was his ability to *coax* performances. And he'd listen to others. The rehearsal period was really unruffled and at the end of it, I think, we all knew we were on the brink of something remarkable.'

It was a memorable first night. The play's fusion of 'What's going to happen next?' suspense, wonderful comedy (there have been many big name Davieses – Leonard Rossiter, Michael Gambon and Jonathan Pryce included – but Pleasence's explanation of Davies' journey to a Luton monastery in pursuit of buckshee footwear remains unsurpassed) and with Woodthorpe's damaged loneliness, suggesting a man locked in the solitary confinement of the soul in Aston's description of his asylum treatment, was masterfully maintained throughout (some productions start on a note so taut that the play's string goes loose before the end).

The critics had a field day with 'interpretations' with many a metaphorical analysis. In the *Observer* Kenneth Tynan, who never quite 'got' Pinter (his intellect and theatrical sense told him this was a born dramatist, his Brechtification blinkered him to the essence of Pinter's talent), suggested that the two brothers might be bifurcated halves of a split personality or that the three characters could stand for the ego, super-ego and the id. Terence Rattigan posited that the three men in that room in a derelict London house represented God the Father, God the Son and God the Holy Ghost. His fellow-Establishment playwright, Noël Coward, also recognising the natural born dramatist in Pinter, was more sensible; he admitted he'd dreaded seeing the play, presuming its 'obscurity' would represent all that he disliked about the New Wave but found that 'somehow it seizes hold of you … Nothing happens except it does'.

The reception – more than a dozen curtain calls from the first night house – and the majority of critics comprehensively overturned the verdict on *The Birthday Party*, and the production went on to the Duchess Theatre (at 500 seats, still suitably intimate) winning the *Evening Standard* Best Play of the Year Award (the first of many to go to a Codron production) and running for over a year.

It was magnificently acted, particularly by Bates who overnight vaulted into a different league. His Mick had a feral edge and all the leather-jacketed, Jack-the-lad cockiness was in focus too, but there was another dimension to this portrayal, subtly suggesting the character's desolating awareness of the hopelessness of his pipedream of transforming a filthy slum into a kind of Austin Powers-style 'shagtastic' pad. Bates, a complex man, once said revealingly: 'I understand these three rather isolated people and their need to belong and to find some kind of purpose. I find them all very moving characters. I understand them. I know who they are'; as well as being a vitally integral element in the play's balancing act as its power games and territorial imperatives are played out, he especially and unsentimentally contributed to the compassion in the play, a vein in Pinter often overlooked.

After just over a year at the Duchess with Pinter briefly standing in while Bates filmed *Whistle Down the Wind* ('Harold was the most frightening,' said Pleasence discussing various Micks. 'Alan was not so frightening but his was a much more subtle performance with Alan's own brand of malign understatement') the play moved to New York (where Robert Shaw played Aston) for another successful run. Michael – after being forced into an unseemly period of bargaining, no fault of Wax's – was finally allowed one per cent for the London production from the Broadway receipts, hardly in proportion, considering the production's London success – making it all the more enticing a proposition for New York – and not to mention that Pinter's London reputation had been very largely created by the Codron management. The reaction of Stevens's co-producer Frederick Brisson (married to Hollywood's Rosalind Russell and known, with little affection, as 'The Lizard of Roz') was typical of Michael's first encounter with Broadway's ruthlessness: 'Fuck the London production!' Michael owned that they had been 'totally outmanoeuvred' when the Americans granted the one per cent 'as if it should be regarded as a great favour'.

Only after *The Caretaker* was established as a hit and when the plans for its Duchess move were in motion was Michael quite able to focus on its success. *The Golden Touch*, his big musical venture, had been – chill phrase – 'in trouble on the road' since its Edinburgh opening during rehearsals for *The Caretaker* and things had not significantly improved.

With *The Boy Friend*, *Salad Days*, *Lock Up Your Daughters* and *Oliver!*, the home-grown musical in the mid-1950s and early 60s seemed to be on the verge of an upsurge (another false dawn). Michael had enjoyed another 1950s British show, *Grab Me a Gondola* by James Gilbert and Julian More, a zestful satire of European Film Festivals complete with venal movie moguls and busty blondes in mink bikinis (its show-stopping number 'Cravin' for the Avon', a starlet's plea to be taken seriously as a classical actress, turned up fifty years later when Michael presented *The Shakespeare Revue*). This new show from the same team was a satirical look at the early 1960s jet set – Callas and Onassis figures and all – and 'drop-out' beatniks (one number was titled 'Beatnikology') on a pre-*Mamma Mia!* Greek island. It had something of the 'rather racy' quality Michael had liked in *Gondola* but *The Golden Touch* had a slack book, a More score not quite varied enough and an untried director of musicals (Minos Volanakis). During rehearsals major troubles were soon evident on a very expensive production – designed, stylishly, by Hugh Casson with all the delicacy of his watercolours but at variance with a somewhat broad show – with Volanakis clearly out of his depth and soon departing, leaving the choreographer, *Pieces of Eight*'s Paddy Stone, in overall control. Julian More and the leading lady Evelyne Ker were in the throes of a passionate affair and so no suggested changes in her material (her pallid performance was not a major asset) were countenanced and 'on the road it played to mostly empty houses'.

The listing vehicle, boosted only by some exhilarating dance numbers (Stone's work on 'Whisky A' Go Go' briefly roused torpid houses to wan enthusiasm) edged its way into the Piccadilly Theatre just a few nights after *The Caretaker* had opened at the Arts (it closed before Pinter's play reopened at the Duchess). Michael stoically had to face a flop, always a grim duty: 'My abiding memory of that show is one of the public dress rehearsal, a kind of preview, the night before opening. I was going down the side of the stalls after a less than ecstatically received performance, aiming for the pass door to backstage, when I was passed by two showbiz queens, both of whom gave me smiles of deep commiseration, one of them adding as an extra token of sympathy: "Oh, Mr Codron, bring back *Valmouth*!"'

The Golden Touch closed ignominiously (its notices were depressing) after only twelve performances at a loss of over £20,000 (a very large sum then – to open *The Caretaker* at the Arts, by way of contrast, cost exactly £1,166): 'But for *The Caretaker* I would definitely have gone under. And I was very grateful for the understanding and help of Geoffrey Russell, my landlord at the Piccadilly, who'd been helpful at the Savile on *Valmouth* too.'

The lessons of these experiences and David's help in confirming Michael's increasing feeling that he should follow his own taste rather than think purely commercially first led to some crucial stocktaking in the Codron office. Never again would Michael produce a big book musical from scratch – revue was another matter – they needed, he decided rightly, a more specialised and larger organisation than his. The 'revolution' following mid-1950s milestones such as *Waiting for Godot* and *Look Back in Anger* could not be said to have transformed British theatre overnight; the West End still had more than its fair share of formula thrillers and light frivols but Michael sniffed something in the wind. And indeed, in the early 1960s with the opening of the Royal Shakespeare Company's Aldwych base in London, the Chichester Festival Theatre, Guildford's Yvonne Arnaud Theatre, the National Theatre launched at last, initially at the Old Vic, new perimeter theatres in Greenwich and Hampstead (where Michael was deeply involved in fundraising and pre-opening events) and a spate of new writing along with, crucially, some other bold younger producers, Michael White among them, the face of theatre in and close to London would be altered.

For much of the four years after *The Caretaker* at the Arts, Michael chose to base most of his work there, with transfers a possibility and launching only the occasional venture directly in the commercial mainstream. It was the ideal theatre for his plans with a capacity of 350, an intimate auditorium, a bar and a club upstairs popular with actors after their shows. Actors were drawn less by the salaries - £50 per week top then - but by the prospect of interesting new work, possibly with a commercial transfer and West End money. There was a marked absence of the gilt and plush 'glamour' of the West End, but that was partly the point; the Arts was a welcoming, informal house, much cheaper than the West End and conveniently central, near Leicester Square Tube.

Another key person central to this period - and well beyond - in Michael's career was the literary agent Margaret (Peggy) Ramsay, perhaps the most crucial of all Michael's mentor figures. Then in her early fifties, she was an ex-singer and actress - she also had worked as a co-manager of the 'Q' theatre - a dynamic, candid figure, fiercely protective of her clients' interests. She, too, was no respecter of persons - she was perfectly capable of finishing discussions on the telephone with a movie mogul like Sam Spiegel saying, 'Oh, fuck off, Sam!' or calling a major critic like Harold Hobson to tick him off soundly for failing to understand a play (*Treats*) by her client Christopher Hampton and telling him to go back and re-review it (he did). She operated, dressed usually in flowing, filmy dresses, scarves and, often, plimsolls, looking like a slightly askew stork, from premises (she liked to claim they were a former brothel) in Goodwin's Court, off St Martin's Lane. Her most significant client when she set up independently as an agent after leaving A.D. Peters was Robert Bolt; gradually she built up an enviable list, which included Ayckbourn, Bond, Brenton, Churchill,

Hampton, Hare, Marcus, Orton, Mortimer, Livings, Nichols, Plater, Poliakoff, Russell, Rosenthal, Saunders and Charles Wood. She first met Michael at Hammersmith and then on the hapless *Why the Chicken?* (John McGrath was her client). She had not failed, with her acute eye taking in everything going on in the London theatre scene, to notice Michael's Hammersmith season (she had recommended Richard Pearson – an actor she knew from her 'Q' days – to Peter Wood for *The Birthday Party* and wrote to Hobson telling him to cover it) and she had also seen *The Caretaker*. She also advised Michael to base himself at the Arts for a time. 'She told me I wouldn't make any money but I would make my reputation.'

Ramsey treated Michael – sometimes calling him 'Codders' or 'Cod' – rather as she treated her clients, scolding ('Don't whimper, Codders') and encouraging in turn. He would agree that it was largely due to Ramsay – crucially in that early 1960s Arts period coinciding with an upsurge in new, iconoclastic writing (Ramsay too was always drawn to work with 'edge', a whiff of danger) – that he was able to build up his reputation throughout the 1960s and thereafter as London's foremost producer of new work. Like David, she buttressed his belief in his own taste rather than encouraging him in trying to follow that of the public or the box office.

The Ramsay office represented a third of the plays Michael presented at the Arts and she came deeply to admire the dedicated, sheer hard slog he put into the job, opening a new play every four or five weeks. To her he was 'small, frail and quiet … he works very hard and, most important of all, he has really good taste allied to genuine modesty … This metier is so hard from time to time that people who survive in it do so by a kind of stoical endurance and, if possible, the retention of some kind of inner life. There is not much happiness from the career itself except hard work, which is a good disciplinary hair shirt for the soul.' Michael would have said the same of her (except, possibly, for the 'frail and quiet') – the pair had some less than cordial exchanges on occasion over the years, but nothing could fundamentally dent a profound mutual respect that continued through their personal and professional relationship until Ramsay's death in 1991.

It was a shrewd move to have Pinter's name associated with the production at the Arts in 1961 of *Three*, the triple bill of which, inevitably, *A Slight Ache* received the most attention (it was also by far the best of the plays). Donald McWhinnie, who worked regularly for Michael over this period (later, sadly, a drinking problem seriously scarred his career) handled the different tones of the trio adroitly but *A Slight Ache* was something special.

Based on an earlier, unproduced radio play, *Something in Common*, it was eventually broadcast in 1958, a tightly written piece in which Pinter, in a first excursion into middle-class territory, once more through his unique lens scrutinised territorial and psychological power struggles, this time between a bourgeois couple and, anticipating Davies in *The Caretaker* perhaps, a broken-down vagrant selling matches just outside the couple's garden. A silent presence, on radio he had to be imagined whereas on stage, in Richard Briers' impassive mute presence, he became a potent factor in the play's equation, ending up being invited in by the wife who smothers him with affection (as Meg embraces Stanley) before he displaces her husband in the home. Pinter's ability to marry the comedic to dread and sexual tension is particularly distilled in this one-acter – not least in an early passage as the couple, breakfasting in their garden, bicker over how to kill an unwelcome wasp hovering over the marmalade pot (incidentally the opening of *A Slight Ache* uncannily anticipates the first scene between the elder couple in Ayckbourn's first success, *Relatively Speaking*, some years later – Ayckbourn too has a middle-aged bourgeois couple in a sunlit garden with a substrain of marital tension over the breakfast marmalade).

With *Three* enjoying success at the Arts worthy of a transfer to the Criterion, Pinter had crucially helped establish Michael's Arts project. His next author there, the Lancashire-born Henry Livings (a Ramsay client) was a personal favourite – he was involved with three of his plays – although his work never quite achieved a major commercial breakthrough. *Stop It, Whoever You Are* (1961) was a very funny comedy set in a northern factory, directed by Vida Hope, always full of energy and enthusiasm, with Wilfrid Brambell (Steptoe *père*) well cast as William Perkin Warbeck, a pensioner now working as a cleaner in the factory's Gent's toilet, a keen cornet player, unfortunately seduced by the fourteen-year-old daughter of a fellow band member. Much of the play revolves round the visit to open a new factory wing by local dignitaries – blissfully led by the peerless Arthur Lowe, bemedalled and chained as Alderman Oglethorpe – who discover the new building lacks a lavatory, much to Warbeck's glee. Like Pinter, Livings fuses comedy with another strain, although his in this play is more violent, with its assaults on the elderly and a voracious underage girl. For some metropolitan critics these elements in the framework of a Northern farcical comedy were simply too sordid, with several suggestions that it was a 'smutty' play (a foretaste of things to come later for Michael in the so-called 'Swinging Sixties'), while audiences laughed themselves silly. It ideally illustrates the exchange between Michael and a radio interviewer who described him as 'a man of impeccable taste with a vulgar streak', sharply corrected by Michael's: 'No, I'm a man of vulgar taste with an impeccable streak.' Throughout his career there would be regularly an alternation between committed, serious new writing and unabashedly broader but equally valid fare (comedy by authors from Livings, Philip King, Ray Cooney and Terence Frisby to Willy Russell, Mike Stott and Terry Johnson, revue, a Beatles musical, Victoria Wood); a core belief was that the West End should be, as it were, a broad church rather than a narrow pulpit. And that King and Cooney should be as considerately cast, directed and designed as Pinter or Mortimer.

Livings's *Big Soft Nellie* was also seen at the Arts in 1961, again under Vida Hope who had a knack akin to that of Joan Littlewood for shaping this kind of Crazy Gang comedy (sadly she died not long afterwards), set in a radio and electrical repair shop full of coloured lights with circus music on tap. There was comparatively little plot but a great deal of verbal comedy, often repeating everyday banalities, frequently leaping into larky physical comedy, including a memorable scene with Roy Kinnear as a very insecure employer miming a Sergeant Major on parade. Again the critics tended to condescend to this populist writer, although audiences responded positively to this play too. Others were beginning to notice Livings; the RSC commissioned a play and the resulting *Eh?*, also with a factory setting, was a big Aldwych success under Peter Hall with David Warner and Donald Sinden. Michael produced his next play (at the Royal Court) with the ESC who had commissioned it.

Kelly's Eye (1963) was a major departure for Livings. Rather sprawling in structure, it was still utterly absorbing, set on a bleak Lancashire coast (imaginatively and sparely suggested by Alan Tagg, who would be a Codron regular designer for over thirty years). Kelly, a magnificent part for Nicol Williamson, is a man haunted by the memory of his seemingly motiveless murder in Ireland of his only friend, and now living a hermit's existence; he becomes involved with a young girl (Sarah Miles), a very 1960s character – spirited, in rebellion against her possessive bourgeois father – who unwittingly causes Kelly's doom. There was a strong vein of unsettling dark comedy and an unexpected use of symbolism – Arthur Lowe played, hauntingly, a choric figure, 'The Eyeless Man'. *Kelly's Eye* completely divided critics and public – although there were no complaints about Williamson's sweaty, tense portrayal of a man on the rack of conscience – but the business did not warrant a commercial transfer.

Other new writers were keen to follow Pinter and Livings to the Arts,

131

one of whom, Giles Cooper, worked happily with Michael before his tragic early death. Cooper also had a background in radio (*Unman, Wittering and Zigo* remains a milestone in BBC radio drama) and he too had worked with McWhinnie at the BBC. Also a man of few words and long silences – how he, Michael and the ruminative McWhinnie ever got through discussions when preparing a play remains a mystery – he had little stage experience except for an odd, dystopian piece from 1955, *Never Get Out*, about a tramp and a middle-class woman together in a bombed house in a deserted village, and so Michael was surprised by the comedic expertise and poise of *Everything in the Garden* (1962), which McWhinnie directed with a luxury cast headed by Geraldine McEwan. From a cosy-ish initial domestic comedy Cooper inexorably established a corrosive, acridly funny satire on the vanity of human wishes and avarice, an unusual modern Morality Play.

McEwan played Jenny, a suburban wife bored with her uneventful life married to a respectable salesman of office furniture. Having answered a job advert she receives a visit from a well-dressed Polish woman, revealed as a Wimpole Street Madam and offering Jenny an 'opening'. After her initial outrage, Jenny takes the plunge only for her husband, puzzled by discovering money stashed away in the house, to blow her cover. A later cocktail party scene, packed with acid observation of consumer-driven suburbia and 'keeping up with the Joneses', uncovers that most of the local wives are on the game part-time with the husbands now mostly complicit. With the return of the Madam the play develops into a viciously shocking fight between the men leading to a murderous cover-up. Although an edgy, abrasive play it was well received (with some carps about the twist of tone at the close) and transferred to the Duke of York's, still with McEwan's teasingly sly ambivalence at the centre.

In retrospect Michael should have opened Cooper's next play, *Out of the Crocodile* (1963) at the Arts but once Celia Johnson and Kenneth More were cast – neither of them would be interested in starting there for £50 per week – it was scheduled, with McWhinnie directing, for the West End. Then the perennial problem for a producer – the lack of available theatres intimate enough for a small-cast comedy but sufficiently large to break even with two percentage stars and hopefully go into profit – forced him into the capacious Phoenix (he comforted himself by remembering that *Private Lives*, with a cast of five, had opened the theatre in 1930 but was not entirely convinced).

Also satirical in thrust, tilting at contemporary social values, Cooper created a tantalising setup in *Out of the Crocodile* – a conman, Peter Pounce, having by chance acquired the keys to both the London flat and weekend Brighton home of the Hamsters, a middle-aged couple of clockwork routine, proceeds to live, unknown to them, in whichever home they are not occupying – but then fails to work out how to develop it, let alone end it. Johnson had some vintage passages – her wide marmoset eyes boggling in baffled bewilderment as she finds herself playing the roles of Pounce's mother and servant in turn were worth the ticket price – but More, prone to the star's disease of wanting to be loved, undercut the aspect of Pounce as ruthless corrupter, going for a laid-back charm, which confused an already rather muddled play. Michael had tried to tackle Cooper about the second act's contradictions and the ending, closing on an unconvincingly contrived dance ('You can't ask an audience to be beguiled for most of the evening and then take the carpet from beneath them', to which Cooper's reply: 'That's the reason I wrote the play' always blocked his efforts). It closed rapidly, although Michael would have been happy to continue the association with a writer he liked and believed in, but suddenly and somewhat mysteriously, Cooper was killed when he fell from a train travelling to his country home after a Garrick Club dinner. 'A fascinating man and I thought he would develop as a stage dramatist,' said Michael; he was also upset by the Broadway production of *Everything in the Garden* (which did not involve him) with the text adapted by Edward Albee who turned Cooper's sly satire into a mean piece of misogynistic camp.

The search for new work sometimes produced plays from unexpected sources. Peggy Ramsay represented one of the modern novelists Michael most admired – Muriel Spark – and when her play *Doctors of Philosophy* (1962) arrived he was struck by its unusual dialogue and keen to programme it for the Arts, although he sensed it might divide opinion. It was unquestionably a literate (and literary) play, its language mandarin and elegant (most of the characters are, admittedly, PhDs), but the charlady is even more articulate than her employers who themselves have an unforgiving candour of speech recalling that of another novelist, Ivy Compton-Burnett. Spark had a splendid opening situation – Charlie Delfont, an eminent married philosopher, deep in study, is visited by his wife's sister Leonora's ghost, who proceeds to give him the strikingly abrupt command that he father her child – but other strands in the play including characters being fished regularly out of the Regent's Park Canal (next to which the philosopher's house stands) were somewhat stuck on to the main story. It had one splendidly vivid character, a cousin of the Delfonts and the happiest of all the characters, played with a sunnily engaging charm by Fenella Fielding. The reaction was fairly tepid and although Michael kept hoping Spark would write another original play (and continued to read all her novels as published) he never received one.

Another novelist whose first play Michael presented at the Arts – Edna O'Brien – did go on to write more plays (*A Pagan Place* for the ESC by far the best) although like many novelists, the dialogue in her plays seemed always stronger than her plots. *A Cheap Bunch of Nice Flowers* (1962) at the Arts emerged as rather a wispy piece, involving an imaginative young girl, Ria, saddled with a dreary boyfriend and an uncaring mother, with whose lover she sleeps, subsequently pretending to be pregnant. Simultaneously her mother is diagnosed as having cancer, Ria believing it is her mother's fake response to her own condition. The daily help exposes Ria, who then retreats into another dream alone with her fantasy. It was cast to the hilt; Susannah York, gawkily graceful as Ria and three magnificent Irish actors – Eithne Dunne, Ray McNally and the incomparable Marie Kean as the sharp-tongued daily. Even they could not quite escape from the prevailing misty Celtic twilight, and an oddly jerky production by Desmond O'Donovan (a director of great promise who later took the cloth) did not much help.

The Arts under Michael could never be accused of predictability or playing safe. Three years before Edward Bond's *Saved* he produced a play of genuinely shocking impact, which involved the kind of deprived underclass then rarely seen on the English stage and that had a scene, every bit as unsettling as that in Bond's play, involving the murder of a baby. *Infanticide in the House of Fred Ginger* – Michael was struck by the Websterian title and then even more by the play – was the last in a series co-produced with the RSC at the Arts (soon under its new lessee Nat Cohen with Michael as its managing director to become the New Arts) in 1962. It was by Fred Watson (he also wrote for television but then seemed totally to disappear), a dramatist, on the evidence of this play, capable of stark, powerful writing. A young misfit (touchingly played by John Normington), now on night work at a factory, rents a room from a hospital porter, Fred Ginger, with his ex-nurse wife (worried by the squalor of their lives and her husband's instability) and baby. Another lodger, a nervy loner, agrees to babysit while the couple go to the cinema, but when Ginger's loutish son and drunken mates return he is no match for them when they turn on the crying baby. In a terrifying scene the baby is given gin to drink and a vicious fight develops between the youths. When the couple return and find their baby not breathing an ambulance is called and Ginger orders his son to accompany the parents, knowing full well the child is dead.

Nothing was spared in a grim, ruthlessly unsentimental and compelling story, which despite the subject and grimy setting was written with both warmth and objectivity. Naturalistic in detail it was given a lacerating production by William Gaskill and cast strongly with Ian McShane, John Hurt and Tony Beckley deeply disturbing as Ginger's depraved son and his mates. For some critics it was merely 'sordid' or 'depressing' while others were deeply affected. Clive Barnes pointed out the elements of Grand Guignol in the play but added: 'Watching Fred Watson's play, I had become absorbed into a strange world … The gurgles of that dying dummy have already haunted me for days.'

At the other end of the scale Michael was able to offer a Christmas Arts show of pure escapist delight. *Cindy-Ella, or I Gotta Shoe* (1962) from the Ned Sherrin and Caryl Brahms team, recast the Cinderella story in the Deep South, simple and sophisticated by turn, designed by Tony Walton mainly using witty back projections to keep the action fleet. Colin Graham from the opera world staged a miniature jewel of a piece, part- musical (using some lovely spirituals), part-revue, with a cast of four black per- formers – Cleo Laine, Elisabeth Welch, Cy Grant and George Browne – all experienced in the worlds of cabaret or revue and so perfect for sharing over twenty roles between them. It sold out at the Arts and then transferred to the Garrick.

During this initial Arts-based period Michael opened productions di- rectly in the West End only rarely, including Mortimer's *Two Stars for Comfort*. A Broadway success, steeped in Jewish ritual – Paddy Chayefsky's *The Tenth Man* (1961) – had a strong appeal for him and he judged its commercial possibilities warranted taking it to the Comedy Theatre. Set in a synagogue, *The Tenth Man* involves a young girl accused of being pos- sessed by evil spirits who has contacted a sceptical lawyer to guard her interests. Gradually the play builds to its climax as ten men in their prayer shawls with lit black candles assemble for the rite of exorcism, complete with sexton and the Cabalist to order the dybbuk to leave the afflicted girl's body. A highly theatrical piece, it began strongly at the box office but after a couple of months spectacularly collapsed. 'We ran out of Jews' was Michael's explanation although it may have also had something to do on this occasion with McWhinnie's production, which did not quite match up to that on Broadway from Tyrone Guthrie, who injected a sometimes lumpen text with a visceral jolt and bravura staging. Michael had, however, noted and remembered amid the mainly Jewish cast (Cyril Shaps, David Kossoff included) a young Gentile actor (a Quaker in fact) playing the Rabbi, Paul Eddington.

Much more commercially successful, although a trial to produce, was *Rattle of a Simple Man* (1962), which had a long West End run at the Garrick, a favourite home for Michael's productions since *Share My Lettuce*. It was run by John Hallett, another of his mentor figures. With a reputation as something of a maverick (he was very suave, like Patrick Mcnee in his *Avengers* heyday), Hallett's background was somewhat mysterious – he was rumoured to have sold a part of Burma to someone and had seen, even if briefly, the inside of an English jail – but he was as much a charmer as his erstwhile partner at the Garrick, the musical star Jack Buchanan. Now he ran the theatre for the Abrahams family, whose property company covered several West End houses; he and his actress wife Valerie White were always extremely kind to Michael and David: 'He became a great, great friend – a benevolent influence on me always.'

Rattle of a Simple Man was by Charles Dyer, also (as Raymond Dyer) an actor, represented by the Eric Glass agency ('that I kept with the play at all was entirely due to my continuing enthralment to the Glass Menagerie'). Glass had invited Michael to catch the play being tried out in rep with Edward Woodward (also a Glass client) in the cast; Michael took McWhinnie with him and both thought the play had possibilities and that Woodward was too good to lose. For the co-starring role – the play is essentially a two-hander – of a good-hearted prostitute, Michael's immediate thought was Sheila Hancock: 'I knew she was gawky rather than the glamorous call girl Dyer wanted and he fought me tooth and nail. Sheila even auditioned for it – and she was an established name then – but he kept resisting. He even came up to London from Bournemouth where he was acting and returned the £100 advance I'd paid to option the play, saying, "There. You're going to ruin my play by casting Sheila Hancock." He wanted Diana Dors, ideally with Harry H. Corbett. I simply kept saying he'd have to trust us and he gave in finally with very ill grace. Just as well – we were already committed to the Garrick by then.'

Both Hancock and Woodward had major success in *Rattle of a Simple Man*, he as Percy, a virginal forty year old, up for the Cup in the big city, she as Cyrenne, the proverbial tart with a heart. It is a patchy play – it flopped on Broadway and while John Alderton and Pauline Collins carried it in a 1980 Savoy Theatre production with their onstage chemistry, a more recent revival (at the Comedy, 2004) with two television stars (Michelle

Collins and Stephen Tompkinson), exposing the play's threadbare stretches, failed miserably. Somehow Woodward and Hancock found a vein of vulnerability, even genuine pathos, underneath the banter of two somewhat clichéd characters, which helped transform the play. It was one never too fondly recalled by Michael: 'My main memory of that production was that Dyer gave us grief throughout the run. And when it closed he said he'd show me how it *should* be done by appearing in it at the Intimate, Palmers Green. He was terrible. He was mainly the reason behind one of my big mistakes when, quite soon afterwards, Eric Glass sent me Dyer's *Staircase*, about two gay hairdressers. No doubt coloured by my lack of any urge to deal with Dyer ever again, I said, "This is awful – these two garrulous queens going on and on. It's unbelievable." What *was* unbelievable was Eric calling me soon afterwards to say Peter Hall was going to direct it at the Aldwych with Paul Scofield and Patrick Magee for the RSC.' Subsequently it was made into a terrible movie with Rex Harrison and Richard Burton, both shamefully bad.

The loss of *Staircase* did not rankle much. In any event, back at the Arts, Michael was about to embark on one of his busiest periods, involving him with some familiar authors, Pinter included, but also some vibrant new voices. He was by now thankful that he had taken Peggy Ramsay's advice to base himself there.

CHAPTER 9

A SECOND HOME

The 1960s, a heady decade for the Codron firm, coincided with a time of often rapid change in British society: with the abolition of National Service in 1962 and Labour's 1963 victory under Harold Wilson at the polls, an energy and a youthful, less metropolitan-biased irreverence and iconoclasm began to infuse British life and culture. Kingsley Amis, Muriel Spark, Doris Lessing, William Cooper, Alan Sillitoe, John Wain and others, often writing of a world outside London, reinvigorated the English novel. There was, of course, the 'Satire Boom' with the magazine *Private Eye* following the impact of *Beyond the Fringe* on stage (and a bestselling LP), *That Was The Week That Was* and its successors on television, and also an upsurge in British cinema, cheekily goosing classics (*Tom Jones*), subverting national shibboleths (*The Charge of the Light Brigade*), viewing sexual freedom in an immediately post-Pill era through Antonioni's lens, in what *Time* magazine dubbed 'Swinging London' (*Blow Up*) or boldly rivalling Hollywood for sex 'n violence and glamour with the first James Bond movie (*Dr No*). While popular music reversed the 1950s domination of American rock 'n' roll as the Mersey sound in the wake of The Beatles for a time headed both transatlantic pop charts. Much of the Codron output of new plays would come to reflect this altered landscape.

Further unbuttoning of the 1950s costive restraints took slightly longer in the theatre. The 1963 *Lady Chatterley* trial was a victory for fiction and publishing freedom but the Lord Chamberlain's Office still dictated the theatre's boundaries and could on occasion be implacably repressive (Edward Bond's *Early Morning* was returned to the Royal Court with no blue pencilling – instead the entire script was banned, suggesting as it did a lesbian relationship between Queen Victoria and Florence Nightingale). But, as noted, when the cuts to *Hang Down Your Head and Die* were questioned, the result was something of a climb-down by the Chamberlain's office. When John Osborne's *A Patriot for Me*, tracing the espionage career of a gay army officer in the Austro-Hungarian Empire, was refused a licence for public performance without massive cuts (including an entire sequence at a drag ball), the ESC management simply turned the Royal Court into a club (for a small extra fee) evading the Lord Chamberlain's jurisdiction for the (sold out) run. The same ruse was used for *Early Morning*. Many of Michael's next wave of dramatists took a much franker, often subversive and sophisticated look at British sexuality and morality, at times almost as if teasing the Lord Chamberlain to see how far they could go.

Together with Pinter in his masterly *The Lover*, Joe Orton and Frank Marcus brought a bracing, invigorating air to sexual matters in the theatre (reinforcing Philip Larkin's playful dictum that 'the sexual revolution began in 1963'). Marcus had a certain middle-European perspective on sex in *The Formation Dancers* (1964), coinciding with a similarly sophisticated attitude in Pinter's *The Lover* (1963), and went on to give the British stage its most candid view to date of a lesbian relationship in *The Killing of Sister George* (1965). While Orton, after a frustrating period of rejection, burst into full polymorphous-perverse bloom with *Entertaining Mr Sloane* (1964). All were presented by Michael originally at the Arts (except *Sister George*) where he continued to base himself during 1963 and 1964, his productions often reflecting the shifting *mores* of the era.

There were occasional, more financially necessary commercial excursions. In 1963 Michael presented one of the few revivals associated with him when he transferred James Roose-Evans's production of Noël Coward's *Private Lives* from Hampstead to the Duke of York's. Coward's reputation was then in one of its periodic troughs (his latest play, a dark-tinged comedy of life in an actors' retirement home, *Waiting in the Wings*, had been comprehensively panned by London critics) but his imperishable 1930 classic (for Michael undisputedly 'the best comedy of the century'), unrevived in the West End since 1944, opened the eyes of a new generation to the piercing and enduring truths about love and sexual relationships under the quicksilver shimmer of the banter as it spins from tender wooing to aggressive verbal and physical combat. It was played in modern dress, which in the youthful, spirited 1960s mostly adapted well to the defiantly hedonistic 'let's enjoy the party' world of the play – Amanda's second act provocative dance became an athletic Twist – and although this *Private Lives* lacked something of the play's insouciant sophistication, minimal as an Art Deco shrug, it had a major asset in the Amanda of Rosemary Martin, recently out of RADA, impudent, sexy and deliciously skewering the male ego. This revival, together with the National Theatre's *Hay Fever* soon afterwards, can fairly be said to have launched the revival of

Coward's reputation ('Dad's Renaissance' he called it) in the last decade of his own lifetime.

Also with a view to boost the firm's accounts, Michael presented an efficient if not especially innovative whodunit, *Licence to Murder* (Vaudeville, 1963) by the respected television writer Elaine Morgan, which met with little success. But a production by Minos Volanakis of Ibsen's *Hedda Gabler*, which Michael brought from the Oxford Playhouse to the Arts proved successful enough to move to the St Martin's (1964). This may not have had the shattering impact of Ingmar Bergman's heavily Freudian interpretation – almost a deconstruction – for the National Theatre with Maggie Smith a decade later, but with Joan Greenwood, costumed in pale chiffon gowns (Timothy O'Brien's set, an elegant circular room, was – as Ibsen suggests – full of light), prowling her territory like a feline thoroughbred and silkily evading an unusually sexually assured Judge Brack (Andre Morell), it was a production that mined a rewarding vein of irony in its approach to the play as social comedy. Greenwood's vocal mannerisms were kept in check; she held the house spellbound in the sequence of burning Lovborg's manuscript, playing it slowly and very quietly as if suggesting that Hedda was self-hypnotised.

Although Peggy Ramsay was by now the agent central to his career ('She's done her best to give me teeth and claws' he said once), Michael was still both loyal and grateful to the Glass Menagerie. It was very much at the Glasses' urging that he chose to revive the wartime farce *See How They Run* (Vaudeville, 1964) by their client Philip King. Also an actor – he played the Bishop of Lax, one of the many clerics (real and assumed) in the play, on various occasions including this revival – King and Michael had originally met through Melville Gillam, the dapper manager of Brighton's Theatre Royal: 'Philip lived on the edge of Brighton in a little bungalow with very manicured gardens. He lived with his musician partner Norman, whom he met when acting in Harrogate where, having tea one afternoon in the White Rose Pavilion, he saw Norman coming up on his Wurlitzer. It was love at first sight. And Philip had a Wurlitzer put in for Norman in this tiny bungalow. If that isn't love, I don't know what is. He was a member of the National Liberal Club, where he always dressed in a faded blazer – you wouldn't have connected him at all with Brighton's gay world. I also met him sometimes at the Glasses at their very smart flat overlooking Hyde Park.' King would become a regular and loyal Codron backer.

King wrote sometimes in collaboration with Falkland Cary (*Sailor Beware!*), but on his own he came up with some intriguingly varied work including a very funny backstage comedy of repertory theatre life, *On Monday Next*, and a brave piece on homosexual blackmail, *Serious Charge*. However, *See How They Run*, first produced in 1946, remains his best, a classic English farce set in a quintessential English village, Merton-cum-Middlewick, in wartime, complete with vicar, ex-actress wife with a staid bishop for an uncle, visiting vicars, Nazi spy, dim maid and snooping censorious spinster. It builds, like all good farce, from one credible basic situation into a spiralling maelstrom of misunderstandings leading to a giddy chase involving all the male characters except the local copper dressed as clergymen, climaxing in the bishop's command: 'Sergeant, arrest most of these people!' Michael fatally allowed one crucial error; King felt that the piece was not yet far enough away from the war for comedy and so, like *Private Lives*, it was given a contemporary setting, cutting all the references to blackouts and rationing and making the Nazi into a burglar. It robbed the play of any serious threat and without a credible background only the geometry of farce was on display, never quite enough. It was packed with comedy talent – John Standing, Rosemary Martin, Joan Sanderson included – but it died at the box office. Although the play toured often to good business it did not have a successful London revival until Ray Cooney directed the original wartime-set version for the Theatre of Comedy at the Shaftesbury (his cast included John Alderton, Michael Denison, Maureen Lipman and Derek Nimmo) in 1984.

The Arts, however, remained Michael's prime focus, his second home at that time. Peggy Ramsay had introduced him to a young writer recently added to her list, James Saunders, who had been a chemistry teacher writing radio and stage plays, mainly 'Absurdist' in vein, but meeting only frustration when dropped by his first agent. Ramsay was intrigued enough by the experimental streak in Saunders's work to take him on and she responded strongly to *Next Time I'll Sing To You*. The play was very much the result of Saunders reading, at Ramsay's instigation, Raleigh Trevelyan's book *A Hermit Disclosed*, the touching story of an East Anglian recluse, Jimmy Mason (coincidentally, Henry Livings drew some inspiration for *Kelly's Eye* from Trevelyan's book, also recommended to him by Ramsay). Eventually Saunders, rebuffed by the BBC when he suggested a television play inspired by the book, found new impetus when he wrote for the leading amateur theatre group, the Questors, based in his local Ealing.

Next Time I'll Sing to You develops into a metaphysical exploration of illusion and metaphor as Saunders bases his piece around a group of actors. The leader of the ensemble, Rudge, who aims to discover the essence of the hermit's existence, casts an actor as Jimmy Mason and then is joined by a somewhat punctilious philosopher, Dust, and by Meff, best described as a cockney joker, a kind of metaphysical stand-up comedian, followed by a scatty dolly bird, Lizzie. Saunders inventively uses devices such as verbal cricket, a trial, and circular games as Rudge tries to break into the hermit's isolation, finally facing the Pirandellian concept that each man creates his own relative truth to make existence tolerable.

Michael was impressed by the play's originality and moved by some of Saunders's more lyrical writing, such as Rudge's attempt to analyse the emotion of grief. At the Arts (1962) it was directed by a new name – Michael was often happy to take such risks – Shirley Butler, Canadian born, tall, elegant and energetic with a strong visual sense, as well as the ability to handle actors with sensitivity. It was imaginatively cast – remembering Michael Caine from *Why the Chicken?* Michael suggested him for the irreverent Meff (his laconic, laid-back scepticism usefully adding to the play's texture) while Liz Fraser, mini-skirted and ditsy, prattled away as Lizzie with the rising Michael Bryant as Rudge, Barry Foster (who had worked in Ireland with Pinter and knew Saunders and Butler) as Dust and Denys Graham ineffably touching as the sad, finally delusional hermit.

At the Arts it created quite a stir, seen predominantly as an English Absurdist play. Some – Harold Hobson among them – reacted like Michael in finding Saunders's work absorbing, rueful and funny while for others, not least the abrasive American critic/director Charles Marowitz (working in London with Peter Brook then), it was a blatant rip-off of all the anti-illusionist devices from Brecht and the New Drama. To him, while recognising the play's debt to Pirandello, it ended up as 'a kind of diarrhoea of the cerebral'. Nevertheless, the Arts business warranted a move (with Peter McEnery replacing Michael Bryant) to the Criterion for a successful run.

For many it remains a haunting play of the 1960s. It has had one revival, at Greenwich in 1980, with a striking but hopelessly misguided Magritte-inspired set (so specific as to ruin the play's tone, demanding a generalised world – Timothy O'Brien's sculptural platform space had worked ideally at the Arts and the Criterion), which disappointed the play's admirers. Michael was keen to continue the association and commissioned another play from Saunders. He was heartened when *Next Time I'll Sing to You* shared the *Evening Standard* Most Promising Playwright Award for 1962; the joint winner, by another Ramsay client, was Charles Wood's *Cockade*, which Michael also produced at the Arts in 1962.

21. Denys Graham contemplates a hermit's life while Michael Caine
(Meff) listens – *Next Time I'll Sing to You*, 1963.

Wood, who had worked as a stage manager for Theatre Workshop had
had, like Saunders, a frustrating period after losing an agent in 1962,
joining Ramsay at the recommendation of his friend and her client Peter
Nichols. The BBC had broadcast Wood's stinging study of army life in
Prisoner and Escort but was dithering over the two other short plays of his
army-centred trilogy. Ramsay swung into action with characteristic brisk-
ness, sending the three plays to Michael who replied within two days to
say he very much admired the crackle of Wood's iconoclastic vignettes of
military life and that he would programme them for the Arts later that year
(*John Thomas* and *Spare* joined *Prisoner and Escort* as *Cockade*).

The associations with Saunders and Wood continued, with Saunders
writing more speedily to deliver the commissioned *A Scent of Flowers*
(Duke of York's, 1964) for Michael, which he produced directly into the
West End after a brief tour, partly because the physical demands of the play
would be tricky to handle at the Arts. Once again he used Timothy O'Brien
as designer; later a leading RSC light but then beginning his serious stage
career, O'Brien had designed for John Barton while at Cambridge before

143

studying with the eminent American designer Donald Oenslager and then working in British television for ABC. Just as he had evoked the abstract landscape of *Next Time I'll Sing To You*, so on *A Scent of Flowers*, an intricately structured piece exploring a young girl's suicide often using flashbacks but demanding speedy transitions, O'Brien came up with a mould-breaking steel and stone structure (stage design was changing rapidly and moving from the painted approach – the RSC's John Bury, originally part of the pioneer work at Theatre Workshop, had recently innovatively used metal in designing the epic Stratford *Wars of the Roses* cycle), which could both accommodate rapid transitions and flashbacks and, vitally, isolate actors from a literal environment. His design was most sensitively lit by Richard Pilbrow and Robert Ornbo, both central to the rise of the Theatre Projects Company, so influential over the next decades in stage lighting, sound and projections.

Risk was written all over this venture, also directed by Shirley Butler. The demanding leading role is that of a young girl, Zoe, who has committed suicide and is watching her own funeral take place. At times she is visible to those around her in poignant episodes leading up to her death, revealed in flashbacks involving her emotionally closed mother, ineffectual father and insensitive half-brother (Ian McKellen in his first West End production). A troubled affair with a married man has brought Zoe into conflict with the Church (Saunders tellingly doubled the roles of priest and pragmatic undertaker), bringing her closer to her Uncle Edgar who becomes the one to tip her over the edge. The play moves into its affecting final act, Zoe mingling at her burial with her grieving but uncomprehending family, finally helped into her grave by the two choric figures of gravediggers.

It sounds a depressing play but in fact it was leavened by an often tart wit and some robust comedy from Uncle Edgar. A more commercially driven producer would have compromised, upped Zoe's age and so cast a star, but Michael rightly intuited that the play's core would be damaged if Zoe were too mature and he cast the gracefully luminous Jennifer Hilary, not long out of RADA (she was 23, her sole West End credit having been to replace Susannah York as the dying heiress Milly Theale in a version of Henry James's *The Wings of the Dove*). He was astute enough to surround her with experienced West End actors – Phyllis Calvert and Derek Bond as her parents – but in any event Hilary was magnificent in the part, somehow finding a resilient core to Zoe that avoided the yawning traps of the fey or the self-pitying. But despite mostly positive reviews for both Saunders and

22. Zoe (Jennifer Hilary) turns to her unheeding brother (Ian McKellen making his West End debut) in James Saunders's *A Scent of Flowers*, 1964.

the central performance, the play – perhaps because of the combination of a hard-to-sell theme and an unknown in the leading role – showed no signs of life at the box office and closed after two months.

Another play by a Ramsay client – Frank Marcus's *The Formation Dancers* – was also taken on for production at lightning speed (even Ramsay, incisive herself and a quick reader, was surprised) after Michael read it. Simultaneously she sent him Joe Orton's *Entertaining Mr Sloane*; she had tired of waiting for a response from Donald Albery and Joan Littlewood (who had been in co-production alliance over several transfers to Albery houses from Stratford, E15) and was startled again by Michael's immediate and enthusiastic acceptance of work by an unknown author.

Both dramatists were tackling sexual themes in an unusually sophisti-cated way on the British stage. As Ramsay shrewdly wrote of Orton to her client Robert Bolt on the day Michael accepted both her submitted scripts: 'I suppose he is the answer to Pinter (NOT Bolt) but his influence is Firbank and Genet, instead of Beckett' whereas the German-born Marcus (named Frank after the dramatist Frank Wedekind) was influenced more by Arthur Schnitzler or Ferenc Molnár (both of whom he later translated). Michael

145

had felt drawn to Marcus as 'a new voice, writing a grown-up play about sex' and had high hopes for *The Formation Dancers*. The title and the headings of the play's separate acts – 'Take Your Corners', 'Honour Your Partners' and 'Grand Chain' – at once suggest the dance of love in Schnitzler's *Reigen* (*La Ronde*). The central character (played with a splendidly preening self-regard by Robin Bailey) is a pompous literary critic; he and his ex-actress wife Maggie decide to enliven their routine sex lives when Maggie suggests he has an affair with some lively younger woman to revitalise him. She is less than thrilled, however, when he lights on Perdita, the personification of 1960s free-spirited Bohemianism, already involved with her best friend's husband, who then tries to get his revenge in the manner of Molnár's *The Guardsman* by becoming in reality the 'phantom lover' invented by Maggie to hit back at her husband. Marcus's comedy of modern marital manners – with its occasional darker undercurrents – did well at the Arts and transferred to the Globe.

During rehearsals and the run Michael came to know and very much like Marcus. Mild-mannered, slightly academic in bearing ('with a tough but sweet wife who looked like a Toby jug'), Marcus occasionally invited Michael to his 'very European flat just off Baker Street'. He hoped he would receive Marcus's next play, which he readily commissioned, before long; he had liked the sexual frankness – unusually bracing on the Anglo-Saxon stage, so often embarrassed or lubricious in tackling sex – of *The Formation Dancers*, which, with its 'phantom lover' element, had shades of both *The Guardsman* and Pinter's *The Lover*.

The Lover was moderately successful at the Arts but – at least temporarily – it saw the end of Michael's close involvement with Pinter's work. One of the finest one-act plays of its time, *The Lover* needed a companion piece and eventually Pinter elected to dramatise his sole fictional work, *The Dwarfs*. The novel remained unpublished until 1990 and so the material was an unknown quantity, and some audiences were left at something of a loss in the theatre. The novel is essentially autobiographical in origin, its male characters largely drawing on Pinter's Hackney friends (and himself), full of local references to 1940s and early 1950s East London. Not to its benefit, his stage adaptation excised the one female character, Virginia, who acts as a focus for the young men's rivalries and betrayals as they pass from youth to manhood (to some the novel, although of course much briefer, is Pinter's version of Marcel Proust – a writer he revered and adapted for Joseph Losey for a film, tantalisingly never made – and a *À la Recherche du Temps Perdu*.

146

Originally written for television in the days when a *Play for Today* could command an audience of millions – it created quite a media stir – *The Lover* still shocks and dazzles with its formal elegance of structure and the poised resonance of its dialogue; watching it and sensing the lava bubbling just below the surface is rather like sipping Martinis on the rim of Mount Vesuvius, as it coolly scrutinises the fissures in English middle-class marriage. Like John Osborne in *Under Plain Cover*, his one-act play involving an incestuous brother and sister, and like Marcus in *The Formation Dancers*, Pinter is exploring the sexual foibles and fetishes of the English bourgeoisie. Richard and Sarah's games with a fantasy lover (Richard himself – again, echoes of Molnár) trace in the play's comparatively brief running time an extraordinary arc from civilised decorum to fetishistic excitement and near-feral lust before a gradual return to a slightly but crucially revised order.

The dialogue – often acutely funny – at times has the double pulse of vintage Coward, in particular *Blithe Spirit* (a play later directed by Pinter at the National Theatre), which in some of the passages between Charles and Ruth Condomine especially has a barbed politesse fused with suspicion, similar to much of *The Lover*'s dialogue (the echoes were especially striking in a Battersea Arts Centre season of critics' productions when Pinter's biographer Michael Billington's production paired a superbly matched Siân Thomas and John Michie). Anglo-Saxon sexual attitudes have rarely been more elegantly impaled than by Pinter here, with – as often in his plays – the female revealing a more pragmatic acceptance than the male.

At the Arts the casts included John Hurt in *The Dwarfs* and Pinter's wife, Vivien Merchant, opposite Scott Forbes in *The Lover* (Alan Badel – mercurial and so subtly dangerous as Richard on television – was unavailable and a major loss). For Michael this was a venture fraught with problems – 'it was a miserable time' – and he felt that a good deal of the trouble stemmed from Merchant: 'She did certainly on that project tend to take on the position of Wife to Famous Dramatist.' He felt always that Merchant rather disapproved of him as some kind of venal showbiz figure. Especially vivid was the memory of a weekend spent with Kenneth Williams in Brighton not long after *The Caretaker* had successfully transferred. He and Williams had not reckoned on Brighton's streets being taken over by a Mods versus Rockers clash and after taking refuge at the Hippodrome where they caught some of a touring matinee of *White Horse Inn* ('Let's be gay, boys/For today, boys!') they took a walk that went past the Pinters' neo-Georgian house in Worthing just as Merchant was approaching her door from the other direction: 'There were a few polite civilities. But we weren't invited in. That was the moment I thought, "Ho-hum, maybe I don't have an ally there." And she was frosty to me all through *The Lover* and *The Dwarfs.*'

Merchant was an extremely gifted actress with a seductive dark voice that had a slight 'crack' in it, but a complex personality. It must have been difficult to watch her husband within a very short time after *The Birthday Party*'s flop become so feted and fashionable, whereas as actors she had been the one with the more lively career. Also, for some reason – partly perhaps to do with her feeling that Pinter had somehow betrayed an old tramp by befriending him and then (as she saw it) exploiting him in *The Caretaker* – she violently disliked that play, previously on the same Arts stage. Moreover, her old friend Guy Vaesen, who worked mainly in radio now, had at one time been slated to co-direct the double bill with Pinter but then was asked (and had agreed) to be assistant director (Merchant blamed Michael for what she regarded as another betrayal, although Vaesen had little experience as a stage director). Nor could it have been easy to be directed by her husband in his own play and, according to Vaesen 'I began to get alarmed because I hadn't appreciated how deeply angry they both were'. It was, indeed, a marriage going through a perilously jagged phrase, not conducive to a relaxed rehearsal period: 'Harold was always chiding the stage- management team for moving things and he was forever moaning about noise from the Arts's kitchens disturbing his concentration (later, when directing David Mamet's *Oleanna* at the Royal Court he was maddened by the noise of Tube rumblings beneath Sloane Square, summoning the Court's director Stephen Daldry to demand "It must be stopped"). Also Mrs P was sometimes a disruptive influence. It certainly wasn't the happy collaborative experience of the first three ventures and I think that was partly why our relationship started to fray slightly. Plus its reviews were not great and business did not build enough to warrant a transfer. It was quite soon afterwards that Harold asked me to lunch – a pricey place close to Harrods, so I had forebodings – and more or less right off he said: "I have to tell you this. I have found the director I want to direct my plays. But he works in the subsidised sector."'

That director – Peter Hall – had recently directed Pinter's one-acter *The Collection*, another study of sexual rivalries, for the RSC and would go on to direct the seminal plays of Pinter's maturity from *The Homecoming* to *No Man's Land* for the RSC or the National Theatre. This was the first instance of what would become a familiar pattern, with dramatists enjoying early commercial success and then having their work taken up by the subsidised theatres. The attractions are clear – prestige, generous commission fees, longer rehearsal periods, deluxe casting and the chances of further exploitation – and Michael grew philosophical about the syndrome ('If they want to leave, they'll leave. It happens to most managements').

Before long Michael would collaborate further with Pinter as the director of several Simon Gray plays and they were united again on a strong revival, teasing out all the comedy in its territorial imperatives, of *The Homecoming* in 1978 at the Garrick ('one I always wished I'd originally produced – I felt as if it was unfinished business'). With a first-rate cast including Gemma Jones, Michael Kitchen (especially fine as the thuggish Lenny – 'I respect him as a father but also as a first-class butcher' as he salutes the play's patriarch – one of Pinter's most memorable creations) and Timothy West, it was directed by Pinter's brother-in-law Kevin Billington ('discreetly helped by Harold') but did puzzlingly erratic business, only surviving because of John Hallet's enthusiasm for the play: 'When I told Harold of John's admiration he said, "Well, he'll get a Christmas card this year."'

The dramatist who made possibly the biggest impact in tackling Anglo-Saxon sexuality in the 'revolution' of the 1960s was the urchin-faced (looking much younger than thirty) donkey-jacketed, bejeaned and Doc Marten-booted Joe Orton, with whom Michael's first meeting, in his office, was memorable, largely because of Orton's disarming candour and unusually in-your-face gayness (Leicester, Orton's home town and Michael's wartime haven, was a useful icebreaker). Ramsay sent Orton – who had come to her via radio's shrewd talent spotter John Tydeman (Sue Townsend's Adrian Mole would be another of his discoveries) – to see Michael once he had committed so speedily to *Entertaining Mr Sloane*.

In this play, perhaps more than any other of its decade (*The Homecoming* and Orton's later *What the Butler Saw*, unrevised at his death, come close), sexual hunger permeates the air, that fixation on the pleasure principle so prevalent in the 1960s. As Orton's biographer John Lahr has pointed out he was the first playwright to dramatise the psychopathic style of the era, 'that restless, ruthless, single-minded pursuit of satisfaction transformed by drugs and rock music into a myth. His plays sported with death in order to expose the dead heart at the centre of English life.' Orton's gloriously macabre comedy takes place in a fussily crowded and knick-knack bedecked lounge (with a waste tip outside), the refuge of a natural born killer (the eponymous Sloane), still under age, who comes to lodge with Kath, a much older, skittish nymphomaniac whom he impregnates. He also kicks to death her father ('The Dada') who has recognised him as a murderer. Kath and her butchly gay brother Ed then turn on Sloane, blackmailing him into sharing his favours with them for six months of the year each in return for their silence.

Originally Ramsay's friend Peter Wood was scheduled to direct and he did some work on the script with Orton, heightening the play's irony (which subsequently suggested the wonderfully apt final twist of sexual sharing). When he proved unavailable Ramsay suggested Patrick Dromgoole who had directed *Cockade*.

Michael coped with the Lord Chamberlain's niggles – not for the first time that office got things endearingly topsy-turvy, on this occasion by blue-pencilling all the heterosexual explicitnesses while passing the homosexual ones, much to Orton's delight – and decided to ask Donald Albery to co-produce. This was not only a gesture of goodwill because Albery had received the play first (although he had not responded); there was the ulterior motive that if the play transferred (and Michael felt 'very positive' about *Sloane*) then Albery, who controlled several of the most desirable medium-sized West End theatres, could be quite an asset. It was cast unerringly; Madge Ryan caught precisely Kath's blowsily tawdry elegance ('I'm in the rude under this dress'), like an overblown cabbage rose (her stalking of Sloane was authentically surprising) and Peter Vaughan was similarly on target as Ed, eschewing all the gay stereotypes of several later productions (no bracelet or pinky-ring here), unmistakably a masculine man who just happens to like boys in tight T-shirts, while to date no later Sloane has come close to Dudley Sutton's air of a corrupt Botticelli angel. Television's Matthew Horne from *Gavin and Stacey* was bland by comparison in a 2009 West End revival, although Beryl Reid, Alison Steadman and Imelda Staunton all have found gold in subsequent productions offering differing splendid Kaths.

Rehearsals first time round were not always easy. Dromgoole from the outset found little favour with Orton who found him distinctly pompous and felt, with some justification, that his production was uncertain in tone (fatal for Orton, who must be directed and played with sure-footed brio) far too often. Michael and Peggy Ramsay came to agree.

Perhaps, unsurprisingly, the notices for *Sloane* were completely divided. The *Daily Telegraph*'s W.A. Darlington, soon to be put out to grass, outdid himself in declaring that he had felt 'snakes writhing about my feet' all evening and quite a few others were thrown by Orton's fiercely ruthless

23. Kath (Madge Ryan) steers her suspicious 'Dada' (Charles Lamb) away from Mr Sloane (Dudley Sutton) – Joe Orton's debut play, *Entertaining Mr Sloane*, 1964.

style (compassion has no place in an Orton play). It also found some champions, among them Michael's old Oxford acquaintance Alan Brien, now critic for the *Sunday Telegraph* who perceptively dubbed Orton 'The Oscar Wilde of the Welfare State'. Like Michael, Brien had especially responded to the formal elegance, sharply counter-pointing the seething violence at the play's core, of Orton's dialogue ('The air round Sidcup was like wine', says his brutish killer describing a journey). *Sloane* transferred to the Wyndham's and then the Queen's, adding to that sense of a New Wave rolling up Shaftesbury Avenue.

There was an unexpectedly strong backlash from the old guard. Led principally by the veteran producer Emile Littler (then president of SWET – the Society of West End Theatre, a tightly exclusive cabal of established producers) and Peter Cadbury, who ran the Keith Prowse chain of ticket agencies in those pre-online times (Littler and Cadbury had commercial television interests in common), it was noised abroad that the West End was suffering and would further decline if this spate of so-called 'Dirty Plays' was allowed to continue. The RSC was also a particular target with productions such as Peter Weiss's *The Persecution and Assassination of Jean Paul Marat as Performed by the Inmates of the Asylum of Charenton under the Direction of the Marquis de Sade* (not entirely unconnected with the *ancien régime*'s fear of the avant-garde and its undoubted jealousy of the subsidised sector and its resources) along with Peter Brook's Artaud-inspired 'Theatre of Cruelty' season. Orton's play lit the touchpaper for the 'Dirty Plays Row' as the press in a quiet silly season liked to call it, while press agents seized on the furore for publicity ('The persecution and assassination of *Entertaining Mr Sloane* is still taking place at the Wyndham's Theatre. Warning: this play is not suitable for the narrow-minded').

Albery, temperamentally more akin to Littler and Cadbury than to Michael, insisted (contractually he had the right) on moving *Sloane* to the Queen's, freeing up Wyndham's for the transfer of Ray Cooney's Whitehall farce, *Chase Me, Comrade!* It was a move too far; although overall *Sloane* went into profit, it did less well at the Queen's. Michael was left seething by Albery's pusillanimity and by the thinly veiled attacks on his brand of productions by his so-called peers in SWET, although worse would come his way on Orton's next play.

In the meantime he held his tongue. He had earned kudos over his time at the Arts from within most of the profession, with four transfers in 1963/4. The most commercially successful was a darkly bitter comedy from Jean Anouilh, *Poor Bitos* (1963), which moved from the Arts to the Duke of York's, one of Shirley Butler's finest productions (she died not long afterwards – another too early demise) with a particularly brilliant Timothy O'Brien design. He used every available inch of the Arts stage, taking the set right up to the theatre walls, to suggest a cavernous cellar space, fluidly easing the staging of another flashback-structure play. The piece was obviously too *grinçante* for H.M. Tennent, Anouilh's usual London producers, but Michael liked the play's fusion of acrid tone and blazing theatricality.

Set in a French provincial town ten years after the end of the Second World War, a 'wig' party is hosted by Maxime, a flamboyant local bigshot, at which his guests will impersonate French Revolutionary figures. This is a cover for his real intent – the humiliation of Bitos, a former schoolmate now prominent in the town, who Maxime hates. Bitos (Donald Pleasence) arrives in unbecoming blue satin as his designated character, Robespierre (others are costumed as Danton, Marie Antoinette, etc.). Slowly the play develops into Bitos's nightmare as Robespierre's life from abject poverty to power, matching his own, is acted out, in the course of which Bitos begins to understand how the battle with his sense of inferiority has killed his capacity for love.

While the play's political implications for post-war France had inevitably less impact in London, Anouilh was enough of a dramatic conjuror to make his play bristlingly arresting, providing meaty roles as the characters act out his clever re-enactments in flashbacks of the Revolution's trials. Pleasence was on top form, devastating in the realisation of his death of the heart, his nervy half-cringing, half-defiant Bitos perfectly balancing the supercilious Maxime of Charles Gray.

Although *Poor Bitos* did well enough on transfer, it had a large cast in a comparatively small theatre. Like most of the Arts transfers, it did not make enormous sums. The commercial failure of *A Scent of Flowers* added to the financial gloom just as his period at the Arts was drawing to a close. Michael may have fulfilled Ramsay's prediction that he would make his reputation there, but she had qualified that with her rider that he would not make much money either. She was proved right there too. Now Michael wanted to continue to find good new work – to be launched in the commercial sector – and although he would not expect to produce the kind of volume of work he had produced at the Arts he would need some solid cash in the bank. He was beginning to find a few friendly and loyal backers including Philip King, Michael Oliver, the *bon viveur* Edward Sutro and Kenneth Hall, Chairman of the Board of Directors at London Management, the powerful West End talent agency. A wealthy man, Australian-born, Hall had many business interests and was mad about the theatre. He had been an enthusiastic supporter of the Arts enterprise and indeed for a while he was Michael's sole backer. For Michael this was not an ideal arrangement – too much responsibility towards one individual – but he was grateful for the implicit suggestion of confidence in him and would remain grateful for Hall's continued backing over the years and for his friendship. Hall and his glamorous wife Bonnie 'lived in great splendour in Albert Hall Mansions and were the most generous of hosts. They became almost surrogate parents to me and David – whose father died when he was a boy.'

In the meantime Michael 'went very commercial' by presenting a popular comedy by Jack Popplewell. *Busybody* (1964 at the Duke of York's) was sheer comedy-whodunit escapism; more by luck than by planning, Michael was able to open it not long before Christmas when *A Scent of Flowers* failed at the same theatre, and so it started strongly, but he also had the trump card of Irene Handl as his star. Handl came late to acting (she had beginner's luck as the gormless maid in Gerald Savory's *George and Margaret* before the war) and specialised in lovably cheery cockneys (she was in fact highly cultured, of Viennese parentage and author of two novels). She had a major hit in the long-running 1961 comedy by Arthur Lovegrove, *Goodnight, Mrs Puffin*, as an irrepressible cockney with prophetic dreams, and Popplewell wrote a similar role for her in *Busybody* – Mrs Pider, an office cleaner who discovers a murder when working late. Running to call the police, she returns to find the body gone and the rest of the play, often divertingly, is taken up with her agog interest in police procedure and her amateur sleuth's way of discomfiting the plods. Nobody – certainly not Michael – would claim that *Busybody* was high comedic art but its plot was ingeniously (and honestly) handled, while Handl had all the malapropisms and apparent dimness married to a mind as sharp as any Miss Marple, which delighted her audiences. *Busybody* had a solid run and replenished the Codron office's finances enough to prepare several ambitious projects, including new plays by Orton, Marcus and David Mercer aimed for the West End.

CHAPTER 10

STARS AND BARS

Having aimed to reduce his exhausting Arts schedule of a new production every few weeks or so, Michael hardly kept to the script; he presented five productions in 1965 and no less than nine the following year. Production costs were still comparatively low and he had by now attracted some more loyal backers, recently including Nat Cohen of Anglo-Amalgamated Films.

As he returned to the mainstream he and David were dealing too with changes in their domestic lives. By now they were established as a genuinely bonded and happy London couple, with a busy social life. Still in his early thirties, Michael – partly under David's influence – now was becoming something of a dandy; he had always been immaculately groomed and occasionally shopped at fashionable 1960s men's stores such as John Stephen or Mister Fish, but tended to dress much more formally than David who favoured casual jackets or blousons in the office and rarely wore a tie. Now they were both regular customers at Blades, the trendy exclusive tailors run by a young London meteor, Rupert Lycett-Green (coincidentally pleasing for Michael he was John Betjeman's son-in-law) just around the corner from the office near Savile Row. Michael's Blades dinner jacket, with its watered-silk lapels and waistcoat, was quite a fashion talking point for a while; he wore it well into the 1980s when middle-age brought some inevitable spread.

They also moved from Chelsea to the more central Cambridge Gate near Regent's Park; Caryl Brahms, who lived at No. 3, had tipped them off about No. 8. It was a property on a Crown Lease, held by Mr and Mrs George whose business was in the East End but who behaved decidedly *de haut en bas* when interviewing Michael and David: 'This is a *cream* position and we don't really want any theatricals.' When asked why, Mrs George replied: 'They throw things against the wall.' Mollified by the news that they were not actors, the Georges finally granted a tenancy (£14 per week) although Michael had a residual scruple: 'I felt I was moving back north of the Park and so closer again to my parents – it wasn't openly acknowledged that David and I lived together.' David never accompanied Michael to the ritual

Friday evenings at the family home. Similarly, while Michael got on well with David's mother she, too, did not acknowledge their relationship: 'My name came up with her bridge circle and when one of her table said, "Isn't that the man who lives with David?" Mrs Sutton sharply replied, "*Works* with. Works with,"' and when we later rented a house in Kent, whenever she came to stay at weekends we had to pretend that my bedroom was separate.'

In preparation at the office were four enticing projects – new work from Orton and Marcus, the first full-length stage play by David Mercer and the revised version of a play by Leonard Kingston, first seen in a Royal Court Sunday night production as *Edgware Road Blues* and now newly titled *Travelling Light*.

Michael and David had become friends with Orton and his lover Kenneth Halliwell and had visited their small studio flat in Islington, its walls densely collaged with reproductions of works by such artists as Hieronymous Bosch, a sometimes uncomfortably claustrophobic experience. The insecure, toupéed Halliwell, such a crucial early influence on and collaborator with Orton from their RADA days, was now watching his younger partner be profiled, interviewed and courted by fashionable London, mentored by Peggy Ramsay, and he felt diminished by contrast. Michael and David were always polite but Michael privately found it difficult to forgive Halliwell for his behaviour after the happy transfer of *Sloane* to the Wyndham's. It was a rainy night and Ramsay, who rarely went on to first-night celebrations, had slipped off before Orton, always respectful of his agent, said, 'Where's Peggy? She'll be so pleased' only for Halliwell to sneer 'Oh, she won't hang around. She's only interested in her ten per cent.' Michael could not help silencing Halliwell: 'If that's what you think of Peggy Ramsay you've got her completely wrong.' But they tolerated him (like most people – except, ironically, for Ramsay, who at one time went to some effort as Orton's star rocketed to help Halliwell find some purpose) while they really took to Orton with his breadth of interests and infectious sense of the ridiculous.

Michael introduced Orton to Kenneth Williams ('I think you'll get on very well with each other' he wrote to Williams) when he arranged a happy supper at Cambridge Gate: 'There's absolutely no doubt that Joe was instantly smitten by Ken, impressed by his erudition, wit and sardonic eye.' Both men were autodidacts, hated pretension and were self-mythists, perhaps why they took so strongly to each other; Williams in turn was vicariously thrilled by Orton's accounts of his feasting with panthers, his

24. Michael and David in Venice, 1958.

stories of orgiastic daisy chains in public lavatories ('Sexually he really is a horrible mess' said Orton of Williams's clenched self-denial).

Their meeting coincided with Orton's work on his follow-up to *Sloane*, originally called *Funeral Games* (it was Halliwell who provided the title of *Loot*). It opens with Fay, a young nurse, serial killer and multiple bigamist (she packs off frail old ladies, colonising the husbands plus their assets before moving on) just completing her latest coup with her victim, old Mrs McLeavy, shrouded like a mummy ready for her coffin, provided by the randily bisexual McLeavy junior, Hal, and his bank-robbing partner and undertaker chum Dennis. The lads have stashed the proceeds of their latest robbery in the coffin. At which point Truscott of the Yard, impersonating a Metropolitan Water Board official, arrives on Fay's *femme fatale* trail. The obsessive, crazed figure of Detective Sergeant Harold Challoner, who detested demonstrators and dissidents and was happy to plant evidence (bricks included) on innocent people ('You're nicked'), was the clear model for Truscott who could, in Orton's opinion, provide a perfect part for Williams.

The star responded positively very quickly, (naturally he loved Orton's language) and then Michael was able to cast Geraldine McEwan as Fay, Ian McShane ('Joe was mad about him – he was stunningly handsome and very

157

good in the part') as Hal and the *farouche* Scots actor Duncan Macrae (perhaps a vocal eccentric too many) as McLeavy. Ramsay, once his champion, vetoed Dromgoole as director (Orton agreed), telling Michael, 'You cannot do it with your little team like before' and suggested her friend Peter Wood. Some prime touring dates were booked and although no London theatre was immediately available Michael, like everyone else involved, felt buoyant in advance about the production – he had had 'something of a *coup de foudre*' on reading the first draft of *Loot* ('Orton was kind of my contemporary and he was also gay – although apart from Stephen Churchett and Peter Quilter much later, he's the only contemporary gay dramatist I've produced').

The saga of *Loot*'s original production has become akin to the Japanese story, *Rashomon*, with different perspectives on and versions of the same events – Williams's and Orton's diaries, John Lahr's Orton biography and other books all cover it in some detail – and untangling the truth is not easy. But two things seem clear. Having begun the play as Fay's story Orton then focused increasingly on Truscott once Williams was in his mind, and despite subsequent rewrites that problem was never entirely solved ('The play became unbalanced' Michael realised in rehearsal). Also Peter Wood got the play completely wrong as he was refreshingly honest enough later to admit. Wood was in New York when he read *Loot* and had just seen and been very impressed by Mike Nichols's off-Broadway production of Ann Jellicoe's *The Knack* with a minimalist set of white floor and steel-frame bed: 'Stylisation was in … and, everybody was worried about *Loot* because it was thought to be a little bit distasteful. And I said: 'Well, we'll stylise it' … I stylised the set. I stylised the acting. Whatever was wrong it was my fault – it was me trying to do something with a piece that just didn't want to have that done to it. I tried to do it as artificial comedy.'

Accordingly Desmond Heeley provided a ravishing set – all white, like a rococo wedding cake with, of course, funereal black costumes, all very 1960s op-art chic – but it was fatally at odds with a play, which, for all its articulately fashioned dialogue ('The contents of your dressing table are an indictment of your way of life. Not merely firearms but family planning equipment', Fay chides the errant Hal), is driven by the gleefully realistic rage of an ex-con (Orton really had been harassed by the police) who saw nothing 'artificial' about the play's props of bodies, false teeth and a glass eye, all of which had exercised the Lord Chamberlain's Office more than Orton's satire of authority and religion. Wood became aware in rehearsal that the text was not bending to his concept of it; at one point he had even placed a metronome in front of his cast, arguing: 'This play is essentially stylistic and I want the dialogue to be delivered in a stylistic fashion.'

Fairly predictably *Loot* opened in Cambridge to virtually no laughs. There were the usual post-performance inquests and endless discussions over tepid coffee and room service sandwiches; the set was swiftly re-painted and redressed (although its basic inaptness was never righted) and Michael returned with David to London in some gloom. They knew the production's root problem: 'Joe's decision to build up Ken's part made it a sort of broken-backed play. He developed Truscott in Ken's image but it really wasn't Ken. I think that was to the detriment of the play but it was due to his absolute hero worship of Ken.'

Orton was shrewd and objective enough to acknowledge the problem and worked heroically, encouraged by Michael and Wood, on the road (altogether there were more than 150 pages of rewrites) while Wood tried to right the errors of rehearsals. Fundamentally it was just too late. Williams described the experience of the rehearsals and tour as like being on a ship that set out with the navigator, the captain and the crew all doing different things, and that they never did quite come together. The nadir of the tour was Bournemouth where the audience expected a kind of *Carry On, Ken* and reduced the cast, faced with stunned silence like *The Producers'* 'Springtime for Hitler' sequence, to a state of near hysteria. But then, as can happen on the road, spirits rose again at Golders Green, often the grave-yard of hopes but on this occasion unexpectedly responsive (Fenella Fielding noted there perceptively, however, that although Williams delighted his public it was largely due to his use of his different voices, common to dead posh – he was not, *au fond*, playing Truscott who must be a genuinely threatening figure for the play to work).

Despite the problems Michael felt that Orton's work on tour had produced a leaner, more balanced text and he would have risked taking it into the West End, gambling on enough encouraging notices (he knew some would be hostile) and Williams's box office appeal to nurse a one-set, small-cast play and build an audience. His co-producer, however, who had kept a significant distance on tour, was clearly less committed: 'I was "obleeged" to do it with Donald Albery as co-producer but he was such a discouraging voice. Yet he did have access to theatres.' As the tour drew close to its final week in Wimbledon it became clear that not only were other landlords not rushing to house *Loot* (the rumour mill had done its work) but also that now Albery was only prepared to offer the slimmest of chances that it might go to the Garrick, where he had *Who's Afraid of*

Virginia Woolf? struggling to meet its weekly break-even figure with its second cast.

The Saturday last night in Wimbledon was a depressing experience – an upset woman after the show came up to where Michael and David were miserably standing to say, tearfully: 'This was Felicity's twenty-first' ('In other words, we were responsible for totally mucking up this girl's entry into womanhood by letting her see *Loot*'). Michael and David had had to huddle near the payphone in a nearby bar at the interval for a call from the Garrick – they were told that the takings had gone up for the week to above the break figure and that *Virginia Woolf* would continue there. Michael was also told by Fred Carter, who booked the theatres controlled by Prince Littler, that although the Phoenix theatre was 'dark' they'd rather it stayed so than house *Loot*. Somehow this was leaked to Bill Bourne, an *Evening News* showbiz hack of the old school who loathed the so-called 'Dirty Plays' and had a field day gloatingly reporting *Loot*'s vicissitudes. Obviously still smarting from the disappointment but making a serious point too, Michael felt that SWET was not supporting new work in the teeth of enemies such as Bourne, along with the diehards Cadbury and Littler, and so resigned from the Society's Board. This created quite a fuss; Michael was startled to read a newspaper placard proclaim: 'Dirty Plays – Producer Quits'. To its discredit the mostly still ultra-conservative SWET was one theatrical body that was against any repeal of the Lord Chamberlain's powers.

Eventually the row abated and some harmony was restored. Emile Littler even became a regular Codron investor; it later rather tickled Michael in light of Littler's fulminations against 'filth' (he felt that the *Marat/Sade* was somehow insulting to the Queen) to visit his office where a considerable quantity of rare Picasso erotica was on display, or to hear such fevered dialogue in the Littler-produced *The Right Honourable Gentleman*, a stilted costume drama on the Charles Dilke scandal, as 'Yes! We slept together – all three of us!'

Sadly *Loot* left some rifts: 'Peter Wood and I were non-speakers for a time. He was very naughty in Manchester going off to the Halle Orchestra instead of watching the play and then trying to persuade the cast to advise me not to bring it to London,' and Wood and Williams ended the tour barely communicating. Peggy Ramsay, not untypically, turned on her suggestion of director too; arriving at the box office in Brighton she announced loudly: 'I'm here to see the play that Peter Wood is ruining.'

Michael did not immediately give up on *Loot*. He approached George

Devine at the Royal Court but he simply refused: 'He said that it was not a Royal Court play – ironic in the light of the Court doing all three full-length Ortons later.' But 'by introducing Joe to Braham Murray I was able to throw Joe a lifeline'. Murray did a sharp production of *Loot* for the Century Theatre then based in Manchester where it was seen by Oscar Lewenstein, a senior fellow producer to whom Michael always deferred: 'He was everything I wanted to be – not frivolous at all – and I revered him. I admired where he came from politically and morally. He was where I would like to be if I had not been so involved in boulevard theatre. He wasn't exactly a father figure – but I was especially impressed by his integrity, his genuine love of women and his extraordinary house on the beach at Brighton. Later when I was on the Board at the Royal Court, I became closer to him.'

Michael and Lewenstein lunched at Wheeler's to discuss a *Loot* co-production but by now Michael felt he was perhaps 'a dead hand' on the project. It went ahead in 1966 co-produced by Lewenstein and Michael White, directed by Charles Marowitz at the Jeanetta Cochrane in Holborn and then at the Criterion (it ran for over 300 performances, won the *Evening Standard* Best Play Award and obstinately refused to go into the black). Marowitz's production was coarse but it had the priceless assets of Michael Bates, who had the delusional Truscott right down to the bristling toothbrush moustache and spit-shined shoes (Bates, aware of Marowitz's somewhat unorthodox rehearsal methods, insisted on a clause in his contract excusing him from any improvisation) and Kenneth Cranham and Simon Ward, a splendid pairing as Hal and Dennis, mop-haired and exuding randy ambivalence. Later, with Lewenstein as the Royal Court's artistic director, the theatre presented all three of Orton's main plays in 1975. Lindsay Anderson steered a first-rate *What the Butler Saw*, rescuing the play from its mangled reputation following the original disastrous posthumous H.M. Tennent production, and Beryl Reid was a hilariously brilliant Kath in a fitful *Sloane*, but Albert Finney, directing *Loot*, made the play seem thin on laughs. Not until the Theatre of Comedy production (1984) by Jonathan Lynn with Leonard Rossiter as Truscott in his final appearance (he died during the interval of one performance) did *Loot* deliver the genuine Ortonian goods, seen at last as a modern classic. Both John Alderton and David Haig have struck peak form as Truscott in subsequent productions.

In New York in 1990, Michael saw a Manhattan Theatre Club production of *What the Butler Saw* with a stand-out performance from Joseph

Maher as Dr Rance, the obsessional Inspector of Asylums. Still feeling 'unfinished business – now I could finish off the trilogy' – he set up a production with Jenny Topper of Hampstead Theatre (where he was still on the Board), which brought over Maher and the director John Tillinger from New York. With Sheila Gish and Clive Francis as the battling Prentices, it transferred to *Sloane*'s old Wyndham's home (1991) where 'it played to excellent business for twelve weeks and then sank like a stone'.

It looked worryingly for a time as if Frank Marcus's new play might have a baptism similar to that of *Loot*. Michael had commissioned the play and it arrived relatively speedily (Marcus wrote it in eight weeks). Michael was delighted with *The Killing of Sister George*, 'a funny but compassionate play' focused on a lesbian relationship, charting new territory in the commercial theatre where plays such as *Maidens in Uniform* and Lillian Hellman's *The Children's Hour* (which found little favour with the Lord Chamberlain) had only obliquely tackled the subject. The Sister George of the title is a cheery District Nurse in a long-running, country-set BBC radio soap opera (from the ripe extracts we hear, not a million miles away from *The Archers*) played by middle-aged actress June Buckridge, whose sliding personal ratings plus a penchant for the gin bottle are alarming her producers. June lives with her lover, Childie, a seemingly waif-like girl (actually in her thirties), in a volatile relationship, the cracks in which widen with the visits of a lethally pleasant BBC executive, Mrs Mercy Croft. Gradually it emerges that she too is lesbian and that her motives come to include an ulterior one; she takes Childie away from June, written out of the series and who is finally left alone, practising her lowing for her new role as Clarabelle the cow in a new radio show for children, *Toddler Time*.

The frank depiction of lesbianism brought Michael into his first direct confrontation with the Lord Chamberlain's Office (*Loot* had involved mainly some cut swear words and copious orders to avoid anything 'suggestive' in handling the embalmed body): 'We simply could not get an answer or the script of *George* back from the Office – they always prevaricated. So finally we insisted on a meeting and had to go to St James's Palace to meet Colonel Eric Penn, a very affable Guards officer in his cosy office with the sound of the guard changing in the background. It became clear that their readers had been totally shocked by the lesbian content (possibly, too, by the satire on the BBC) but could not find any direct reference to it anywhere in the play' (Marcus had been extremely clever and the script, with a licence demanding no cuts whatsoever, was duly returned). 'It's almost incomprehensible to think now of all the hoops one had to go through – it really was a nanny-state mentality.'

Similarly many theatre owners were leery of the play and finally Michael went to see Eddie Horan who then ran the Duke of York's. Horan resembled an American B-Movie hoodlum: 'If you took him a play he would usually weigh it, not read it. But he *had* read *Sister George* and said it was OK because people could see it without realising that it was about lesbianism at all, so it was acceptable for the Duke of York's.'

When Michael commissioned Marcus he had made only one stipulation, that he create 'a meaty role for a star actress' but he mentioned no name. Marcus himself thought on completing *Sister George* that Hermione Baddeley could be a possible June (and she did indeed play it later) but Michael's thought had always been Beryl Reid; ever since seeing her during his Jack Hylton days in variety and revue he had wanted to tempt her into a play. She took some wooing – she began to capitulate when Michael took her to see *Sloane*, which she adored (subsequently she played Kath in a revival) – but once she was signed the clever, acerbic Lally Bowers was cast as Mrs Mercy Croft. It was David who suggested and pushed for Eileen Atkins for the difficult part of Childie – the delicate Jill Ireland, then making something of an impact in movies, had been the front runner – and for her it was the breakthrough from supporting roles to stardom. She and Reid made a really believable couple, especially in a larky sequence when June and Childie rehearse a Laurel and Hardy mime (Marcus was a friend of Marcel Marceau) before they go off to a lesbian club. Reid, after some initial problems easing into her first (and daunting) big stage role (she could only ever begin to find her character when she 'got the shoes right' and her June shoes took some finding) was magnificent – bullying, frightened, often very funny (not least when explaining an unfortunate incident involving assaulting two nuns in a taxi) vulnerable and, at the close, indomitable.

Sister George began at the Bristol Old Vic directed by the artistic director Val May and then went on a tour where the lack of response on most dates (a sullenly silent Hull was the lowest point) – audiences perhaps expected from the title a thriller or a comedy featuring Reid's 'Monica' persona from Variety – lowered spirits all round. It was a somewhat nervy Duke of York's opening. Uncharacteristically, Michael – largely because of the chill apathy towards *Sister George* on tour – had had a slight nervy wobble himself ('It had all been rather bumpy on tour and I got a bit edgy about bringing it in on my own'). He allowed the show business mogul Bernard

25. The Lesbian trio of *The Killing of Sister George* – Beryl Reid (George),
Eileen Atkins (Childie) and Lally Bowers (Mrs Mercy Croft) 1965.

Delfont to buy part of the production (it cost Delfont £250 – the entire
production for which Bristol provided the set, was budgeted to open in
London for £3,000) – he was a major Beryl Reid fan – an investment that he
was to get back in spades. The first night was packed but from early in the
evening clearly divided between the Stalls and Circle, together pleasingly
responsive, and the Gallery. In those days the Gallery was still a force to be

reckoned with; on first nights they consisted largely of a fearsome group (others belonged to a more civilised organisation known as The Gallery First-Nighters) mainly of elderly women (their unofficial leader was a squat Madame Defarge figure known as 'Fat Sophie') and rather waspish gay men, all deeply conservative in taste (Anna Neagle and Celia Johnson were particular favourites) and frighteningly knowledgeable about all the West End's doings. Michael, as producer of plays like *Sloane*, was on their hate list and they were audibly aghast to see their beloved Beryl cast as a domineering dyke, commanding her lover when guilty of any misdemeanour to be punished with orders such as 'Drink my bathwater' or (to particularly outraged mutters from above) 'Eat my cigar butt'. Michael had worried about the sometimes hostile reaction to such lines on the road but Ramsay – sensing his unease – advised 'don't cut them, dear. You'd be drawing the teeth from the play'.

The Gallery then liked to let its opinion be known and there was some booing at the curtain (booing vanished when galleries were tarted up and their benches replaced with proper seating, and when the hardcore regulars died off) although drowned out by the cheers from below. *Sister George* had a long run and was eventually a Broadway success too (it was the Broadway co-producer, Morton Gottlieb, who introduced Michael to the phrase 'a nervous hit', which indeed *Sister George* was to begin with in New York) before being filmed (coarsely) with Reid in her original role. When Reid left for Broadway, Hermione Baddeley replaced her and continued when the play moved to the St Martin's. Baddeley could be almost as good as Reid when sober but her tippling made her wildly unpredictable. Sadly watching her well-oiled display during the last post-West End performance in Brighton, Michael and David finally, unable to watch more, retreated to the sadly vanished 'Single Gulp' backstage bar of the Theatre Royal, soon joined by the redoubtable Margaret Courtenay, who had just finished in her supporting role of Madam Xenia, a medium, with her last scene opposite June, and clearly in need of a stiffener: 'My God, the management! You can't take it either. It's like being onstage with one of those excavator trucks – you see it coming towards you and you duck out of the way, but you forget it can turn round and still dump it all over you!'

Most of Michael's productions at this period seemed problem-ridden and it was a particularly fraught time on David Mercer's first West End play, *Ride A Cock Horse* (Piccadilly, 1965). Mercer, a respected television dramatist, was another Ramsay client; she tended to bracket those of her writers – Livings, Alan Plater, Peter Terson *et al* – who lived anywhere north of Watford Gap as 'Northern', and so Mercer, Wakefield-born al-though now settled in London, was numbered among them. An epic boozer and womaniser, Mercer's brooding personality and hard early life gave him a romantically Lawrentian aura for Ramsay, who acted like a surrogate mother towards him and worked hard to help him realise the potential as a stage writer, which she was convinced was in him; she did not succeed – although much supported by David Jones at the RSC later, Mercer never came up with anything for the stage to match the quality of such screen work as television's *Where the Difference Begins*, and *Providence* for Alain Resnais, or *Morgan – A Suitable Case for Treatment* for Karel Reisz (had David Warner, Morgan on screen, played the lead in *Ride A Cock Horse* it might have had a different fate).

Both Michael and David had particularly admired Mercer's polished television play *Let's Murder Vivaldi* and when Michael approached Ramsay to express interest in a stage play from Mercer she soon afterwards sent him *Ride A Cock Horse*. He was daunted by its length but recognised the fierce passion behind much of the writing, staking out new territory in its exposure of an author's psyche. Its leading character – a huge role, never offstage – is Peter, a classic example of a displaced person, working class and northern-born, now a famous writer, tormented by a continuing am-bivalence towards the repressive regional world of his boyhood and guilt over the rejection of his parents whose sacrifices educated him 'out of his class'. Alan Sillitoe and David Storey had mapped out some aspects of this world in fiction but Mercer took into the theatre those big 1960s themes of class consciousness, religious scepticism, Marxist philosophy and sexual confusion. The play offered a potentially rich role in Peter, involved with three women – his withdrawn doctor-wife and two mistresses: a highly strung actress and a pragmatic computer programmer – in the tracing of his progressive decline into breakdown, allowing the actor bravura scenes of crockery-smashing, mistress abuse and even dressing up as a Nazi (how he came by the uniform is never revealed), ending with Peter in an infan-tilised foetal crouch as two mute older figures, presumably his parents, come to comfort and/or reclaim him.

The Lord Chamberlain's Office had quite a bit to say before *Ride A Cock Horse* was licensed: 'There were endless deletions, mainly to do with "language" (i.e. swearing). I had to have another meeting at St James's with Colonel Penn, this time with Mercer, sober and arguing his case well. A great deal of time was taken up with one reference in the play, to a man being in a punt with a girl and rhapsodising about the position she was in.

Penn said this must be cut. When we questioned it, genuinely bewildered, with "But why?", he spluttered, "Well, come on let's face it chaps – this is a straightforward case of rogering", adding rather revealingly, "As if rogering can ever be described as straightforward!" Another of that Office's ludicrous stipulations.'

Peter O'Toole, a bankable huge star then, expressed interest in the play, summoning Michael and Mercer to Paris where he was filming, ensconced in luxury at the Georges V with his business manager Jules Buck ('like a movie gangster played by Rod Steiger'). Over drinks, with O'Toole's commitment confirmed, when Michael suggested Peter Hall as director 'O'Toole made a theatrical gesture of revulsion and fell off his sofa, then looked at me and said, "You could direct it", which should have made me see the writing on the wall. We ended up with a pleasant Scottish television director, Gordon Flemyng, who was – just as O'Toole wanted – of the "Yes, sir, no sir, three bags full" school. Barbara Jefford (wife) and Wendy Craig (computer expert) were terrific but against me, David and even Flemyng, O'Toole insisted that as the actress we cast Yvonne Mitchell who was totally wrong. By which time I'd had to reach a financial agreement with Jules Buck that Keep Films (O'Toole's film company, of which Buck was a director) would co-produce. Now that we were so committed I thought it was the practical thing to do – it was always going to be the case on this one that the star was "the muscle" as they say in America. After about a week of rehearsals, O'Toole summoned me to his ravishing Hampstead home one evening to say he'd been wrong about Yvonne and that he wanted me to fire her the next day, adding, "Oh, by the way, I've just found out that Siân (Phillips, then Mrs O'Toole) is free and she'll do it." So I then had the painful task of meeting Yvonne Mitchell for coffee – it was an awful thing to do to a sensitive woman, even if she was miscast. It was widely seen as victimisation, especially among many Gallery regulars, for whom Yvonne was something of an icon. The production was, as it were, marked.'

O'Toole continued wayward. Two Nottingham weeks and two in Bristol, where his career had taken off, had been booked: 'It was he who'd wanted two weeks at the Bristol Hippodrome and he then insisted he'd play only one so we had to cancel a sold-out week.' At Nottingham Michael was alarmed not only by a slack production and O'Toole's self-indulgent performance but also by the lack of work done on the script – 'it seemed to play as long as *Götterdämmerung*.' Afterwards with a somewhat worse for wear Mercer, Michael insisted on cuts and back in London worked on them with Mercer to take to rehearsal in Bristol: 'We went down with Kika

Markham, who was Mercer's girlfriend at the time. She'd seen it in Nottingham so said she'd go off to visit her uncle, a cleric, and join us after the show for dinner. Mercer and I went to the Hippodrome to see O'Toole before the curtain and give him the cuts but we were greeted by his bodyguard (another Peter), a ferocious fellow in one of those T-shirts so tight the nipples stare at you accusingly and he said: "Message from Peter. He's having a dinner at Harvey's after the show for the whole company. The play can't be discussed – it's a social occasion. Oh, one other thing – Peter also says that if there's any more talk of cuts you'll be opening in London with John Mills."'

The only recourse for Michael was to take his seat in the stalls and for Mercer to watch his play from a handy spot near the Stalls bar: 'It wasn't any better than in Nottingham. Then we went to Harvey's, joined by Kika who was sat on O'Toole's right. She was talking of her uncle and how she too had once contemplated going into the church, to which O'Toole said, "Maybe that's why you're such a rotten actress." She burst into tears and ran out. I said to Mercer, "Follow her – she's in distress" to which his response, well drunk by now, was "No, no – you've got to get Barbara Jefford into my bedroom tonight. It's the management's duty!" All I could think of to say was, "Don't be silly, she's an OBE."'

Sanity – of a sort – was restored the next morning when 'we went through the cuts with Flemyng – although there were still less than I wanted'. The play was opening in London 'to a very sizeable advance' with a glamorous first-night audience (O'Toole's *Lawrence* co-star Omar Sharif and Tom Courtenay included). Beforehand Michael was sought out by 'Fat Sophie' at her toughest, buttonholing him with: 'Oh Mr Codron, we've just had a word with Felix Barker (critic for *The Evening News*) – he thought we were booing the other week at *Sister George* and we told him we weren't really booing.' She paused then added, 'But we're booing tonight.'

Michael passed on the warning to his Piccadilly landlord Donald Albery, who rapidly got every theatre fireman in his London theatres posted up in the Gallery to deal with any incident. There was a palpable tension in the house although the first act – largely because of Barbara Jefford's assured performance – passed without incident, but in the second there were regular calls of 'Speak up!' or 'Can't hear!' to O'Toole and a visibly edgy Siân Phillips, clearly directed at the star's late-replacement wife, ousting a Gallery favourite. There were some vociferous 'Boos' from the top level at the curtain calls but no major incident.

The notices were mostly dreadful – and O'Toole's semaphoring, vocally

26. A soulful Peter O'Toole in David Mercer's *Ride a Cock Horse*, 1965.

monotonous performance deserved them – although Harold Hobson found, not for the first time, signs of an allegory of Christian redemption in an often windily rhetorical play (illustrating the occasional truth of Penelope Gilliat's wicked crack that 'the characteristic sound of an English Sunday is that of Harold Hobson barking up the wrong tree'). 'But because of O'Toole's fame we were critic-proof – we didn't even have to have a library deal' (producers often boosted advance sales by selling blocks of tickets to ticket agencies or 'libraries') and every night the cheerful box office manager John Hulbert would announce, 'We're full again – even up to Row Q for Queen'. Then, once we were up and running we were told that Princess Margaret and Lord Snowdon would be coming and then going for drinks in O'Toole's dressing room. They came to the show but not the star dressing room, leaving him fuming: 'They've got no fucking breeding!' That was just about the last we saw of him. Jules Buck called me to say he'd got a bad throat and would not be well enough to come back. The understudy had to play until we could work out our two weeks' notice with the theatre. The scenes in the foyer were like the outbreak of World War III. O'Toole compensated the production for the contractual weeks he did not play, but the whole thing was a truly miserable experience.'

By contrast, Leonard Kingston's genial comedy was a comparative

27. A 1960s triangle – Michael Crawford (Arnold) Julia Foster (Tricia) and
Harry H. Corbett (Brian) in Leonard Kingston's *Travelling Light*, 1965.

breeze. *Travelling Light* (Prince of Wales, 1965) also chimed with shifting
1960s sexual mores with a triangle of two roommates, an ebullient soap
salesman, Brian (Harry H. Corbett) and a gormless young man, Arnold,
working as a waiter and sublimating sex in religion (Michael Crawford, in
a preliminary sketch for his Frank in *Some Mothers Do Have 'Em*) together
with the salesman's young girlfriend, Tricia (Julia Foster). Brian sleeps with
Tricia whenever he can persuade her to stay over (the Lord Chamberlain
was particularly insistent that no obvious 'bed work' went on) and, inevitably, Arnold falls for her in what develops into an engaging
rites-of-passage play. It was slightly swamped in the wide open spaces of
the Prince of Wales (where smoking in the Dress Circle was still permitted

in those days), but it was truthfully, tellingly acted. Along with the happy success of *Sister George* it made up for the *sturm und drang* of *Loot* and *Ride A Cock Horse*. But Michael still made a private vow to avoid stars who flexed their 'muscle', let alone cast any who hired bodyguards with tight T-shirts in which to display their own.

CHAPTER 11

NEW VOICES

The later 1960s and early 1970s marked one of the most active periods of Michael's entire period in management. Some old alliances continued; he had had the shock of Orton's death, murdered by Halliwell who then took his own life (Michael did not produce the first version of Orton's posthumous *What The Butler Saw*), but Marcus and Wood both had plays on the stocks for him, along with some new writers with whom he would go on to form strong alliances. In 1968, the year after the Wolfenden Report's recommendations finally saw the reform of the laws regarding homosexuals, the Lord Chamberlain finally released his grip on the British theatre; led by the American musical *Hair* there was a brief flurry of shows featuring nudity, mostly – like *The Dirtiest Show in Town, Let My People Come* or Kenneth Tynan's 'erotic revue' *Oh, Calcutta!* – more tedious than genuinely arousing, but no floodgates opened and no end of Western civilisation seemed imminent.

Most of the Codron office's work continued to focus on vibrant contemporary writing. Donald Howarth, another former actor, initially encouraged as a dramatist by the Royal Court (he was its literary manager for a time in the 1970s), directed his own delicate play, *A Lily in Little India* (St Martin's, 1966). This was a poignant study in escape from repression with Jill Bennett radiant as Anna, dutiful daughter of a retired clergyman in the 'Little India' sector of a Northern town, somewhat unfamiliar territory then on the British stage. It also featured Ian McKellen confirming the promise of *A Scent of Flowers* as Alvin, a gauche young stamp collector retreating from a dominant mother and her many 'lodgers' to reach out to Anna. The public responded to Howarth's play much more than to one which Michael and David both thought would fare better and that also put an unfamiliar, younger world on to the stage.

Little Malcolm and his Struggle Against the Eunuchs (Garrick, 1966) was by Yorkshire-born David Halliwell, still in his twenties. Set in a shabby Leeds bedsit, among a group of disaffected art students led by the wonderfully named Malcolm Scrawdyke, a nonentity with dreams of domination and revenge on a society blind to his talent, *Little Malcolm* contained some terrific scenes, shot through with a raw energy and wild, anarchic comedy as Scrawdyke forms his neo-fascistic political party, consisting of misfit hangers-on, including the faithful but scorned disciple, Nipple. Eventually Scrawdyke is exposed as the sad fantasist he is by the one girl he unwisely allows into his circle. John Hurt was outstanding in the title role, his voice – querulous and reedy – hilariously at variance with his self-obsessed vaunting visions, but the critics (all much older than the characters in a very young play) condescended to the piece from a lofty height and it folded rapidly, as it did on Broadway (retitled *Hail, Scrawdyke!*, also with Hurt). Only when Ewan McGregor – a bigger young star than Hurt had been in 1966, of course – appeared in a Hampstead revival, transferring to the Comedy (1998) did *Little Malcolm* receive anything like its due. Not for the only time, Michael was slightly ahead of popular taste.

With Orton's death black comedy of manners seemed in decline, although Michael saw something of Orton's glittering ferocity in Bill MacIlwraith's *The Anniversary* (Duke of York's, 1966), seen then as outrageous in its pitilessly unsentimental view of motherhood. MacIlwraith created a memorable monster in Mum, an eye-patched matriarch (one eye was lost when her favourite son, as a child, was playing games with her) of appalling selfishness. She treats one son, a voyeuristic knicker snatcher, with contempt and the pregnant wife (Sheila Hancock) of her adored younger son with breathtaking spite ('Do you mind sitting further away, dear? I don't care for body odour'). 'There was a play reading of *The Anniversary* in my flat with Peggy Ashcroft, Michael Crawford, Jack Hedley, June Ritchie and James Cossins and the reading went very well but somehow Peggy Ashcroft didn't land in our net.' It opened with the same cast minus Ashcroft but it gave Mona Washbourne – more usually cast as loveable biddies – a series of juicy opportunities, every one of which she grabbed with relish, oozing malice as this domestic ogress before her inevitable comeuppance.

Hancock graduated to Mum's role in a 2005 revival (Garrick); it was a clumsy production and the play's fangs seemed no longer to drip blood. What had shocked, even outraged, nearly forty years before in this production had lost its sting.

Never given a revival – although it deserves one – Charles Wood's *Fill the Stage with Happy Hours* (Vaudeville, 1967) was a welcome return to form after his full-blooded flop with *Meals on Wheels* at the Royal Court directed by John Osborne. The ESC stayed loyal as did Michael who willingly joined

28. Michael, Jill Bennett and Lindsay Anderson at a Garden Party.

forces to co-produce Wood's new play in the West End (the Royal Court was taken up with the visiting *America Hurrah* from Jean-Claude van Itallie). Steeped in the world of provincial repertory theatre, *Fill the Stage with Happy Hours*, directed with loving scrupulousness by William Gaskill, featured Harry H. Corbett (comprehensively laying the ghost of Harold Steptoe) and, equally fine, Sheila Hancock, as Alfred and Maggie, manager of a run-down rep and his ex-actress wife, now pulling pints behind the bar. Forever promising to programme Ibsen and Strindberg, Alfred presents tacky nudie revues to fill in until his next Arts Council grant instalment. Wood also created a ripe part, ripely taken by the Music Hall veteran great, Hylda Baker, in Molly the stage-struck dogsbody, and a touching subplot involving an ageing 'guest star' (Faith Brook) and her fancy for Alfred's and Maggie's young son. Hancock was heartrending – revealing a remarkable emotional range – when remembering her acting glory days, while she and Corbett created in these defeated but still somehow gallant figures a sense that they now are people who know only one reality, that of performance. Like so many plays about the theatre itself, *Fill the Stage* was another that obstinately refused to pull in the patrons. At the end of the short run Hylda Baker left at the stage door an envelope with a £1 note inside for William Gaskill. It is normal for actors to tip dressers or stage doorkeepers like this; nobody was sure whether Baker's gesture to her director was an innocent mistake or an uncharacteristically subtle insult.

The same short-lived fate – although less surprisingly – awaited David Pinner's *Fanghorn* (Fortune, 1968), a satirical take on modern theatrical themes involving sadism, sex and sacrilege – plus the unusual sight of

Glenda Jackson clad in *Avengers* style tight black leather – set in the country home of a Ministry of Defence bigwig deep in Daphne du Maurier country (somewhat unexpectedly designed by Philip Prowse, later a Glasgow Citizen's triumvir and regular Jackson director). As Cornish gales lash mullioned windows the politician's wife and her Sapphic ally Tamara Fanghorn (Jackson), seemingly to take revenge against the entire male sex, plot his humiliation and destruction, involving flagellation and symbolic castration until a fairly predictable climactic twist. The whole farrago – directed with a heavy hand by Charles Marowitz – seemed like an extended revue sketch parodying Jean Genet or Orton, without the imagination of the first or the wit of the other.

On occasion a production could come about obliquely. Returning to Regent Street one afternoon Michael passed a middle-aged couple looking into the window of Garrard, the jeweller's, then opposite his office, and was struck by how close and manifestly still in love they were before belatedly realising they were Hugh and Margaret Williams. An established and polished actor, Williams had formed a successful partnership with his wife, writing a number of successful light comedies including *The Grass is Greener* and *The Irregular Verb to Love*.

Back at the office, Michael began to wonder what had happened to the duo's latest play, a four-hander comedy produced and directed by Jack Minster on tour. Laconic, usually drawing on a cigarette, seemingly permanently hatted and resembling a lugubrious Basset hound (he was affectionately nicknamed 'Jolly Jack'), Minster was a much underrated director with an agile comedic touch, given to terse notes ('No use looking at the floor, old chap' he told one laid-back actor, 'You won't find anything there except the play'). Michael enjoyed his company and listening to him on actors ('He's of the old school – and it's one that should have been pulled down years ago'), or to his views on comedy (he believed – and had on occasion proved – that an iffy play could sometimes be saved by a strong final ten minutes, sending the audience out forgetful of previous *longueurs*). Minster had moved on to other projects but he told Michael that the Williamses' play had some excellent scenes but had not been strongly enough cast to bring into London.

On reading *The Flip Side* Michael realised that it was old wine – central stylish couple, a Kentish oast-house setting out of *House and Garden* – in a new bottle – a background of sexual 'swinging' and wife-swapping – as the Williamses caught up with contemporary mores. But if their efforts to be with it seemed sometimes strained, Michael could see the play's commercial potential and that they had created a real original in the character of Candida, an insecure middlebrow among the sophisticates. He cast Anna Massey who gave the part a deliciously apprehensive comedic edge.

Her conditions made the other casting in the play unusually tricky. Her current boyfriend, Ronald Lewis, was also cast but then her stipulations about the other roles included (a) nobody with red hair like hers (b) nobody ever previously involved with Ronald Lewis (c) nobody ever previously involved with her brother Daniel Massey to whom she was then not speaking and (d) nobody ever previously involved with her ex-husband Jeremy Brett. All these provisos combined, plus the fact that Brett was bisexual and had not been exactly a monk, led to a casting equation that Michael rapidly realised, 'ruled out quite a chunk of Equity membership'.

Eventually, opposite Patrick Allen, for the other female lead the film world's Dawn Addams (dark-haired) was cast but early in rehearsals the director, Robert Chetwyn, was reporting to Michael that she was making life awkward, insisting for instance on being placed to favour her 'best side' in profile. Finally, Addams summoned Michael for a meeting at which she tearfully claimed that she was not being handled sympathetically and suggested that she might 'want out', an Americanism Michael hadn't heard before. But he knew exactly what Addams, expecting to be soothed and coaxed back to rehearsals, was implying and then promptly spiked her guns by saying that he would be 'happy to accede to that'.

Rapidly Michael organised her replacement – the clever Canadian-born (and dark-haired) actress Toby Robins – and *The Flip Side* (Apollo, 1972), despite some criticism of the pale Xerox of Coward with its foursome in a cocktails-before-adultery world, went on to be a public and commercial success, running for over a year. During its run, Michael was able to enjoy some *schadenfreude* in a piece of belated score-settling:

'During its successful run at the Apollo, I got a call from Freddie Brisson who was staying at the Savoy and said having seen the production he'd like to take it to Broadway but that it had to star Anna Massey. Freddie Brisson was the co-producer of the US version of *The Caretaker* on Broadway who had ventured the opinion "Fuck the London production!" in response to our requesting the smallest of royalties. Reluctantly I had to mention this offer to Anna Massey and tea was arranged at the Savoy for Brisson, Anna and me. The tea arrived and Anna was pouring it into our cups when Brisson told us he was the producer who transferred Peter Shaffer's play *Five Finger Exercise* to New York but had replaced "the awful actress" who played the mother – Adrianne Allen. In real life Adrianne Allen was Anna

Massey's mother; on hearing this she paused in her pouring and I knew then to my relief and I must confess with some delight, that Brisson's project was out of the window.'

Inevitably some projects went awry. The novelist James Kennaway, author of *Tunes of Glory*, which Michael had admired, wrote a fitfully striking family drama set in his native Scotland, *Country Dance* (Edinburgh Festival, 1967), but even with a well-disposed local audience, the play's unevenness told Michael to take it no further. At this stage in his career, with some seesawing periods, Michael estimated that financially 'I expected to make personally about the same annually as an averagely successful dentist'. All that altered with two productions in the late 1960s, both snatched from the jaws of incipient disaster.

Always on the lookout for work – of whatever genre – reflecting the contemporary world, Michael had spotted something interesting about a young new dramatist, Terence Frisby. Also an actor and director, Frisby had directed his own play, *The Subtopians*, a bleakly funny play of family tensions set in suburbia, at the old Bromley Rep, which his friend Sheila Hancock, having admired it, persuaded Michael to see. There had been some rival managerial interest in *The Subtopians* (the producer Peter Bridge subsequently had an option on it for a while) but Michael passed ('It belonged really in the fifties') although he relished a good deal of the writing and some time later, with a gap in his Arts Theatre schedule, let Frisby set up a moderately successful production of his play (with a ripe Bill Fraser leading performance) there. Subsequently he arranged a meeting with Frisby and the writer recalled 'this awe-inspiring figure only a year or two older than I, who had brought exciting new work actually into the middle-class, middle-aged, middlebrow West End', noting the immaculate grooming and well-fed hamster cheeks ('Everything he did was smooth and tasteful; he loved the pause technique'), comparing him to a cat in the way he might pick one up and drop one with a feline's apparent indifference. Frisby was considerably elated, however, when Michael closed the meeting abruptly (a favourite technique) but not before saying, 'Send me your next play and I'll do it.'

When Michael received the script of *Mr Danvers's Downfall* from Frisby's agent Harvey Unna he was at once intrigued (despite his dislike of the title) and optioned it quickly ('I told you I'd do your next play' he reminded Frisby). Originally written for television but rejected by a new BBC broom, Frisby's play initially seemed a promising example of the standard West End light comedy structured round an older man's pursuit of a younger woman; the classic ingredients of clashing sexes, classes and generations were all in place, but what intrigued Michael was that Frisby, instead of following the conventional formulae of similar earlier 1960s pieces, such as William Douglas-Home's *The Secretary Bird* (1963), somewhat subverted the genre by making his very contemporary, streetwise girl both innately brighter and more ruthless than his self-centred seducer, even having her walk away at the play's close.

Michael called it a 'bridge play' spanning the Old Wave and the New – certainly the character of Marion, the female lead, very much of the King's Road and an irreverent, classless, spirit ('the prey devouring the predator' in Frisby's new take on the sex war) could not have been written previously – and was genuinely enthused by the piece. Frisby took greatly to Michael and David ('David played bright-eyed ingenuousness to Michael's Machiavelli; they combined perfectly') during the pre-production period.

It proved a nightmare to cast. Robert Danvers, a lawyer, was ageing and preternaturally vain – not attributes calculated to attract middle-aged stars conscious of their 'image'. An early thought, Donald Sinden, had liked the play but was frustratingly unavailable for some time. Frisby came to realise that 'one of Michael's admirable characteristics was his commitment'. Other producers might have tried to persuade Frisby to cut some references to Danvers's thickening waistline or thinning hair in order to attract a box office star but that would compromise the play, which was never Michael's way. After a depressing period of many rejections, Michael decided to wait for Sinden although he was not then a proven major stage star who was guaranteed to sell seats. There was also the factor that in order to cast the female lead at the right age and to make maximum impact the actress should ideally be relatively unfamiliar. There was a long list for the blithely outspoken Marion, with Michael totally agreeing with Frisby and the director (Robert Chetwyn once more) that she should be someone young and convincingly derisively indifferent to Danvers's seduction techniques of flaunting his luxury pad and lifestyle, more drawn to her spaced-out rock band boyfriend. Seeing a fizzingly vivacious ex-dancer, who had also worked with Joan Littlewood, when she appeared in Bond's *Saved* at the Royal Court, persuaded all involved that Barbara Ferris was perfect for the role.

Only just prior to rehearsals did Frisby realise, with considerable surprise, that in 1968 Michael Codron, respected producer of Orton and Pinter, had not been able to raise the full capitalisation (around £10,000 – Hutchinson Scott's fashionable split-level set was pricey) for a play by a virtually unknown author with no major bankable star presented by a management which, however respected, had produced very few long-running, money-minting successes. In fact Michael, with Frisby's consent, had to allow his investor Nat Cohen of EMI Films a matching clause for the film rights to persuade him to invest more heavily. He also eventually contributed more of his own money than he would customarily consider.

The finance was finally in place but essentially the work had just begun on a play illustrating the old adage that often successful comedies are not so much written as rewritten (best described by Moss Hart in *Act One*, recounting the pre-Broadway tribulations of *Once in a Lifetime*, his Holly-wood comedy co-written with George S. Kaufman). A read-through revealed glaring flaws – too many side issues, too much undigested and undramatised sermonising on 1960s sexual double standards – and Frisby almost literally took his script apart. There were major rewrites in rehears-als and during a decidedly bumpy tour. Danvers no longer practised law but became an example of that new 1960s phenomenon, the celebrity cook with a TV show (Robert Carrier and Graham 'Galloping Gourmet' Kerr were, so to speak, flavours of the month). However, on the road Sinden – as he owned himself – had not plugged fully into his character. He was, of course, dealing with daily rewrites and re-rehearsals, never easy on tour while also playing eight performances each week, but his Danvers cru-cially lacked the root of the character's magnificent self-obsession. Frisby felt that Anglo-Saxon culture, guilt-haunted as it is, demanded that depic-tions of philanderers had to be distorted to fit a false morality and, as he noted: 'The term "male chauvinist pig" had not yet been invented but Robert Danvers was to be archetypal.' During their final touring week in the vault of a depressingly echoing, sparsely populated Golders Green Hippodrome, the actor's breakthrough came as Sinden found and began profitably to mine the gloriously amoral self-satisfaction that fuelled Dan-vers, in what developed into a major performance. There had been other problems on the road – the replacement (twice) of a key supporting role included – and the rumours around town of a problem-beset piece meant that few were anticipating a long stay on Shaftesbury Avenue. Michael had only been able (at no small price) to snare The Globe, pride of H.M. Tennent's empire, because Tennents had in the pipeline a production earmarked for that theatre a short time ahead and because John Perry, who had caught a grisly accident-jinxed performance on tour, felt that it might manage a short 'fill-in' run largely because his chauffeur had found it 'quite funny'.

The play – at Chetwyn's clever suggestion it had been retitled *There's a Girl in My Soup* – became a long-running megahit with 2,547 performances at the Globe (Tennents had to see several productions through before that theatre was freed up for them again) and then the Comedy. Amazingly – and bizarre as it may seem now – it provoked one of the last vestiges of the old Gallery opposition to innovation when on opening night a few die-hards booed their objections to the girl flouting tradition by not marrying the man. *There's a Girl in My Soup* may not be an enduring classic but it struck that vital spark of recognition about human behaviour in its audiences. It went through several West End casts and eventually made a so-so British movie with Goldie Hawn imported to play Marion opposite Peter Sellers's smoothy-chops but curiously gelid Danvers. Casting him was similarly difficult on Broadway where Arnold Saint Subber ('like a whispering Japanese gnome') co-produced with Michael, and although it had a successful enough run – with Ferris decidedly outshining a soft-centred Gig Young – it was nothing like the phenomenon into which it developed in London.

It made Frisby (and Michael) a great deal of money and indubitably boosted the Codron name in the eyes of backers, but sadly the two fell out over Frisby's follow-up, *The Bandwagon,* in 1969. Originally a TV play it was the story of the South London working-class Botterill family, of which all the female members are pregnant, the youngest with quintuplets and already negotiating lucrative media deals; trouble arises when she lets slip on television that her five will be illegitimate, adding defensively but disastrously in the media's eyes, 'My friend Sylve told me it was safe standing up'; this line, which Frisby refused to cut, led the BBC to cancel the broadcast of the play, which Frisby then reworked for the theatre.

With a cast of seventeen it was impractical to tour and – yet again – no suitable West End house was available. *The Bandwagon* ended up at the Mermaid at Blackfriars and although plays often moved into the West End from there, Frisby felt it was wrong for his play, and then became further exercised when he found out it was set up as a Mermaid production with the deal that Michael would come in on transfer (which would not have been cheap). It was the end of a friendship with Frisby seeing the deal as demonstrating, on this occasion, a lack of commitment from Michael. The play opened successfully – Peggy Mount as the Botterill matriarch amply demonstrated that she was much, much more than the foghorn-voiced dragon of *Sailor Beware!* – while Frisby married his frank comedy to a perceptive take on the dichotomy between the Botterills as they are and the image of the family as presented in a prurient media. But it did not transfer – and no other producer picked it up – to Frisby's continuing disappointment.

One of Michael's own disappointments was the failure of his third collaboration with Frank Marcus who in *Mrs Mouse, Are You Within?* (Duke of York's, 1968) took unfamiliar London territory as his setting (rather like Mortimer in *The Wrong Side of the Park*), here 'the No Man's Land' between Holland Park, in the 1960s all restored houses for smart progressive liberals, and North Kensington where the stucco is leprous and the houses carved up into flats for immigrants and singletons. The Mrs Mouse figure is Anita, touching thirty and employed in a department store, who has twice weekly trysts with her a-wooing frog, Hob (a brilliant study of arrested development, a selfish man, played by John Warner, late of *Salad Days*, still tied to his mother,) but who in a one-night stand becomes pregnant by a local charmer, Sean O'Hagan (despite the name black, not Irish). While the self-centred Hob and Anita's feckless sister offer no help (O'Hagan has scarpered), it is her Marxist Scots landlord who comes to her rescue. A slender but poignant piece with some genuinely hilarious episodes, Marcus clearly is on the side of cheerful disorder rather than the increasingly regimented and mechanised efficiency of the times in this ruefully affecting scrutiny of the nature of friendship.

Like *Sister George* it opened under Val May at Bristol where the Anita of Barbara Leigh-Hunt was a triumph ('we all fell in love with Ba Leigh-Hunt – she was stupendous in Bristol'). Michael had qualms: 'We knew this was not the most robust of plays – it was a wing-and-a-prayer venture that gambled on rave notices for her and the *réclame* of *Sister George*.' But odd things can happen on the night; for whatever reason – a nervous cast, a seemingly passive house after Bristol's warm glow – *Mrs Mouse*'s endearing but special world (rather like a marriage between Anita Brookner and Bridget Jones) just did not come over on the performance that mattered. The reviews were kind enough but nowhere near warranting a big success and it closed after a brief run.

The other Codron production of that time to emerge as an unpredictable and lucrative hit was even more unlikely than *There's a Girl in My Soup*. Philip King had written a new comedy with Falkland Cary, called *Big Bad Mouse*, with a business setting: 'I thought it was obviously a rather weak play but after the disappointment of *See How They Run* I was keen to do another with him. I tried it out at Worthing where it was seen and liked by Jimmy Edwards – a great stroke of luck. Then Eric Sykes contacted Eric Glass who represented the Georges Feydeau estate – it was a Feydeau

Sykes wanted to do and Eric Glass had to tell him no suitable one was available, shrewdly adding: "But the Feydeau *de nos jours* is Philip King, and Michael Codron has a new one, so you should call him." And he did, and when I told him Edwards was keen he came on board too.'

Luckily in light of the way the play developed, Michael had planned a very long tour, opening at Coventry: 'That was truly grim. It opened to not a laugh, except at the end, when Jimmy and Eric came forward for their call and started to ad-lib and got laughs, largely at the expense of the play. And gradually the ad-libs grew into the play.' Michael felt guilty about what was happening to his friend's play – a Manchester critic described it as 'a shotgun wedding between farce and burlesque' – but if King minded, he said nothing and took the royalties. Michael asked Glass if he could bring in Ray Cooney and John Chapman as 'play doctors': 'So they came to Golders Green and said, "No, sorry, we can do nothing with this. But these two men are brilliant together so if you commission us we'll write a play for them."' Michael agreed, and very soon received the team's top-flight farce, *Not Now, Darling!*, which, to his surprise, both Edwards and Sykes promptly turned down ('No, it's too vulgar – we can't be seen with near-naked women'. Set in a posh furrier's showroom with some models involved in the action). In effect Michael – lucky man – got two hits out of one potential flop. He sent *Not Now, Darling!* to Donald Sinden and Bernard Cribbins who made a dream team for classic farce: Sinden all breezy rantipole confidence, Cribbins subservient and twitchy, playing with what Sinden called the 'prestidigitorial speed' required in farce, most demanding of *genres* and craftily directed by another adroit farceur, Patrick Cargill. It ran with great success at the Strand (now Novello) for well over a year from 1968.

Meanwhile with *Big Bad Mouse* by now altered out of recognition on the road, still on his hands, Michael began negotiations with Charles Clore, then owner of the large-capacity Shaftesbury theatre: 'It was regarded as a bit of a graveyard but buoyed by the success of *Girl in My Soup* I said we'd take it, sell it at popular prices (£1 top) and I managed to get a very advantageous rental deal.'

Big Bad Mouse played for two years at the Shaftesbury, with Edwards and Sykes in effect doing something similar to *An Evening of British Rubbish*, or Spike Milligan's deconstruction of what was originally intended as a straight version of the Russian classic *Oblomov*, subverted into a kind of *Hellzapoppin'* evening of mainly improvisational lunacy. Edwards in particular loved anarchy and the abolition of audience stage barriers; once, in

29. Saved by improvisation – Eric Sykes (Mr Price-Hargreaves)
with boss Mr Bloome (Jimmy Edwards) in *Big Bad Mouse*, 1966.

a terrible Harold Fielding revue, *Hullaballoo*, set in a reproduction of Piccadilly Tube Station's Gents' lavatory and headlining the then popular
drag duo of Rodgers and Starr, he found himself in a grisly number dressed
in tight lederhosen amid an oompah band and Tyrolean dancing girls,
turning in the midst of it to say to the first-night audience: 'I must have been
pissed when I said I'd do this.' In *Mouse* he had a field day especially when
showing up the inadequacy of stage props (unplugged telephones, blank

183

letters, etc.) or castigating latecomers in a manner the arch anti-illusionist Bertolt Brecht himself would surely have adored. The crumbled masonry of the original play remained – set in the Chunkibix Ltd factory in which a mild clerk is mistakenly identified as a sex offender, so becoming an unlikely heartthrob at an inhibition-loosening office party – but Sykes and Edwards (as his choleric boss) built a whole new edifice on top, ad-libbing outrageously and in effect debunking the whole notion of theatre. On their best nights – which could add up to half an hour to the running time – they were the delirious equal of Olsen and Johnson or Morecambe and Wise.

If this represented the 'vulgar' Michael then the 'impeccable streak' was still pulsing. Three new dramatists – Christopher Hampton, David Hare and Simon Gray – and the recently established Tom Stoppard all came into the Codron fold.

It was Ramsay – again – who alerted him to Hampton, then just twenty and still at Oxford. She sent his play *When Did You Last See My Mother?* to Michael who was then discussing with William Gaskill, artistic director at the Royal Court succeeding Devine, the possibility of jointly leasing a West End theatre (the plan came to nothing) and who responded positively at once. At the same time the Royal Court's script, which had been dismissed by one of their panel of readers, was read by an ambitious young Scottish assistant director at the Court, Robert Kidd. He asked Gaskill (a great admirer of Hampton's play also) if he could direct it and was given two Sunday night performances at the Court while Michael arranged its limited season transfer to the Comedy.

It was very much a young man's play, verging at times on the melodramatic, but written with truth, conviction and that innate sense of vibrant theatrical language which always made Michael's antennae react. He could recognise, too, the authentic emotion in its situation of two ex-public schoolboys (Hampton had been to Lancing) in pre-university limbo, living in London's bedsitter land, loving each other but confused about their feelings. One sleeps with the other's mother – touchingly played by Gwen Watford – who later kills herself. A young actor – he was twenty-one – who would go on to extraordinary work, mainly at the Royal Court, before his early death, Victor Henry, also gave an astonishingly mature performance. Hampton wished to finish his Oxford course but Michael was happy to commission another play and he would wait if necessary.

Tom Stoppard was nearly a decade older than Hampton but still, in the wake of the overnight sensation of *Rosencrantz and Guildenstern Are Dead* at the National Theatre, regarded as a *wunderkind*. Michael had met Stoppard before: 'I was interviewed by Tom, then a journalist on a Bristol paper, in the Establishment Club in Soho – a night club in daylight is not a salubrious place – and I knew he wrote, or wanted to write plays. Then the Oxford Theatre Group had a triumph at the Edinburgh Festival with *Rosencrantz and Guildenstern*. I was in Edinburgh, very much because of Jim Haynes, a dynamic and articulate American whose fingers were in many pies, and we went to see it together. Unfortunately we didn't see past the wrinkled tights. Very short sighted of us. I saw the second night at the National and felt somewhat ashamed of myself. But I did recognise Stoppard as a coming man and wrote to him saying "mea culpa" or words to that effect, adding that if he ever wrote anything right for the West End, I'd love to see it. And then later he sent me *The Real Inspector Hound*. I laughed out loud reading it – Kenneth Ewing, Tom's agent over many years, remembered me sending him a one-word telegram saying simply "Dazzling". Then with my usual shortness of vision we took it – largely because of *Girl in My Soup* – to Bob Chetwyn and J. Hutchinson Scott. They said the design – the play was set in a theatre during a performance – prohibited touring so we decided to do previews – the first in the West End. There were ridiculous grumbles – with SWET about prices and with the Critic's Circle behaving most high-mindedly saying we could only have ten previews and then they'd come, invited or not – but we made a little bit of history, announcing "Reduced Price Previews". What took the gilt off the gingerbread was pairing it – because *Hound* ran just over an hour and a quarter – with Sean Patrick Vincent's *The Audition*, which had had a modest success at the Arts and being slightly Absurdist, we thought might match *Hound*. But it really didn't.'

At times rehearsals were uneasy, especially when Michael and his two stars, Ronnie Barker (in his last stage acting role) and Richard Briers, wanted some textual trims only for Chetwyn to turn on them: 'He stamped his foot saying, "You're dealing with Stoppard here, not a West End farce." He became somewhat intransigent, which he'd never been before – it was then I got the first sign of what Coral Browne, who had a tricky time on that misbegotten first production of *What the Butler Saw*, which he directed, called his "Hitler Syndrome". And Stoppard didn't mind little cuts at all.'

The Real Inspector Hound (Criterion, 1968) was surprisingly critically undervalued on its first outing. Its wickedly funny picture of two theatre critics writing their notices during the performances and rehearsing choice aperçus ('It has *élan* while avoiding *éclat*'), did not find universal favour; a decidedly literal Milton Shulman retorted that critics simply did not behave like that. But undoubtedly only Peter Shaffer's *Black Comedy* or Ayckbourn's *Gosforth's Fete* from *Confusions* can rival it as the funniest modern short comedy.

A truly dire Christie-ish whodunit is taking place – the *trompe l'oeil* set had the Criterion audience facing a stage with more seats and a dress circle surrounding it – complete with an exposition-fuelled comic charlady opening the action on the telephone ('This is Lady Muldoon's drawing room. One morning in early spring'), while two critics, Birdboot and Moon, are covering the play. Birdboot lusts after the actress playing the tempting Lady Muldoon and Moon is a typically jaded second string; as the play progresses they write their reviews but gradually fantasy takes over when Birdboot finds himself on stage pursuing Lady Muldoon before the play repeats itself – this time with many lines revealing new meanings – and Moon also becomes involved before both men end the play dead, as Stoppard pursues the link of the subtle relationship between actor and audience to its logical conclusion.

Michael was right about *The Audition*, which involved three actors doing a backers' audition for a new musical. Certainly when *Hound* was revived in 1985 at the National Theatre, paired with Sheridan's *The Critic* – both plays involving a play within a play, inside a surrounding critical framework – it seemed, although still hilarious, less a mere diversion and more an ingenious Pirandellian exploration of illusion and reality (Chichester in 2010 mounted the same pairing). The same was true when it was paired in an agile Greg Doran production (Comedy, 1997) with David Tennant and Selina Cadell among a clever cast, with Peter Shaffer's *Black Comedy*. But no two actors have yet quite matched Barker and Briers who made an imperishable critical double act.

Michael and David came to be good friends with Stoppard and his then wife Miriam, occasionally visiting the couple at their house in Buckinghamshire. Michael liked his company – 'I got on very well with Stoppard although I suppose I was a little daunted by and in awe of him as much as I was by Michael Frayn.' Stoppard's next play – *Jumpers* – was already promised to the National Theatre, but both Michael and Stoppard were serious about future collaboration.

CHAPTER 12

NO MUSICIANS, ACROBATS OR PERFORMING ANIMALS

Patience, as Michael always owned, was not a virtue for which he was famous; he felt sometimes that was why he so especially enjoyed revue, its rapid changes ideal for a low-boredom threshold. But he had to have patience in waiting for Stoppard to write a new play that would bring them together again. Everyone else was after Stoppard too – *Jumpers* (1973) was a major National Theatre success, and *Travesties* (1976) a similar RSC sell-out, while his slyly satirical *Dirty Linen* (1976) ran for years at the Arts for Ed Berman's Inter-Action group with which Stoppard was associated. It would be nearly ten years after *The Real Inspector Hound* when Stoppard delivered the goods but it proved worth the wait.

In the meantime in the 1970s the firm of Michael Codron Limited had produced some of the finest work of the decade with plays from an extraordinary range of dramatists – Ayckbourn, Bennett, Bond, Churchill, Frayn, Hampton, Hare, Gems, Gray, Russell, Wood – and had long since replaced H.M. Tennent (which had declined even before Beaumont's death in 1973) as London's leading management: 'After the success of *There's a Girl in My Soup* we were seen as such good tenants at the Globe – as indeed we were, paying twenty-two per cent rent with a break-even figure fixed at £3,000 per week, which seemed a fortune then – that we were kind of taken up by Binkie and John Perry. Occasionally Binkie took me to Scott's – very posh in Piccadilly, then – and advice would be given over Haddock Monte Carlo and I thought, "This is great, it's what I'd like to do when I'm in his position – have my own table here." Then soon afterwards Scott's went under and anyway I realised I was happier doing my kind of plays. Sometimes we got invited to Knott's Fosse, the country home in Cambridgeshire, a cottage with beautiful grounds, the only hazard being the newly installed sauna and the worry that a straying hand might wander. But I realised that even he was vulnerable: once we were staying when *Not Now Darling!*, which we had at the Strand was well into its second cast and tottering a bit, and I had heard on the grapevine that Binkie had been

approaching the Strand to put Alastair Sim in *The Magistrate* there. No
mention was made of it all weekend so on the Monday morning I said,
"Look, Binkie, I know you're after the Strand. Why didn't you say something?" And he said, "Well, I really don't want it at all. But you see, I
thought the Lyric, which was our first choice, was all fixed but now Prince
Littler says he'd rather have Rex Harrison in *The Lionel Touch*." A salutary
lesson – to think that even someone like Beaumont could be treated like
that when theatre owners play you around.'

With the financial bonanza of *Girl in My Soup*, (it recouped its costs
within ten weeks at the Globe, regularly beating previous box office records) as Michael said, 'Our lives changed completely.' In London they
moved in Regent's Park to nearby Chester Terrace: 'I was driving back to
Cambridge Gate and came through the arch off Albany Street and saw
someone at the front door of an absolutely beautiful house. I stopped and
said, "I think your house is terrific" and he said, "Well, I'm talking about
moving but my buyer is in a rush and I need time." That suited us. We
couldn't afford to buy it but the company could. The sale was being
handled by a very upmarket estate agent (called Rupert Delavigne) based
opposite the Connaught Hotel where, in the nicest possible way, we were
asked if we were good for £165,000 (quite steep for a long Crown Lease
even then). We got it and we loved it – it was Nash's own house, built with
his crippled sister in mind and so on only two floors with a superb
double-cube drawing room and a sunken front garden.' Quite a lot of
furniture came thriftily from past productions, while even some soft furnishings were recycled – 'a hugely expensive Thai silk dress Julian More
made me get for Evelyne Ker in *The Golden Touch* provided some beautiful
cushions'.

Michael and David had a busy metropolitan social life and were regularly generous hosts at Chester Terrace. They were marginally involved in
the capital's gay lifestyle; there had been a rapid proliferation of gay or
gay-friendly clubs and restaurants in London since 1968, with the Casse-
role in the King's Road and Belgravia's La Popote especially successful.
The latter, its wildly camp pink and purple décor with quantities of swag-
ging and ruching matching its clientele, and hopelessly incompetent but
tight-trousered waiters serving food only marginally more palatable than
the red wine that tasted of iron filings, had something of the air of a private
club. Always packed in its 1970s heyday, it was still then something of a
hangover from the pre-Wolfenden world, its candlelit tables echoing to the
gossip of what were then called 'screamers' (one, a respectably married

tycoon in the outside world, was known there as 'Decibelle'), many affecting that ultra-refined vocal style now rarely heard except from art critic Brian Sewell.

Although occasionally enjoying forays into that world, both Michael and David favoured less-exclusive venues; for most of the 1970s Michael's favourite restaurant was The Grange in Covent Garden's Henrietta Street, which pioneered traditional English food in the teeth, as it were, of Nouvelle Cuisine and which drew a more mixed clientele. The same area's underground Boulestin's, enjoying its final flowering before its transformation into a pizza parlour, was another regular haunt, along with – nearer the Regent Street office – the rather faded Chez Victor off Shaftesbury Avenue where the somewhat hefty French food was fine if one did not mind the occasional mouse scurrying around the tables (one food guide, reacting to the restaurant's boast above the door – *'Le Patron Mange Ici'* – speculated that *le patron* must be deranged). It too became a pizza joint.

Before long there would be a country house for weekends. Michael was not such a workaholic – nor was David – as to forget the importance of what Ramsay called 'the inner life', the renewal of mental batteries with dogs, walks, friends and books plus occasional breaks to the South of France or visits to friends such as Edward Montagu, away from London's pressures. John Hallett and Valerie White, who had a charming cottage in Burwash, asked them to look over with them a house they were contemplating renting in Rolvenden: 'We weren't that familiar with Kent apart from occasionally visiting John Schlesinger and Geoffrey Sharp and when the Halletts didn't take the house – their housekeeper said firmly that it was too far from the West End – we took it on because we both liked it so much. There was only an eleven-year lease (at £500 per annum), so all the petrol and driving there and back probably ended up more expensive than the house but the medieval Kent Hall House, called "Rawlinson", was a happy home for twenty-one years (the landlords – very benevolent – extended the lease, alas not on quite the same terms).'

Professionally David had confirmed Michael's feeling that his impulse to ask him to join the business was one of the best decisions he had ever made: 'He was always the one the accountants went to; he submitted the company accounts much better than Richard Eastham and I had and he sorted out complicated things like pensions. I could coast along being the Poet and Dreamer but David coped with more of the blood, sweat and tears. Someone once said, "The nicest thing about Michael Codron is David Sutton" and I had to agree.'

Financially the firm was on more solid ground than most and its standing steadily increased with a string of memorable productions throughout the 1970s even, paradoxically, as that began to seem a strange, volatile decade, jagged with unpredictabilities, riven by bifurcations. Some dynamic new shoots – the Women's Liberation movement, major progress in Gay Rights campaigning – forced themselves through in a period often scarred by industrial action (the three-day week under Edward Heath's administration, severely restricting power supplies, had a devastating impact on London theatre), which later in the decade, coinciding with the IMF crisis and the Winter of Discontent under James Callaghan's Labour government, reached the theatre world in an unlovely, at times violent, manner on the South Bank as the National Theatre, moving from the Old Vic to Denys Lasdun's new building, struggled to open its doors under Peter Hall. This curiously ragged period was the staccato overture to Mrs Thatcher's victory in 1979 and a long period of Tory rule with combat against the unions – the miners' NUM most memorably – taken to a new level of aggression in a gradually socially transformed Britain.

Unsettled, unsettling decaying landscapes of social disorder haunt the work of so many 1970s writers – for a while even the restrained Morningside tones of Michael's favourite Muriel Spark were cloaked in an urban or international background of sinister threat, while the London of Paul Theroux's *The Family Arsenal* resembles a *Blade Runner* world, and Margaret Drabble's 1977 novel *The Ice Age* describes a Britain chilled by 'a huge icy fist, with large cold fingers'. Her vision was echoed by other novelists such as J.G. Ballard and by younger meteors in fiction including Martin Amis and Ian McEwan, all creating atmospheres as disturbingly menacing as those suggested by some emerging dramatists – David Hare, Howard Brenton, Stephen Poliakoff, Christopher Hampton – who likewise reflected this queasily tense era in a Britain shrouded often in a pall of rancid conflicts, corruption (the 1970s became an era of major civic and local government scandals) and violence (even in Hampton's urbane comedies of manners or in Bennett's *Enjoy* and Frayn's *Make and Break*, an offstage public violence often hangs over private events). A kind of dystopian vision informed much of the decade's output – on screen also with such mordant takes on contemporary culture as Lindsay Anderson's *O Lucky Man!* or Derek Jarman's *Jubilee*, bringing startling new images of Punk to the cinema. And, as journalist Andy Beckett pointed out in his perceptive survey of the 1970s in *When the Lights Went Out*, for those who wanted some comedy to lighten this brooding vision, two popular TV series of the

190

time – *Fawlty Towers* and *The Rise and Fall of Reginald Perrin* – featured middle-aged men trapped in a tumbledown nation, both fuelled by a similar kind of impotent cosmic fury and dreams of escape. By contrast with what now seems the innocent, carefree world of the 1960s, popular music was rudely shattered, irrevocably altered, by a similarly toxic anarchy and aggressive energy from Punk – the Sex Pistols appeared in 1975 – its banshee howl drowning out the harmonies of Beatles and Beach Boys alike. Often the work out of the Codron office reflected the shaky, insecure mood of the period; *Siege* (Cambridge, 1972), an intelligent, somewhat Shavian piece by David Ambrose set in a long-established Pall Mall club, with Alastair Sim in top slippery form as a wily ex-Liberal Prime Minister, took place against a background of angry youthful insurrection in London's streets. A mordant three-hander with Michael Bryant, powerful as a reactionary PM, and Stanley Holloway in his valedictory stage performance as an ancient club-land waiter almost stealing the evening from the great Sim, it sadly faded away in the vault of the Cambridge, the only theatre available.

Other producers envied Michael his stable of writers but like them he too had periods of marking time, still having to keep the office busy between commissioned plays or those scheduled for future productions. By the 1970s it was also clear that both the big subsidised companies alongside the ESC in Sloane Square were becoming serious rivals in the field of new writing. As Michael wrote to fellow producer Peter Bridge: 'Good new plays are becoming rarer and rarer all the time – and in fact all of us commercial producers are staring at rather bare cupboards.' Some of his output around then had deeply disappointed; a Dora Bryan vehicle, more a ramshackle revue than a play, allowing her to portray nine different domestics, *They Don't Grow on Trees* (Prince of Wales's, 1968) by Ronald Millar, later Mrs Thatcher's favourite speechwriter ('The lady's not for turning' came from him) was a low point. As was another star vehicle, featuring a strenuously unfunny, toothy turn from Tommy Steele in an ill-judged revival of Goldoni's *The Servant of Two Masters* (Queen's, 1968); nobody would necessarily expect a production such as Giorgio Strehler's legendary Milan Piccolo Theatre version in the West End, but this was barely a pantomimic plod, marked by clichéd acting of the worst kind – desperate 'comic' servants with blacked-out teeth, supposedly funny walks and endless running entrances and exits.

Michael gave two unknown stage writers crucial breaks; Kevin Laffan, later prolific on television, came up with an intermittently sharp piece structured round the pressures, on women particularly, of post-Pill Catholic marriage set among Liverpool's Irish community (with an excellent Prunella Scales performance) in *It's a Two Foot Six Inches Above the Ground World* (Wyndhams, 1970), but David Percival's *Girlfriend* (Apollo, 1970) with a potentially rich contemporary comedic situation of gender confusion, boosted by Rolls-Royce casting including Margaret Leighton, ditsily myopic, and John Standing, sputtered out of genuine invention after the interval and ran only briefly.

Work like this was not entirely satisfying Michael either; he knew it was not 'in his own handwriting'. Partly for that reason – he greatly admired the work – he took the risk of transferring David Storey's beautifully fashioned play *The Contractor* (Fortune, 1970) from the Royal Court. Fellow producers were surprised – the play had not been doing especially strong business in Sloane Square – and even Helen Montagu, the Court's manager, when preparing what she called a 'guesstimate' of transfer costs, asked David why Michael was so set on moving Storey's play ('He wants to get his self-respect back' was David's reply).

On paper it seemed a questionable proposition, a piece of Royal Court naturalism, set in the West Riding, structured round the erection of a marquee and then its dismantling, the seemingly minimal plot involving workmen erecting the tent for the marriage of the boss's daughter. There had been some earnest critical theorising – was it an allegory of the English leaning towards unconscious revolution? Or was the tent a metaphor for the rise and fall of the British Empire? – all of which masked the fact that the play's seeming ease and delicacy of surface, in Lindsay Anderson's lucid, loving production, had a family play of subtly suggested tensions and shifting class divisions below. It was graced with precision-fine performances from Bill Owen and Constance Chapman as the parents, and Martin Shaw as their ambivalent son.

Michael responded – rather as he had to the double pulse of Pinter – to the poetic strain in Storey's writing beneath its prosaic surface. He luckily had an ally in John Hallett: 'He always really listened when I said I wanted to do something. When I said I was tired of producing the purely commercial plays I'd recently had to do and wanted to move *The Contractor* to the Fortune, which he managed, he was the only one to want it (Donald Albery ran a mile).' Business initially at the Fortune was somewhat patchy: 'So then John Hallett and I thought of charging only half price on top-price tickets. We did it and it was working well but then SWET called me in and I was well and truly carpeted: "You have broken a rule. There can be no

30. The team prepare for the match in the first act of
David Storey's *The Changing Room*, 1972.

price alteration such as this without ratification by the Society." The old guard was aghast. So I said I'd resign from the Board of SWET but I wasn't going to stop the Fortune experiment. I made life difficult for them because I was Chairman of the SWET/Equity Committee, which was in the midst of crucial negotiations on pay and conditions. The anomaly was that they kept having to get me into the Boardroom to discuss the details of those, so in the end they had to bring me back.'

The Contractor's business picked up – very much by word of mouth – and it eventually made a decent profit, as did Storey's larger cast *The Changing Room* (Globe, 1971), which Michael also transferred from the Royal Court. The plot again seemed similarly anorexic – the changing-room preparations for and aftermath of a Rugby League match – but once again in a scrupulous production from Anderson, the master of poetic naturalism, it evoked a whole world of schisms and alliances shifting like tectonic plates beneath. Its nude sequence (somewhat disappointing Noël Coward – 'Fifteen acorns are hardly worth the price of admission'), three years after the removal of the Lord Chamberlain's censorship power over the theatre, raised hardly an eyebrow.

Writing of this quality was matched throughout the rest of the 1970s by that presented by Michael from a string of writers from Alan Ayckbourn to Charles Wood, produced out of Regent Street. However, Michael always felt that he had mismanaged Wood's *Veterans* (Royal Court, 1972), co-produced with the ESC (Michael now sat on the Royal Court Board – George Devine's main ESC credo, that every decision made on a play must stem from the author's text, was very much akin to Michael's own regard for writers). Based on Wood's experiences as screenwriter on Tony Richardson's movie *Charge of the Light Brigade*, it was a hilarious, jaundiced account of life on a Turkish location with some gleeful, thinly veiled portraits of the film's personnel – the director Trevor Hollingshead ('Tall, thin and utterly happy. He could be thought of as shy – he isn't') was clearly Tony Richardson (played mischievously by James Bolam) while John Mills was Trevor Howard and John Gielgud, disproving again Tynan's hoary old *obiter dictum* that he could not play comedy, essentially played himself (never funnier than when nervously trying to ride a model horse before the camera). Some of the on-set language was authentically blue, much of it from the sweaty technician Bernie the Volt (Bob Hoskins).

'Rehearsals under Ron Eyre were a bit tricky, because from the outset Gielgud was nervous about everything. He was always on the phone saying, "Can't you just possibly drop by?" I did occasionally, but they were rehearsing in the King's Road, miles away. I went for a run-through – it was pretty good – then went to have a pee. Gielgud appeared at the next urinal and began peeing and apologising – "I'm sorry I've been such a nuisance. But the only thing I'm worried about now is John Mills" – breaking off when sensing someone on his other side – "Oh, hello Johnny."'

'We made every wrong move we possibly could' was Michael's feeling after the event. 'We should either have opened directly at the Court or toured and come into the West End. As it was we got the worst of both worlds. Gielgud got nervous again, especially in Brighton when the "language" got to the audience a bit (after about the hundredth Hoskins "fuck" a man rose in the stalls to yell before stamping out, "Don't use that word in front of my wife!"). Gielgud outwardly retained his composure but I knew he was saying before the Court opening to his agent, "Get me out of this" – he felt he was upsetting his public. *Veterans* was rapturously received but Gielgud called me to say, "Lovely reviews. But I can't transfer with it, I've got a film!"' Gielgud was probably soon regretting his movie choice – the classic turkey of a musical remake of *Lost Horizon*, set in a hilariously polyglot Shangri-La ('I never miss a Liv Ullman musical' – New York wag). Playing a sage old Lama he looked, by his own admission, like Erich von Stroheim's grandson by Yul Brynner (he called the film 'Hello, Dalai!').

Some months after the sold-out limited Royal Court run Michael and David were in New York, as was Gielgud: 'We took him to an expensive lunch at La Grenouille and worked round to suggesting that now the dust had settled perhaps we could revive *Veterans*. But he replied at once, "Sorry, boys – it's yesterday's kisses" and without drawing breath went on to detail which of the Eighth Avenue male porno-cinemas were the best, describing in that matchless voice to us and to suddenly silent agog executives and Ladies Who Lunch, the odd conjunctions of graphic anatomical

31. Great Actor standing – and sending himself up. Sir John Gielgud
as Sir Geoffrey Kendle in Charles Wood's *Veterans*, 1972.
watched by Bob Hoskins as 'Bernie the Volt'.

manoeuvres on screen against the background of "The Skater's Waltz". *Veterans* – sadly – remains the only time I worked with him.'

Stoppard finally sent Michael a new play in 1977. They had kept in touch over occasional lunches and letters; in 1975 Stoppard had written to thank Michael for his congratulations on *Travesties* for the RSC, adding, 'I would not wish to open in the West End under any other management', later that year writing, 'I'll try to write a play but don't want to be commissioned – it would be fraud since I seem to be empty of ideas at present!' Two years later he was in full spate: 'I've written about an hour of play … no huge set pieces and you won't be needing musicians, acrobats or performing animals. Don't let it be said that I fail to appreciate the problems of management' before the qualification of 'the whole caboodle has to make way for an empty stage and sky cloth in a three second blackout. In other words I am writing one of these nightmare technical weekends.'

Technical challenges – the play opens with the headlights of a jeep shining through mist in an African outback before it drives off to reveal a complex main set – were undoubtedly there, but Michael was happy to take these on board when he read *Night and Day* (Phoenix, 1978): 'I was very excited indeed to get that one – an urgent, topical subject and terrific parts.' The jeep did indeed contribute to major difficulties. In the first place the initial choice of theatre did not work out; Toby Rowland, who then controlled the Stoll Moss Theatres, including Michael's preferred Her Majesty's, found the play 'too wordy' and the jeep was jinxed by the theatre's cramped wing space ('No jeep, no play' became Stoppard's war cry). They ended up at the Phoenix in Charing Cross Road, suitably large in wing space for the jeep and in capacity for an expensive production (it was capitalised at £60,000). Then, twenty-four hours before opening, the jeep failed spectacularly as Michael wrote to Alan Ayckbourn (who would eventually suffer his own worse technical problems on *Way Upstream* at the National Theatre), 'it was something to do with selectors, gear boxes and transmissions, new hazards to add to first-night nerves. At the last minute an understudy jeep was winched through the dock doors and gave a star performance.'

The richness of texture in *Night and Day* – dealing with post-colonial African politics, press freedom and a love story – satisfied Michael's penchant for plays with different layers, and its crackling, high-octane dialogue appealed to him also from the start. Set in the fictional former-British colony of Kambawe whose bullish President Mageeba, trying to crush a border communist rebellion, is clearly modelled on Idi Amin (coincidentally John Updike's novel *The Coup* also focused on journalists in a dictator state in insurgent Africa), Stoppard has three journalists covering the conflict, a photojournalist ('Information is light' he remarks near the close), a young, ambitious idealist (Milne) and the Australian-born Dick Wagner, a hard-boiled Fleet Street veteran to whom Milne, who refused to join a journalists' strike at home, is 'The Grimsby Scab'. Their hosts are the Carsons, a local mining engineer (with a handy Telex) and his abrasive, unhappy wife Ruth who has had a brief fling back in London with Wagner ('Hotel rooms constitute a separate moral universe' is her perspective) but who finds herself now drawn to Milne.

Diana Rigg 'jumped at the part' of Ruth and John Thaw was cast as Wagner. Peter Wood, who had directed *Jumpers* and *Travesties* was Stoppard's choice of director and despite being 'non-speakers' since *Loot*, Michael had no quarrel with that, knowing how suited Wood's firecracker mind was to Stoppard's work – 'Yes, fine, that's a given' was his reply ('We took over where we left off. We're the same generation, both gay, we live in parallel universes. And we're both fond of something slightly destructive'). Even well before rehearsals Michael's keenness was evident; he wrote to Stoppard in May, 1978 with rehearsals still some months away, 'Daily reports from Zaire and rumours of the possible closure of the *Observer* in today's papers make one of course want to do the play sooner rather than later.' The 1970s had seen turbulent revolutions in the newspaper industry; the fall-out from disputes over new technology as the press began to move from Fleet Street, together with the concerns over Rupert Murdoch's growing grip on newspaper titles, all informed the background to the play.

Many critical comparisons were made with Evelyn Waugh's *Scoop*, also set in an imaginary African dictatorship under rebel attack and featuring a variety of English journalists; a less frequent but better comparison was with Bernard Shaw. *Night and Day* has something of the exhilarating give-and-take crackle of Shavian argument and, like Shaw, even if it is impossible to agree with everything Stoppard says, it is also impossible not to join in argument with it. Just as in his piece for actors and orchestra, *Every Good Boy Deserves Favour*, Stoppard argued for freedom from totalitarianism, so here he powerfully argues for a free press. Milne believes that a free press 'is the last line of defence for all the other freedoms' to which Ruth snappily responds, 'I'm with you on the free press. It's the newspapers I can't stand.' Some were perplexed by Stoppard – like Shaw – airing opposing arguments so readily but, as the dramatist said himself, 'I write plays because dialogue is the most respectable way of contradicting myself.'

Alongside the theme involving press ethics – Stoppard, once a journalist, had a professional command of pressman's lingo – ran the parallel story of African freedom and the gradually evolving emotional strand in the play involving Ruth, beautifully played by Rigg with an assured aplomb masking a desolate sexual yearning. She handled especially well the knife-edge timing of Ruth's switches from inside the play to direct voicing of her inner thoughts.

As most of Stoppard's work tended to in the 1970s, *Night and Day* received polarised notices, ranging from Bernard Levin in the *Times* ('deeply disappointing') to Jack Tinker's *Daily Mail* verdict that 'this is a play to set alongside the finest in contemporary theatre'. Michael's regard for the play remained undimmed as he told Stoppard, who wrote in reply: 'I'm touched that you place *Night and Day* so high. I have felt for years – and occasionally said – that the vitality of the English-speaking theatre owes as much to the Codron office as to any management or person in London, the subsidised lot included.'

The Phoenix had a long-running success, helped by powerful casting: Maggie Smith (who would go on to lead a separate Broadway production under Wood), and Susan Hampshire in turn replaced Rigg, while Patrick Mower ('The Lawnmower' to Dame Maggie) took over from Thaw. The road to Broadway was rocky, with poor reviews on its Washington opening and two cast replacements. Frank Converse's Wagner did not find favour with the Dame ('Well, Michael,' said Smith in her dressing room, 'I'll say this for you – you sure can pick 'em') and Paul Hecht took over. Wagner had proved difficult to cast (Michael's notes on auditions put 'Too young?' next to Converse) with one favoured actor being elbowed aside by general manager Liz I. McCann as 'overly ethnic', which Michael always felt sounded like a Cotswolds village.

Housed in the bleak Anta Theatre ('like pitching a tent in the Sahara' said one critic), the Broadway *Night and Day* received notices more divided than in London, although the debate on press freedom there, in light of Murdoch's acquisition of the *New York Post*, was equally urgent. Smith received some love letters ('Oh, that Maggie! She is divine!' gushed Douglas Watt in the *News*) but others carped – *Newsweek*'s Jack Kroll felt that 'she is in danger of parodying herself and playing to the Maggie claque'. Opening in late November it was an expensive venture (capitalised at $400,000 with a high weekly break-figure of $66,000 – without

32. Diana Rigg at the Phoenix – *Night and Day*, 1978.

royalties to author and creative team); it had strong advance bookings but slowly business slipped and after Christmas it was losing money, even on royalty waivers.

Michael was grateful for the commitment from the Broadway producers

199

– James Nederlander (his closest friend among New York's theatre owners and producers), Roger Stevens and executive producers Liz McCann and Nelle Nugent. He wrote to Nederlander and his wife Charlene: 'Knowing you both and being associated with you is the nicest part of having a show in New York.' And in an interview with the *New York Times*, betraying something of his impatience with SWET's conservatism, he reflected: 'It's easier to produce in New York than in London. Your marketing methods are much more advanced. London producers have a lot to learn. We have been talking about a discount ticket booth and a telephone charge system (both long established in NY) but we're not quite organised.'

The next Codron/Stoppard collaboration – Stoppard's biggest commercial success – came about, unusually, from a commission. Michael and David were among the guests at a big lunch party at the Stoppards' Iver house, both rather low after reading a nasty review for Simon Gray's just-opened *Quartermaine's Terms* in *The Sunday Times*. They were taken aside by Stoppard's brother, an accountant, who asked if they would be interested in commissioning a play from Stoppard, adding that the fee would be £10,000. Michael assumed Stoppard 'must have needed a quick injection of capital. It was a very large fee for a commission. We took a gulp and said yes, we would. And we did know from something Tom had said that there was an idea hovering for a play that would involve Felicity Kendal' (the first rumours of a romantic relationship between Stoppard and Kendal had begun to circulate).

The play – *The Real Thing* – turned out to be about love, and the problems of love. And the difficulties of writing about it. And the difficulties of writing itself. Again Michael reacted immediately: 'When the play arrived and I read it I kind of knew this one would be a success. I felt – as some critics did – that this was Tom Stoppard showing his heart at last.' The 1980s saw several plays by major British dramatists on passion and romantic love – Pinter's *Betrayal*, Peter Nichols's *Passion Play* included – and *The Real Thing* focuses on a dramatist, Henry (Roger Rees) whose wife is appearing in his latest play with his friend Max. Henry is having an affair with Max's actress wife Annie (Kendal) and their passionate relationship and separations from their partners before their own love comes under pressure, take the piece into a complex skein of commitments and loyalties, professional and private, under stress as Annie leaves for a play in Glasgow where she becomes attracted to a younger actor and where her attachment to the cause of a firebrand young political activist, Brodie, increases.

The play begins with a dazzling piece of Stoppardian pyrotechnical panache in a witty Coward-esque scene of adultery discovered, followed by a sequence that gradually reveals that it was 'in reality' a scene from Henry's latest play. When Max discovers Annie's 'real' adultery with Henry, he behaves very differently from his assuredly aphoristic stage persona, reduced to inarticulate, tearful abject pleading. These dislocating, glintingly funny early scenes prepare the way for the rest of the play, which reinforces that love, adultery and betrayal are never simple or to be taken for granted. The Stoppard hallmarks of glittering wordplay, puns and references to other plays – Strindberg, John Ford (we glimpse Annie rehearsing *'Tis Pity She's a Whore* in Glasgow) and Wilde – are all there, and Henry has a wonderfully, articulately passionate speech using a cricket bat as an analogy to illustrate his ideal of good writing to Annie. All the comedy is yoked, however, to the play's serious spine. The problems with *The Real Thing* tend to be that Annie's character can seem manipulatively self-absorbed (both Kendal and Glenn Close in New York mostly managed to overcome that) and that Brodie, the radical whose shoddy polemical play Annie asks Henry to help put into viable order ('Cut it and shape it? Henry of Mayfair' is his first response) never quite convinces as a real character when he belatedly appears.

Again the critical jury was hung. John Peter hailed *The Real Thing* as 'one of the best English plays of the century' in *The Sunday Times*, while Irving Wardle's *Times* review was a comprehensive pan, describing it as 'cleverness with its back to the wall' (when Michael called Stoppard the morning after opening and mentioned Wardle's notice, Stoppard replied: 'Forget it. He's missed it by a country mile'). But the box office was extremely busy from the outset and the play ultimately went through three West End casts. Its 1999 Donmar Theatre revival (transferring to the Albery) with Stephen Dillane and Jennifer Ehle was also successful, the play this time receiving virtually unanimous praise. Another revival, at the Old Vic in 2010, saw Toby Stephens take on the role of Henry opposite Hattie Morahan's Annie; once again the play was hailed as a modern classic.

Broadway on this occasion was a triumph. Originally the plan had been to reproduce Wood's West End production with Kendal and Rees (a Broadway name since *Nicholas Nickleby*) with James Nederlander again co-producing with the McCann/Nugent team and Michael. But Frank Rich of the *New York Times*, before whom all Broadway producers then seemed to tremble, when writing his annual roundup of London productions was highly (and somewhat too sweepingly) critical of Wood's work ('a prepos-

33. Henry uses cricket as an analogy for writing – Stoppard's
The Real Thing (Roger Rees and Felicity Kendal, 1983).

terously gimmicky production'), causing a swift revision of plans, accelerating when it became known that Broadway's Golden Boy Mike Nichols was keen to direct *The Real Thing*. This together with Rich's review and the financial failure of *Night and Day* in New York, called into question the wisdom of proceeding as planned, although Wood's contract had a clause giving him first option on any Broadway production.

Michael was in a difficult position: 'There began the most delicate discussions with Tom who had met Nichols, very drawn to him directing but not wanting to be the one to tell Peter Wood. But that's part of a producer's job. I met Peter and advised him that on this occasion he should stay in England, take his reduced percentage and use it to put a roof on the barn he'd bought in Somerset. There were even more delicate discussions in New York in Nichols's Carlyle Hotel apartment along with his *über*-agent Sam Cohn of the then giant ICM agency ("I don't work for ICM – I have my own boutique within ICM"), Meryl Streep (a Cohn client, interested in playing Annie) *et al.* Finally Streep decided Henry was the better role – we were very lucky to land Glenn Close to play opposite Jeremy Irons. Without hurting feelings, all those decisions were in the circumstances the right ones for Broadway.'

Eventually, understanding the situation, Nederlander backed out of the equation and *The Real Thing*'s principal producers became Emanuel Azenberg and the Shubert Organization. Nichols's production was predictably extremely glossy with Tony Walton sets much more realistic than Carl Toms's West End designs, stressing the play's emotional journeys (Stoppard revised the text somewhat for Broadway) more than its intricate Pirandellian structure as Wood had done in London. The Broadway version was sometimes less subtle – the opening play-within-the-play scene was played with such knowing underlining as a Coward parody that it made both actors seem somewhat coarse and robbed the following scene of elements of its irony and surprise – but it was undeniably crowd pleasing, with the Irons/Close pairing making for rich emotional interplay. It became a major Broadway 'event', a several times Tony Award Winner and a financial blockbuster. Budgeted at an extremely high $800,000, it recouped its costs within twenty weeks and became one of the most successful Broadway plays of the 1980s. It remains a Codron favourite: 'It will endure, I think – that speech Henry makes to his daughter says so much so pertinently about love.'

Before another new play from Stoppard, Michael presented one of his rare revivals with *Jumpers* (Aldwych, 1985) another piece that he wished at the time he had produced. Another multi-levelled play (like its startling opening pyramidic image of the Radical Liberal Jumper acrobats), it dazzlingly blends philosophical debate, murder mystery, vaudeville, a striptease on a trapeze and acrobatics physical and philosophical. George Moore, the angst-ridden philosopher at the heart of the play, senses the world around him fracturing into absurdity (the critic Hilary Spurling on radio once astutely compared the Stoppard of *Jumpers* with the Lewis Carroll of *Alice in Wonderland*); the image of the acrobats in perfect symmetry before one is shot and the pyramid crumbles parallels the fragility of human reason. George's gorgeous but fragile wife Dotty, once a cabaret singer, is spiralling increasingly into mental disarray by watching the moon landings on television, shaking her ethical system further ('We are no longer the still centre of God's universe') as she is courted by the protean and Mephistophelian figure of Archie, vice chancellor of the university at which George teaches.

The play seemed very different seen thirteen years after its premiere, much less 'difficult' to begin with; as Wood perceived 'audiences have caught up with Tom'. Also, in a later 1980s climate when the country was beginning a slow slide into recession, the play's philosophical concerns seemed less urgent than its personal dilemmas. Paul Eddington's George, less eccentric than the great Michael Hordern, had a real sense of the philosopher's compulsion to pierce to the core of the fundamental question of God's existence but it was his parallel dread of being cuckolded that had a heart-stabbing anguish for the audience. Felicity Kendal as a glamorous, lost Dotty and Simon Cadell's sinisterly suave Archie made up a strong cast under Wood for the West End. This revival played to consistently strong business throughout its six month contracted run.

When Stoppard's new play arrived, its title – *Hapgood* (Aldwych, 1988) – gave little away, but Michael soon recognised how different this one was going to be: 'I didn't quite understand it all at first reading and I could see it was going to need a brilliant design to contain a play in lots of short scenes but I was totally absorbed by it.' In some ways *Hapgood* was kin to a 1968 Stoppard television play, *Neutral Ground*, in which a double agent becomes a stateless redundant spy. *Hapgood's* title character (Kendal once more) leads a British counter-intelligence unit, a single mother with a schoolboy son by a defected Russian scientist, Kerner (Roger Rees again), and with a mind so sharp she can play mental chess. Her urbane colleague Blair (Nigel Hawthorne), worried by the leaking of quantum physics secrets, suspects a 'mole' in the unit who could be a double agent, Kerner, or a 'turned' British agent Ridley (Iain Glen).

Hapgood begins as high-octane farce – at an East End swimming baths with an intricate near-ballet of briefcase exchanges between agents watched by CIA men (staged brilliantly by Wood to Bach's Suite in G Minor) – then moves across London (Carl Toms's clever set used large-scale A-Z map sections and other projections to move the play swiftly) as Kerner at London Zoo explains to Blair how the enigma of light particles can leave room for our understanding of an apparently random universe. When Hapgood's son is kidnapped, Hapgood uses her twin sister to trap Ridley, finally exposed as the mole in a clever 'sting'.

Wood neatly described *Hapgood* as 'like a great philosophical pantomime'. Stoppard saw a relationship between quantum mechanics and human behaviour – 'There is a straight ladder between the atom and a grain of sand. At the top is classical physics and below particle physics. In the centre there is metaphysics' – the point being that as further research goes on it seems increasingly likely that there are random elements making up matter, which makes nonsense of causality, suggesting we may have reached an age in which science cannot explain everything. The play manages to marry a scrutiny of Heisenberg's Uncertainty Principle to a twisting John Le Carré-style plot, Stoppard once again stressing the value of human bonds in the face of the uncertain qualities of virtually everything else.

34. Felicity Kendal on the moon as Dotty in the *Jumpers* revival, 1985.

The try-out at Wimbledon was technically tricky, irritatingly giving rise to some snide press speculation in advance of the London opening that it was somehow a very 'difficult' play ('Actually, once it was up and running audiences would come out saying, "Well, it wasn't as abstruse as all that."'). Hawthorne was never happy as Blair but Kendal had a fine time as

laser-precise Hapgood and her much raunchier sister, and the play survived its predictably divided notices to fill the Aldwych for its scheduled
run. It never played Broadway but one of America's finest actresses,
Stockard Channing, illuminated a fine Manhattan Theatre Club production
for which Stoppard revised the text, highlighting Hapgood's scrutiny of
the fallibility of human perception.

There would be still more partnerships with Stoppard, whose variety
never ceased to surprise and delight Michael, but only one further original
piece launched in the West End. *Indian Ink* (Aldwych, 1995) remains one of
his most beguiling plays, less pyrotechnical than most perhaps but still full
of surprises and narrative twists. Stoppard wrote extensively for radio
early in his career and returned to the medium in 1991 with *In the Native
State* (Peggy Ashcroft and Felicity Kendal headed the BBC cast), subsequently revised and expanded for the theatre as *Indian Ink*. His central
character Flora (Kendal, who grew up in India and to whom the play is
dedicated), is an early twentieth-century poet, best known for her erotic
verse, dying of lung disease in India, her story meshing with scenes set in
Shepperton half a century later with her sister (Margaret Tyzack) sifting
through Flora's papers with a thrusting American biographer (Colin Stinton) and debating the contrary evidence of two paintings of Flora with the
son of their Indian artist. The parallel time schemes take in diverse themes
such as the traps of biography (as in Stoppard's *Arcadia*), the ironies of
literary reputations, the British abroad and, once more, the problems of
language in what Stoppard described as 'a play about the Raj'.

Flora, always scornful of the British rulers in India and their grandiose
sense of the British Empire ('I wouldn't trust some of them to run the
Hackney Empire'), encourages the painter Nirad Das (Art Malik) to assert
his Indian identity. As much as E.M. Forster in *A Passage to India* (Flora is
very much an Adela Quested figure) or Paul Scott in *The Raj Quartet*,
Stoppard is portraying a kind of quest – that of an outsider trying to pierce
the elusive mystery of the Raj and its equivocal attitude to the Empire –
thwarted often by Nirad, a romantically blinkered Anglophile who remains bound to his prelapsarian vision of an England all greensward, linen
shirts and tweeds and Bloomsbury attitudes. The whole play seems suf-
fused by the spell India clearly had for Stoppard; in 1942, escaping the
advancing Japanese forces, he and his brother were evacuated from Singa-
pore to Darjeeling for four years – when later relocated to Derbyshire the
continent exerted the tug of an idyllic lost domain.

Much as Michael admired the play he was anxious about aspects of the production on its pre-London Guildford run, constantly chivvying Peter Wood about various details, particularly the need to tighten the play's ending. He wrote to Wood: 'My roles consist either of Mistress Scold (from *Gammer Gurton's Needle?*) or the other part I seem to be cast in, Mr Badger, continually badgering poor Moley for his own ends.'

However, he was delighted with the production as it opened at the Aldwych, much enhanced by Wood's use of haunting Indian reed music (Michael was always impressed by Wood's use of music in his productions), Carl Toms's gauzy, gliding sets and fine performances from Kendal, Tyzack ('she was brilliant in it') Stinton and Malik: 'There had been a lot of pre-opening talk that it was not a commercial play but when we got it I said we'd do it at once. It was one of the happiest experiences of all the Stoppards.' Its run was extended – Niamh Cusack taking over from Kendal – at the Aldwych where it ran for a year.

His admiration for Stoppard's work was such that Michael also transferred two large-scale ventures from the National Theatre to the West End. Prior to *Indian Ink* he brought Trevor Nunn's masterly production of *Arcadia* to the Haymarket (1994) where it seemed to sit more happily than in the bleak concrete box of the National's Lyttleton auditorium. Pyrotechnics were here in abundance – an exploration of Chaos Theory was built into the very architecture of the play, zigzagging between past and present, binary contrasts infusing the entire piece through to the ending, one of Stoppard's most thrilling scenes, a haunting Mozartian dance to the music of time, which is 'chaotic' only in the sense that both time scales simultaneously co-exist on stage, a climactic coup essentially possible only in a theatre.

Arcadia may sound daunting but although sophisticated in structure, audiences seemed to find it accessible – certainly it tells an absorbing story, or stories. The Stoppardian jokes are there ('Do you think God is a Newtonian?' 'An Etonian? Almost certainly, I'm afraid.') but they are integrally part of a story of literary sleuthing in the present (Kendal and Bill Nighy originally as competing academics) and those scenes set in the scientifically curious but still Romantic era of the early nineteenth century, all set in Studely Park, a gracious Derbyshire pile with its landscaped grounds by 'Culpability' Hawks (glimpsed tantalisingly through the windows of Mark Thompson's seductive design). Stoppard always claimed, 'My interest in chaos maths is an artist's interest, not a scientist's.' Some critics found the play over-cerebral but the public adored it; *Arcadia* ran successfully enough to survive a cast change and ran profitably for over a year. Its 2009 revival

(Duke of York's) was less glitteringly staged and designed – and decidedly patchily cast – but the play once again was mostly favourably received.

The Invention of Love (Haymarket, 1998), directed by Richard Eyre – Michael's period on the National Theatre board was mainly during Eyre's regime – was on an even more expansive scale with a big cast for the commercial stage, but Michael strongly believed that Stoppard's study of A.E. Housman's smothered life and its scrutiny of late nineteenth-century homosexual love should be seen beyond a limited subsidised theatre run. This time the Haymarket seemed less ideal; on the National's open stage Olivier Theatre, the play's imaginative journey (including Charon, resembling a London cabbie, ferrying his passengers on the Styx to the Underworld) seemed to move more freely than behind the proscenium arch, despite John Wood's movingly restrained elder Housman, nursing his unvoiced aching love for Moses Jackson.

If *Arcadia* and *Indian Ink* at times seemed like companion pieces (Peter Wood described them as 'brother and sister') with their similar divided time schemes and the Proustian overtones in their reflections on time itself, then *The Invention of Love* makes a triptych, imbued as it is also with the rueful compassion behind Stoppard's comprehension and communication of the unpredictability, even inscrutability, of both time and the world.

The Haymarket was never as busy as it had been for *Arcadia* and it closed at a slight loss but Michael never regretted his association with *The Invention of Love*. Eight collaborations with Stoppard had brought them close – even if Michael claimed he was possibly more close over the years to directors (of whom he tended to see more) than dramatists – and Stoppard undoubtedly enriched his life both privately and professionally. He had one regret – that the sheer scale and logistics of Stoppard's *The Coast of Utopia* (National Theatre, 2004), his ambitious trilogy, ruled out any question of a transfer to the commercial sector, now crowded with musicals or 'celebrity'-starring plays, a world utterly altered from the comparatively carefree times of *The Real Inspector Hound* in a West End of nearly forty years before.

CHAPTER 13

SHADES OF GRAY

Another dramatist who first came into the Codron stable in the later 1960s and, like Stoppard, stayed more or less exclusively within it for nearly thirty years – occasional excursions into the subsidised world aside – arrived out of the blue. Although a keen reader of contemporary fiction, Michael had not read any of Simon Gray's four 1960s novels when the script of his first stage play, *Wise Child*, landed on his desk in 1967.

It came from Gray's agent Clive Goodwin, one of the most prominent of the period (later Gray would follow Pinter to the firm set up by Judy Daish after the death of Jimmy Wax for whom she had worked). Goodwin was a very 1960s figure: 'These characters just don't exist any more. He was very good-looking, married to the pop-artist Pauline Boty and friends with Peter Blake and all the modern art set in London, all rather different, racy and quite exciting, probably temperamentally a bit more suited to Michael White than me. I had quite a good relationship with him – he looked after David Hare early in his career too.'

Gray had been born in England – in Hayling Island, Essex – but spent most of his formative years in Canada before returning to study at Oxford, subsequently teaching at London University's Queen Mary College. *Wise Child* was something of a wild card, a strange and unclassifiable play with echoes of Gray's favourite Dickens (most critics dubbed it a black comedy) about a criminal on the run disguised as a woman, 'Mrs Artminster', with a young accomplice passed off as his/her 'son' in tow, holed up in a seedy boarding house, the creepy born-again proprietor of which soon betrays more than a passing interest in the 'son', while 'Mrs Artminster' has an eye on a lively black housemaid. Michael at once recognised a new talent – again the dialogue, spare but freighted with subtext and often unvoiced thought with some heightened passages of desolation and doubt, was a major draw – and he was undeterred by the central ambiguous relationship, which might well fan the embers of the 'Dirty Plays' row.

At least he could argue as he put *Wise Child* (Wyndham's, 1967) into production that nobody could possibly accuse his simultaneous production of the slightest scruple of smut. Producing the first London revival of Sandy Wilson's *The Boy Friend* (Comedy, 1967) was a labour of love and although Wilson's own production basically followed Vida Hope's original to the last eyelash flicker, it was beautifully cast (Marion Grimaldi had a sophisticatedly Gallic insouciance as Madame Dubonnet while Cheryl Kennedy's Polly Browne genuinely beguiled audiences with her unforced innocent charm and pure voice). It was certainly streets ahead of the next revival in the 1980s when, surprisingly, Cameron Mackintosh allowed a brassy, garishly designed version – as coarse as the Feuer and Martin distortion on Broadway – to play London.

An unknown author's risky debut play would need a carefully considered production and casting, and on *Wise Child* Michael decided to go for broke and start at the top: 'One of my good friends and supporters was Dennis Van Thal of the London Management agency, very much – like his literary agent brother Herbert Van Thal – an 'old school' gentleman-agent. It was he who introduced me to Kenneth Hall, Chairman of London Management, who was such a crucial early investor and friend. Dennis lived in Queen's Gate Gardens with his wife Mary but he was very, very discreetly gay. When I read *Wise Child* I talked to Dennis, who screened the offers for all the major stars he represented, and asked, "Is there the remotest chance that Alec Guinness would nibble at this or would he bridle at the thought of going into drag and being on the run?" At the time I'd never even met Guinness.' The star's multi-role virtuosity in *Kind Hearts and Coronets* had involved (briefly) a D'Ascoyne battleaxe ancestor in drag and later the film of Graham Greene's *The Comedians* saw him both in black face and *en travesti* but it was a bold move of Michael's at that time.

The play intrigued Van Thal enough to send it on to Guinness and then he arranged a lunch at Prunier's in St James's – a great Guinness favourite along with the Mirabelle in Mayfair and Soho's L'Epicure – with Michael and his client. Inscrutably polite as always, Guinness revealed little about his feelings towards the play and 'Mrs Artminster', until in the middle of some generalised chat about it he suddenly said, 'I know who can guide me into how to play this part!' He mentioned, somewhat to Michael's surprise, the name of a leading London interior designer based in the Pimlico Road, Geoffrey Bennison. Ostensibly an Establishment designer with a successful line in discreet classical good taste (he had 'done' Terence Stamp's set in Albany and provided chic Proustian cork-lined walls in Guinness's Smith Square London base), it transpired that Bennison had a double life, regularly climbing into full drag in which he often was to be found at the all-night coffee stall on Battersea Bridge attempting to pick up burly leather-clad bikers (reputedly with some success).

An appendix to this is that having accepted 'Mrs Artminster' Guinness suggested that Bennison might help 'do up' Cambridge Gate for Michael and David: 'So Geoffrey Bennison came along with his young assistant Terry "to have a recce" as he put it. He had Jean Shrimpton, *the* model of the 1960s, in tow but she waited in the car. He apologised for being late – "Sorry, but I had a lumber last night." I thought he meant a lumbar puncture or something and commiserated but he explained that 'a lumber' is what you get when you pick someone up and bring them back and then expect them to go but you find yourself lumbered making breakfast. Anyway, he had a look round the flat and said what he could do and what he would put where and for what price. My face must have dropped or betrayed my reaction, and young Terry chipped in with: "Look, Mike – if you go to Geoffrey you've got to open your handbag." I chose not to.'

In fact Bennison was most helpful to Guinness over the choice of clothes for *Wise Child* (including an appropriately tatty fur, reminiscent of the drag artist Mrs Shufflewick's 'untouched pussy'), even helping with shoes and advising on wigs (conscious always of his baldness, the star insisted on a ginger crew-cut job – only briefly revealed – underneath 'Mrs Artminster's' greying curls). As usual Guinness fussed about most things. He said firmly in advance that he did not want 'a university director' – he had not enjoyed his most recent play, Arthur Miller's *Incident at Vichy*, under Peter Wood – but seemed fairly happy with Michael's suggestion of John Dexter ('a good old pro') and it was cast quickly with Simon Ward, Gordon Jackson, creepily clammy as the Bible-besotted landlord, and an effervescent Cleo Sylvestre, splendid in a tricky scene in which 'Mrs Artminster' persuades her to undress.

Guinness felt his way slowly into the role – eventually he actually enjoyed being in drag ('I'm going to miss the old bag' he said towards the end of the run, and he could be quite skittish backstage, once saying to Gordon Jackson, 'Oh, my dear, I don't feel like it tonight – I've got the curse!') – and gradually he built up a brilliant study of a thuggish man inhabiting a genteel persona, to at times hilariously contradictory effect.

At Michael's suggestion the whole venture 'deliberately kept a low profile' – blandly unrevealing press releases, few interviews, no pre-West End tour, and before opening cold in London in those days prior to previews, only one public dress rehearsal (usually, to regular moans from most of his directors, those for Michael's productions would be filled mainly with what seemed to be invited audiences of the extremely apathetic and depressed, often residents of nurses' hostels – Alan Ayckbourn called them 'The Three Weeks to Live Society' – probably chosen so that even a tepid opening would seem better). The first night of *Wise Child* actually went very well, with an audience delighted by Guinness's minutely observed study and intrigued by the play's unsettling world. But the run was marked by regular audience protests; Kenneth Williams was watching the play one evening when an elderly man shouted out as he and his wife noisily departed – 'I'm ashamed of you, Sir Alec!' – and Michael found himself visiting the star dressing room more frequently than usual to reassure him: 'Alec was never entirely happy during the run because of the audience reaction. But it was very popular – the occasional outbursts from the stalls all helped publicity – and it ran to very good business for the six months he'd agreed to. Although Alec and Simon never quite struck up a rapport, I became friends with him and his wife at the time, Beryl, and it was kind of understood that I should get his next West End play.'

Secretly Michael was rather glad that both *Dutch Uncle* (Aldwych, 1968) and *Spoiled* (Haymarket, 1971) were already spoken for. The former, a gruesome black comedy involving a Christie-like murderer, had a first-rate RSC cast (John Alderton and Warren Mitchell included) but, in an uncharacteristically messy production from Peter Hall, was a full-blooded disaster. *Spoiled* reworked a previous television play by Gray, a small-scale study of a marriage in crisis when a schoolteacher husband becomes dangerously absorbed in the life of a pupil (Simon Ward once more). It too was a rapid failure and also greeted coldly was Gray's ambitious version of Dostoevsky's *The Idiot* (Old Vic, 1970) for the National Theatre, with Derek Jacobi as Prince Myshkin, directed by Anthony Quayle. None of these ventures had yoked Gray to an ideal director, but Dexter's success with *Wise Child* made him the natural choice to steer Gray's next play which went to the Codron firm.

'When *Butley* arrived David and I were very excited by it and we were convinced that John Dexter would share our view.' Dexter read the play – whether he was excited or not by it was never made clear – 'but then through his agent Michael Anderson of ICM he made demands – huge fee, zonking weekly percentage and he wanted to be put up and paid for at the ritzy and very pricey Stafford Hotel in St James's, claiming he was domiciled abroad – impossible to meet. His *Wise Child* fee (£5,000) had been high then and indeed Binkie wagged his finger at me about it, saying I was "spoiling the market", which was nonsense – the market dictates its own terms in the theatre. It was David who then came up with the inspired suggestion of Harold Pinter.' David remembered how well Pinter had directed *The Birthday Party* in Scarborough and he and Michael had recently seen Pinter's revelatory production of James Joyce's *Exiles* at the Mermaid, staged with a burning-glass lucidity of focus.

Pinter was sent the script: 'He accepted it with alacrity, so we went round to discuss it at Hanover Terrace, all very palatial with everything on a sumptuous scale and a gleaming new black Mercedes outside matching Harold's all-black clothes. It was the first time I'd been inside a Pinter residence and a bit surprising. We felt very much the ones on the wrong side of the park, still in Cambridge Gate then. Vivien was there, graciously, in the shadows.' From the start Gray and Pinter made a good pairing; cricket was a shared passion and Gray, still a lecturer in English at Queen Mary's College at London University, was also passionate about some of the same writers (Yeats, Eliot, Beckett) as Pinter. There was one later rift when Pinter was offended by the portrait Gray painted of him in a television play but the friendship was happily repaired. Michael, who always enjoyed the pre-production process, particularly enjoyed putting *Butley* together, although it was a tricky one to cast, particularly the title role, a college lecturer in English. Heavy smoker and drinker, sexually ambiguous, articulately caustic, witty often at others' expense, Ben Butley is a man pressing increasingly on a self-destruct button during the one day in his office during which the action passes.

Alan Bates was Pinter's first suggestion: 'Then began the long, long courtship of Alan through his agent, Judy Scott-Fox at the William Morris Agency. She regarded Alan really as Mother Goose regarded the Golden Egg; occasionally she would let you glimpse it, even let you hold it for a moment but it would always be snatched away.' Bates was prone to vacillation in any event and was also touchy about any light falling on his deeply closeted bisexuality. He had decided qualms about playing Ben Butley and the associations that might be made with Butley's ambivalent nature (Noël Coward when told by Bates that Scott-Fox was advising him to turn down the role because of Butley's anti-feminist remarks advised crisply, 'Have you told her to put on her brogues and go for a sharp walk?'). Eventually – for ten per cent of the box office – he signed for six months.

'Then a struggle to find somewhere to house it began. We didn't want to tour because of Alan's limited availability so had to book a theatre – and it couldn't be too big for a play that rarely had more than two characters on stage at the same time – before signing people. So I had yet again to deal with the dreaded Donald Albery. Sardonic as ever – I never really took to his patrician, somewhat sinister air – he always gave one the impression if one got into one of his theatres that one was a naughty, inky schoolboy in an exclusive school. Producers today who complain about theatre owners – most of whom are understanding about producers' problems and are ready usually to negotiate – don't know how lucky they are. With Albery, to get the Criterion you had to pay twenty per cent of the takings as rent (no negotiation was countenanced) and accept the fact that you could be given or give notice after three weeks of the opening if the box office figures hadn't reached the agreed break figure, but if you didn't do that then you had to wait another nine weeks, which could be awfully risky on a play that was initially uncertain at the box office. Risky for the producer, that is – Albery would always get a weekly rent. Albery had turned down Hampton's *The Philanthropist* when I wanted to transfer it from the Royal Court and he wasn't at all keen on *Butley* either. But I had an ally in the camp with Anne Jenkins, Albery's PA, who was a chum, and she gave the script to Albery's then wife Heather to read under the drier at the hairdresser's. She liked it and then persuaded Albery to let us have the Criterion, the perfect theatre for it. With the rent at twenty per cent plus percentages (to author, director, designer and star) also amounting to twenty per cent, I was paying out forty per cent of the take before paying the other actors, stage management, advertising and the theatre's contra (in addition to the rental – the fixed costs to producers of heating, cleaning, etc.). So *Butley* had to be more than usually carefully budgeted in a small capacity theatre. But it worked – despite mixed notices – enough to recast twice.'

Butley saw Bates on peak form as the flailing academic losing his wife and his friend (and, implicitly, ex-lover) on the same day. Bates deflected any suggestion that Butley was bisexual in interviews, as did Gray when interviewed shortly before the Broadway opening. But the character's sexual ambivalence seems part of the fabric of the play and certainly was widely seen as such in the first production. Later, for a 2002 version of the text Gray reinstated a passage cut from the first production, which would suggest that Butley indeed is bisexual. Bates was especially adept at handling Butley's vituperative wit, seizing on any chink in another's armour to probe, niggle and hurt, suggesting that even in semi-drunken despair his mind is always intensely, vividly alive. He professes to loathe Byron's work – he is splenetically rude about Byron to an older female colleague who has just published a book on him, her long-time obsession – but his mind is exactly like the description Byron gave Keats's – 'a fiery particle'.

35. Academic contemplation – Alan Bates in *Butley*, 1971.

Magnificently insulting to virtually everyone else in the play – two students, his wife, other staff and Joey, who shares his office and had shared his life – Bates was certainly a devil, but he did have wonderful tunes. Richard O'Callaghan as Joey was superb opposite him – flinty, vulnerable but able occasionally to score points himself and with a crucial touch of prissiness.

After six months of capacity business Bates left for Broadway (and a Tony Award as Best Actor) and Richard Briers took over. He was Michael's suggestion, somewhat to the surprise of those who saw the actor as the quintessential cardiganed sitcom man from television and *The Marriage Lines*; Michael had always highly rated Briers's work and realised 'his range was much wider that what was seen on television. I wasn't surprised that people were surprised but I knew he had that capacity for bile in him.' After that it was the turn of Alec McCowen – more acid in intellectual combat but equally valid – to keep *Butley* running profitably for well over a year altogether.

Gray's following play, *Otherwise Engaged* (1974) ran for even longer and 'it was a joy, except for its genesis, again to do with casting Alan Bates'. The central role of successful publisher Simon Hench was very different from Butley in energy; this was, essentially, a reactive role. Arriving back at his smart London address – Hench and his wife are childless and own the whole house but rent a self-contained flat to a student – he is looking

215

forward to an evening alone with a Scotch and a new recording of a favourite Wagner opera, *Parsifal*, when his plans are disrupted. A string of visitors including the cadging student, his brother, a cocksure writer crony, an old boy from his old school with an ambitious girlfriend, and finally his wife, informing him she is leaving him, all ruin his evening, leaving him alone with his music at the close. A man who has always successfully edited his own life (somewhat akin to Philip in Christopher Hampton's *The Philanthropist*), Hench has a wit much more cool but just as lethal as Butley's, part of his insulating self-erected carapace to shield him from others' griefs and troubles. On stage throughout the play, the part presents a formidable acting challenge.

'Again it was offered to Alan, now represented by Ros Chatto and Michael Linnit and again it was a bit of a nightmare. Alan was a bit shocked that after *Butley*, in which he never drew breath, he was now being asked to play a more passive role and again was undecided initially. And then Clive Goodwin, who still looked after Simon Gray, was on holiday in the Caribbean and passed the script to Peter O'Toole – of all people – who immediately said, "I want to do it." I really couldn't face all that again and besides I thought Alan better casting, so I tried to lean on Pinter a bit to put the pressure on Alan. Then, back in London, O'Toole simply turned up in my office one day to say, "I'm not going to set the dogs on you but you should let me play this part." I said that the decision rested with Harold as the director to which O'Toole responded, "Harold Pinter can't direct the traffic." That didn't really do any cause he might have had much good.'

Eventually Bates made up his mind and agreed to play Hench, coming up again with a magnetic performance. Quietly still for a good part of the evening, his listening was an object lesson for younger actors; patiently and with ineffable politeness attending to his 'guests' while his life slips slowly into disorder, his eyes were a constant index to his thoughts. Gray claimed that he never set out consciously to write with Bates in mind but he said perceptively of him: 'He's the most human actor of his generation … there's a gorgeous vulnerability about him.' The best episodes involved Hench and his brother Stephen, a schoolmaster desperately hoping – and needing – to be appointed an assistant headmaster, secretly resentful of Hench's Oxbridge background and enviably comfortable lifestyle (Nigel Hawthorne and Bates played these scenes – cringingly funny often – with the finesse of two brilliant tennis champions, masters of spin and slice). Julian Glover as the dreadful hack writer, Ian Charleson the truculent lodger and Mary Miller, crisp and cool as Hench's wife ('You're one of those men who only give permission to little bits of life to get through to you') were also strong in Pinter's pitch-perfect production in Eileen Diss's carefully neutral apartment (she was Pinter's most regular designer, with a special gift for giving a fairly conventional setting a crucial dislocation or nudge from naturalism).

Otherwise Engaged played a week at the Oxford Playhouse prior to opening at the Queen's on Shaftesbury Avenue. The Oxford opening was tricky: 'Harold came with Antonia Fraser. We'd only just begun to grasp the situation that he and Vivien had separated. The *paparazzi* began to hover and the situation got much worse at the Queen's with photographers sneaking into the stalls during rehearsals, so much so that Harold and Antonia had to skip the previews. They waited for us to report afterwards in a nearby restaurant. Peter O'Toole *was* at the first preview, however. Despite all that peripheral fuss, *Otherwise Engaged* went well from the start, with good reviews and strong business. Then we replaced Alan with Michael Gambon (my idea – I still regretted we hadn't got to use him in *Collaborators*) and then, after him, Hywel Bennett (another Gray favourite).' Altogether it ran for over 1,029 performances at the Queen's and sub-sequently the Comedy and was also successful on Broadway where Tom Courtenay played Simon Hench. A Criterion revival under Simon Curtis in 2005, with Anthony Head's monster of a writer rather stealing the show from Richard E. Grant's Hench, was less successful.

Gray covered similar terrain in *Dog Days* (Oxford, 1977), which also had two brothers in the cast (Gray had an adored brother, Piers, a T.S. Eliot specialist at Hong Kong University, who shared his battles with alcohol and tobacco and about whom he wrote in a later play, *Japes*) and had a similar background in publishing. Michael chose to pass on that one, which brought him a ticking off from Gray's friend, the editor and critic Ian Hamilton who told him, 'You are Simon's producer and as I expect as a writer my publisher should publish everything I write so you as a producer should do all Simon's work.' Michael argued that the relationship between the author and publisher is different from that of writer and producer ('If one produces something it must have something of oneself in it'). Also – and he was not alone – he found *Dog Days* inferior to *Otherwise Engaged*.

Gray seemed to feel no resentment and the team of Gray, Pinter, Diss and Codron reunited for *The Rear Column* (Glove, 1978): 'There was little advance word about it. Harold had read it first and, for him, was hugely enthusiastic. I knew the play involved Stanley and colonialism, which sounded intriguing but when I read it I honestly couldn't say I was excited by the subject. It was absorbing and very well written but somehow not attention grabbing. But I liked it well enough to do it – it was certainly a departure in some ways for Simon – and we were offered the Globe. I suppose I felt that it wasn't a very intriguing theme for a West End play, especially following *Otherwise Engaged.*'

Nineteenth-century Africa is *Rear Column*'s setting, in the Yambuya Camp in the Congo where, under the command of Major Barttelot, a rear column is being assembled instead of, as most expected, joining up with Henry Morton Stanley's relief expedition to Emin Pasha. Also present is a mild and polite amateur, Jamieson, who has paid to join the expedition. Stanley's orders are for the men to wait until enough porters have been supplied by the local Arab slave trader to take supplies through to Stanley. Although their own supplies are inadequate Barttelot refuses to allow food for Stanley to be touched. His obsession with Stanley – he sees the orders as a form of persecution and with increasingly manic logic is determined to see them through – turns the men against him. After a year the slave trader Tippo Tib has still not provided enough porters; Barttelot's bottled tension has exploded and even Jamieson, a virtuous but fatally detached man, has taken part in a cannibal feast, part of the gradual decay of reason and honour throughout the play. Once again Gray tells a story the events of which cloak the most awful human darkness. Perhaps on this occasion Pinter was not the ideal director. The cast included some of his favourite actors including Barry Foster (his Barttelot pulsing with edgy energy) and Jeremy Irons (just before his screen breakthrough in *Brideshead Revisited*) as Jamieson, but for all the appeal of such performances and the evening's potential interest it seemed funereally paced (not helped by much crucial action occurring offstage) and often low in wattage. One of Michael's investors said to him, 'You had to do it, I suppose, but was it worth the doing?' Michael thought that it was and that his relationship with Gray and Pinter added to that, but he had to agree that for all its virtues and fine performances 'it never really caught the audience's imagination'. It ran for less than a hundred performances, closing at a loss.

Perhaps to restore his commercial credentials, or perhaps just to amuse himself, Gray's next play, *Stage Struck* (Vaudeville, 1979), mapped out completely new territory for him, certainly surprising Michael, with a comedy thriller. One of the few theatrical genres of which Michael felt unsure was the thriller. He had no snobbery about them but, not uniquely, he found them difficult to gauge on the page, just as others find it tricky to judge farce – both genres depend so much on physical action and development in rehearsal without which the text can seem like a form of geometry. He had turned down the most successful thriller of its era when he passed on Anthony Shaffer's *Sleuth*, even although Joe Scott-Parkinson, no slouch in assessing a script, told him to persevere with it ('I found it all a bit precious – it was called something like *Anyone for Tennis* then'). Afterwards, whenever he rejected a thriller he always added a consolatory PS – 'Remember that this comes from the man who turned down *Sleuth*'. He presented only a few in his career. He had high hopes of *Silhouette* (1997) by the able whodunit novelist and radio writer Simon Brett, crucially dependent on a vital piece of doubling. With Stephanie Beacham as the threatened heroine, it did good touring business but provided too few twists and surprises to keep audiences absorbed and it closed on tour.

His one major success in the field was from a reliable veteran, Francis Durbridge, famous from radio's *Paul Temple* and TV serials such as *The Scarf*, watched by millions. Durbridge's *House Guest* (Savoy, 1981) paid off its production costs even before it opened in London; an eighteen week pre-West End tour with a cast headed by Gerald Harper and Susan Hampshire (both with major television followings as well as stage names) did help that, of course, but it continued to do strong business at the Savoy also.

Michael invested in this project just as much attention and time as in anything by Ayckbourn, Gray or Stoppard. It was clear from early performances on tour that there were problems: 'It was decided that the second act needed radical alterations, an extra scene and a lot of rewriting. I can think of many much younger writers who would insist on the play being taken off to give them more time. Not him.' On the road as Durbridge refashioned the play, Michael was beadily vigilant, writing a particularly long list of 'notes' to director Val May after seeing an Eastbourne performance. These covered major questions of emphasis – he nagged especially about a crucial drop in tension during the penultimate scene – but there were detailed notes too on lighting, costumes, shoes and props, including the size of a vital dagger.

Slowly over the tour a conventional, seemingly routine thriller, set in classic territory for the genre, in a sumptuous house on St George's Hill in Weybridge, with its film star owners caught up in a kidnap plot, was refashioned into a constantly twisting affair in six scenes, each ending with a cliff-hanger, combining what Alan Bennett called Snobbery with Violence with some genuine and effectively theatrical surprises. It received totally polarised notices but it undoubtedly pleased its audiences. Emile Littler, whose investment was returned with considerable interest, wrote to Michael: 'I do congratulate you on having the pluck to do it. So many of us might have said, "Oh, this is impossible …" but whatever it is, it is mighty good entertainment. The audience ate up the proceedings with a knife and fork.'

Stage Struck was Gray's attempt at an out-and-out commercial thriller, adding a vein of knowing comedy very much in the style of plays like *Sleuth* or Ira Levin's *Deathtrap*. A decidedly rum affair, *Stage Struck* was set in a Home Counties converted barn (with a vital trapdoor in the ceiling) where Robert, an ex-actor and now resentful, unemployed stage manager is cooking dinner for (while planning a horrible revenge on) his exacting diva actress-wife, soon to return from her current starring West End performance. Alan Bates, surprisingly, had already agreed to star although Pinter passed ('with impeccable tact') on this occasion. Stephen Hollis, a friend of Gray's, directed an increasingly implausible tale of bluff and double bluff, some involving a creepy Australian tenant from a cottage in the grounds (cue rather too many anti-Oz gags from Robert) and some supposedly Gothic climactic effects (including something nasty from the attic), which had few authentic thrills. Bates's star power saw *Stage Struck* through six packed months but he refused to extend his contract ('I can't stay, much as I love you all' he said to the cast, 'this really is donkey work'). Michael recast with Ian Ogilvy as Robert. At that time Michael Codron Ltd owned the Vaudeville, bought from Peter Saunders (another of Michael's regular investors) and so a success such as *Stage Struck* solved, at least in the short term, any scheduling problems.

Much more to his taste was *Quartermaine's Terms* (Queens, 1981), for many Gray's best play, again reuniting the Codron/Pinter/Gray/Diss team, this time with Edward Fox, in an outstanding performance, as the star. Gray again went to the past, although one more recent than in *The Rear Column*. The setting was a Cambridge School of English in the early 1960s staffed by people initially chipper enough on the surface before we gradually sense that they all are living lives of quiet desperation (there are occasional echoes of Rattigan's *The Browning Version*, another study in English emotional repression set in a school). Loomis, co-owner of the establishment, fearful for the health of his gay partner (unseen); Anita, saddled to a blatant philanderer of a husband; a failed novelist; a spinster with an exploitative old mother; an accident-prone Northern newcomer; and deputy head Windscape, with a neurotic wife and unloving children, a weak man who reveals a cruel streak near the close. Most memorable is St John Quartermaine, another of Gray's detached men, of whom the aspirant novelist says, 'You have an amazing ability not to let the world impinge on you', a bachelor seemingly happy and unaware of all the heartache, agony even – love affairs, abortions, death – going on around him. It is a play of relatively little action; there were some critical comparisons with Chekhov (indeed, teasingly, there is a running joke in one scene about which Chekhov play is playing at the Cambridge Arts Theatre). There was some justice in the analogy; language supposedly is the tool of communication, but this becomes rather ironic in light of the play's setting in a school of language, with Gray's characters – like Chekhov's – often speaking but not really listening to each other.

The in-depth study of Quartermaine, deeply courteous, full of accommodating good nature (a useful confidant/babysitter/possible convert), but a hopelessly inept teacher, drifting seemingly only half-consciously through life, more than any other character in the Gray canon catches that sense of the strange or the inexplicable in the quotidian, never more affectingly than when in a scene with Melanie, the spinster teacher, he makes an odd speech – superbly scored by Pinter and Fox – full of hesitations, ellipses and even moments of seeming near-aphasia, about his memories of swans seen on childhood visits to an aunt, and tries to articulate some atavistic inner terror. But Melanie, too, is mostly unheeding; like the others she fails to comprehend that Quartermaine, who seems to be waving, is slowly drowning. Gray deliberately ends the play somewhat abruptly; Loomis, after his partner's death, retires and the school is left under Windscape. His first act is to fire Quartermaine, a shocking moment; the curtain falls on Quartermaine alone, sitting in silence, an unforeseeable future before him, no longer protected by the innocence that he has worn like a magic cloak.

The play was not universally admired. B.A. Young in the *Financial Times* liked the acting but felt short-changed ('A good play would have offered a bit more'), while Gray's old adversary James Fenton, then on *The Sunday Times*, fairly put his boot in. But others saw the poignancy in the play and the compassion behind its unsentimental scrutiny of drifting misfits and nobody could fault the acting – Prunella Scales, James Grout (with a splendid Iago smile for Windscape), Jenny Quayle and – hauntingly – Robin Bailey as the slightly old-maidish Loomis – which backed Fox's magical legerdemain as Quartermaine. It had a healthy seven-month run at the Queen's.

It was almost a decade before Gray's name appeared again on a Codron production. He had written a good deal for television in the meantime but

36. Dancing on thin ice – Edward Fox (Quartermaine) observed
by Robin Bailey (Loomis) in Simon Gray's
Quartermaine's Terms, 1981.

his main stage play from that period, *The Common Pursuit*, tracing literary friendships from Cambridge to metropolitan success (figures akin to Kenneth Tynan and Ian Hamilton, who had provided the Leavisite title, were featured along with an imperishable gibe at James Fenton) was not one picked up by Michael after its first production with a fine but not especially star-laden cast including Simon Williams and Nicholas Le Prevost at the Lyric, Hammersmith, directed by Pinter. Both author and director initially wanted Michael to produce – for Gray he was simply 'the best producer in the West End' – although Pinter predicted (accurately) that its cast of six equally sized roles would be a deterrent. The Lyric wanted to produce it under its own steam in the West End after Hammersmith, but the combination of a lack of available theatres and the Lyric's inexperience of commercial production forbade that. Later, with a younger cast mainly famous from television including Stephen Fry, Rik Mayall and John Sessions in Gray's own production, *The Common Pursuit* had a lengthy West End run.

For Michael *Hidden Laughter* (Vaudeville, 1990) represented the best of Gray. Like *Quartermaine's Terms* this was a play of people masking secrets and troubles, with some of that play's rueful compassion but with an even more troubling dark undertow. Wryly aware of his reputation in some eyes – as a purveyor of middlebrow plays for a bourgeois public – Gray had a central character in *Hidden Laughter*, Louise, a novelist, describe her fiction as 'marriages, infidelity, children – the usual middle-class stuff'. He also, in an interview, described *Hidden Laughter* as 'the most English play I have written'.

The play has two teenage children in the cast and their laughter from up a tree is the first sound we hear – the title, referring to the hidden laughter 'of children in foliage', is from T.S. Eliot's Meditation on Time and Memory in *Burnt Norton* ('Time present and time past are both perhaps present in time future'). It takes place in the garden of a Devon cottage ('Little Paradise') to which for over a decade at weekends come Louise, her literary agent husband Harry, a serial philanderer and their children, all observed by Ronnie the local vicar ('an agnostic vicar') who acts as caretaker in their absence. Towards the end of the first act Nigel, the son, is gored by a bull and maimed for life. Also Louise is diagnosed as having a brain tumour but by the close of the play is miraculously cured (Harry confides to Ronnie that the recovery is somehow disrupting her writing). A subtle study in selfishness, a deeply unsettling play emerges from the initial dappled seductive sunlight on the greenery.

Ronald Eyre had been scheduled to direct but he became ill and Gray decided to take over himself, not the wisest notion; he was not helped by a setting by Robin Don less beguiling than it might have been but Gray directed rather stiffly. And it had proved obstinately difficult to cast. Both Gray's top choices, Tom Courtenay and Edward Fox, turned Ronnie down, as did Michael's favourite idea, Derek Jacobi. When Felicity Kendal agreed to play Louise the process accelerated; Kevin McNally as Harry, two promising younger talents making West End debuts (Michael particularly enjoyed the casting process for untested actors) Sam West and Caroline Harker for the children, and a very funny Sam Dastor as Draycott, a permanently irate novelist seeking an enormous advance for his new novel (called *Bugger All*). Michael worked very hard to lure Peter Barkworth for the crucial role of Ronnie, the innocent and introverted vicar, and finally succeeded. It made the evening; nothing is harder to act without boring the audience than genuine goodness but Barkworth – an undervalued actor by many – brought to Ronnie a substrain of unvoiced but palpable despair, which made him the most interesting person on the stage, as he quietly insinuated himself into the interstices of the family's lives.

Once again, the critics were divided on Gray although it was a box office success. *The Sunday Times*'s John Peter saw in it a sad divine comedy while others found aspects of its symbolism (a hollow stump with a rat hiding inside, last evidence of a rotten tree) over-strident, missing the way that 'Little Paradise', intended as a restful haven, instead becomes a repository for obligations. Yet again the suggestion of Gray as a literary, witty writer of civilised plays set on country lawns or in comfortable drawing rooms, set the tone (admittedly his awkward staging of *Hidden Laughter* did not help). What the more perceptive saw was what Michael had seen from *Wise Child* in Gray's work – the underlying darkness, ferocity, even savagery in the writing (speaking of students, one of *Quartermaine's Terms* teachers remarks as they play genteel croquet, 'They'll discover how much incivility is possible on our tranquil English lawns'). After all, the seemingly archetypal Oxbridge-educated, literate Gray spent his formative years out of England, charging his perspective with the eye of an outsider (something which often – as with Pinter, Orton, Livings, Marcus and Stoppard – made an impression on Michael) and his wit with its acerbic edge. Written in 1990 it could be said of *Hidden Laughter* that its scrutiny of moral equivocations, casual adulteries, greed and confusion make it Gray's epitaph for the 1980s, to him as well as to others an unattractive, mean decade.

It was the last Codron/Gray collaboration, although Michael was a keen reader of Gray's non-fiction – first his series of incomparably funny, sometimes bilious books covering specific productions (Michael comes in for some ribbing in *An Unnatural Pursuit*, Gray's account of the first production of *The Common Pursuit*) and then the glorious sequence of memoirs under the umbrella title of *The Smoking Diaries*, detailing Gray's often baffled battles with the theatre, machinery, officialdom, doctors, drink and cigarettes. His funeral in 2008 Michael found 'very moving – so many memories, mostly happy ones. And Harold, although ill himself and very frail – he died later the same year – spoke beautifully.' A small consolation was that Gray had left one last volume – *Coda* – of the sequence to be published posthumously.

CHAPTER 14

THE LANCING BOYS

The novelist Ford Madox Ford – also a great editor (*The Transatlantic Review* was his creation) and talent spotter, early publisher of Ezra Pound and James Joyce – was once splendidly dubbed 'The Only Uncle of the Gifted Young', a description that would have well suited Michael as he grew older. Like Ford – 'simply mad about good writing' – he came increasingly to enjoy, alongside continuing existing producer-author relationships, spotting and fostering emergent talent. This would remain a hallmark of the Codron operation into his old age.

The 1970s made an especially fruitful time during which he developed his association with Christopher Hampton and became the first commercial producer to champion another young writer who took the pulse of the period so acutely, Hampton's contemporary and school friend David Hare (Michael called them 'The Lancing Boys'). Both writers were also originally associated with the Royal Court – at one point Hare was Hampton's assistant during the latter's period as the ESC's resident dramatist and later literary manager – on the Board of which Michael sat as a governor.

Michael had taken to Hampton from the start – 'he was rather lanky and spotty and studenty but we struck up quite a rapport' – and had commissioned a new play from him after *When Did You Last See My Mother?* However, when the resulting play was delivered Michael chose not to produce it. Written during a year spent in Hamburg and Paris before finishing at Oxford, *Total Eclipse* (1968) was a tightly structured piece, written in intense short scenes, tracing the turbulent and ultimately destructive relationship between Paul Verlaine and his astonishing, precocious fellow poet Arthur Rimbaud. Michael admired it but he felt, partly because of its cast size (fourteen), that its commercial chances were slim. He was right as it transpired – the original Royal Court production, despite an incandescent performance by Victor Henry as Rimbaud (convincingly suggesting genius – rarely easy on stage) in Robert Kidd's production, designed by the artist Patrick Procktor, played to sixty per cent capacity in Sloane Square. It was a play particularly championed by Peggy

Ramsay who, unusually, threw a party for its opening. She also helped engineer and support its 1981 revival at the Lyric, Hammersmith directed by David Hare (by then also her client) with her adored Simon Callow as Verlaine. It was a handsome production, ravishingly designed by Hayden Griffin (painted masterfully by David Laws) and the play received better reviews than in 1968, but it fared even less well at the box office.

Hampton's next play – *The Philanthropist* (1970) – remains one of Michael's personal favourites, occupying a special place in his affections ('It came as a delightful surprise'). Written in what Hampton described as 'the climate of abrasive candour' characterising the elision into the 1970s, set in an ivory-towered Oxbridge remote from a background of metropolitan unrest and violence (a fair percentage of the Cabinet has recently been mown down in the House) matching the world of Molière's *Le Misanthrope*, similarly peopled by bright, articulate characters in an insulated environment, *The Philanthropist* was astonishingly 'finished' a play from a young dramatist. Impeccably crafted, with strong finishes to every scene (including two startlingly vivid visual coups), packed with aphoristic wit and intellectual energy, with total success the play achieves Hampton's aim of applying classical method (Molière's scrutiny of a character stamped by one defining negative characteristic – misanthropy, hypochondria, avarice) to the examination of what might be labelled a virtue. His protagonist, philology don Philip, aims to be affable to everybody and to cause no offence but instead, whether discussing a student's play, dealing with unwanted sexual propositions or handling a self-aggrandising novelist at a dinner party, succeeds only in unwittingly offending people.

It was superbly cast – 'For once everything fell into place. It rarely happens but here *all* the first choices – Alec McCowen as Philip, Dinsdale Landen his fellow don, Charles Gray, Jane Asher, Penelope Wilton as the voracious Araminta – they all worked out with unusual felicity'. McCowen gave a masterly performance as the detachedly urbane Philip ('My trouble is I'm a man of no convictions. At least I think I am'), adept at anagrams (late in the play he comes up with a new corker – 'Imagine the theatre as real', an anagram of 'I hate thee, sterile anagram'), who comes to realise that brilliant though he may be academically, he is hopeless at human relationships. His absorption in his philological vocation has come to be simpler and safer than any immersion in life.

The Philanthropist packed the Royal Court – 'It was crystal clear that it was a play of real quality and worth a transfer. But not according to Donald Albery. I was naturally looking for a middle-size house like the Criterion or Wyndham's, which he controlled, but he simply said, "It has no future resonance" and that was that. So I said to the Royal Court, "I'm going to take a very deep breath and go to the Mayfair."' This was a major departure and a gamble. The Mayfair was simply a basic space with about 300 seats beneath the Mayfair Hotel off Piccadilly, near Berkeley Square. It was used mainly for daytime business conferences; it had a small stage with little wing space and no fly tower, there were few dressing rooms and it was off the West End beaten path. Furthermore, taking a play there involved striking the set after every evening performance to leave the theatre available for conferences.

The theatre was managed then by James Wollheim representing the Grand Metropolitan group, with Dallas Smith (later Hampstead Theatre's general manager before becoming a leading agent) as front of house manager, both hugely helpful over *The Philanthropist*. 'I got quite bullish about it – it must have come at a time in my life when everything was going well and it made me determined to overcome all the odds against it not working. We even had to set up a proper box office at the theatre, and so it was splendid when it really took off.' The play ran for nearly four years with, following McCowen, Nigel Hawthorne ('I was very taken with him') and George Cole ('I had a very good relationship with him – he was very fine in the play and he stayed for two years. You'd never get that now').

The New York production used most of the London cast although Victor Spinetti, known there from *Oh, What a Lovely War*, could not match Charles Gray's magnificent self-regard as the boorish novelist Braham. It seemed to promise success during previews but the all-important *New York Times* notice, from Clive Barnes, although fairly favourable, was headlined 'Literary Import'; Michael's co-producer, the *monstre sacré* David Merrick, regarded this as 'the kiss of death' and rapidly lost all interest in *The Philanthropist*. It ran only a few weeks on Broadway. It has had two West End revivals. In 1991 (Wyndham's) a somewhat flaccid production, seen first at Chichester,starred Edward Fox and in 2005 the Donmar revived yet another play first produced by the Codron management with Simon Russell Beale as Philip. On this occasion the play seemed as sharply funny as ever, with Russell Beale almost matching McCowen's suggestion of an echoing loneliness inside an apparently contented man, one who describes himself as a man with a memory full of rooms, all of them – except for himself – empty.

Ramsay was always distinctly patronising about *The Philanthropist*, referring to it as Michael's 'little play' ('How's it doing, dear, your little

37. 'A cast of first choices' – Tamara Ustinov, Alec McCowen,
Jane Asher, Charles Gray, Dinsdale Landen, Penelope
Wilton in *The Philanthropist*, 1970.

play?', to which he would always remind her during the long run that it
may have been small in size but was 'doing very well, thank you, and
making a good deal of money for all of us, including your client. And you').
But then Ramsay was always ambivalent about success and the perils of a
commercial theatre in which money must be a prime consideration, although she was equally wary of the subsidised world's use of public
money and of its safety nets, such as generous commissions, of which she
never entirely approved.

She was rather taken aback by Michael's strong support for *Savages*,
which he co-produced with the Royal Court in 1973 before transferring it
to the West End. Hampton indeed surprised many with the play, a passionate, eloquent piece set in early 1970s Brazil, centred round the kidnapping
of a British writer, Alan West, by a rebel outfit set against the background
of the genocide of Brazilian Indians. The play begins with torch-lit preparations for the tribal feast of the 'Quarap' and is punctuated by scenes
tracing the stages of the ceremony – one conducted by most Indian tribes
whose culture had not been eradicated – giving the play an enthralling
backbone of ritual, acting out legends of creation mixed with those of the
tribe itself involving procession and masquerade.

Alongside, Hampton traces the growing relationship between prisoner and kidnapper – one as complex as that between Winston and his torturer in Orwell's *Nineteen Eighty-Four*. He also widens the portrait of West in flashback scenes between him and characters including an anthropologist and, memorably, in a superb scene recalling something out of Conrad (later Hampton would work on David Lean's abortive *Nostromo* movie project) or of Evelyn Waugh's *A Handful of Dust* later episodes, in which West is entertained by a leathery old planter, Major Bragg, at his colonial bungalow with Gilbert and Sullivan on the gramophone.

Savages clearly involved an enormous amount of anthropological research – Claude Lévi-Strauss's work had become better known in England – but throughout it wears its learning lightly to become a play of piercing power, subtly probing one of the main themes of so much 1970s writing, a sense of sad disillusion with well-intentioned liberal champions of noble causes. Fusing eloquence with visual flair it remains, with Hare's *Knuckle*, one of the most potent plays of its time, surprisingly unrevived.

Again Hampton's work attracted a top-flight cast, including Geoffrey Palmer as an unctuously superior American missionary and Tom Conti the Brazilian kidnapper. But inevitably the evening was dominated by Paul Scofield's West, the unique voice of soft dark velvet bound with brass never more arresting than in the passages in which, choral-style, West participates in the ritualistic episodes throughout the play. *Savages* remains another high on Michael's list of favourites: 'It gladdened my heart when I read it. A piece of sharp, but totally accessible political writing.'

Its Royal Court run coincided with a nightmare time for the Codron firm. They had an established hit at the Globe with Charles Laurence's comedy *My Fat Friend*, a clever confection of an overweight girl (books such as *Fat is a Feminist Issue* were not uncommon in that period of burgeoning feminism) aided in her love life by her outrageous gay neighbour, played by Michael's friend Kenneth Williams. The old neurotic Williams had never gone away – he had left the cast of a West End comedy *The Platinum Cat*, shortly after it had opened to poor notices in 1968 (although it was by his friend Beverley Cross) and he was now playing up again. He had been difficult through *My Fat Friend* rehearsals, at times openly contemptuous of his director Eric Thompson, had quietened down after good personal notices but now was testing his friendship with Michael to its limits with endless complaints: 'I was subjected to the possible defection from *My Fat Friend* of Kenneth and I knew we were standing on the edge of the abyss. He'd taken violently against Eric Thompson again and also his leading lady Jennie Linden, egged on by his chum Maggie

Smith, appearing in *Private Lives* at the Queen's next door. All the time he was moaning more and more and being less well with his old colon problem. I said to our Globe landlord Toby Rowland of Stoll Moss that I had a feeling Ken was going to jump ship and he said, "No, no – he won't do that, he's your friend" – but I got a letter from Peter Eade, his agent, saying Ken was ill and definitely would not be returning. So I thought, "Well, now I have to act quickly and tell Toby Rowland the bad news about Ken's defection from *My Fat Friend* but also, thankfully, the good news that I could bring in *Savages* with Scofield from the Royal Court to the Globe." On the way to Toby's office I passed the Warner Cinema with a long queue waiting to see Lindsay Anderson's film *If.* John Gielgud was in the line and saw me, so I told him I was just going to tell Toby that Ken would be leaving the show to have an operation because he had this thing up his arse. To which Gielgud replied, holding the cinema queue enthralled, "The trouble with Kenneth Williams is that he's never had *anything* up his arse."

'Then, when I met Toby, he floored me by turning down *Savages* (that old chestnut – "too wordy") so I now had to face playing out *My Fat Friend* with the understudy to zero business (heavily cutting into the profit the play had made so far), find another home for *Savages, and* tell Paul Scofield, who liked the Globe, that we couldn't go there. So I met him at the Goring Hotel near Victoria – his train always came into Victoria and the Goring is forever associated for me with him – but he took the alternative proposal of the Comedy Theatre very well. And although it was a tight squeeze with a large cast, it did look very well there and we did terrific business.'

Three years later Hampton's *Treats* (1967) presented Michael with a dilemma: 'I felt an obligation to do it even although I didn't think it was a wonderful play', although he cloaked his doubts and co-produced it with the ESC. Short, taut, again in brief scenes punctuated this time by 1970s pop (including The Monotones with 'The Book of Love' – also prefaced to the published text), *Treats* is a three-hander play on love, centred round a young woman, Ann, living with the amenable but dull Patrick, whose life is invaded by the Lawrentian figure of her ex-lover Dave. Also set in an enclosed world – Ann's barely furnished flat – while outside there is urban unrest (anti-IRA protests in the distance here), *Treats* traces the triangular shifts and readjustments, slowly letting the audience see the power struggles illustrate that a seemingly exploited character may emerge as the strongest in the play, through some acidly funny episodes (especially those involving the extravagant Dave). It is a play easy to admire but difficult to warm to – all three characters can seem similarly solipsistic – and although

38. Paul Scofield in *Savages*, 1973.

Michael transferred it to the Mayfair (following *The Philanthropist*) it never built into a solid success. It was a strong cast – Jane Asher, James Bolam and a gangly Stephen Moore especially fine as the hapless Patrick – but never an especially happy one, and the reviews were so-so at best. Ramsay was infuriated by them and even called Harold Hobson to point out what his review had missed, ordering him to go back and then re-review it ('He did and he wrote a review somewhat more enthusiastic, but it still didn't save us. Audiences just didn't take to it so the word of mouth didn't build business'). *Treats* has had a revival at Hampstead (1987) and was also seen again in the West End (Garrick Theatre, 2007) with ex-pop singer and *Dr Who* star Billie Piper as Ann, but it did only patchy business even with considerable publicity surrounding Piper.

It would be nearly a decade before Hampton's next play – he worked on screenplays and translations in the meantime – which was his worldwide success of *Les Liaisons Dangereuses* adapted from Laclos's epistolary novel for the RSC. Michael's life had changed in that time. It saw some of the peaks of his professional career – at one stage in 1974 all four Shaftesbury Avenue theatres (Lyric, Apollo, Globe and Queen's) were occupied by Codron productions, while Michael Frayn's *Noises Off* at the Savoy was one of his biggest ever and longest-running successes. But at the time of *Les Liaisons*: 'I was in the middle of the worst phase of my life with David, when I was having an affair involving all sorts of subterfuge and secrecy. Peggy had told me about *Les Liaisons* so I went up to Stratford to see it at The Other Place and – I don't know – I don't think my judgement was then at its most acute and also it was all about intrigue and it was an adaptation rather than an original play, and altogether I just wasn't able to enthuse enough to commit to it. So Frank Gero, the American producer, got it and yes, it was a hit in the West End and on Broadway but I couldn't shed many tears over it.'

There were tears and anxieties over his private life throughout the volatile 1980s. In 1981 he had the appalling shock of his parents' deaths together in circumstances never entirely resolved. Haco and Lily had been out for dinner; Lily drove them home and, leaving her to park the car in the integral garage, Haco went through the door from the garage into the house. Then, whether by accident or design the engine was left running and next day both bodies were discovered in the carbon-monoxide filled house and garage. Lily's depression, never totally allayed since her mother's death, had resurfaced (on one occasion leading to ECT treatment) but on balance the likelihood is that the deaths were due to a tragic accident.

It was a devastating shock for Michael and for his brother. David was married happily with children –'he did the Jewish filial thing and gave my parents the grandchildren they wanted so much' – while always the unvoiced issue of Michael's homosexuality coloured his relationship with his parents. But it had done nothing to break the bonds between them and the love he felt for them. It marked for him a very low period indeed – as many friends and colleagues noticed – during which David was always there to provide comfort and support.

Also unfailingly, David backed Michael in some radical changes for the Codron firm. The closest Michael had come to managerial control over bricks and mortar was a time spent as a director of Theatres Consolidated, part of the Abrahams family property group for which John Hallett worked. Then in 1983 Michael Codron Ltd acquired (for £600,000, a good price, helped by the National Westminster Bank) from Peter Saunders (still then producer of *The Mousetrap*) the Vaudeville Theatre in the Strand. In excellent repair and in a prime position, the Vaudeville with 700 seats was an ideal size for much of the kind of new work favoured by Michael. He knew very well the headaches of theatre ownership – lack of suitable 'product' at the right time particularly – but as he said at the time: 'When I do find a play, now I don't have to go cap in hand to any theatre owner. Far from being a deterrent to producing, owning a theatre myself will be a spur.'

The following year the Aldwych Theatre came up for sale and John Hallett suggested that Michael buy it from the Abrahams Group but Michael did not have ambitions to become a property tycoon. He did, however, tell Hallett, 'it's not for me but I know who would want it' – his friend James Nederlander who at that time owned ten Broadway theatres. Michael had partnered the Nederlander organisation on Broadway co-productions happily and now he entered into an agreement whereby he would manage the Aldwych for them, initially for three years (a quarter of a century later and the arrangement continues). Peter Saunders had retained his Vaudeville offices, entered from Maiden Lane behind the theatre, as part of the deal when selling the theatre, and so the Codron outfit now moved from Regent Street to the spacious high-ceilinged offices above the Aldwych, previously occupied by the Royal Shakespeare Company. Michael had a large, light room on the Aldwych/Drury Lane corner while David (when it was suggested he and Michael share an office, his immediate response – it was important not to live in each other's pocket all the time – was 'Not in a million years' – 'which I took to be a No') had an equally

234

attractive room on the next floor, still leaving space for secretaries, production manager (Gareth Johnson, a former admired and efficient company
manager on many Codron productions, proved equally popular when he
succeeded Joe Scott-Parkinson) and in-house accountants.

Professional consolidation was not matched in his private life, which
began seriously to unravel in the 1980s (to many observers, undoubtedly
triggered by the deaths of his parents), ending with David leaving him
(although they continued as professional partners for a time subsequently).
Michael had begun an affair with a good-looking and quick-witted young
cockney, Mark Brough, who had sold fruit from a stall outside the Strand
Theatre (now Novello) just down from the Aldwych. Based in Romford
with his common-law wife and child, Mark had also done casual backstage
work at the Strand before working as one of the theatre's stage doormen.
Michael had Stanley Price's comedy of a midlife redundancy crisis in an
increasingly technological age, *Why Me?* with Richard Briers playing there
in 1985 (no *Boys From the Black Stuff* perhaps, but a West End first in tackling
professional unemployment) and, always keen to discreetly monitor his
productions, he slipped into the auditorium one afternoon to watch an
understudy rehearsal ('I have to confess I was particularly interested to see
how the rather comely ASM/Understudy Nick Berry was coming along').
On leaving he stopped by the stage door where Mark told him they had a
birthday in common, proposing, 'How about a birthday drink, then?'
Rather taken aback Michael reminded him, 'You do know I'm gay?' 'But
then Mark said four words which more or less changed my life: "I have my
moments." It was, no doubt, some kind of male menopause thing, but I
suddenly realised that my fantasy of a good-looking cockney boy with a
big smile could come true. It genuinely unhinged me – it was, without any
doubt, a *coup de foudre*. It may sound rather naïve but it showed me a whole
new aspect of myself – I was in my fifties and I'd begun to think that
nothing would ever really happen to me again.'

The giddy intoxication of his affair with Mark Brough could make life
difficult at times, when it could be 'something of a hide-and-seek existence,
with a kind of furtiveness which was not always pleasant like when I went
up to see *Les Liaisons* with Mark in Stratford where we were seen by
Duncan Weldon and his driver who both knew Mark from the Strand. And
then when I was working on the film of Michael Frayn's *Clockwise* with
John Cleese and some favourite actors, Alison Steadman, Michael Aldridge
and Penelope Wilton included – I'd never done a movie before, and you go
on location where there are all sorts of opportunities for infidelity. So Mark,

39. Mark Brough.

who rather liked the intrigue, would come up. I really was totally besotted – he was mad about history and battles and I'd go off with him to battle sites like Culloden.'

After twenty-five years together it was unlikely that David had no idea that something was afoot. And shortly after an assignation with Mark in the Mountbatten Hotel in Seven Dials, Michael and David were dining in Mon Plaisir more or less opposite, when the restaurant manager – unaware of making any *gaffe* – mentioned having seen Michael and his friend in the Mountbatten. As David reminded Michael: 'Don't you realise that this is a village we're living in?'

Gradually but inevitably their relationship foundered on the rocks of the deception and untruth involved in infidelity rather than the unfaithfulness itself. David moved out of Chester Terrace into a Redcliffe Gardens flat. The shock of the physical move made Michael comprehend 'I'd made a mess of it all' (constantly he kept recalling a friend's remark: 'There's no fool like a middle-aged fool'). There were occasional meals together – 'I would beg him to come back – don't forget I was seeing him every day still. But I began to comprehend that David was not going to return.'

A sympathetic shoulder was provided at this time by Simon Cadell, then undergoing a similar personal crisis (happily repaired) in his marriage. Michael recalls: 'I cried a lot and then came to realise that you have to bounce back no matter how much you've mucked things up.' Michael came to an amicable financial settlement with David ('so we wouldn't have to squabble over the house and things like that') and also gave him half the business that he had helped run so efficiently, taking on the lion's share of administrative work on the Vaudeville and Aldwych ventures, which Michael had to learn after David decided to retire.

The affair with Mark Brough – 'he moved in with me for a few months but it didn't really work out' – gradually came to an end, compounding a miserable domestic time living in houses in London and Kent, which held such resonant associations with David. Also their physical parting, perhaps inevitably, somewhat reduced their professional symbiosis. No longer were there such long discussions about plays, playwrights, and casting – the whole 'marriage broking' of production .

David had enthusiastically supported Michael over Christopher Hampton, for instance – he often cited Scofield's West in *Savages* as one of his Desert Island performances. And he was if anything even more positive about the talent behind the early plays of David Hare with which the Codron management was involved. Before he became the knighted principal contemporary writer for the National Theatre, Hare was associated with radical theatre, with Hampstead Theatre, with the Royal Court (both with Michael's support on the Board) and with the West End. Of Michael's Lancing Boys he was the more precociously poised theatrically: 'He was very young when I first met him but he was already married and socially extremely adept, certainly more than the rather diffident student the young Hampton was.'

It was Hare's first agent, Clive Goodwin, who alerted Michael to this new voice, the most distinctively lucid of that generation of writers including David Edgar, Trevor Griffiths, John McGrath and Hare's occasional collaborator Howard Brenton, whose work in the unlovely, compromised 1970s through the era of Margaret Thatcher and into Tony Blair's New Labour, took the national temperature. In the late 1960s Hare had helped to found Portable Theatre, a radical touring company (later it restructured into Joint Stock) with his Cambridge friend, composer Tony Bicat, with writers including Brenton and Snoo Wilson soon coming on board. Hare seems to regard his Portable work, including his first plays *How Brophy Made Good* or *What Happened to Blake?*, as juvenilia, opting rather to cite Brenton's *Christie in Love* (1968), which he directed – confrontational, fuelled by a ferocious comedic energy – as the best of Portable, whose work he once defined as addressing 'closely knit social situations in a process of extreme decay'. This would seem initially to have little to do with the commercial theatre, and yet as Hare's voice established itself in the 1970s his recurrent fascination with insulated communities and institutions seemed to chime increasingly with a wider audience.

Even the prentice *Brophy* – Hare later described it as 'a primitive satire on the unlikelihood of revolution in Britain' – had attracted Michael's attention when Goodwin sent him the script and he immediately commissioned a play from Hare. *Slag* (1970) was first produced at Hampstead Theatre, when its picture of three teachers at the exclusive Brackenhurst School for Girls, opening the play with a collective vow (echoing *Love's Labour's Lost*) abjuring men and to establish 'a truly socialist society', was generally and rather myopically viewed as a genial satire on feminism and the wilder shores of Women's Liberation. But, not unlike Pam Gems's all-female play *Dusa, Fish, Stas and Vi* (Hampstead and Mayfair, 1977), which Michael also produced, its writing is too layered to be labelled so simply.

Written in six sharp scenes (Noël Coward made Hare laugh when he described *Slag* as five very good scenes and one bad one – 'I'm afraid he was being generous'), it is charged with Hare's unmistakable theatrical energy, which informs dialogue and the script's strong element of play and games alike. It is also – which certainly appealed to Michael – often very, very funny (indeed Hare wrote some of the best comedy of the 1970s, contrary to his often aloofly mandarin image), not least in its picture of the sheer bitchiness of public school life. The Hampstead production was well cast but slackly directed, never quite finding Hare's comedic tone. Much happier was its production the following year, co-presented by Michael and the ESC at the Royal Court in a fast razor-sharp production by Max Stafford-Clark and a cast of Barbara Ferris, Lynn Redgrave and Anna Massey (Michael was happy to join the venture, even knowing that all the cast were unavailable to transfer). This time *Slag*'s special atmosphere, suggesting at times a marriage between Jean Genet and Angela Brazil, was securely in focus; it played to very strong Sloane Square business and definitely established Hare's name.

Michael was involved with Hampstead also in the production of *The*

Great Exhibition (Hampstead, 1972), a play which seems to have slipped through the net into oblivion. Hare's central character is Hammett, an increasingly disillusioned Labour MP ('Can you imagine a disillusioned Tory?' asked David Warner, who created Hammett, sensibly pointing out that while Labour tends or pretends to be idealistic, Tories are practical). The play's structure (Act One is described as 'Public Life' and Act Two as 'Private Life') may have confused some, together with some of its bold, vaudeville-style leaps beyond naturalism, as a rapidly unravelling Hammett hires a private eye to investigate the possible adultery of his casting director wife Maud. The first act has some terrific comedy riffs – at one point considerable quantities of marijuana are being smoked when a visitor arrives ('It's the Home Secretary'). Quizzed on his seeming withdrawal from the Party, Hammett turns on his visitor – 'Show me one MP who resembles a man. Not a pedant or a hypocrite or a mental cripple or a liar or an egomaniac or a performer or a fool but a sort of well, let's say human being.'

It is a technically demanding play – the whole set of Hammett's study has to disappear on the instant to transform the stage into Clapham Common where Hammett's disintegration sees him take up 'flashing', ending with his exhibiting himself to an ex-deb friend of Maud's. And it is a flawed piece, certainly – the character of Maud's lover, a spaced-out Australian ex-banker who has enthusiastically joined the Alternative Society, rather outstays his welcome and the second act never quite matches the invention of the first. *The Great Exhibition* began Richard Eyre's association as director with Hare and the cast included David Warner as Hammett and Penelope Wilton, with a good line in withering scorn, not least for the contemporary theatre world in which Maud works. Michael admired both play and production but sensed that its commercial chances were slim (it did not fill Hampstead to overflowing and did not transfer).

When Michael received the script of *Knuckle* (1974) – which he had also commissioned – he was at once delighted by it. At this time Hare moved to Peggy Ramsay (after Goodwin's less than committed response to the play) and she too was enthused, to a degree that led to her breaking a personal professional rule of never investing in a client's play (Michael's rule for investors was that they had to invest in all of his productions rather than pick and choose but on this occasion he made an exception for Ramsay). For Ramsay, Hare became for a time a cause as well as a client, rather as David Mercer had been, as Michael noticed: 'I don't quite know why Peggy championed him so much. Her campaigning on his behalf was much more active than for any other writer I can recall. She saw – and it was very bright of her – that he was going to be a major political dramatist. But she didn't have to persuade me about *Knuckle* – I thought it had all the ingredients of a good, solid commercial success'. Ramsay, for all her passion for the play, was more pragmatic; when Hare asked her if she thought *Knuckle* would be a success she retorted, 'Good Lord, no. It's going to be a disaster ... it's way ahead of its time.'

Like so many early Hare plays *Knuckle* begins mysteriously, unsettlingly – it takes time for an audience to realise that a play that has a mercenary and hard-boiled international arms dealer (Curly) as a central character investigating the mysterious death of his beloved sister Sarah, with scenes set in a shadowy nightclub is not taking place down the mean streets of Los Angeles familiar from Raymond Chandler or Dashiell Hammett but in Guildford and leafy Surrey. Something of the world of Roman Polanski's *Chinatown* hangs over *Knuckle*'s daring recasting of the staples of an American pulp thriller or *film noir* in a Home Counties setting, with Curly's tough neo-Senecan stoicism often echoing Philip Marlowe as incarnated by Humphrey Bogart, not least in some acrid, direct address monologues. But, as Michael noticed, just as *Slag*'s agenda went beyond clever satire, so *Knuckle* transcends parody or hommage to locate Curly's attitude in a very specific moral climate rooted in an England tainted by the rot and corruption of the scandals of venal characters like John Poulson or John Bloom. Curly may sell guns but Patrick, his father – as confirmed in a wonderful near-climactic scene between them, one of the best episodes in all Hare's work – is directly implicated, through his grubbier drug deals, in Sarah's death. Jenny, a friend of his sister's, whom he meets in the Shadow of the Moon Club and to whom he becomes close, tells him in a scene set on a moonlit Eastbourne beach as she conjures up ghosts of Guildford, that people like Curly and herself are the spiritual inheritance of the south, 'children of John Bloom and Jack Cotton', heirs of a new breed of ruthless self-made entrepreneurs. As Hare later said of *Knuckle*: 'It is organised round the two types of British capitalism which ten years later were to clash so violently: the paternalistic kind with its old social networks and its spurious moralising, and the new aggressive shameless variety, which would gain such ascendancy in the 1980s, giving the play a prophetic quality not immediately recognisable in those years before the emergence of Thatcherism after the election of 1979.'

Despite the tense, tight writing and the staging challenges – it covers quite a few locations, interior and exterior – *Knuckle* proved problematic to

40. 'Down these mean streets …' Curly and Jenny
(Edward Fox and Kate Nelligan) in the Shadow of the Moon Club
in David Hare's *Knuckle*, 1974.

set up. The Royal Court was barely lukewarm about a co-production (Lindsay Anderson, still involved at the Royal Court and prone to see himself as its conscience, was never keen on Hare's work) and so Michael decided to go it alone in the West End. Surprisingly he had several refusals from established directors before Michael Blakemore agreed to take it on, although that may not have been the ideal choice. A superb director of text, Blakemore can on occasion be let down by his visual sense – Michael felt that his production of Anthony Minghella's *Made in Bangkok* was damagingly over-designed, as was Frayn's *Afterlife* for the National Theatre, and that on *Knuckle* the design which John Napier and Blakemore came up with was both dull to look at (a drab unit box into which units trucked or flew) and clumsy. Also, while nominally a box office draw after *Day of the Jackal* on screen, Edward Fox never quite captured the ruthless core of Curly, although Douglas Wilmer as his father – a still, quietly spoken Henry James reader cloaking an articulately lethal exploiter – gave a knock-out performance. Jenny was played by a newcomer to London after some striking Bristol Old Vic work, Kate Nelligan. Her then agent Norman Boyack had pushed her heavily for the role and after her audition Michael agreed 'we must have her – it'll be worth any risk'; Blakemore certainly gave her a dream entrance for a West End debut, slowly revealing her as smoky lighting came up on the Shadow of the Moon Club with 'We'll Gather Lilacs' swelling on the speakers, sitting on a barstool drawing on a cigarette like a modern incarnation of Lauren Bacall. Her performance of Jenny was startlingly tough and tender, matched perfectly to the writing (it was not surprising that Nelligan should go on to *Licking Hitler* on screen and *Plenty* on stage for Hare).

The air of a slight hex over *Knuckle* continued; it opened on 4 March, 1974, the evening of the day Edward Heath eventually resigned to allow Harold Wilson to form a Labour government after the rancorous 'Who Runs Britain?' General Election, following a period scarred by strikes and a three-day working week. The reaction was not quite the disaster predicted by Ramsay but was still bitterly disappointing. Despite a few exceptions (Harold Hobson included) the reviews for *Knuckle* were poor and often patronising, certainly not enough to give a sluggish box office a kick. Ramsay tried to cheer up a depressed Hare ('Fuck the critics. They've all compromised or sold out. They are failures'), as did Michael who kept it running for much longer than was commercially sensible (until late June) but he too felt that this was a new play by a young writer that should be seen by as many as possible. Unquestionably a key play of post-war British theatre, *Knuckle* has had one UK tour but no major London revival.

The ESC and Michael combined again on Hare's *Teeth 'n' Smiles* (1976), a play with music (by Tony and Nick Bicat) directed by Hare ('Written 'n' Directed' was his billing) first at the Royal Court and later at Wyndham's for a successful run. Again Hare initially slightly wrong-foots the audience – only gradually is it clear that the setting is Cambridge at a College Ball (specifically set on the night of 9 June, 1969). The rock band at the heart of the play, hired for the evening, includes a Janis Joplin-ish lead singer, Maggie, finger pressed on a self-destruct button (played – and sung – with a raw, nervy vitality by Helen Mirren) and the composer Arthur (Jack Shepherd and, subsequently, Martin Shaw), a man of acute intelligence under his rock 'n' roll cool. *Teeth 'n' Smiles* hurtles along with even more than the customary Hare energy – and was even more vital after Hare put in cuts before the West End re-opening – as the band gets busted for drugs while, out of it on Johnnie Walker, a drunk Maggie loses control, insulting the audience and torching the hospitality tent. But as Arthur makes clear towards the close (the play ends with the evening's best song, 'Last Orders on the Titanic') it is not really Cambridge that has been damaged, rather the band itself. Its supposedly liberating music comes off second best from the encounter. Arthur can see that the deep-rooted hierarchies of closed institutions such as Cambridge will be there still after the band members follow Maggie to collapse in a morass of self-indulgence and useless recrimination. A Manchester Royal Exchange production in 2008 demonstrated that the incisors of *Teeth 'n' Smiles* were still sharp, still dangerous.

Michael much enjoyed his encounters with Hare and their collaborations on aspects of England. Peter Hall took Hare into the National Theatre with *Plenty* (1977) and after Richard Eyre succeeded Hall, the dramatist's star rose even higher on the South Bank, continuing to feature strongly in Nicholas Hytner's regime. To Michael's regret *Teeth 'n' Smiles* marked their last partnership although not the end of their friendship (both are Trustees of the Peggy Ramsay Foundation) and he tried to revive the association: 'I thought *Racing Demon* was a really tremendous play and I made some noises about moving that from the National but it came to nothing.' Then after Ramsay's death when the office combined with Jenne Casarotto's agency to become Casarotto-Ramsay, her former business partner and successor Tom Erhardt 'sent me David's two-hander *Skylight* (1995), which I loved. Tom said it would probably go to the National especially if Michael Gambon could be lured for the male lead about which he was undecided. Tom asked me to talk to Mike about it which I did and he did finally accept the part with Lia Williams opposite him. But then I got a call from Richard

41. Sex 'n' Drugs 'n' Rock 'n' Roll – Hugh Fraser and Helen Mirren
in David Hare's *Teeth 'n' Smiles*, 1976.

Eyre saying Robert Fox's solicitor had been in touch saying that as I was on
the National's Board and was already producing Patrick Marber's *Dealer's
Choice* in the West End after the National, that for me to transfer *Skylight*
too could be described as a kind of 'insider trading'. Richard said he was
sorry but we'd have to accept that *Skylight*, which he was directing, would
be produced by Robert Fox should it transfer. Which it did. There was a
little residual hurt – and I'd love to have produced David's *Amy's View*
instead of which I could only be a sort of landlord when Robert Fox moved
it to the Aldwych – but there was a rapport between David, Richard and
Robert, they were closer to each other in age and Robert is more high
profile in New York and on film.'

244

Patrick Marber and the National similarly later went to Fox on *Closer*'s commercial transfer. But Michael insists, 'I feel very strongly that writers don't really defect, they go if they want to. I used to hear Binkie Beaumont rail against Peter Shaffer when he took *Black Comedy* to Chichester, calling Earl's Terrace (where Shaffer lived) "Traitor's Gate", and I'd hate to think like that.'

The loss of rising writers to the subsidised sector was not exactly new to Michael when both Hampton and Hare began to move towards the National Theatre or the RSC. And in any event there were other writers in Michael's sights, some already known and others yet to make a mark.

CHAPTER 15

ALAN, ALEC, WILLY, MIKE, ETC. ... AND MICHAEL

Alan Bennett, a writer whose work Michael wished he could have presented from the start – he was later involved with four of his plays – was another who moved from Shaftesbury Avenue to the welcoming embrace of the National Theatre where all his work from the double bill of *Single Spies*, including *The Madness of George III*, *The History Boys*, and *The Habit of Art* has been first produced.

And yet his initial dramatic effort, *Forty Years On*, which he had first offered to the National Theatre, was promptly turned down by Kenneth Tynan, then the National's literary manager, on the grounds that 'it wasn't their cup of tea but might have commercial possibilities'. The veteran director Frith Banbury suggested that Bennett send it to Toby Rowland, the cheerful, always optimistic American-born producer, then with the Stoll Moss theatre group, who snapped it up and presented it in the West End (Apollo, 1968) with John Gielgud in hilarious form as the old-style headmaster taking his farewell of a rather faded public school, Albion House, metaphor for a changing England. It was Michael's sort of play – multi-layered, a kind of play within a play as the boys and staff present 'Speak for England, Arthur', part-revue, part-play, interlocking periods of English social history from 1900 to the present.

Bennett combined clever parodies – Wildean comedy, 'Snobbery With Violence' derring-do based on John Buchan and 'Sapper's' work, Bloomsbury satire with characters based on Lady Ottoline Morrell or Harold Nicholson and Vita Sackville-West – with the headmaster's aghast reaction to this new irreverence ('When we have to resort to the lavatory for our humour, the writing is indeed on the wall'), his own designated contributions ranging from a wicked send-up of Lawrence of Arabia backing into the limelight to an elegiac close to the first half on the eve of war in 1939 with which Gielgud – voice here like the 'silver trumpet muffled in silk' of Alec Guinness's phrase – rarely failed to bring a collective lump to the audience's throat. Fusing nostalgia with subversive comedy, *Forty Years On* for Michael confirmed Bennett as a major coming dramatist.

Of all the *Beyond the Fringe* boys, while Jonathan Miller had an international career as director of opera and theatre and Peter Cook and Dudley Moore were a successful double act on British and American stage and screen, Bennett then seemed to have the lowest profile, despite some excellent sketch comedy for television in *On the Margin* (which Michael admired). *Forty Years On* would rapidly change that.

Stoll Moss had contracted Bennett for three plays but the second, *Getting On* (Queen's, 1970), with the same *Forty Years On* director (Patrick Garland) and designer (Julia Trevelyan Oman) was a much less happy experience. It was a tighter and tougher play, perhaps confounding expectations in that although often funny, it was at root a serious study of 1960s compromise and political idealism. The central character, George Oliver, is a self-absorbed Labour MP, blinkered domestically and often unfeeling; like *Girl in My Soup*'s Danvers it was the kind of part calculated to make middle-aged, image-conscious stars run a mile and indeed several leading actors politely passed. Kenneth More was finally cast and proceeded, rather as on *Out of the Crocodile* for Michael, subtly and sometimes most unsubtly to manipulate the text to keep Oliver sympathetic. As Bennett came ruefully to grasp, 'Casting Against the Part' rarely works with stars but on *Getting On*, More even began to alter lines, eventually barring Bennett from the Theatre Royal during a fraught try-out in Brighton (as Bennett wrote of Brighton audiences then – 'It sometimes seems that their chief pleasure in going to the theatre is in leaving it as noisily as possible'). Inevitably relations between the producers, Garland and Bennett became strained but there is little any director or producer can do with a certain kind of star – Rex Harrison, Robert Morley and Ralph Richardson were others – set on going their own way, secure in the knowledge that their name is mainly selling the tickets.

Contractually Bennett owed Stoll Moss another play but the experience of *Getting On* made him reluctant to deal with them again. He sought advice from John Mortimer who suggested he write 'a play impossible to produce'. When Rowland received the resulting play – set in a teashop with its chief characters the members of a ladies' string quartet, the script insisting that all four had also to be able to play to the very highest of standards – he had to say he could not produce it, letting Bennett off his contractual hook. Bennett – on Mortimer's advice – did tell Rowland that he wanted Michael Codron, with whom his then agent Michael Linnit had been in touch, to produce his next play. In turn Michael felt morally obliged, given Stoll Moss's investment in Bennett to date, to allow the firm 'a substantial stake' in its production, also agreeing to play a Stoll Moss Theatre (by no means every producer would have made such gestures).

What arrived on Michael's desk was initially teasing – a play with practically no stage directions of any kind beyond specifying a seaside Hove setting.

Habeas Corpus (Lyric, 1973) is another play of the varied texture to which Michael so responded; superficially it is a farce complete with the classic British farcical staple ingredients of dropped trousers, adultery *interruptus*, comic charlady, etc. (but without the usual accoutrements of slamming doors and concealments), set in the Hove household of Arthur Wicksteed, a middle-aged GP. The spiralling complex plot also involves the large-sized, sex-starved Mrs Wicksteed, daughter Connie (sadly flat-chested) hypochondriacal son Dennis, local vicar Canon Throbbing (usually arriving on 'his trusty Vespa'), rival medico Sir Percy Shorter, a falsie-fitter (Andrew Sachs) and, returning to a changed England from the colonies, the redoubtable Lady Rumpers ('When I hear the word 'arse' I know which way the wind is blowing'), and her gorgeously pneumatic daughter Felicity. Like Joe Orton crossed with Donald MacGill *Habeas Corpus* is often deliriously funny – not least in an inspired episode of crossed wires when a visiting falsie-fitter mistakes the awesomely bosomed Mrs Wicksteed for Connie after her enlargement from previously delivered falsies and advances on her admiringly ('These are magnificent!'), asks permission to adjust them, leaning forward with 'May I?' before being clutched to her embonpoint as she exclaims, 'At last – a tenant for my fallow loins!' But also throughout, mostly in Betjamesque reflections from Wicksteed solo on Brighton pier, there is a potent substrain, a constant suggestion of the skull beneath the skin, a strain of *memento mori*, the awareness of the transitoriness of the flesh.

With director Ronald Eyre aboard, casting began: 'Alan and Ron Eyre came to see me and said they wanted Denholm Elliott as Wicksteed. I said I'd had a hunch from first reading it about Alec Guinness for the part; even if maybe he didn't have the rampantly lusty quality the name suggests, I could envisage him in the slyer and also more reflective sides of Wicksteed very clearly. I suggested we at least explore the possibility and if he declined then we'd go to Elliott.' Guinness was sent the play via his agent Dennis Van Thal, who thought it a good part for his client but the star took time to commit, as he owned: 'I was doubtful. I havered. I wondered whether I should do it or not.' He was always drawn to lack of excess in design and so liked the notion of a very simple staging for the play, but a niggle remained ('I just couldn't help thinking there was something missing').

Nevertheless he eventually signed for the play. 'Then we got our first rebuff when Patricia Routledge smartly rejected Mrs Wicksteed apparently finding the play a bit smutty. We were lucky to get Margaret Courtenay.'

Most of the casting was inspired – Joan Sanderson at her most magisterially vinegary as Lady Rumpers (thawing when recalling her 'mad magenta moment', her seduction and impregnation beneath a table in wartime blacked-out Bristol under bombardment and lamenting never seeing her lover's face: 'Alas, I glimpsed him only fitfully in the post-coital glow of a Craven A'); Patricia Hayes as the Puck-like choric figure of Mrs Swabb, the daily ('hoover, hoover, hoover') in headscarf and Nora Batty stockings; John Bird as the splenetic, height-obsessed Sir Percy Shorter and the formidable Courtenay ('I grow more like the Queen Mother every day') included.

Rehearsals were mostly smooth as Bennett described: 'I wrote it without any idea of how it could be staged, and rehearsals began with just four bentwood chairs. The big revolution occurred after two weeks' rehearsal when Ronald Eyre decided we could manage with three'. But Guinness was still subject to his customary shivers. He had already given the team including Michael a nasty moment; in a gap between auditions one morning during which there had been some chat about *Habeas Corpus* as a title, Guinness 'suddenly appeared in the row behind us and whispered "Cold Feet". Alan said, "That's a wonderful title, Alec," to which the star replied, "No, no – *I've* got cold feet."'

Then, quite late in rehearsals, by which time the cast had heard the seaside barrel organ music composed for linking the scenes by Carl Davis: 'Guinness asked to take Ron, Alan and me to dinner at Leith's – very upmarket – and he said, "I think there's still something missing. I think I ought to finish the play with a *danse macabre*, a kind of *totentanz*." There was a pause before Alan responded, "All right. You can try it but I won't put it in the text when it's published."'

The original script ended with a 'walk down' sequence to rhymed couplets with the cast in wedding finery for the marriage of Dennis and Felicity and a closing Wicksteed jest:

'Whatever right or wrong is,
He whose lust lasts, lasts longest.'

From the outset Guinness had incorporated into the body language of his performance, usually when Wicksteed feels the stirrings of late-life lust ('King Sex is a wayward monarch'), a kind of involuntary physical tic like an embryonic buck-and-wing dance step as if Wicksteed's impulse were to dance. Late in the day Fizz Fazan choreographed a haunting solo dance after the walk down to Davis's music for Guinness, initially jaunty and elegant like a Sussex Fred Astaire in his top hat and tails wedding gear, before slowly the music began to grind down and the lights fade on his gradually deflating figure while a spectral voice echoed, 'Arthur' into the inky void. It brilliantly encapsulated the play's double pulse of life-enhancing celebration of sex and an omnipresent awareness of decay and mortality. Guinness could on occasion be an awkward customer but this instance is an illustration of how an actor – unlike the kind of case with Kenneth More – can enhance a play as indeed Bennett did, after all, fully acknowledge in the published text.

Still the star fretted. The out-of-town opening at the Oxford Playhouse was less than triumphant with tentative performances and a house slow to grasp the style of the evening. Afterwards Guinness was decidedly grumpy – he had personally received fewer laughs than expected – and David did not greatly lighten his mood by suggesting, with the utmost tact, that occasional inaudibility might have been part of the problem ('This is the first time,' retorted Guinness, 'that my diction had been called into question'). Most involved were dining afterwards with agents or loved ones at the Randolph Hotel; Guinness with his wife Merula and Dennis Van Thal, Michael and David together, Courtenay with her agent and so on. There was a sudden unexpected simultaneous lull in most tables' conversations during which was heard – the Randolph's high ceiling provided excellent acoustics – the murmur of Guinness to his agent: 'This time I mean it, Dennis – you're going to have to get me out of this one', followed by the crash of cutlery from suddenly nervous hands to various tables. But during re-rehearsals in Oxford he began to find the necessary insouciant tone for some scenes – Courtenay helped him by telling him to try swinging the sponge bag he was carrying by the strings when packing to leave in disgrace, which gave his cross-stage exit a big laugh – and by the time *Habeas Corpus* was due to open at the Lyric, his performance was fully projected with the right jaunty edge while Eyre had fine-tuned the text with precision timing.

It was a major success in the West End with Guinness finally very happy in it – 'He became even quite larky – he was naughty sometimes and during his final performances, knowing Robert Hardy, a passionate falconer, was to replace him he would try to 'corpse' the cast by playing it with an invisible falcon on his shoulder'. Bennett himself climbed into Mrs Swabb's wrinkled support-hose and pinny to give a wickedly funny performance with the second cast. The New York production – Michael had no significant involvement – was disastrous, even with Donald Sinden's potentially ideal Wicksteed. He and everyone else (Richard Gere as Dennis included) were scuppered by a crass production – with potted palms, musicians and real doors all over the place – which put in all the stock physical ingredients of farce unnecessary and indeed damaging for the play. Similarly, a Donmar revival in 1996 – surprisingly heavily directed by Sam Mendes – failed to unite a glitzy cast into a cohesive style with only Celia Imrie's dreadnought Lady Rumpers catching the authentic Bennett tone.

Bennett's next play would also star Guinness – they became firm friends – although it did not surface until 1977. In the meantime Michael produced two plays with the star he rated 'supremely high' among the actors he presented, both of which I directed. The first was Julian Mitchell's expert adaptation of Ivy Compton-Burnett's *A Family and a Fortune* (Apollo, 1975), a basilisk scrutiny of kinship, jealousy, the corrupting power of money and cruelty in a landed Edwardian household, a superb distillation of that unique novelist's unforgiving world in dialogue of sometimes disconcerting candour, poised, articulate and on occasion quivering with malice. It was an expensive production with a large cast and period costumes, and I remain still not entirely sure why Michael risked the venture with a relatively inexperienced director – I was still in my twenties and my professional experience then consisted solely of four years at the Mermaid where my work included a brace of new plays, two Shavian revivals including the rediscovery of *John Bull's Other Island*, and the revues *Cowardy Custard* and *Cole*, co-devising both and directing the latter with David Toguri's dazzling choreography. I was invited to lunch – kidneys in sherry at Martinez, a long-vanished Spanish establishment near the Regent Street office – to meet Michael (contrary to the pause-charged meeting I'd been warned to expect he was friendly, frank – and often very funny). Later, when he had read and liked *A Family and Fortune* I had to be screened by Guinness – this time it was Lamb Provençale at La Poule au Pot in Belgravia – when we seemed to agree about the play, especially its need for an essentially simple staging and fluid, unfussy movement between scenes. It was a dauntingly stellar cast – Margaret Leighton, Rachel

Kempson (beautifully gauging a strange, almost surreal deathbed scene that closed the first half), Nicola Pagett, Jill Balcon and Anthony Nicholls included, designed with stylish understatement using *trompe l'oeil* painted flats and descending chandeliers by Margaret ('Percy') Harris, last surviving member of the great Motley trio. It was an unusual evening, not too loved on its pre-London tour when audiences were somewhat put out to find Guinness playing – even if first among equals – in an essentially ensemble play while their glamorous Leighton was cast as a malevolent bitch (by 1975 Leighton was crippled by multiple sclerosis but her character was disabled and she could play – with whiplash command and courage in her valedictory stage appearance – with a cane) and Brighton manifestly missed the glitzy Beatonesque glamour of H.M. Tennent's period productions. Guinness's Dudley Gaveston was a masterly performance of a man who has always controlled his own life until a surprise legacy transforms his circumstances and it opened in London to positive notices (more than a few remarking on Codron's risk in putting such a large-scale piece on the commercial stage during a recession) and packed houses. It recouped its production costs within only a few weeks.

This was my first opportunity to observe Michael at work. My boss at the Mermaid had been Bernard Miles, Lord Miles of Puddle Dock, often inspired but as batty as a brush and ruling his fiefdom from his office near the Thames, which he shared with his malodorous *Treasure Island* parrot (Stevenson's yarn, often with Miles as Long John Silver, was a Puddle Dock perennial Christmas treat for decades) who seemed happy enough to leave me alone on productions, even although I must have started out there decidedly green. Although no meddler, Michael always liked to know how work on the design was going; he approved immediately of the notion of few hold-ups for scene changes and the non-naturalistic approach. On casting there were auditions for the supporting and younger roles always attended by Michael and on occasion David too. These were always meticulously organised, usually in a theatre, by Joe Scott-Parkinson, with each actor given a decent amount of time and leaving a period at the end of each day for full discussion of the candidates; from his comments, brief but decisive, it was evident that Michael fully understood the need for precise vocal clarity and sharpness for Compton-Burnett's articulate dialogue.

First rehearsals were held in a dreary Fulham church hall. I had not been at all nervous until I walked in to see most of a predominantly starry cast already there with Michael, David and author arriving shortly afterwards at which point I felt suddenly decidedly wobbly. Clearly it was up to me

42. Cross-gender casting – Alan Bennett (with Mike Carnell as Mr Shanks) taking over as Mrs Swabb in his own play *Habeas Corpus*, 1973.

to launch the venture; only too conscious of all eyes on me I got through some preliminary chat about Compton-Burnett and her world (only the first volume of Hilary Spurling's superb biography had then been published) before the first (encouraging) reading of the play.

Rehearsals moved after a week to the more congenial Petyt House, an airy and clean rehearsal space attached to the St Thomas More church on Chelsea Embankment, one of the most expensive to hire in London but a favourite for many years with the Codron management. There would be a telephone call each Sunday – I am sure the company manager and Guinness too would have kept him informed – 'just checking' that rehearsals were on track. Which they were; this was a genuinely happy rehearsal period – everyone came to love Leighton, often scabrously funny – with Guinness seemingly less beset than usual by nagging anxieties. He picked up at once on the notion I had of using sounds throughout the play (such as the clink from turning over coins in his pockets by a venal, calculating younger son) and it was he who suggested the opening sound of an imperious gong resounding as the curtain rose, summoning the Gavestons to the opening breakfast, first of the several family rituals of the play.

During the last rehearsal week Michael and David attended a run-through; with no costumes and only token furniture and props, the visual aspect of a multi-scene period play was hard to envisage but both were experienced enough to take that into account. Michael's few notes when we had a drink afterwards had only one real worry, an anxiety that Guinness in the opening scenes before his life-changing inheritance might be possibly too self-effacing (this niggle evaporated once Guinness had an audience).

He was similarly watchful but supportive in Bath where a pre-Apollo Theatre tour opened. He watched a rather rushed and accident-prone dress rehearsal with the equanimity of experience and a remarkably smooth opening performance. He gave an after-show drinks and buffet food party for the company – understudies and stage management were always included in all such affairs on any Codron production – in the upmarket Popjoy's restaurant then next to the theatre, having called a meeting after breakfast next day at the Francis Hotel for Mitchell, Harris and me to join him. Again he was brief but cogent; rightly he felt that the set needed some highlighting including architraves around the downstage side doors ('Percy' Harris agreed) and he made a fervent plea that somehow and hopefully prior to the next date at Brighton we solve a blip in the second act when an otherwise smoothly flowing evening was stalled for a time-

43. A family discusses its fortunes – Rachel Kempson, Margaret Leighton, Graham Swannell, Bruce Bould, Anthony Nicholls, Alec Guinness, Nicola Pagett, Donald Eccles in *A Family and a Fortune*, 1975.

consuming change for another breakfast scene, undeniably breaking the rhythm of the play. I had said to Michael some time previously that somehow we had to 'spellbind' an audience into Compton-Burnett's unique world. Before leaving Bath for London he left a note that I found at the hotel after the second performance saying, simply but hearteningly, 'We were spellbound and I think others will be too.'

Brighton, by marked contrast, was not remotely spellbound, even though by some swift rewriting and restaging the hiatus in the second act had been solved by turning a breakfast scene into one set after dinner with coffee in the drawing room, removing the busy scene change of bringing on table and chairs. Audiences coughed, wheezed and generally communicated their disappointment that Guinness and Leighton (who actually had little stage time together) were not delighting them in some airy comedy and cast morale was not helped by the famously stony reaction of local thespian luminaries; Dame Flora Robson ('Oh dear, Alec') and the legendary old drag star Douglas Byng ('I'm Doris, the Goddess of Wind') could barely cloak their disapproval of the austere staging and lack of glitz. Two weeks there was a little too long; grasping the situation, Michael came down with David during the second week, saw a perfectly fine show (despite the chill indifference wafting from the stalls) but called the cast

255

together afterwards in Leighton's stage-level dressing room for a brisk talking to, warning them that confidence must not droop because of Brighton's notorious audiences and that the evening should not slacken ('like a Dorothy bag, it must be kept tight'). Guinness was rather naughty for the rest of that week, urging those waiting in the wings for their first entrances to 'tighten your Dorothy bag', but actually Michael was right to sense at that point on tour prior to London that the company, particularly those less seasoned than his stars, needed to see their producer and recognise his authority again, even if fundamentally the production was in strong shape.

There was no first-night party after the Apollo opening (there was no house rule but generally the Codron method is to allow everyone to be with wives, husbands, loved ones, agents and friends then and to give dinners for the company after 100, 200, 300 performances and so on). One unfailing ritual is that Michael at 'the half' (thirty-five minutes before the stage manager calls 'Beginners' – those in the opening of the play) does the rounds of all the dressing rooms, from those of stars to stage management, knocking on each door and briefly popping in to wish each occupant 'Good Luck'. The males in the company also always receive champagne, the women bouquets in their dressing rooms.

Early next morning I received a call (Michael has been a lifelong early riser) to tell me how good the reviews had been. He was obviously pleased – clearly *A Family and a Fortune* was going to be a success at the box office but a critical success meant even more. His judgement – and appreciation of his risk in putting on a large-scale play (and not an easy one at which audiences could check their brains at the cloakroom) in tough economic times – was being consolidated. More touching, he sounded genuinely pleased on my behalf too, reading out some fulsome quotes about the production; he must have had occasional qualms about a director of limited experience compared with those he worked with often, but then some risk was stamped on most Codron ventures and it pleased him when those risks seemed justified. Virtually all the productions that I have directed for him have seen the same pattern and other directors mostly would tell a similar story, and all would admit to respecting his opinion and notes, and yet, when necessary he can be tough although never brutal; it could not have been easy dropping James Roose-Evans from *Re:Joyce!*, for instance. And when Roose-Evans later on a new play on tour, which never came to London, was having major problems from a difficult and time-consuming dramatist, Michael came swiftly from London to deal with the problem and restore harmony.

With Guinness – after a genuinely happy time at the Apollo – I then wrote an 'Entertainment' (it was not exactly a play) called *Yahoo* (Queen's, 1976) based on the life and work of Jonathan Swift, a favourite of both of us. Aiming to concentrate on Swift's gift of adopting different *personae* in his work, an ideal neo-ventriloquial technique for irony (most memorable in his guise of writing as a population-control expert in his satiric master-piece 'A Modest Proposal', quietly and with inexorable deadly logic positing the eating of babies as a solution to the woes of Irish poverty and overpopulation) and to play down the received image of Dublin's Gloomy Dean of St Patrick's fuelled exclusively by *saeva indignatio*, it was hardly conventional West End fare but Michael willingly put it on. Even with Guinness, whose career had had its flops (most recently including Arthur Miller's *Incident at Vichy*) it was a dubious prospect at a time of West End recession and anti-Irish feeling in the wake of increased IRA activities.

Michael made sure – as always – that the production values were right. The production often was thrilling to look at – Bernard Culshaw's design, based on eighteenth-century portrait conventions, backed by sepia screens of *Gulliver's Travel's* maps, a great, soaring carved pillar and a huge swagged crimson curtain, was equally imaginatively lit, often subtly evoking candlelight and brilliantly using strobes for *Gulliver*, by Nick Chelton. On the road this time Guinness was his customary bundle of frets and fusses. Frightened by the reaction to 'A Modest Proposal' – he gradually froze the house into a rictus of horror, precisely Swift's intention – he wanted it cut, leading to a major disagreement between us during the Bath run (Michael, with enviable tact and patience, supported me – many producers would have taken the star's side at once – and the piece remained, as a major highlight). Although that piece, together with a chilling, Beckettian glimpse of the immortal Struldbrugs showed the star – as Bernard Levin described him in his *Sunday Times* notice – to be 'the leading Houyhnhnm of our stage', Guinness was always happier with the lighter episodes when the evening explored the region of Swift's satiric fantasy – sublimely dotty as a senescent Emperor of Lilliput walking on his knees with false 'feet' attached, or in a card party *en travesti* with Angela Thorne, Nicola Pagett and Mark Kingston gossiping about Mr Gulliver before the party developed into a bravura performance of 'Verses on the Death of Doctor Swift', with Guinness swooping in with a triumphant trump card on the last couplet.

44. 'The leading Houyhnhnm of the English stage' – Alec Guinness
prepares to play Jonathan Swift in *Yahoo*, 1976.

The reviews for *Yahoo* were divided – inevitably some found too little of
the misanthropic Swift of popular imagination – although several echoed
Levin and B.A. Young in the *Financial Times* who wrote that '*Yahoo* reinforces one's admiration for the commercial theatre in this country, for it is
in no way designed to pack the house with coachloads come to guffaw or
swoon over the heroes of television'. Guinness reflected this in writing to
Michael: 'My grateful thanks for your courage in presenting such an odd
evening, and so splendidly.' The risk proved justified: *Yahoo*, at a £3.50
top-ticket price, opened on 6 October, 1976 and recouped its costs by the
week ending 30 October, less than a month after opening.

By the end of *Yahoo*'s run Bennett had completed his new play, which
had a strong central role for Guinness, even if not written specifically for
him. *The Old Country* (Queen's, 1977) posed a Hare-like mystery initially,
with only tantalising hints as to where the play, set in a comfortable
wooden house, full of books, surrounded by birch and pine, might be
taking place (John Gunter's design was teasingly ingenious) as a middle-
aged man and his wife potter about, Elgar on the record player, the talk
covering such topics as Pathé News or E.M. Forster. Only when Guinness's
character, Hilary, wonders what he and some other neighbouring men
have in common and his wife replies, 'You're all traitors' does the penny

drop and the audience grasp that *The Old Country* is set in a Russian *dacha*. Some claimed that Kim Philby was the model for Hilary but Bennett here is essentially much more interested in exile than in espionage or betrayal as Hilary, an ex-Foreign Office official in exile, is faced by official visitors including his brother-in-law come to persuade him to return to London.

Guinness was at his lapidary best in crumpled cardigan and comfy shoes, beautifully conveying the sense of a man in Russia geographically but spiritually still in the England he betrayed, his oboe-voice giving the play's brand names (Fuller's Walnut Cake, Gamages, Dickens, King's College, Cambridge) a haunting resonance. Through the prism of this performance emerged a very Bennettian scrutiny of the English character, most tellingly of that bred-in-the-bone but often fatal penchant for irony that weakens it, insidiously compromising its certainties and the worth of its basic tenets. The ending, with Hilary following the others off to the car waiting to begin the journey 'home', calling out 'Poop, poop!' like Mr Toad (soon Bennett would look at the English character again in adapting *Wind in the Willows* for the National Theatre) was heart stopping. Supported by Rachel Kempson as his clear-eyed wife and with Faith Brook imperiously befurred as his snobbish sister-in-law bewailing the democratisation of their beloved Spain (now 'Costa del Tesco'), Guinness took *The Old Country* to another capacity-house success. Its 2006 revival (Whitehall) with Timothy West as Hilary, reinforced the play's appeal for a British public so often drawn to plays on espionage or betrayal.

The Bennett-Codron partnership's third time out was sadly not so fortunate when his *Enjoy* (Vaudeville, 1980) was a major flop. It was a signally undeserved one – there was even at the time a widespread feeling within the theatre world that the critics really had got it very wrong, or were cutting Bennett down to size in an instance of Tall Poppy syndrome – as proven when it was generally critically praised in its popular revival (Gielgud, 2009), with a trimmed text directed by Christopher Luscombe with Alison Steadman and David Troughton.

Bennett always has been sceptical about the 'Heritaging' of England. He wrote, echoing Philip Larkin's 'Going, Going', of a 1989 article in the *Guardian* reporting that a Victorian school building in Yorkshire was to be demolished and then, brick by brick, re-erected in Bradford Museum, 'where it is to be visited by, among others, patients suffering from Alzheimer's disease in the hope, one presumes, of jogging their memories'. He added wryly that he had predicted just such an event in *Enjoy*, written as the 1980s began. Its old couple – Mam and Dad – live 'in one of the last back-to-backs in Leeds' with Mam's memory disintegrating (as was that of Bennett's mother, chronicled in his *Diaries*) and Dad disabled with a steel plate in his head after an encounter with local gang violence (*Enjoy* evokes a strong sense of offstage urban threat and violence). By the close he is in hospital (after a presumed 'death') while Mam resides still in the back-to-back, now reconstructed inside a museum. Amongst the social workers – a breed familiar but rarely emerging with much honour from several Bennett television plays – who have organised the move, is the initially silent, soberly suited, enigmatic presence of a young woman ('Ms Craig') who emerges as the couple's son, estranged and absent since the disclosure of his homosexuality and now in drag, acting and behaving as a woman. Their daughter, Linda, announces that she is off to marry a Saudi prince but in fact she is a calculating, chill-hearted whore. Late in the play Mam is reconciled to her 'son' as the set slides away leaving them to dance together to 'I Can Give You the Starlight' by her favourite Ivor Novello ('We'll Gather Lilacs' also turning up briefly again).

It was cast easily: 'We went to the best names for the play and got Joan Plowright, Colin Blakely and Joan Hickson. It all looked very promising, at least on paper, with Ron Eyre back with Alan. There was a hiccup in rehearsal when Joan Hickson said, "I've made a mistake", feeling miscast as the nosy neighbour, but we got Liz Smith to take over and she was very funny.' Richmond audiences prior to London were guarded in response and Bennett was alarmed when, after four days away, he returned 'to find it has turned into *A Girl in My Soup*, with the actors hopping from laugh to laugh with no thought for what's in between'. Eyre made sure that was righted by the Vaudeville opening and both Plowright, button eyes oddly vacant and hilarious with Liz Smith laying out Dad's 'corpse' (with an inconvenient – and unexpected – erection) and Blakely were very fine in *Enjoy*.

London's critics were, almost universally, seemingly baffled by the play – descriptions such as 'Expressionist' were tossed about pejoratively and inaccurately – and put it comprehensively through the wringer: 'They were almost jubilantly bad reviews for Alan, one has to say, particularly Milton Shulman'. Sheridan Morley's *Punch* review tore it apart – at great length – ('two and a half endless hours') while some others were tinged with prurience in their suggestions that 'Ms Craig' represented a closeted aspect of Bennett, possibly a deep-rooted desire to stroll around NW1 in cardigan, pearls and sling-backs. Worst of all was the *Sunday Times*'s James Fenton;

the poet had for some reason been given the newspaper's drama critic post (Simon Gray had a character remark of a Fenton-like critic in *The Common Pursuit* that his *Sunday Times* bosses were 'impressed by his lack of qualifications') and he panned *Enjoy*. Bennett took later eloquent revenge in his *Diaries*: 'James Fenton, I am told, even referred to the drag character as "the writer". Mr Fenton's subsequent abandonment of dramatic criticism to become the *Independent*'s correspondent in the Philippines was one of the most cheering developments in the theatre in the eighties, though when President Marcos claimed to be a much misunderstood man I knew how he felt.'

Always ready to be self-deprecating, Bennett – at least publicly – blamed himself (suggesting that *Endure* might have been a better title and wishing he had persuaded Eyre to cut more). He once commented 'An article on playwrights in the *Daily Mail*, listed according to Hard Left, Soft Left, Hard Right, Soft Right and Centre. I am not listed. I should probably come under Soft Centre'. But he is wrong – *Enjoy*, for all its delirious comedy, has a diamond-hard Swiftian *indignatio* at its core. Bennett certainly did not hold Michael in any way responsible for the flop – it had been impeccably produced in every way – but the reviews, even with a star cast, resulted in silent box office phones and Michael was forced, reluctantly ('I was intrigued from the start by *Enjoy* and the sex-gender aspect of it and its mix of comedy and pathos'), to close after only six weeks.

A favourite writer, Franz Kafka – he turns up too in Bennett's television film *The Insurance Man* – is at the centre of *Kafka's Dick* (1986), which Michael presented at the Royal Court in a co-production with the ESC ('I thought – as did Alan – that this should have a launch and the Court was keen'). Not only Kafka but his father, mother and biographer Max Brod all appear in a suburban London house in this dream-within-a-dream play, with a first act of ceaselessly inventive comedy as Sydney (Geoffrey Palmer), an insurance man, dreams of being a Kafka expert and of what it would be like if Kafka appeared in his house, ignorant of his posthumous fame. Kafka similarly dreams of Sydney; he has asked Brod to incinerate all his manuscripts when he dies; in his dream he projects seventy years ahead to find his biographer has not obeyed his request so that now he is the centre of a worldwide cult, discussing everything from his loathing of his parents to the size of his penis (Sydney has similar worries). The double-dream structure allows Bennett the freedom to take on and juggle different themes, not least (like Stoppard in *Arcadia*) those of posthumous fame and literary biography.

Richard Eyre directed a quality cast with Alison Steadman as the wife of a pseudo-intellectual (much brighter than he, it emerges), hilarious when blooming like a late flowering hothouse orchid under Kafka's attention, a nerdily cadaverous Kafka from Roger Lloyd Pack, and Andrew Sachs a laconic Brod. The notices were disappointing, tending to echo Michael's main qualm ('the second act never really fulfilled the promise of a brilliant first act – I think audiences came out slightly deflated'). He did not transfer it – 'Alan was upset that I didn't bring it in but I really wasn't convinced it would work'. Peter Hall directed a 1998 revival (Piccadilly Theatre) with Julia McKenzie, John Gordon Sinclair and Eric Sykes (scene stealing with his Zimmer frame), but it too received somewhat downbeat notices and played to only average business.

The production ended the Bennett-Codron professional partnership – perhaps the failure of *Enjoy* and the lack of a transfer for *Kafka's Dick* combined to take the playwright across the river to the National – although he remained both grateful to and fond of Michael ('He wrote a most touching letter after David died, saying he looked back on that period in the 1970s and 1980s when we were producing him as a happy time'). They continue to keep in touch; Michael found himself much moved at the end of *The Habit of Art* in 2009 at the National Theatre when Bennett's play recalled, briefly, Ronald Eyre, reminding him of the many happy times on *Habeas Corpus* and *Enjoy* and wrote to tell the writer, saying he hoped he hadn't reacted 'too much'; on a postcard Bennett replied: 'There can't be too much emotion. As I once said to Routledge, "There's not enough of too much these days."'

Those excursions with Bennett were only part of a varied output from the Codron management during that time. He was involved with a good deal of new work, much of it at the Royal Court, including A.E. White-head's *The Foursome* (1971), a Liverpool-set piece of a quartet of contemporary young lovers, which he transferred to the Fortune and an early Caryl Churchill play, *Owners* (Royal Court Theatre Upstairs). In this 1972 play, commissioned by Michael at a time when Churchill had written mostly for radio, which introduced London audiences to her work, Chur-chill – somewhat like Ayckbourn in *Absurd Person Singular* at the same time – seemed to anticipate that urge towards a ruthless individualism soon to come in England, with a toughly realistic capitalist landlord (a forerunner of her Marlene in *Top Girls*) at its centre. As Michael observed, few British writers understand money with Churchill's perception. He was very drawn also to Edward Bond's strange, absorbing *Tempest*-variation *The Sea*

(Royal Court, 1973). This was given a production he admired greatly by William Gaskill, charged throughout with the sense of violence suffusing the piece and full of memorable stark imagery, including a funeral service set on a cliff edge with only a piano, one chair and the mourners in deepest black set against a boundless, empty sky, the congregation singing of peace while an artillery range booms its aggression from across the bay. Coral Browne was in majestic form as the town queen bee, Mrs Rafi, with Ian Holm a quivering mass of neuroses as the unsettled haberdasher Hatch. Michael regarded *The Sea* highly; he was somewhat disappointed by what he found a rather too muted 2008 Haymarket Theatre revival.

When he and David saw David Rudkin's *Ashes* (1974) at the tiny Open Space (then on Tottenham Court Road) they at once began negotiations for its transfer, although it was often a harrowing play, tracing the efforts of an infertile couple to have a child, the first time the subject of IVF had been scrutinised in the theatre. But somehow the new production by the RSC's Ron Daniels – not helped by the open stage of the Young Vic – with Ian McKellen and Gemma Jones replacing Peter McEnery and Lynn Farleigh, could not quite recapture the claustrophobic intensity of the original production or fuse it with Rudkin's ironic comedy. Likewise a somewhat clumsy physical production undercut Howard Barker's *Stripwell* (Royal Court, 1975), co-produced with the ESC. This began with promising panache in a startling opening scene – a criminal vowing awful vengeance on the eponymous Judge (Michael Hordern) sending him down – but subsequently became bogged down in a meandering plot involving the Judge's son and drugs smuggled in elephants' vaginas and the Judge's involvement with a young, iconoclastic go-go dancer. Hordern as always was a delight, jowls a-quiver in eloquent dismay; he, Constance Cummings as his wife and a fizzing Patricia Quinn as the stripper helped keep the play just about afloat.

The decade also saw some major commercial successes for the Codron management, including Royce Ryton's long-running Abdication drama *Crown Matrimonial*, produced fittingly at the Theatre Royal, Haymarket (1972). Michael was well aware that the writing, although adept, was basically superior soap opera but there had been a few failures (*Siege* included) beforehand and he knew that if a top-drawer cast could be tempted for the play, and with a superior design (Finlay James gave Queen Mary's Marlborough House apartments the most discreetly sumptuous works) it could be a commercial success. To his delight Wendy Hiller accepted Queen Mary; he then worked hard to woo Peter Barkworth, who recently had become disenchanted with the theatre, to play Edward VIII, even taking the script to deliver personally to the actor in Hampstead. Barkworth's friend, Michael Redington the producer, later told Michael of the actor's reaction: 'Well, the good news is that I've just had Michael Codron trotting up my path with a new play. The bad news is that it's one of the worst plays I've ever read.' Nevertheless, Barkworth too spotted the play's commercial potential, he admired Hiller and was drawn to the technical challenge of playing an inhibited man, at his most clenched faced with his formidable mother, a marbled personification of Duty.

Some major players in the Abdication drama – Stanley Baldwin, Archbishop Lang, Wallis Simpson herself (one wag suggested a musical version to be called *Hello, Wally!* – later there even was one, a disaster called *Always*), Ryton wisely kept offstage to tighten focus on the family. The air of Madam Tussaud's was never entirely absent but Peter Dews's cunningly paced production, helped by superbly crafted work from Barkworth (suggesting an incipient stammer when with his mother), and Hiller as two people with ramrod exteriors evoking worlds of interior turbulence, papered over many of the play's cracks.

Barkworth rediscovered his zest for stage work, as he wrote to Michael: 'I feel renewed, ready for fresh challenges – your firm is the most perfect management imaginable.' But Michael was always watchful on a production's progress, even a runaway success and especially in the director's absence; alarmed by the increasing running times indicated on the stage manager's nightly show reports he revisited the Haymarket, subsequently writing tactfully but firmly to Wendy Hiller to voice 'my concern at the slowness of the whole performance, the tempo of which must of course stem from Queen Mary'. He also immediately spoke to Amanda Reiss (Duchess of York) when she seemed to be playing less a protective wife, more an overt bitch.

Sometimes Michael would, only mock deprecatingly, refer to it as 'my shame' and relate how audiences loved it 'especially all the locals in Kent where my stock has risen considerably since the play opened'. *Crown Matrimonial* received some unexpectedly warm notices – nobody could fault the acting – and it ran to packed houses, surviving a cast change (Phyllis Calvert) to go into a second year. Subsequently Ryton's rather laborious farce of inconvenient bodies, *The Unvarnished Truth* (Phoenix, 1978), had a cast of adroit comedy players – Graeme Garden stood out – but never built up solid momentum at the box office.

On paper a success similar to *Crown Matrimonial* seemed likely for *Alice's*

Boys (Savoy, 1978) starring Sir Ralph Richardson. Written by the team of Felicity Browne and Jonathan Hales it had been scheduled for production by H.M. Tennent who had presented their previous play, *Family Dance*. But a change of directorship when Helen Montagu suddenly left Tennents gave Richardson – who had rarely appeared for any other commercial management – some anxiety and so his powerful and wily agent, Laurence Evans at ICM, got his client out of his commitment and took the play to Michael. Knowing it was a thin piece but keen to present Richardson, Michael surrounded the Knight with deluxe support – Michael Gambon, Michael Jayston and Gary Bond included – and lured Eric Thompson to direct.

It all went very wrong. The faults in the script emerged in rehearsal but major rewrites were throwing to a star of Richardson's age (his memory had been a problem on *What The Butler Saw* previously); he took strongly against Eric Thompson (his attitude to directors was simple – 'I give them three days, then if they don't know more than me I go my own way') and Lindsay Anderson who had directed him with Gielgud in Storey's *Home* was brought in. However, it was clear during the Richmond try-out that this comedy of espionage (Richardson's 'Alice' was an MI5 chief) was never going to work, not helped by Murphy's Law kicking in, as it tends to do – with extra malevolence – on doomed projects. One Richmond performance saw a chair spectacularly collapse and the cast – no doubt because of pent-up tension – dissolve into such giggles that for a while the play could not continue. Its West End opening was a chilly occasion; Alice and the boys were checking out of The Savoy in less than a month.

It was his old ally Peggy Ramsay, as indefatigable as Michael in truffle hounding the gifted new, who alerted Michael to the talent of her Liverpool-based client Willy Russell – she had taken him on on the basis of a couple of TV scripts and the recommendation of television executive Barry Hanson – when he wrote a Liverpool Everyman Theatre show, *John, Paul, George, Ringo ... and Bert* with Beatles music.

Michael instantly loved the show in Liverpool when he saw it with Ramsay and the pop-music impresario Robert Stigwood who had recently acquired the rights to the Beatles' songs. It was presented in London (Lyric, 1975) as a co-production between Michael and Stigwood (uniting Michael with Bob Swash, his successor at Jack Hylton's, now controlling Stigwood's theatrical ventures). Remembering *Salad Days* and his recommendation to Hylton to use the Bristol cast and not 'star it up', Michael agreed that the Everyman team, directed by Alan Dossor, must be brought in its entirety to

London – it was quite some cast in any case, including Trevor Eve, Antony Sher, George Costigan, Bernard Hill, Philip Jackson and Barbara Dickson.

Popular, populist, directed and acted with the committed truth characteristic of Everyman work at this peak of its existence and with high musical standards, *John, Paul ...* looked by no means a 'provincial' show in the capital where it was an instant success. Russell's tight, economical script drew vivid portraits of four young men, for a time the most celebrated, adored and privileged people on the planet, and then traced the collapse of it all with Costigan as their devoted fan Bert McGhee acting as a kind of choric Everyman figure, a Dante taking the audience through what developed, despite or because of ever increasing riches and success, into a latter-day Purgatorio. Russell also made sure there was due focus on the crucial figure of Brian Epstein (who had ambitions as a theatre producer) and his death; with the loss of the one constant figure they could genuinely rely on only in-fighting, rancour and bitterness lay ahead. The songs – Dickson's rich voice was present throughout at the piano upstage – funny, exhilarating and plangent by turn, were often used to unexpected effect, not least when Ringo's catchy ditty 'A Little Help from My Friends' became, in a slower tempo, an ironic counterpart to the ruthless dismissal of Pete Best as the group's first drummer.

Dossor's work on *John, Paul ...* impressed Michael, as did his ebullient production of Mike Stott's comedy *Funny Peculiar* (Mermaid, 1976 transferring to the Garrick). This young man's play coincided with one produced by H.M. Tennent from the veteran Ben Travers, *The Bed Before Yesterday* (written earlier but unproduced because of the Lord Chamberlain's edicts), both celebrating unbuttoned and fulfilling sex. Set in a Pennine village *Funny Peculiar* saw Richard Beckinsale, an actor of unaffected charm who excelled in 'Mr Average' roles before his early death, play grocer Trevor Tinsley, happily enough married but keen for more adventurous sex from his wife Irene (Julie Walters). In this genial, beguiling play, Stott's cast list includes a character who in less politically correct days would have been called the village idiot or 'softie' (the tall, goofily gangly Matthew Kelly), the modern emancipated Shirley, and Desmond Ainsley, a baker, played by Pete Postlethwaite who memorably partnered Beckinsale in an hilarious slapstick scene set in Trevor's shop when Ainsley turns nasty with the gobstopper dispenser after Trevor, in a fit of frustration, demolishes two dozen custom-made cream cakes. Inventive throughout, *Funny Peculiar* closed with Trevor, having broken several bones escaping from an encounter after Shirley has extended his amorous education, in hospital with his

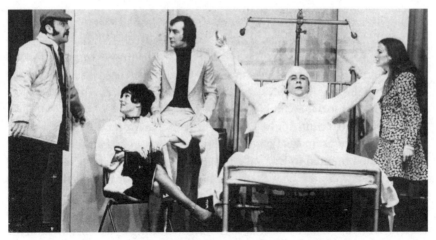

45. The close of Mike Stott's *Funny Peculiar* (Richard Beckinsale
and Julie Walters at right), 1976.

arms in traction while finally, behind a screen, Irene is persuaded to try
what is still possible in that position.

The popularity of Stott's comedy – its Garrick run was immensely
successful – was in part responsible for Michael taking on Russell's *Breezeblock Park* (1977), which had been seen two years previously at the
Everyman and now took the same route, playing the Mermaid prior to the
West End. This was a more rueful, sad-edged comedy, set on two virtually
identical council houses on a Liverpool housing estate with similar families. The wives are sisters, Betty (Wendy Craig) and Reena (Eileen
Kennally), bound in a long-standing rivalry with each other over status,
taste and 'respectability' and both with untidy but amiable husbands. Each
couple has a teenage child; Reena and Ted's John is stifled in the competition to suggest the perfect family unit, while Betty and Syd's daughter
Sandra threatens to collapse the household's house of cards by leaving to
'live in sin' with the student by whom it is revealed she is pregnant. There
were some comic highlights – a vibrator mistaken for a drinks mixer, Julie
Walters as a whiningly genteel sister-in-law ('Ooh, don't say that word,
penis. It goes right through me!'), balanced by David Neilsen's quiet
dignity as the decent, undervalued John – but the tone darkens throughout.
In particular Betty emerges in Russell's handling as a quasi-tragic figure,
trapped between her conditioning to a 'keep up with the Joneses' lifestyle
and an inarticulate urge to reject all these values when she senses that her
daughter might be escaping in a way that she herself was never quite bold
enough to do.

The Mermaid production was edgy – partly because Wendy Craig could not totally master the Scouse accent – and Russell fell foul of some critics (rather as some early Mike Leigh projects were prone to), accused of patronising his characters, a charge as false in his case as with Leigh. Prunella Scales, more securely anchored in Liverpool's rhythms, replaced Craig as Betty for the Whitehall Theatre transfer.

There would be no more Russells for Michael after *Breezeblock Park*. *Educating Rita* was an RSC commission and Michael admitted that he did not spot the potential in Russell's *Blood Brothers* musical, which he saw in an early, short version (he was disinclined to produce larger-scale musicals in any event) before its first West End run presented by Bob Swash and its later Bill Kenwright production, still running after two decades, often revitalised by inventive, successful casting including Spice Girl Melanie C.

There remained other writers, however, whose loyalties, with occasional forays into the subsidised sector, stayed firm to the commercial theatre and to Michael Codron Ltd in particular.

CHAPTER 16

PHILOSOPHY AND THE HUMAN HEART

Of all the dramatists presented under the management of Michael Codron Ltd. by far the most constant were Michael Frayn and Alan Ayckbourn, both associated with the firm for more than thirty years. Although at times working within the subsidised sector, principally at the National Theatre, they maintained a fundamental loyalty to and friendship with Michael.

Once Frayn wrote: 'I suspect that producing plays is harder than writing them; at any rate there are fewer good producers in the world than good playwrights', calling Michael 'a prince among producers'. While Ayckbourn, similarly not given to extravagant statements, described him at the time of *Taking Steps* (1979) as 'in my opinion, undoubtedly the best producer there is.' With Frayn, whose early theatrical work was encouraged by Michael, there were thirteen collaborations, including two Chekhov translations and a Chekhov compilation. With Ayckbourn – counting trilogies as one venture – the total is an astounding twenty. Only the Broadway producer Sam Harris's long association with George S. Kaufman's work really rivals these collaborations.

The mutual loyalties covered major hits (*Noises Off* for Frayn, *Absurd Person Singular* for Ayckbourn) and crushing disappointments (the flop of Frayn's *Look, Look* and the box office failure of *The Revengers' Comedies* from Ayckbourn) but in both cases the partnerships seemed strengthened by setbacks. Only in 2002 when Ayckbourn was upset by the handling of his trilogy *Damsels in Distress* at the Duchess, disillusioned by what he viewed as especially poor handling of a cherished project by the theatre's then-owners and co-producers the Really Useful Group headed by Andrew Lloyd Webber, also co-producing with Michael, was there any sense of a rupture in the Ayckbourn/Codron alliance. Thereafter Ayckbourn has bypassed the West End with new work (during which time he suffered and recovered from a stroke) and when he returned with revivals of *Absurd Person Singular* (2007) and *Woman in Mind* (2009), both originally Codron productions in London, it was under Bill Kenwright's management. The professional partnership may have frayed but happily the personal friendship survived intact. Throughout both partnerships Michael was constantly delighted and surprised by the sheer unpredictability of the work of both men, never quite knowing what was in store when he opened a new script.

Ayckbourn seemed destined from the theatre from Haileybury schooldays, earning his spurs as ASM and actor, then apprentice dramatist under the remarkable Stephen Joseph, champion of theatre-in-the-round, before his plays began regularly to travel south from Scarborough. Whereas Frayn at first sight seems an unlikely figure in the madcap world of showbusiness – donnish, a brilliant philosopher (Michael once said, 'I've always been rather in awe of Michael Frayn, as I am of Tom Stoppard – these extraordinary intellects') – more seemingly suited to the books of philosophy or the probing fiction he has also written, in a career overall almost as prolific as that of Ayckbourn.

However, Frayn has also given occasional glimpses of a stage-struck boy in South London suburbia; he built and operated his own puppet theatre ('I had ambitious plans, delayed only by lack of Arts Council funding, to extend the gold-painted cardboard until my entire bedroom had become an auditorium, with gold cardboard boxes, circle, upper circle and gallery, all filled to capacity at every performance with my parents and sister'). He was also a keen conjuror, dicing with the danger of recalcitrant props, he adored radio's *ITMA* and *Happidrome* with their puns and linguistic-confusion jokes and, like Michael, loved Variety, becoming a regular at the Kingston Empire.

Growing up deflected Frayn from the theatre – he was thirty-six before his first West End venture. As he wrote later, 'what held me up was early failure'. At Cambridge he was active in undergraduate theatre, writing a 1957 spoof musical *Zounds!* and for the Footlights, not long before the Golden Age of Peter Cook *et al*. In his last year, à la Bamber Gascoigne, he wrote most of the entire May week revue with lofty aims – no dancing and no showbiz jokes – but heavily influenced by the neo-abstract style of *Cranks* ('But *Cranks* made people laugh. My imitation of it did not'). Then, when studying Russian (Alan Bennett among his fellow students) he had a nightmare experience in a small role in Gogol's *The Government Inspector* (in Russian) when a door stuck, prohibiting his exit, leaving him on stage while stagehands tried to unstick the door and the audience began a slow handclap. Not surprisingly Frayn 'turned against the theatre' and as a journalist on *The Guardian* then *The Observer* regularly satirised its conventions in his columns. Then, resembling the atheist who comes to mock but remains to pray he was 'gradually reeled in'. Television plays – *Jamie on a Flying Visit* included, a delightful scrutiny of English embarrassment when a couple find themselves entertaining an old friend for much longer than anticipated – proved his ability to write good dialogue. The expansive Broadway producer Alexander Cohen invited him to submit a piece for a projected evening of short plays on marriage for London (Ayckbourn was one of the eventual contributors to *Mixed Doubles*) but rejected the play, about a young couple with a baby revisiting a Venice very different from their idyllic honeymoon (apparently the great producer would not countenance a play in which a nappy was changed onstage).

Michael came into view for Frayn soon afterwards. He had briefly come across the writer when he helped his friend Bamber Gascoigne polish some *Share My Lettuce* material and had been a constant admirer of Frayn's idiosyncratic columns: 'I'd finally thought, "Well, Bamber Gascoigne isn't going to be a dramatist but Frayn might be." He lived then in Blackheath with his first wife Jill and daughters and it seemed a very attractive writer's existence. Every time I suggested an idea for a play he'd say, "I must ask Peter Nichols" – his friend, neighbour and fellow dramatist, who looked rather like him and for whom he was regularly mistaken – and it became a constant refrain. But then, rather diffidently, he proposed the idea of an evening of short plays.' One-act plays had slumped from favour, regarded as box office poison, but Michael rarely took notice of such superstitions and encouraged Frayn to go ahead. He came up with *The Two of Us* – designed for two actors to play eleven roles in three short pieces and one longer one-act play.

Frayn kept for *The Observer* a brief diary of the highs and lows of the venture, aptly titled 'On the Roller Coaster', tracing the arc from the initial euphoria of a Café Royal lunch with Michael (a dicey prospect since one of the plays involved a repellent producer lunching an appalling writer) and Michael's enthusiastic response to the first three pieces through rehearsals and a seesawing tour to the Garrick opening. His lunch with Michael was in the Spring of 1969 when a July start was suggested. It finally opened in August, 1970. Casting had its vicissitudes. Initially seeking Richard Briers and Lynn Redgrave they had to accept his unavailability and her pregnancy. In the meantime seven directors came and went. They ended up after all with Briers, now free, and Redgrave (having been delivered of her baby) and the eighth director, Mark Cullingham, better known from television.

The rest of Frayn's brief journal has distinct anticipations of his *Noises*

271

Off as *The Two of Us* lurches through rehearsals and a bumpy tour – a depressing run-through taking place in total silence ('Michael is very firm afterwards; I feel as if I'm up before the headmaster'), a later run ('Smiles, congratulations all round'), a sticky Cambridge opening with Binkie Beaumont over from Knott's Fosse ('Oh, Binkie, we've been thrown in the deep end!' wailed Briers, soothed by the veteran impresario with 'I know, dear, but you do such lovely strokes') much rewriting of the ingenious dinner-party farce *Chinamen* involving multiple quick changes, which will finally be the jewel of the project, deep depression in Brighton – not for the last time - with a blood-freezing silent audience ('The whole show has become a dust bowl!' wrote Frayn), the jettisoning of the producer/author lunchtime-set play, the swift writing of a new one, its celebration with a Ritz lunch (appropriate location given that it was the setting for the now-cut play), euphoria dashed again in drizzly Southsea where John Dexter is brought in to polish *Chinamen*'s staging (for Michael 'Mark Cullingham, Dexter's protégé, didn't really deliver the goods') and through to a West End opening.

The Two of Us had an edgy Garrick first night. The gallery – not best pleased that a Marie Lloyd musical, *Sing a Rude Song*, starring their beloved 'Babs' (Barbara Windsor) had closed to house this new whizz kid's plays – gave it a rough reception with some old-style booing. Frayn passed 'three rather camp young men coming out of the Gallery exit' afterwards, one of whom turned to shout 'load of bloody rubbish!' and his critical reception was not significantly better. But Briers and Redgrave were strong box office names and after a slow start business improved and carried Frayn's roller-coaster ride (it would not be his last) to a strong run. It was mostly a happy time: 'The only unpleasant memory of that venture was Lynn's husband, John Clark, who tried to take it over and get the U.S. rights. Then he didn't pay Frayn's option money and also wanted to use more than two actors, destroying what the evening was designed to do. We couldn't understand why she was shackled to such an unpleasant man although, who knows, it may have been that she was cocking the gun but he was firing it, not an unfamiliar scenario with star actresses and their husbands. Oscar Lewenstein, whom I revered, said to me "You're very lucky – you've got away with it" and I realised that was what producing involves sometimes.'

Michael and David both had enjoyed working with Frayn, admiring his work ethic as well as finding him excellent company. Keen to work with him again Michael, who had read *Towards the End of the Morning*, Frayn's novel of pre-technological revolution Fleet Street – rivalling *Scoop* and A.

N. Wilson's *My Name Is Legion* as the funniest English novel of journalistic life – suggested a play with a newspaper background. The resulting *Alphabetical Order* (1975) was small in scale (one set, seven characters) but large in resonance. Set in the disordered Cuttings Library of an ailing provincial paper, presided over by the earth-mother figure of Lucy to whom the staff bring their problems (more is involved with two of the male members). It creates a sense of a warm, womb-like world invaded by a new assistant, Leslie, a brisk younger advocate of efficiency who wastes little time in transforming the office as well as Lucy's current attachment, the languidly charming John, a man with a brilliant Oxbridge future behind him. It is Leslie who leads a staff revolt at the suggestion of closure, even after the others – in the assumption that their jobs have no future – have reduced her order and classification in a defiant, anarchic burst of rebellion to utter chaos again. Understandably the play is detested by stage management who have to tidy furiously at the interval and then re-arrange everything at the close. Twice on matinee days.

As soon as he had read it and liked it ('Plays with a background of work are always fascinating') Michael began a shrewd piece of marriage broking: 'At that time I was very involved with Hampstead Theatre and I'd been on the Board since the opening. I thought the stage there would suit the play and, also still playing matchmaker, that Michael Rudman who was the artistic director then, would direct Frayn well.'

His instincts were right and Rudman, aided by a choice cast, served Frayn extremely well. He understood, as did Frayn's subsequent regular director Michael Blakemore (there always seemed a plethora of Michaels around on any Frayn production) that although of course while it is possible to claim a didactic intention in his work – *Alphabetical Order* could be seen as Frayn championing generously slapdash warmth against soulless efficiency, or as a metaphor for contemporary society, the office a microcosm of a laissez-faire England in need of change and efficiency – a much more crucial aspect of Frayn's perspective is that fundamentally his plays are, as he has said, 'attempts to show something about the world, not to change it or to promote any particular idea of it'. It would be rubbish to say that there are no ideas in them but essentially they revolve round the way in which we attempt to impose our own ideas on to the world around us (in the case of *Alphabetical Order* it would be classification).

The original production captured all that Michael found appealing in the play: 'I rate it highly among Frayn's plays. It really showed his voice – wry, scholarly but accessible.' There is, too, a vital compassion in it – for misfits, the lonely, the old, as much for the tidy-minded Leslie as for the muddled mess that is Lucy and her love life – which Rudman and his cast teased out. 'We were very lucky to get Billie Whitelaw as Lucy – she was quite a box office catch. And Barbara Ferris was a lovely Leslie, always the outsider. And for a time Dinsdale Landen (John) became known as M.F.A. (My Favourite Actor) because of the look of him – he had something of the air of the Captain of Cricket – the wickedness of him, that naughtiness, which no other candidate for the part could quite match.'

Landen's was indeed a tour-de-force performance. Draping himself over filing cabinets like an etiolated Spy drawing, reeling off John's long, tapeworm sentences like a Bernard Levin of All Souls, suddenly in parenthesis slipping in the occasional disconcerting compliment ('I love the little as it were hollows in the back of your knees'), like a bowler with the occasional googly, he delivered a wonderfully original comic creation. He could be a naughty boy on stage – 'Billie and Dinsdale didn't get on really. He was rather mischievous and she very serious. And he would provoke her by leaving bits of chewing gum attached to the filing cabinets and things' – but while in his later career he could go over the top (there was something recalling Michael's great early favourite, A.E. Matthews, about Landen) he remained mostly consistent on *Alphabetical Order*.

The Hampstead notices and business were strong – 'It well deserved a transfer and this kind of play had my signature on it. We took it to the Mayfair – in those days it was possible to make money there, even although it would never be millions, with just over 300 seats, and we more than recouped with *Alphabetical Order*.' Although widely seen in regional theatres the play had to wait until 2009 for a London revival when Hampstead included it in its 50th Anniversary season, now in its new building at Swiss Cottage, which Michael then co-produced for a brief tour. It had bad luck – Annette Badland's knee injury forced her to withdraw just before previews – and somehow just failed to live up to expectations.

Frayn found himself back on a roller coaster with *Donkeys' Years* (Globe, 1976). Eventually a long-running success, it was in its first outing a classic instance of a play 'in trouble on the road'. Set during a reunion dinner weekend at an Oxbridge College – with remarkable ingenuity Alan Tagg managed to squeeze on to the stage a college quadrangle and then two different sets of rooms – middle-aged men come to face up to changes in their contemporaries (and themselves) after two decades, at times having to adjust their preconceptions. Once again Frayn explores the way in which we project those preconceptions on to other people and on the world around us. To increasing comedic returns he reveals how his characters to varying degrees have had to shed aspects of their old personae and that when for one gaudy night they try to climb back into them 'the effect is as absurd as wearing outgrown clothes would be'.

Donkeys' Years provided glorious acting chances, not least the one female role, Lady Driver, once a much-pursued (and frequently caught) undergraduate, now married to the (absent) Master of the College. Keen to see an old flame, a one-time college idol (who fails to attend the reunion), she tumbles into a nightmare night of forced concealments, trapped often behind doors in potentially hideously embarrassing circumstances and is finally forced, after ripping her dress attempting to repeat her youthful escapades by climbing over the railings, to get into male attire to escape. The second act is a dazzling construct of timing – doors opening and closing feverishly on Lady Driver while a camp cleric relives his glory Footlights days (Frayn gleefully parodies the arch world of 1950s revue in the number, with the vicar playing a naughty nun, 'Nun The Less').

When he heard about it Michael was at once intrigued. He had wanted to produce Frayn's *Clouds*, also written in 1976, and had hovered benevolently over its Hampstead production with Nigel Hawthorne and Barbara Ferris. Set in Cuba with two writers as central characters – their notions of an unfamiliar country constantly unsettling them - *Clouds* had been successful at Hampstead under Rudman, but it was generally felt that Ferris was miscast. When Felicity Kendal agreed to play it she was very keen to have Tom Courtenay co-star – they had been looking for a play to do together – but Michael felt morally committed to Nigel Hawthorne and so finally Ray Cooney produced *Clouds* in the West End.

Donkeys' Years delighted Michael ('a sharp and very funny academic comedy') and he put it smartly into production. Initially both Frayn and Rudman were unsure about Michael's strong advocacy of Penelope Keith as Lady Driver, possibly unconvinced that she could break away from the persona of Sarah, the control-freak bourgeois wife she had played so memorably in *The Norman Conquests*: 'They kept saying, "But there are other actresses. What about Judi Dench? Or whoever." And I just kept saying again and again, "It's got to be Penny Keith."' Eventually I arranged a drink for us all at the Café Royal near the office. And then they agreed.' Other casting was comparatively easy with Peter Barkworth taking on Headingley, an M.P. and Parliamentary under-secretary (in the last scene, with a monstrous hangover, absently spreading shaving foam on his toothbrush, Barkworth was a special delight): 'Getting Barkworth was a great coup – *Telford's Change* was on television and very popular then'. Peter Jeffrey, John Normington (very funny in 'Nun the Less') and Jeffrey Wickham played other guests, with Andrew Robertson as the always-forgotten outsider Snell and the veteran A. J. Brown as the archetypal Head Porter, obsequious on the surface but not to the extent of calling off industrial action by College staff.

Then – 'Off we set on tour – the play was in three acts with two intervals then – and opened in Bath. Very shakily indeed. Business was poor too and audiences just didn't seem to respond. After a show there I heard one of my backers, Edward Sutro, say, "Well, that's £250 down the drain!", which wasn't very encouraging. We persevered – luckily it was a co-operative cast – with Frayn doing a lot of tightening – staggering on to our penultimate date in Holy Week in a very rainy Brighton, the only date then when one played Good Friday. The Globe was promised for London and all should have been well but it was a very dismal week indeed. On Good Friday we were all standing at the back of the stalls – me, David, Frayn and the theatre manager Melville Gillam – when a man came up the aisle, stopping beside Frayn: "Michael Frayn?" "Yes.'" "Congratulations." "Oh, thank you very much." "On writing the worst comedy ever written." He moved off and Gilly said, "Oh, don't mind him, he's on drugs" but it still lowered spirits further.'

Another depressant followed: 'A great friend of Peter Barkworth's was the magisterial Patience Collier who came to see the last Brighton performance. They drove back afterwards to London in total silence until Gatwick, when she turned to Barkworth to say, "Now, I'm going to tell you why you must never appear in London in that play."' Luckily Barkworth ignored her advice.

During the miserable Brighton week Toby Rowland, controlling the Stoll Moss chain, contacted Michael to say that of course they would honour the commitment to the Globe but ('definitely to deter me – he obviously hadn't liked what he'd heard on the grapevine about the play') there would be a nine-week gap before it could open. Still convinced of *Donkeys' Years*'s merit, Michael told the cast of the hiatus while they played their last touring date in Richmond and, similarly committed to the play all (except John Normington, replaced by the equally fine Harold Innocent), agreed to wait, with the proviso that nine weeks be taken off the contracted West End run should it be a success. Further work went on during the re-rehearsal period, especially on the first act, originally over-expository but as reshaped, and with Barkworth and Jeffreys giving object lessons in deftly underplayed comedy in a long, early duologue consisting mainly of repeated pleasantries ('My word!', 'Well, Well', Goodness me' etc.), cleverly lighting the fuses for later explosions. Keith in the second act – her tall, commanding figure constantly subjected to indignity – helped take the play into a deluxe comic zone. Played now with only one interval, the play also seemed more satisfyingly shaped. Not surprisingly, however, Frayn said to Michael during the run: 'I've now made quite a lot of money from this. But I've earned every penny for the obstacles we had to overcome.'

The obstacles had gone on to include mostly downbeat notices ('I remember Jack Tinker in the *Daily Mail* more or less saying why were we all bothering with this'), apart from a glowing review from Robert Cushman in *The Observer*. But *Donkeys' Years* began to build strongly at the box office – clearly a word-of-mouth success – going on to survive various cast changes (Anna Massey and then Amanda Barrie for Keith, Paul Eddington for Barkworth) during its Globe stay of eighteen months. A 2008 Comedy Theatre revival produced by the Ambassador Theatre Group featured a strong cast (Samantha Bond included) and had a healthy run and long post-London tour. The play itself was received much more enthusiastically than in 1976.

Few plays have been so ill-starred as *Balmoral*, Michael's next outing with Frayn. Its central trope is that the 1917 Revolution took place not in Russia but in Britain; Balmoral Castle in 1937, chilly and ramshackle under the totalitarian regime, is a Writers' Residence, currently occupied by something of a B-list including Enid Blyton (with dreams of writing children's books rather than the 'curiously erotic verse' for which she is known) and Hugh Walpole. The once-stately pile is also a war zone between its officious Warden, Skinner, and the wily factotum McNab, who finds himself forced to impersonate an inconveniently dead Walpole just at the time of the government inspector's arrival (the play's comedic variations on identity owe not a little to Gogol).

Michael set up its first production in 1980 at Guildford with Fulton McKay – then featured in television's *Porridge* sitcom – as McNab but Eric Thomspon's production never quite gelled and it travelled no further. In a revised version titled *Liberty Hall*, I programmed it (Michael hovered benevolently over the venture) at Greenwich Theatre in 1982 with Alan Dossor directing an ace cast led by George Cole's Skinner and the great Scots star Rikki Fulton (his long, lantern-jawed face often resembled that of a mournful camel) as McNab. Frayn has written eloquently of the contrast between its wildly enthusiastically received preview, that audience 'on' to every facet of the play's prismatics, and the cool, even chill, reaction on press night resulting in mixed notices; despite a strong Greenwich box office, a transfer was not warranted.

Frayn's luck with the play sadly remained consistent on a Bath production that I directed for the Peter Hall 2009 Season (Michael was not involved). All seemed set fair during rehearsals until Rik Mayall's illness forced him to pull out late in rehearsals; despite an heroic understudy as Skinner, post-Bath plans were abandoned as the play (*Balmoral* once more) again sank from view. Frayn occasionally sighed for Michael's producer's strengths in Bath but remained extraordinarily supportive in the midst of the *sturm und drang*.

Not long after *Donkeys' Years* Michael Rudman left Hampstead to join the National Theatre as an associate director under Peter Hall and Michael rather assumed that Frayn's plays might follow him there: 'Indeed in 1979 Frayn told me, "I've written a play about industry and it has a big cast, you probably wouldn't want to do it so I've offered it to Rudman at the National." I was, I must admit, a little bit hurt. But then Rudman, for reasons I have never completely understood, turned it down. So after reading it and liking it – another work play – despite the cast size (thirteen) I said I'd do it. Peter Wood was offered it to direct but said he'd only do it with Colin Blakely in the lead and he turned it down. It was Frayn who said, "We aren't getting very far with Peter Wood so can we show it to Michael Blakemore?" and I replied, "But he's Peter Nichols's director" – Blakemore had directed Nichols's first three plays – "Are you sure?" And Frayn, with his customary tact said, "Well, I have a feeling that relationship isn't as strong as it was." I found that Blakemore had been contracted to direct three plays for the recently refurbished Lyric, Hammersmith and that he would include Frayn's play, *Make and Break,* in his season if he could have Leonard Rossiter with whom he'd had such a success in *Arturo Ui,* to star.' Despite some grumbles from the American producer behind that Lyric season, *Make and Break* (1980) began there, the highlight of Blakemore's trio.

The play charted new territory for Frayn although as in most of his work a philosophical basis, unforced but omnipresent, underpins its scrutiny of the world of salesmanship and business ethics at a Frankfurt Trade Fair. Set in a hotel suite doubling as a showroom for a company selling partitioning systems of walls and doors for offices (cleverly designed by a fourth Michael on this production, Michael Annals), its central figure John Garrard, the firm's managing director, is one of Frayn's most memorable creations, unforgettably inhabited by Rossiter, his hooded eyes and sense of internal solitude creating another Frayn character dedicated to efficiency. But this time personal identity has become nearly subsumed in a professional one, his driven sales ethic threatening to intrude on basic human decencies. Yet there is here too a sense of compassion for the near-manic obsessive, which came through Rossiter's portrayal of Garrard, full of telling detail as in a beautifully shaded scene, funny and sad by turn, in which he seduces a loyal secretary, Mrs Rogers, played with delicate finesse by Prunella Scales, using all the efficient strategy he puts into his business (even glancing at the label of her shoe as he removes it from her foot).

A world of subterranean urban chaos is suggested by a background of exploding terrorist bombs 'out there' in the city and some shifts from naturalism incorporating the moving walls of the partition systems. Against this background is the business world of a decaying materialism and a sense that polished professional salesmanship can only mask, not prevent, the pain and messy muddle of real life; this emerges forcefully in Mrs Rogers's description of the quiet goals of an unfulfilled, lonely existence and in the figure of Tom Olley, Garrard's Catholic deputy (subtly played by James Grout) not yet totally corroded by the commercial ethic.

Make and Break was written just as Mrs Thatcher was coming to power and elected Prime Minister (its background of urban violence echoing many other plays of the 1970's and 80s). Like other dramatists produced by Michael – Caryl Churchill in *Owners*, Ayckbourn in *Absurd Person Singular* (as early as 1972 and 1974) included – Frayn presciently seemed to anticipate something of the ruthless business ethic that would stamp much of her time in office, one reason perhaps, why audiences seemed to respond so immediately to the play. Its Hammersmith opening went well and at once Michael began plans for its transfer: 'We had trouble. Both Toby Rowland and Donald Albery refused to give it a home. We were rescued at the very last minute when the Haymarket had a flop with *Reflections,* a play about Robespierre (Donald Pleasence once more), which had to be whisked off and so we went in there for a long run, although not an especially happy one' (Rossiter and Scales were 'non-speakers' most of the time – 'He was a marvellous actor but not an easy man'). Surprisingly – Michael suspects because of its complex set and large cast – *Make and Break* has not had a major revival.

A Drury Lane fundraising evening for the Combined Theatrical charities in 1980 included a short play (titled *Exits*) from Frayn about staging a farce, its cast including Dinsdale Landen. Michael heard about it and asked

279

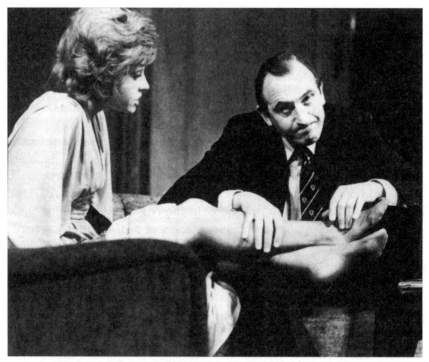

46. Leonard Rossiter's seduction technique (with Prunella Scales)
in *Make and Break*, 1980.

to read it, then commissioned Frayn to expand the idea into a full-length play. The resulting *Noises Off* (1982) was bonanza time for everyone involved including the Lyric, Hammersmith where it opened, despite reservations from the theatre's director Peter James (with his long straight hair, sad eyes and sandals, he was known irreverently to the reunited team of Michaels as 'Creeping Jesus') but, as Michael noticed 'he came round to loving it when the royalties started to roll in for the Lyric after we'd moved'.

Baldly described *Noises Off* may not seem the stuff of theatrical gold. The first act covers the grinding technical rehearsal in Weston-Super-Mare of a formula oops-there-go-my-trousers British farce, *Nothing On*, starring a one-time soap star (also co-producing), Dotty Ottley, with a failing memory ('It's like a fruit machine in there … I never know what's going to come out, three oranges or two lemons and a banana') and having a fling with the younger actor Garry Lejeune. The aloof director Lloyd Dallas also has to cope with a drunk old ham, Selsdon Mowbray, a dim ASM whom he is bedding and a doggedly 'Method' actor, Frederick Fellows ('All my knowledge of world drama is at your service' his director assures him when he agonises over motivation). The second act – Frayn's triumph – takes us to Ashton-under-Lyne a month later, now backstage with *Nothing On* about to begin (we see the back of the twin level multi-doored set and the wings). Dotty is drinking and rowing with Garry who is convinced she is pursuing Frederick, Selsdon is trying hard to fall off the wagon, Lloyd has unexpectedly appeared to see both Poppy (pregnant) and the sexy juvenile whom he has also been bedding, with the matinee audience befuddled by contradictory front-of-house calls. The real joy begins when backstage action and the performance of *Nothing On* combine – some inspired silent comedy played against faintly heard 'onstage' farcical action and a series of sight gags involving props. such as a fire axe, shoelaces knotted together, whisky bottles and (an oldie but a goodie) a phallic cactus – building to mayhem with murder at times only a nano-second away. The third act originally seemed anti-climactic but Frayn continued to revise it through cast changes and revivals and it now has its own comic wattage when we return to *Nothing On*, by now a ragged shadow of its former self, in Stockton-on-Tees near the tour's end two months later. Murphy's Law has kicked in spectacularly – Dotty's lines bear only a faint resemblance to the original, her handling of her crucial prop of a plate of sardines is now in oily disarray, while the telephone has taken to malfunctioning with almost human malignity.

In performance the play can reduce the strongest of men to helpless laughter, although it was hard work getting it to that pitch originally ('When I read it I had to go and lie down' said Blakemore, realising the work and energy the staging would demand). Casting was comparatively stress-free – Patricia Routledge as Dotty, Paul Eddington playing Lloyd with an increasing air of a man travelling into Purgatory, with strong support from such comedic experts as Nicky Henson (Garry) Michael Aldridge (a splendidly sozzled Mowbray) and Roger Lloyd Pack as a much put-upon stage manager. Rehearsals were tough – the second act depends on split-second timing the spontaneous-seeming effect of which demands hours of gruelling repetition. Also: 'The text we started rehearsals and even opened with was much more Pirandellian. It was one of the reasons Eddington accepted Lloyd, which originally gave him a showier role, including a key long speech full of Pirandellian allusions to mirrors and such. But it was – at least I thought it was and Blakemore agreed – a bit self-conscious, a bit of a killer in the third act – so Michael willingly cut and Paul took it well. I went to see the play in Hammersmith the night the cuts went in, and on the way David and I had a row of such magnitude that he got out of the car at Shepherd's Bush roundabout so I saw the play on my own. I suddenly looked at what I had produced and realised this was going to be the kind of smash hit I'd always wanted, even bigger than *Girl in My Soup*. Even my worry that we may have booked too big a theatre with the Savoy proved unfounded. The only flies in the ointment were really just the need to bring the third act up to snuff; and a bit of a downer when we had to line up to meet Princess Margaret after the show on stage and she said to Frayn, "I see you've decided to change tack and amuse us for a change", yet another instance of Frayn being mistaken for Peter Nichols'.

The business was 'colossal' at the Savoy from the outset: 'And, perhaps understandably after a year, the original cast's last performance, which Frayn and I watched, was way over the top. Especially that supposed purist of purists, Ms Routledge, who at one point I thought was about to run up the proscenium arch. Afterwards she rather took my breath away when she said very seriously to me, "You will never see this play performed better than it was tonight." We'd organised a farewell Savoy supper after which I felt I should escort her to a taxi. The driver took a look at her formidable presence and asked, "Will I be safe?" to which she retorted, "As safe as with the Leeds Building Society" and disappeared into the night.'

Altogether *Noises Off* ran for seven years at the Savoy with regular cast changes (Hugh Paddick, Benjamin Whitrow and Christopher Godwin all fine Lloyds, Stephanie Cole a memorably muddled Dotty), with the central joke only occasionally missed ('There were sometimes a few Americans who left after the first act saying, 'We'll come back when they know their lines.'''). It was a big 1983 Broadway success with James Nederlander heading the producers, including Michael, featuring Dorothy Loudon's ripely outrageous Dotty. A National Theatre 2000 revival, with Patricia Hodge cast against the usual grain but very funny as Dotty, and a gloriously pickled Mowbray from Christopher Benjamin, transferred to the Piccadilly (when Lynn Redgrave took over Dotty). Revived in 2001 on Broadway with Patti LuPone as Dotty, it did not quite match up to the first Broadway version but still had a good run.

Few plays combine *Noises Off*'s superbly observed view of the theatre (Frayn had clearly squirreled away a lot from his own experiences), physical comedy and sight gags. He was – as he always acknowledged – lucky with a director like Blakemore and his cast. But what supports the intricate edifice and gives it classic status is that extra dimension in the substrain, appearing in most of his work including his meditative books such as

Constructions. As he put it: '*Noises Off* is not just about the problems actors have with props and doors that won't close – although it is about that – but to do with the problem everyone has with keeping their act going – the panic they feel that everything may become unstuck.'

Although Frayn's next play, *Benefactors* (Vaudeville, 1984) was predominantly a quieter, more reflective play, seemingly at a polar extreme from *Noises Off*'s riot, it spun a variation on its predecessor: 'What most farces have in common is panic – the feeling that things may become unstuck. To some extent *Benefactors* is an exploration of that sense of panic and unease but this time without the cushion of farce.' Michael was immediately enthusiastic about the play, as was Blakemore.

The name most commonly invoked comparatively in the reviews of *Benefactors* was that of Ibsen (fleetingly alluded to early in the play). *The Master Builder* particularly was mentioned – both plays have architects as central characters and both dramatists trace a connection between architecture and life, between the ambition to build high and the expression of personal aspirations and ambitions. Certainly there are echoes of Ibsen in the way *Benefactors* shows domestic life affected and altered by the 1960s push to high-rise architecture, but the analogy cannot be pushed too far.

Technically the play is far from Ibsenite, putting two households on stage simultaneously (Michael Annals's contrasting, steeply raked stripped pine and dark kitchens were striking to look at but hell to play on) and cutting in a filmic, sometimes almost Expressionist style between both time and place, with flashbacks and scenes switching from dialogue to direct address (each of the four characters has a crucial monologue). It traces the way in which four middle-class people mess up their lives. David Kitzinger (Oliver Cotton) is a dedicated, idealistic architect given the challenge of transforming a neglected South London site into a modern housing complex. Not unlike Solness in *The Master Builder*, his professional ideals have led to neglect of his personal life, although his pragmatic wife, Jane (Patricia Hodge) has retreated less into isolation than Mrs Solness, coping in her stride with the crush on David developed by their needy, unfulfilled but draining neighbour Sheila (Brenda Blethyn) married to Colin (Tim Piggott-Smith) an ex-classical scholar whose early Cambridge promise has evaporated, a chill, negative presence. When David compromises all his principles and changes his plans in order to build tower blocks for high-rise living, Jane opposes him and joins the conservationists.

That awareness of human inconsistency at the root of much in Frayn emerges clearly in *Benefactors'* shifting, uncertainly balanced relationships.

David revises his Utopia, Colin develops from weak bystander to become a man of zealous mission, Sheila switches her loyalties to David while by the close Jane has become a kind of spiritual support to Colin. Once Frayn suggested that this wry comedy of (mainly good) intentions is a kind of grandson of his unsuccessful 1971 Greenwich play *The Sandboy* (later revised but never staged as *Up*), which had a city planner as its main character although it lacked *Benefactors'* complex layers of irony as it observes reversals and alterations of convictions. Blakemore talked perceptively about *Benefactors* when readying its Broadway production, indicating that while the play generally was perceived in England as a social comedy for him it seemed more to explore the way so many political solutions and attitudes, which people hoped would lead to amelioration in fact proved somewhat moribund and that people do not know any longer in which direction to put their good will. He felt that *Benefactors* was a truly important play in that it summed up the dilemma of our times, often viewing 1968 from the sadder perspective of the 1980s.

The English reviews were mainly positive with some strange reservations (John Peter in *The Sunday Times* said that Oliver Cotton was not Jewish enough – Cotton politely wrote to the newspaper to point out that he was, in fact, half-Jewish) but the emphasis tended to be on the Ibsenite overtones. It ran profitably, with a cast change (Polly Adams, Nicky Henson) after the first six months, for a year.

Intriguingly, on Broadway with a mainly American cast but still under Blakemore, there were far fewer literary comparisons and the play was examined through a different lens. *The New York Times*'s Frank Rich said after *Benefactors* had opened successfully: 'I don't know a single American, myself included, who saw *Benefactors* in London who imagined that the play would last a month in New York.' It was Rich who almost single-handedly had caused *The Real Thing* to be totally reconceived for Broadway whereas *Benefactors* was seen in the same setting and staging. Reviewing the New York version he remarked on a sea change noting that what on the Vaudeville stage had seemed a social play about urban planning emerged now as much more a play about character and the nature and price of change. Most American theatre critics – who tend to be less literary in bias than the English – concentrated less on Ibsen comparisons than on the way *Benefactors* conveys the disillusionment and the death of innocence of a post-1960s era (applicable to America just as much as to the UK) in which shining visions of Utopia or benevolent Camelot-style democracies faded away.

Its New York cast – Simon Jones as Colin was the only British actor – did mostly well by Frayn (especially Glenn Close as Jane, exploring profitably the character's darker side) although there were more than a few carps over Sam Waterson's elusive British accent as an architect very different from the one he had played in Woody Allen's *Hannah and Her Sisters*. The *New York* magazine critic John Simon felt Waterson was 'a black hole smack at the centre' of what he still found 'a wonderful play', one which captured not just the ironies of existence but 'the multiple bottomedness of life' as it traces the changes caused by human benignity as well as malignity. Helped by the release of *Fatal Attraction* with Close, a runaway movie hit, *Benefactors* became, unexpectedly to many, a major Broadway success; over its Christmas period, the two holiday weeks piled up a total of $142,000 above the break figure, remarkable then for a serious new play. *Benefactors* was unusually lavishly garlanded; it won the Olivier, *Evening Standard* and *Plays and Players* London Theatre Critics' Awards for Best Play and the New York Drama Critics' Circle Award for Best Foreign Play of the 1985-86 Season.

For Michael it only increased his respect for Frayn's work: 'Our theatrical values seem very similar. In *Benefactors* one line had a profound impression on me, when Colin says to David, 'The thing is you imagine everyone is like you. But they're not.' I think I'd always thought it but *Benefactors* confirmed it – Michael Frayn knows more about the human heart than most writers.'

Benefactors made a fascinating counterpart, although it was oddly not remarked on, to a play produced by Michael the previous year, Stephen Fagan's *The Hard Shoulder* (Aldwych, 1983). First presented at Hampstead this acerbic comedy, centred round a middle-class entrepreneur who moves from the wine trade (cue inevitable gag about being 'in hock') into property speculation with dreams of developing a decaying Islington square, nearly going under when his gamble that a planned motorway will be cancelled goes awry, had some strikingly perceptive writing, opening strongly with Toby (Stephen Moore) on the rooftop surveying his development prospect. It cleverly avoided being a simple anti-capitalist piece; beautifully constructed (Fagan was at one time a carpenter), gradually the play began to suggest that the desire for financial security can become a sole goal leading only to spiritual diminution, revealing itself by its close as a potent metaphor for a greedy, get-rich-quick era.

Michael knew that a playwright's West End debut without a star cast and with some uncomfortable home truths piercing the comedy was a risky project, calling for tight transfer budgeting (it was eventually capital-ised at £57,000) and hoping for very good notices. In the event they were very mixed, ranging from Michael Coveney's enthusiasm in the *Financial Times* ('From a narrow base it builds to a reverberative comment on our times') to Milton Shulman's disappointing dismissal in *The Evening Stand-ard*. The *Daily Telegraph*'s Charles Spencer, while admiring the play and its construction, added – pointedly for any producer at that time – 'I am not sure whether such well-crafted qualities are any longer a guarantee of West End success.' They were not for this play; very soon after opening Michael had to put royalty waivers into operation but even reduced running costs could not save Fagan's play from closure after only two months.

In the later 1980s the Codron/Frayn bond strengthened when Michael, who rarely contemplated revivals, produced in the West End two Frayn translations of Chekhov as well as *The Sneeze*, a kind of Chekhov revue. In 1988, with Blakemore directing he assembled a mouth-watering cast (Mi-chael Gambon and Jonathan Pryce as Vanya and Astrov, Greta Scaachi and Imelda Staunton as Ilyena and Sonya) for *Uncle Vanya* (Vaudeville). The design, by Blakemore's then-wife Tanya McCallin, was awkward on the small Vaudeville stage. McCallin said to Michael who then owned the theatre: 'I don't know how I'm going to do this. You've got the smallest opening in London.' At the same time he was trying to lure the producers of the Broadway success in *M. Butterfly* – the set of which, including a great curved staircase, presented sightline problems in the stalls – to the Aldwych, which he managed for Nederlander, only to be told, 'We can't come there. You've got the lowest overhang over the stalls of any London theatre.' For a time Michael liked to claim that 'I was the man with the lowest overhang and the smallest opening in London'.

Despite the promise – it can happen with starry projects – this *Vanya* did not delight unanimously, although Michael admired it very much. For some, although individual performances were mostly fine (Benjamin Whitrow an especially vivid, solipsistic Professor) and while Gambon and Staunton combined most touchingly at the close overall, they did not quite cohere into a sense of a shared world. But it was a major box office success for the cast's six-month contracted run.

The Cherry Orchard (Aldwych, 1989) had the jewel (and box office mag-net) of Judi Dench as Ranevskya, although Michael was equally pleased to land the new *wunderkind* on the block, Sam Mendes, as director. The design, by another new young name, Paul Farnsworth, was ravishing, eschewing the cliches of forestry and silver birches for an adaptable space

47. Timothy West and Rowan Atkinson in 'The Inspector General' in
Michael Frayn's Chekhov evening of *The Sneeze*, 1988.

swiftly moving from interior to exterior, while Mendes' production was swift, refreshingly unsentimental and often very funny. Dench was captivating throughout, in the first act especially when returning to her home like a child arriving for the holidays, giggling, weeping, teasing, flirting and scolding by turn. Not since the great Franco-Russian Lila Kedrova (with whom Dench had appeared in the West End production of *Cabaret*) played Ranevskya in a Prospect Theatre 1960s production had an actress so surely captured the emotional turn-on-a-kopeck Slavic volatility of the character. As often on productions with companies led by Dench it was a very happy atmosphere; for a time her dressing-room door had affixed to it the cover of Jeanette Winterson's *Sexing The Cherry* (this Ranevskya was quite a flirt) and the Aldwych backstage corridors echoed to considerable laughter.

More genuinely involving for Michael was *The Sneeze* (Aldwych, 1988). Frayn always stressed that Chekhov saw himself as a comic writer; he paid his Moscow medical-school fees by writing squibs and skits for comic papers. His plays for Frayn were the logical extension of them, likewise studies in the human comedy. Very adroitly Frayn assembled an evening including Chekhov's short plays (*The Bear* and *The Proposal* included) and adaptations of short stories or sketches, the whole project combining to make a kind of vaudeville or revue. It was Michael who suggested casting Rowan Atkinson ('I'd really taken to him when he appeared for me in revue at the Globe – a special talent') and its pre-London tour opened in Atkinson's hometown, Newcastle ('My abiding memory of that time is trying to get a cup of Earl Grey Tea in a hotel which had a statue of him but of whom nobody on the staff had ever heard'). The tour had its strains: 'Tim West was initially a bit shaky on his lines and Ron Eyre, directing, got worried. West's wife Pru Scales came up to give moral support. But I don't think she cared for much of it – she left a note about it all for Ron but luckily it got put into the wrong pigeon-hole and he never got it. But I rather enjoyed the process on *The Sneeze* – it was rather like the old days of revue and I was quite involved with the running order and the balance of the evening. We decided to end with *The Bear*, which was very generous of Rowan because that piece was really Tim's big chance and finally he was terrific in it.'

The designs, by the emerging Mark Thompson, were a major plus – a tottering towering framework of books framing eight brilliantly coloured sets, fairly minimal but always witty. Michael was touched – 'I took it as a real compliment' – when Thompson said to him, 'I hadn't realised that working in the commercial theatre could be so pleasant.'

By the time *The Sneeze* reached London, Eyre had worked it into splendid shape, both capitalising on and at times usefully subduing Atkinson's innate anarchy. The star was especially splendid – creating some epic laughs – in the title-piece as a lowly government official at the Bolshoi seated behind West's ursine big-wig, unguardedly sneezing snot over his superior's bald pate and then trying unsuccessfully to remove it. This was a superb piece of pre-*Mr Bean* mainly silent comedy.

There probably had to be a blip in Frayn's successes, if only a temporary one and *Look, Look* (Aldwych, 1990) illustrated the old saying that if you have to have a flop you might as well have a big flop and this was massive. Expectations, of course, were very high. Like *Noises Off* this had its origins in a benefit evening (for the family of Colin Blakely after his too-early death) at the Lyric Theatre when Frayn provided a short play with the audience looking at an on-stage audience at a play (including Penelope Keith, Jeremy Irons, Patricia Hayes) and as it were eavesdropping on their secrets, guilts and liaisons. Perhaps thinking that lightning might strike twice Michael again suggested a full-length play from the idea. He was 'a bit baffled' when he read it, although reminded himself that *Noises Off* had been often difficult on the page, not quite sure of the Pirandellian strain, finally downplayed in *Noises Off* but which surfaced strongly in the later stages of the new play. 'Then we had a series of warnings that it might not work. We tried hard to get Michael Blakemore and it was a great blow when he politely declined. And we heard about an Italian production which hadn't worked. I was then quite enamoured of Mike Ockrent who'd done a good job on the Stilgoe and Skellern revue for me and he'd directed *Me And My Girl*, also revising the book with Stephen Fry. So we were buoyed up again when we got Ockrent to direct and, although it meant a long wait, Stephen Fry to star in it.'

It was cast strongly throughout – Margaret Courtenay as a fearsome dowager, Gabrielle Drake her attractive daughter and Robin Bailey as a quiveringly lecherous old queen bent on the seduction of an only seemingly innocent young man – but early into rehearsals it was evident that the play seemed leaden-footed, especially in the second act as the 'audience' becomes involved in the play they were waiting for and then looking at in the first with Fry as director trying to organise events. 'There was constant rewriting during rehearsals and the previews, some of which passed in grisly silence. The opening night was awful to sit through and when I overheard afterwards the *Standard* critic Nicholas de Jongh say to a fellow-reviewer, 'I'm going to put the boot in' it only confirmed my fears that we were dead in the water – mind you, I can sometimes find myself in sympathy with that sort of review, being a curmudgeon myself. Anyway, after the virtually unanimous rotten notices Frayn, nobly I think, asked me to take it off, very rare for an author. But the business – practically non-existent – would have dictated it soon anyway. We had a jolly cheer-ourselves-up dinner at Luigi's up the road – I took a private room for the company – and Fry made a very good speech ('OK, it was a turkey. But it had fine plumage').

Soon afterwards Michael presented the only revival of a play he had revived previously when he produced *Private Lives* (Aldwych, 1990) once again. He had tried to lure Joan Collins into *What the Butler Saw* (at a lunch her agent said to Michael while the star powdered her nose, 'Forget it – she's only here because she knows you have the rights to *Private Lives*'). I had suggested the play to Michael – I had directed a successful production at Greenwich and then in the West End for the play's 50th Anniversary in 1980 with Maria Aitken and Michael Jayston and was keen to tackle it afresh – but I passed on the chance to direct Collins in it and perhaps was irritatingly purist in reaction when Michael told me he was going ahead with her as Amanda; there was something of a *froideur* between us (never reaching 'non-speakers', however) for a time. In the event Sara Crowe's gurgling Sybil ran away with the comic honours (I agreed with Michael Coveney on *The Observer* who found both Collins and Keith Baxter as Elyot 'common', rightly adding that while Coward can be vulgar he is never common). But Michael – and David – were right about its commercial viability; given ravishing Carl Toms sets it received acres of publicity and played to strong business. Michael wisely kept out of a subsequent U.S. tour and brief Broadway run, a financially rocky venture.

The magazine *Plays International* at the time speculated that Michael, 'not normally perceived as a revivalist', had produced Coward's play as a reaction to *Look, Look*, adding the hope that, if so, it was only a temporary expedient – 'It is very bad news indeed for the West End if it is not'.

In the event Michael was soon back in the business of producing predominantly new work, although *Look, Look* undoubtedly had been a jolting experience. Its financial failure also coincided with one of the less happy times in his life following the end of his relationship with David (who remained in the business until 1996) and then when his affair with Mark Brough finished. Casual flings now had little appeal – he really always preferred the continuity of a relationship – and his life at this stage seemed somewhat aimless. At the wedding of his nephew Stephen, the reception

"No Ma'am, Joan Collins has that part"

48. Michael receiving his CBE (despite *Crown Matrimonial*) –
his advertising agency's version.

was held at the Roof Garden above Barker's, Kensington on a glorious
summer day. As a waiter with canapés approached Michael once again felt
a *coup de foudre* – 'My heart literally stood still. He was very friendly, tall
and blond with a wide open smile. We had quite a talk – he later told me

291

49. Gary Woods with marsupial in Australia.

that back in the kitchens he'd told the other staff, 'You'll never believe this – I'm being chatted up by the bridegroom's father!' I asked him out for a drink that evening to be told, 'OK, but it has to be on my manor'. So we met at a bar on The Highway near Tower Bridge and that started the Gary Woods affair.'

This never had the settled air of previous or subsequent attachments. Gary – extremely good-looking, rather like a young Steve McQueen – never moved in with Michael who perhaps invested more in the relationship than Gary, always an independent spirit and on occasion rather moody. They travelled (Australia, Israel, the USA) a good deal – Gary was a sun-worshipper, and adored sunbathing rather more than the theatre, in which he had only a passing interest – but although they often seemed happy together Michael's friends tended to feel that this was not a partnership that fundamentally assuaged the loneliness he had felt since the split with David. Superficially it was business as usual and he seemed his chipper self most of the time, but on occasion at that time at unguarded moments, he could seem abstracted, almost at a remove from the company he was in.

By the time the Codron/Frayn team was reunited later in the 1990s the affair with Gary had ended, with Michael now seemingly contentedly settled in a new relationship and living a different lifestyle. Chester Terrace was sold and in London Michael moved into a compact duplex on the Thames near St Katharine's Dock, with a splendid view of Tower Bridge while in Kent he finally bought his first freehold property, an attractive, mellow half-timbered house near Sissinghurst with beautiful gardens (with pool and tennis court) running down to a small lake. The moves were definitely part of an urge to begin afresh. His new young partner, Mark Rayment, was an aspirant director, dark-haired (unusual for Michael), very bright and quick-witted. He did not care for the Rolvenden house, with its associations with David and with his excellent eye he supervised the redecoration of both the London apartment and the house in Kent.

Mark also occasionally worked for Michael – he assisted Simon Gray and Alan Ayckbourn and solo he directed the only revival of one of his own previous productions which Michael has produced, a production of *The Killing of Sister George* (Ambassadors) with Miriam Margolyes. In 1995 the play seemed tamer than in the 1960s and the production was neither particularly happy nor critically praised. On tour prior to London, Michael felt that he must not combine the personal and the professional; Eddie Kulukundis took over the day-to-day production of the play (sometimes prone to mix up names, he sent his manager to Richmond to see it, calling it *The Killing of Susan George*, suggesting possibly a more intriguing evening). Mark also directed a less than successful new Stephen Churchett play, *Heritage*, at Hampstead – but had he really been ruthlessly ambitious, it is likely that he would have asked to do so much more. At that time his energy was ideal for someone whose life had needed a new sense of direction. Now it was Mark who accompanied Michael to Scarborough for the latest Ayckbourn or during the winter to a favourite retreat, La Gazelle d'Or, an eccentrically stylish hotel in Morocco near the Atlas Mountains to which John Mortimer had introduced him.

In business Michael still missed David – they had had an ideal symbiosis and Michael had been able to bounce ideas off him – and found solo producing harder than it had seemed when he was on his own at the start of his career. The Vaudeville was no longer an additional workload – it was sold in 1996 to Stephen Waley-Cohen who owned the Victoria Palace – but there was the continuing management of the Aldwych to deal with, which David had coped with so easily. Michael now began occasionally to co-produce, usually with Lee Dean, a quiet, dapper younger producer with a background mainly in touring productions but with a good business head and access to investors at a time when some of Michael's were beginning to retire or die.

50. With Mark Rayment at Bodiam Castle.

The new-found energy sparked by his new life with Mark activated Michael for a reunion with Frayn and a return to the revue format with which he felt most creatively involved as a producer. *Alarms & Excursions* (Gielgud, 1998) with Blakemore directing and using an ingenious young designer, Lez Brotherston, was an evening of eight sketches and short plays most of which touched on aspects of an increasingly technological gadget-driven age, another angle on a basic Frayn theme, our hopeless, hapless attempts to comprehend or find at least some kind of order in an unsettling universe. This is best illustrated in a blissful episode involving a vital telephone call from a tetchy tax inspector unable to believe that the burglar alarm, the baby alarm and the smoke alarm are simultaneously disrupting his call. Best of all for many was the climactic 'Immobiles' with Robert Bathurst excelling as an ineffably courteous German landing at Gatwick to find that his host is waiting for him at Heathrow, and then hearing (on another accursed machine) his hostess setting him off on a journey that gets him mugged and taken into the arms of the NHS, but still polite ('Hello, this is Dietrich'), a piece of enjoyably Feydeauesque heartlessness. Some pieces misfired – Felicity Kendal was less than convincing as a rabid Thatcherite figure having a speech destroyed by a misfiring autocue – but much of the evening, scored to an intricate soundscape of telephone bells, buzzers and alarms and with Nicky Henson and Josie Lawrence completing a versatile quartet, was teasingly diverting.

Alarms & Excursions had a tricky pre-West End tour, often to disappointing business. After an early shaky performance at Guildford Michael wrote in crisp detail to Blakemore with a list of notes (counselling against too much 'funny' acting principally) and insisting 'we *must* tighten at Malvern'. The work on the road pulled the evening together just in time, but it met with a mixed reception (although only the stand-in *Standard* reviewer, Nick Curtis, dismissed it out of hand as 'a waste of time'). After a strong box office start it struck a sticky patch with oddly seesawing business but, helped by a revised rental deal with the Really Useful Group, now controlling the Stoll Moss theatres, it recouped its costs over the six months of the run.

No bigger contrast to *Alarms & Excursions* could be imagined than *Copenhagen* (Duchess, 1999), the next Frayn play to appear in the West End under the Codron management (Lee Dean co-produced) and, for Michael, a special one: 'I think it's one of the best things I've ever done. It was sent to me at the same time as it went to the National with Frayn saying, 'A play about two philosophers and Uncertainty Theory may not be too commercial'. Both Michaels – Frayn and Blakemore – were getting fractious because they couldn't get a commitment date out of Richard Eyre. I was on the Board of the National so I had a way in to urge Eyre to programme it and he did. The understanding was that I'd have first refusal on it for transfer, although I'd still have done it even if the National turned it down. And I knew with absolute certainty after the first preview that – barring an unlikely poor reception – it would be a success.'

A mind-expanding play about a meeting – Frayn's fictional speculation – between nuclear physicists Werner Heisenberg and Niels Bohr in the latter's Copenhagen house in 1941, Copenhagen centres round the hypothesis that Heisenberg might possibly have held back data on the atomic bomb from the Germans, convinced that Hitler would have used it. But the thrust of the play is based on *un*certainty (and the chances of any producer presenting two plays drawing on Heisenberg's theories – Hapgood was there before Copenhagen – must be most uncertain); the questions hovering over the scientists' motives are counterpointed by Heisenberg's own scientific observation that the very act of observing something prevents us from knowing precisely how it will behave. Throughout the play is packed with philosophical subversion, inevitable perhaps from a writer like Frayn, educated in a Cambridge still shadowed by Wittgenstein's legacy ('I think there's a drop of philosophy in everything I've written' Frayn once owned).

Blakemore gave what could have been a static, wordy play a production of electrifying, fizzing clarity, at times sending his actors across a nearly bare stage in echo of the nuclear turbulence at the play's core. He saw that two seemingly utterly contrasted plays – Noises Off and Copenhagen – both took an incident and then repeated it from different perspectives in later scenes, both as it were different takes on reality. In Noises Off it is one collapsing in smithereens and in Copenhagen one which becomes ever more elusive the nearer the truth of events the scientists reach. It can sound arid in description but audiences could connect with quite dense material because the production and performances matched the lucidity of the writing. They could see that the way perceptions of reality can be altered impacts on their own lives. This was much helped on Copenhagen by Michael having the Duchess reconfigured (even cladding its cream Art Deco walls in black) to provide the same intense crucible in which to focus the play as was the case at the National's small Cottesloe auditorium. With the tightly disciplined performances from David Burke, Sara Kestelman and Matthew Marsh it packed the Duchess, absorbed a cast change and proved that the commercial London stage could still house serious drama without major stars in the teeth of an ever-swelling number of musicals and encroaching 'celebrity casting'. On Broadway, co-produced by James Nederlander and managed by Liz McCann, Copenhagen confounded its many sceptics and survived some downbeat notices (including John Simon in New York magazine) to have a satisfying run.

Of course the National Theatre imprimatur had helped the further commercial chances of Copenhagen. Frayn's next play in this Indian Summer for his work, *Democracy* (2004), also began on the South Bank, but things had changed there: 'The understanding was that it should follow the same path as *Copenhagen* after its Cottesloe run. But now Nicholas Hytner and Nick Starr were the National's artistic and administrative directors. When *Democracy* opened I said very early that I should like to transfer it, co-producing with Lee Dean, and Blakemore was definitely given the impression that it would move after the Cottesloe, as were the actors. Then the National said they didn't necessarily after all want to follow that route and also that they'd got an unexpected gap in Lyttleton Theatre scheduling so they wanted to take *Democracy* there for a run of performances (thirty-nine in all), not playing in repertoire. This meant it was seen by another 39,000 people before we could move it. Then we went to the Wyndham's – the revised design for the Lyttleton ruled out the Duchess or a small house – where it started well but quite soon began to sag. It really never took off as a solid hit there and it didn't recoup – it only nearly washed its face – in the West End.'

For some *Democracy* was even finer than *Copenhagen*. At that time the British theatre, stirred by disillusion over New Labour and by the Iraq war, was seeing an upsurge in political writing – David Hare's *Stuff Happens* and *The Permanent Way*, and a series of provocative docudramas (including *Guantamano*) at North London's Tricycle Theatre. There was a school of thought, including the young-Turk dramatist Mark Ravenhill, which held that our loss of the Brechtian ability to make direct contact with an audience in what Ravenhill called 'our formulist, shapeless, non-ideological world' made political theatre today able to reach only the converted. While the director of the Out Of Joint company and of *The Permanent Way*, Max Stafford-Clark would counter that there is nothing wrong with a good preach, that it is still possible to do so, and even change things by doing so, in the theatre.

Democracy does not preach but it proved that against the conventional odds, 1970s German coalition politics and the career of Chancellor Willie Brandt could make riveting political drama and reach a large audience. And like most first-rate political drama, its meshing of a scrutiny of political treachery and one of devious human nature inevitably raises wider questions. For some, *Democracy* served as a metaphor for the Blairite era, seeing parallels in the dilemmas of Brandt's Social Democrat government and those of Blair's New Labour, but that was not at the forefront of Frayn's mind when writing; although he could see that both men were charismatic leaders who lost their glamour (he was in Berlin for *The Observer* when

Brandt's fall began) he wrote the play prior to the Iraq war, which rapidly began to tarnish Blair's allure.

Set in Brandt's private office (Roger Allam was superb casting, never quite at ease in his body and beautifully conveying the man's internal isolation) and in the Bundestag in Peter J. Davidson's Escher-inspired split-level set, *Democracy* traces a spy story in the way an East German Stasi 'sleeper' Guillaume (Conleth Hill) is planted in the West Germany of 1956, rising through the Social Democrat ranks to become Brandt's closest aide, assisting with his policy of Ostpolitik, attempting to bring the two Germanies of his era towards some kind of rapprochement, and then to the 1969 election and the start of Brandt's fall as Guillaume is exposed as a spy.

Frayn humanises his historical figures, often wittily and on occasion with piercing insight. Few episodes in his writing are as affecting as the scene in which Brandt kneels at the shrine of the Warsaw Ghetto against Guillaume's overheard words: 'The German who has no cause to kneel went back into the lowest depth of German history and knelt for all of us.' Also stunningly effective was the climactic fall of the Berlin Wall, the bewildered politicians gazing out into the auditorium, which gradually fills with the noise of crumbling masonry, peaking in the collapse of the walls of the set. Like so much of Frayn, it was a quintessentially theatrical scene, impossible to reproduce with the same devastating impact in any other medium (even *Noises Off* became a mostly mirth-free zone on screen).

In his totally absorbing and accessible portrayal of an ideologically divided Cold War-era Germany and its sometimes compromised coalitions he built another metaphor for those human contradictions and paradoxes which, in the end, make democracy 'the least worst' kind of government. But it is essentially a human story, humanely handled, which comes over so potently in the theatre, one at which, as with *Copenhagen*, audiences can take on the complexities to see their own involvement plain, realising Frayn's aim: 'I wanted to write something about the complexity of the human decision-making process and I suppose politics is the most dramatic exemplar of that. How does a democratic country reconcile the viewpoint of millions, especially in a country with a federal system dependent on coalition.'

Prior to its opening Frayn self-deprecatingly described *Democracy* as 'a play about ten men in suits' but in actuality the play has genuine stature, living up to his model of Schiller; *Democracy* both grips and stimulates throughout. It came at a time when the West End stage seemed in danger of starving for want of good, provocative new plays; the American theatre writer Matt Wolf had described the West End then as 'set on a collision course … a once-crucial nexus of talent gone on Kamikaze autopilot'. The play opened in the West End with Michael, although buoyant at its success, sharing some of Wolf's concern: 'Plays are having a tricky time unless they are under the subsidised banner – the audience for new plays in the West End is more limited than it has been. And there's also the total absence of the single play on television.'

The ties between author and producer remained strong; Michael was deeply fond of Frayn and always enjoyed meals with him and his second wife, the writer, Claire Tomalin. He had high hopes for the National Theatre's production of *Afterlife* (2008), Frayn's play on the extraordinary career of Max Reinhardt and his theatrical collaborations which to a degree, as Frayn acknowledged to Michael: 'I intended in part as a tribute to Michael Blakemore and to you. There are some slight echoes of Reinhardt in both of you.' But sadly the production did not succeed, partly (as Frayn admitted to Michael) because he 'did not find another character strong enough to test Reinhardt' (Roger Allam once more), partly because of a misguided physical production. Like others Michael felt that the more intimate sections of the story in particular were stymied by a soaringly grandiose set by Peter J. Davidson, impressive but one which simply dwarfed the human figures. He had found the play intriguing on reading it and had sent Frayn a rhymed note of thanks and congratulations: 'In your depiction of Max Reinhardt/ You have made a Work of Art./ I knew that he had filmed 'The Dream'/ With Mickey Rooney, way off beam,/ But I was held in total thrall/ By your mastery of it all.' It says understated volumes about their firm mutual loyalties that Frayn could write back after the icy shower of most of the reviews: 'Anyway, it was worth writing *Afterlife* just to get your response in verse.'

CHAPTER 17

THE SCARBOROUGH CONNECTION

For almost half a century Alan Ayckbourn has been the most consistently successful dramatist on the London commercial stage. The National Theatre also presented his work regularly under both Peter Hall and Richard Eyre – often larger-scale plays including *A Small Family Business* and *House & Garden* – while the RSC produced one of his more unsettling pieces, *Wildest Dreams*. But Michael has been by far Ayckbourn's most regular collaborator; between 1970 and 2002 the Codron office oversaw twenty Ayckbourn productions.

Statistics seem to dominate surveys of Ayckbourn's career – over seventy plays including musicals, revues and children's plays – but more remarkable than numbers is his work's consistency of invention, its technical innovation yoked to an almost unerring understanding of stagecraft (his book on playwriting is tellingly called *The Crafty Art of Playmaking*). More, perhaps, than any other contemporary dramatist he has had – and kept – his finger on the pulse of British life and *mores* since the 1960s, whether the plays are set in the present or the future, in kitchens, bedrooms, living rooms, garages, attics and gardens (a favourite location – usually with serpents in the shrubbery), in City boardrooms, Savoy Hotel suites, Spanish villas, Docklands apartments, television studios or on board a cabin cruiser. From the seemingly brave new world of 1960s idealism personified by Theresa the frustrated young wife in *How the Other Half Loves* (1969) through the prefiguring of a ruthless 'Greed is Good' business ethic from Sidney, the self-made developer in *Absurd Person Singular* (1973), the scrutiny of a divided social fabric in *Way Upstream* (1981) or of a dystopian futuristic world in *Henceforward ...* (1987) to a blackly comic survey of domestic and social corruption in *A Small Family Business* (1987), to probing television's role as it feeds – and feeds off – a public avid for celebrity culture (*Man of the Moment*, 1988) through to the world of luxury London waterfront apartments as the economic climate slides again towards recession in *Damsels in Distress* (2002), Ayckbourn has beadily, hilariously and compassionately monitored the national moral consciousness.

Always unpredictable (Ayckbourn's boredom threshold is low) – Michael enjoyed especially this aspect of the collaboration ('I was never quite sure what surprise might be in store next') – Ayckbourn never really was a lightweight *boulevardier* as he was initially labelled critically. Even an early piece as apparently soufflé-light as *Relatively Speaking* (1965), his first commercial success, pivots on duplicity, deception and that perennial Ayckbournian theme, man's inhumanity to woman. The politics of daily personal life, of Christmases, tea parties, mealtimes, anniversaries and birthdays around which classic rituals so many of his plays revolve, occupy him more than overtly political issues. The one play that was widely labelled a 'political' play – *Way Upstream* (1980) – is actually not in his top-flight vein. It was generally seen – to his dismay – as a plug for a middle-way political path at a time of political extremes, a period in British society which he described as infused by 'nebulous hate'. The play was hexed in its National Theatre production with a much-postponed (and much-publicised) opening due to the leaking tank containing the cabin cruiser on which much of the action is set, and also by Alan Tagg's uncharacteristically gloomy, heavy set, partly why Ayckbourn's allegory was misinterpreted as a kind of commercial for the recently formed Social Democratic Party. Far more convincing was *A Small Family Business* (1987) in which a London clan becomes a Mafioso-like 'family' enmeshed in a spiralling web of corruption from prostitution to the drugs which will destroy its youngest member. This dazzling play was described, intriguingly, by a much younger and supposedly more 'radical' playwright, Mark Ravenhill (author of *Shopping and Fucking*) as '*the* political play' of its era.

Any writer who casts his net as widely as Ayckbourn is inevitably going to face political material, although virtually always in his work that is refracted through the personal or the domestic. Rather than a political writer he is better described perhaps as a moralist. He is unusual among modern dramatists in that he has clear perceptions of good and evil, both of which can figure markedly in his work. Evil can be a palpable presence in an Ayckbourn play – at the close of *Absurd Person Singular* Sidney has become a near-Satanic figure as he compels the other characters to dance, literally, to his tune in its climactic *walpurgisnacht*, plays such as *Man of the Moment* suggest modern morality plays in their opposition of centrally contrasted characters, while the Devil even makes personal appearances, in different guises, in *Woman in Mind* (1980) and, most seductively, in *A Word from Our Sponsor* (1995). This awareness is just one more aspect of Ayckbourn that can make much of his work unsettling, another way in which he can shift the goalposts of comedy; like so many of the dramatists associated with the Codron name, his plays tend to be layered, often containing controversial or complex themes but never abstruse, always – vital for Michael – accessible. Ayckbourn has never forgotten his mentor Stephen Joseph's advice that one of the keys to writing plays for his Scarborough seaside resort venue was to remember that they had to lure disgruntled holidaymakers in from the rain and then keep them diverted for two hours.

Michael and Ayckbourn met first in the early 1960s. David Sutton had acted with Ayckbourn at Scarborough and also with Ayckbourn's first wife Christine Roland (with whom, under the joint pseudonym Roland Allen, he wrote his first produced plays). It was when David and Ayckbourn acted together at Birmingham that Michael met the writer who would become so vital to his career: 'It was in a David Campton play – Campton was a kind of English Absurdist and I was then in my James Saunders Absurdist vein.' Both men tended to be shy socially on first meetings but Michael's enthusiasm for such new, offbeat work as Campton's helped establish an initial bond. Subsequently, when Ayckbourn had become a Peggy Ramsay client Michael went with her to see *Mr Whatnot* (1963) at Stoke-on-Trent under Peter Cheeseman. The title character is one of Ayckbourn's anarchs, a libidinous piano tuner causing chaos in an upper-crust household, who never speaks in the play, much of which – reflecting Ayckbourn's love of silent-movie comedy, Buster Keaton especially – is in mime, including a virtuoso tennis match: 'It wasn't entirely my cup of tea – just a bit twee now and then, although all the sound-score for the mime was brilliant. Peggy talked incessantly all the way there, but she wasn't trying to sell me the play. Peter Bridge had optioned it, although Peggy was her usual ambivalent self about him. Maybe even then she had a notion that he wouldn't last.'

Bridge, a prolific producer then, brought in a new production team and mostly new cast (including Ronnie Barker as a sublimely dithering aristo) for a misguidedly over-arch Arts Theatre production of *Mr Whatnot* (1964), which was crucified by the press. Afterwards Ayckbourn took himself off for a while to Leeds as a BBC radio producer (the period certainly increased his mastery of sound, so potent for in-the-round staging). Returning to the theatre for Joseph at Scarborough, he remained loyal to Bridge on the West End production of *Relatively Speaking*, first directed as *Meet My Father* at Scarborough's old Library Theatre by Joseph who died not long after-wards, with Ayckbourn succeeding him as Director, a position he occupied in various premises, directing the premieres of all his plays there as well, until 2008. Bridge waited for nearly two years to secure the luxury casting of Celia Johnson, Richard Briers, Michael Hordern and Jennifer Hilary, directed by Nigel Patrick, and it ran in the West End for over a year, admired by all connoisseurs of comedy, Michael included ('It was a truly accomplished play – I admired it very much').

There was a troubling volatility in Bridge's personality, with mood swings and fast decisions which could lead to some messy production problems. *How the Other Half Loves*, co-produced by Bridge and a new name from a Greek shipping family, the expansive and well-liked Eddie Kulukundis, was even more successful than *Relatively Speaking* but its casting was the first major illustration of what would become on occasion an issue with Ayckbourn's work in London. Writing usually for a small regional theatre company virtually all his plays – with rare exceptions such as *Woman in Mind* – tend to be ensemble pieces rather than plays with one or two dominant roles suited to the prevalent West End star system.

Playing the benign, bungling businessman Frank Foster in the West End production of *How the Other Half Loves* (Lyric, 1969) was the rampant personality of Robert Morley, a big star used to having his own way (he often wrote or adapted his own vehicles), loved by his public and unlikely to change his habits. The result was an outrageous 'Look At Me' central performance, often very funny, but one which left this ensemble play of all ensemble plays bleeding at the stumps while a cheerfully unrepentant Morley laughed all the way to his bank for eighteen months. It is one of the most difficult Ayckbourns to get right – I have directed it twice, lucky to have had two different superb Franks in Christopher Benjamin and Nicholas Le Prevost, neither of whom unbalanced the play, and Ayckbourn revived it in Scarborough in 2009 – and its author, richer but wiser, remembered the London production's lesson.

The relationship with Bridge foundered on Ayckbourn's *The Story So Far* … (1970), an intricately structured family – play of a middle-aged couple's anniversary weekend with their three very different daughters and their partners going through different permutations, which Kulukundis produced on tour. Bridge angrily refused to co-produce – he was also having financial problems at this time – but Kulukundis did not bring the play, retitled *Me Times Me Times Me*, into the West End.

It was Peggy Ramsay who effectively 'married' Ayckbourn to the Codron office. She could be cavalier about her clients (she disconcerted the young Simon Callow who on first meeting her was asked directly, 'Do you think Alan Ayckbourn will ever write a first-rate play?') but in truth she was perceptive about Ayckbourn's work and anxious to take care of his central dilemma of writing company-structured plays and then seeing them commercially produced in a star-system West End. She had affection for Bridge, not least for his consuming passion for the theatre, but as a producer she found him erratic. Understandably he was furious when Ramsay steered Ayckbourn towards the Codron firm but she was characteristically honest to him: 'The choice of a manager must be made absolutely ruthlessly ... Michael has been entrusted with at least half a dozen of our new writers and has handled them with consummate delicacy as well as efficiency.'

It was a tricky situation for all concerned, Michael included: 'Peter Bridge bore resentment against me to his dying day. At one point not long after *Me Times Me Times Me* he was seeing a psychiatrist, an old St Paul's friend of mine, Montague Joyston-Bechal, who wanted to know what on earth I'd done to Bridge so he could mollify him. For a time after I was elected to the Garrick Club I was scared to go in just in case I met him. But it happens. I didn't poach Alan. Authors do leave.'

Ironically the first Codron/Ayckbourn outing was unsuccessful. Michael took on *Me Times Me Times Me* in a fresh production with a new cast headed by Celia Johnson which foundered on tour largely on the rocks of that old devil 'star'; Johnson, unlike Morley, remained impeccably within the play but could not help but disappoint her fans by appearing, despite her top billing, as only one of an ensemble, and often offstage at that. Dame Celia was aware of the problem. She had very clear ideas about her career too: 'Any play I do has to be judged by the decision whether or not it's worth driving down the A4 from Henley six days a week. And this one isn't.' Wisely Ayckbourn decided to put the play on ice; revived as *Family Circles* in 1978, properly cast as a company piece and played in the round, as in its original Scarborough production, it was much more appreciated at Richmond's Orange Tree Theatre.

After reading *Time and Time Again* (1971), which he liked immediately, Michael was even more enthusiastic when he saw Ayckbourn's own Scarborough production and it was at once put into preparation for the West End. Peggy Ramsay's counsel was wise; she agreed with Michael (and Ayckbourn) that they should approach Tom Courtenay, a rare star actor whose persona usually did not overbalance plays, to play Leonard, an ex-teacher charmer and cause of much emotional mayhem (another in Ayckbourn's line of sometimes unwitting male destroyers) although she had her reservations (worried that Courtenay might be too fey she insisted 'the pixies must remain strictly in the garden') but to avoid stars in the other roles. Courtenay responded positively, as did director Eric Thompson, known to Courtenay from Manchester's Royal Exchange and whose revival there of R.C. Sherriff's *Journey's End* Michael had much admired, beginning for Thompson – ex-actor and television's *The Magic Roundabout*'s British voice – a happy association over four Co-dron/Ayckbourn productions. At this stage and for a while to come the author seemed happy for others to take charge of his London productions: 'What was *never* revealed in these early years of our association was his dictum that he wrote plays mainly so he could direct them. And that remained hidden for longer because of the rapport between Alan and Eric.'

It was rapidly cast 'with Tom Courtenay's only stipulation that Joan, the young girl, be played by someone "not available" so he couldn't do his usual and fall in love. We cast Cheryl Kennedy, then involved with an electrician on the show, but Tom still fell in love. And married her.' Thompson proved an adroit director of Ayckbourn, staging it in Alan Tagg's inventive set, which managed to combine lawn, pond with gnome, conservatory and slice of recreation ground on the Comedy Theatre stage. The central Ayckbourn wobbly marriage – Graham, a domineering mid-dle-manager and Anna, seemingly happy but filling an empty life with busy domestic routine – was subtly played by Michael Robbins and Bridget Turner while Courtenay was a delight as Leonard, manipulating Joan away from her dull fiancée without seeming to but refusing to commit himself finally (his essential passivity makes him a cousin to Simon Gray's Quartermaine). One or two sharper critics mentioned the shadow of Chekhov (Ayckbourn's master – he directed a superb production of *Uncle Vanya* at Scarborough the following year) across this suburban garden with its hints of loss at the centre of the lives portrayed, but it was more widely seen as a whimsical light comedy. It enjoyed a happy and profitable West End run.

'By the end of *Time and Time Again* it was kind of tacit that Alan, Eric and I made a unit.' So it was understood that Michael would take on, whenever mutually agreed, Ayckbourn's West End productions after Scarborough. He was thrilled to receive *Absurd Person Singular* (1972), its basic symmetry involving three couples over three Christmases in three kitchens – all spanking modern with white goods and Formica in the upwardly mobile Hopcrofts, battered pine for the Jacksons, a flagrantly unfaithful architect and his miserable wife Eva, and faded grandeur at the Brewster-Wrights,

51. Michael outside the Criterion during the run of
Absurd Person Singular, 1974.

a bank manager and his tippling wife, their marriage by the third act as cheerlessly defunct as their failed heating system. Class inevitably informs the play – 'Maroon three Englishmen on a desert island and they will start a class system' Ayckbourn once remarked – and the play does suggest the period's shifting social scales, but it also contains some of his most shrewdly penetrating insights into English marriage; Ronald Brewster-Wright's rueful, baffled attempts to articulate his inability to comprehend women were decades before *Men are from Mars, Women from Venus*. There is, too, an underlying perception of the opportunistic business ethic just beginning in the 1970s as England began to swing back to the politics of self-interest ('Dog eat dog' as the emergent entrepreneur Sidney explains, wheedling a bank loan from Ronald) through a decade of social unrest.

The second act is commonly seen as the play's triumph, with an increasingly desperate (and mute throughout) Eva in her messy kitchen trying to kill herself (gas, defenestration, pills, etc.) only to have her intentions misunderstood by her guests, a classic instance of Ayckbourn's special ability to catch audiences between wind and water. But the final act (set 'next Christmas'), moving from the sad sight of two ashen marriages into the energy of the Hopcrofts' entrance, flushed from a local bigwig's party, to galvanise the others into a grisly game of Christmas forfeits, is even more impressive in its orchestration of mood swings and change of pace.

Michael perceived at once that the play marked something of a sea change in Ayckbourn's writing: 'One could see that it was comic but also very perceptive about human frailty and self-deception. The darker strain didn't bother me. I really felt Alan was developing as a writer, always encouraging when you're developing a growing relationship with a dramatist.'

Michael had one residual scruple, shared with Peggy Ramsay, even after seeing the Scarborough production, after which he wrote to the author: 'I still don't find the Hopcrofts dramatically the peers of the Jacksons or the Brewster-Wrights and this makes me somewhat regret that we have to spend the first third of the play principally with them.' Ayckbourn stood his ground in reply, while granting that 'the Scarborough *production* might be a different matter'. He felt that the balance between the couples was right and that the Hopcrofts were a recognisable everyday couple who live on a purely material level with no apparent problems because, simply, they ask no questions. He stressed that the ending was not merely the Hopcrofts dragging the others down to their level but that it contained a moral – 'a very important moral – symbolic in a way. That, in the modern world, the ones who go out of the way to compete will always win over the ones who live life on a deeper, emotional level.' He later remarked to a German critic: 'Beware! The age of Hopcroft is nigh.' Ayckbourn saw the play as 'like an onion', peeling away as it proceeds 'with a light first act, a heavier if farcical second and a quite heavy close.'

In production it was 'a cast of all the talents' – Richard Briers, with a little bristling moustache, slightly reptilian and Bridget Turner as his compliant wife, mostly allayed any lingering scruples from Michael or Ramsay about the Hopcrofts, with Michael Aldridge, resembling a dyspeptic bloodhound with baffled, pouchy eyes, outstanding as the well intentioned but emotionally inept Ronald and Sheila Hancock beautifully charting Marion's decline from visiting condescension to embarrassing, alcoholic wreck.

The first London cast made a real ensemble at the Criterion where yet again Michael found Donald Albery a less than benevolent landlord. He deeply hurt Michael by the insult of sending his son to approach him standing at the back of the circle on the second night (a Friday) after very positive reviews to whisper: 'Tomorrow night second house looking rather thin. Permission to paper the house?' meaning to distribute free tickets before giving the box office even a chance to build. After a year and a

52. Richard Briers and Bridget Turner as the upwardly mobile
Fosters in *Absurd Person Singular*, 1973.

sudden dip in business, Albery gave the production notice and forced Michael to transfer to make way for that classic *There Goes the Bride!* Ayckbourn's play had been capitalised at £25,000 originally, with a weekly break figure of just over £4,000 and had recouped quickly. Michael could have taken the profits and had a long holiday – the move to the Vaudeville and recasting costs would not be cheap – but he told Albery, who was sceptical of its chances of a longer run: 'The business is still such and my relationship with Alan Ayckbourn is such that indeed, I must transfer.' He was able to write gleefully to Ayckbourn when business jumped again just before the move: 'I was pleased to see that our figure at the Criterion was up on the equivalent week last year, so I hope this gives a certain landlord, who keeps scientific graphs of rises and declines in business, food for thought.'

Recasting (for what proved a long Vaudeville stay) saw the old problem of disturbing the essential Ayckbournian ensemble resurface. While Paul Eddington gave a beautifully understated, perplexed Ronald, Fenella Fielding's languorous delivery as Marion not only added to the running time (Ayckbourn reckoned she took about two minutes just to say, 'Oh, look – lovely deep drawers') but tended to unbalance the play. With immense tact – he was very fond of her – Michael tried to help rein her in, writing to say that while he thought she was excellent in the later stages: 'I wish I had the power to convince you that it isn't necessary to feel you must "sell" Act One so strenuously. Your personality and your talent can do it on their own without the additional stretching which I think you are giving the part at the moment.'

Michael's ability to act as diplomatic intermediary was in heavier de-mand on the Broadway production of *Absurd Person* co-presented at the Music Box in 1974 with The Theatre Guild under the venerable but perma-nently doleful Lawrence Langer ('The Walking Sonoril' to Michael and Ayckbourn). With Thompson directing a strong American cast headed by Geraldine Page, Richard Kiley and Sandy Dennis, it began promisingly on the pre-Broadway tour ('It is going to be very big' reported *Variety* from Washington) but the Guild, who had only been able to raise their capitali-sation from many small investors, became 'very antsy'. They had resisted Ayckbourn's suggestion of casting a black couple as the Jacksons ('It would be nice for once to have black characters in a play that never refers to them once as such'), had suggested changing the title and then, bizarrely, pro-posed switching the order of the second and third acts on the grounds that their 'monitors' reported that the second act got most of the big laughs.

Unsurprisingly, Ayckbourn refused, asking Ramsay why the producers had bought the play if they wanted to change it: 'It's like buying a Volkswagen and then pointing out that, by an oversight, those silly Germans had put the engine in the back instead of the front and had they noticed?' The producers also suggested bringing the final curtain down on a 'big finish' with the collapse of the set. Michael spent a good deal of time assuaging the fussed producers, as Langer later acknowledged ('Let me express my great thanks to you for your help in smoothing over our out-of-town activities').

The Broadway production proved a major success, running for nearly 600 performances. Still Langer could not relax, panicking at the merest blip at the box office, prompting Michael to write: 'In a way it is refreshing to find a fellow producer whose pessimism matches my own. Usually I am known as the friendliest manic depressive in the business but I have to tell you that even I would be delighted with the general press reception and box office takings that seem to be flowing into the Music Box.'

The New York critics tended to echo their London counterparts in stressing Ayckbourn's comedic expertise. Only a few – as in London – had spotted the play's substrain, illustrating what by now is the commonplace that many of Ayckbourn's comedies contain potential tragedies. Ronald Bryden in *The Observer* took up cudgels on Ayckbourn's behalf against the familiar suggestion in more radical sections of the British theatre that Ayckbourn succeeds (*Absurd Person Singular* finally ran for 973 West End performances) therefore he cannot be any good ('I put this down to our theatre's odd lack of a genuine, by which I mean populist, left wing') and the equally persistent criticism that he is mainly a skilful technical wizard who manipulates his characters as a geometrical equation inside his dramatic symmetry. Similarly – and generously – fellow dramatist Frank Marcus, then critic for *The Sunday Telegraph*, noted that Ayckbourn was patronised by some more intellectual critics and that his work was unlikely to turn up at, say, the Royal Court, but if one can see past the laughs in *Absurd Person Singular*: 'You will find a more clear-eyed and devastating mirror image of the unpleasant and unacceptable face of capitalism than anything enacted on the stages of our so-called committed theatres.' In this Marcus was glossing Bryden's suggestion that under the fun this dramatist worked stealthily as 'a political propagandist who works on people's minds without them knowing that he's doing it.'

The play has been revived in the West End successfully, its impact still as strong, if not more so, both in 1990 (Whitehall Theatre) in Ayckbourn's

310

own fine Scarborough revival production and in 2007, (Garrick Theatre) when I had a first-rate cast including Jane Horrocks, Jenny Seagrove, David Horovitch and Lia Williams. Both productions were produced by Bill Kenwright.

By this stage Michael and David had become close to Ayckbourn and his partner (later second wife) Heather Stoney, regularly visiting Scarborough, often staying in their sprawling, comfortable Victorian house high up near the town's ruined castle with its stunning views over Scarborough Bay. They also became very fond of Ayckbourn's mother, the outspoken and often outrageous Lolly: 'She was a terrific personality, always engaging and affectionate to me and David. Years later, after David and I had parted I was in Scarborough for Alan's fiftieth birthday with Mark Rayment and she said to me, "You're giving every appearance of being in love. Isn't it wonderful! I know what it feels like! I'm in love!" – and she named an actor who had been in Alan's company but whose tastes I was certain lay in different directions. My face must have registered something because she went on: "Oh, no! Don't tell me you've had him!"'

Initially Michael was uncertain about the viability in the West End of *The Norman Conquests* trilogy (1974). Ranked particularly high by Ayckbourn devotees the plays cover the events at a dilapidated house in the country over one weekend showing the action in the dining room (*Table Manners*), living room (*Living Together*) and outdoors in *Round and Round the Garden*. The owner – unseen but omnipresent, hovering over proceedings from upstairs – is an elderly invalid woman (more than a few detected hints of Lolly in references to this mother's racy past), looked after by her unmarried daughter Annie, courted (in his vague, uncommitted Ayckbournian manner) by Tom, the local vet. On the Saturday Annie's brother Reg and his bossy, house-proud wife Sarah arrive so that Annie can have a short break but Sarah quickly ferrets out that Annie's weekend away is actually an illicit assignation with Norman, married to Ruth, sister of Annie and Reg. Norman is an assistant librarian with 'a rather aimless sort of beard' and a decidedly overactive libido; prevented from enjoying his dirty weekend with Annie Norman instead, like other Ayckbourn males, creates emotional havoc over the weekend as he pursues both Annie and Sarah, beadily eyed by his caustic, long-suffering wife.

Constructed with interlocking ingenuity, each play can stand alone but the joys of seeing the trilogy in sequence include realising what was going on at times in other locations; each play is, as it were, the offstage version of the others. The set pieces – although they are not written as such – have become legendary, including Sarah polishing glasses and rapidly folding napkins into rigid perfection with accelerating Fanny Craddock-ish displacement activity before finding her table seating going hopelessly awry (climaxing in Tom forced to sit in a ridiculously low chair), Reg's sudden fury when the logistics of one of his invented board games are questioned, Ruth's alarm when Tom (labelled 'the creeping vet' by Norman) grasps totally the wrong end of the stick when she tries to coach him in wooing technique, and Norman's clever approach to Sarah, deeply vulnerable under her starched, uptight exterior.

Although the trilogy made for a sell-out success in Scarborough, Michael, like other producers, was unconvinced that the repertoire schedule rotating the plays' performances would work in the West End; this was prior to the real rise of marketing in the commercial theatre, only launched seriously in the wake of *Cats* and the blockbuster 1970s musicals, which saw the ascent of the Dewynter firm for Cameron Mackintosh initially and then the success of other companies entering what by the 1980s had become a competitive field. Greenwich Theatre under its first director Ewan Hooper took on *The Normans* and Eric Thompson began preparing them. Before long Peggy Ramsay went on a full-frontal offensive, set on seeing her client's work best taken care of.

She was aware of Thompson's anxieties about going it alone at Greenwich and wrote to his agent, Irene Dawkins: 'I rang up Michael Codron and said wouldn't he like to take on the play straight away. He asked me if I thought it would be helpful and I said I thought it would. He has therefore agreed and we are drawing up for Michael a straight West End contract. He is the ideal manager for the play in that he twice before used the team of Alan and Eric and because it will be possible to get a considerably better cast at Greenwich if actors know that Michael has acquired the play.'

Ramsay was at her most toughly persuasive ('Don't whimper, Codders') on the telephone to Michael: 'Peggy rang me to say they'd got themselves in a bit of a muddle down at Greenwich – it was difficult casting three plays for what would be a longer than usual run there without at least the possibility of a transfer as a carrot – so I said I'd help out. I agreed to pay for a central London rehearsal room and to expedite the casting. Alan and I seem to talk the same language in that regard – we hardly ever had major issues over casting. We always seemed to agree.' And Ayckbourn was grateful for Michael's care in the casting process. At this time Peter Hall was wooing him heavily to bring a play to the National Theatre ('You can do without the National Theatre but can the National Theatre do without

53. Confusion in the dining room – *Table Manners*, the first of *The Norman Conquests* with Penelope Wilton, Felicity Kendal, Penelope Keith, Tom Courtenay, Michael Gambon, Mark Kingston, 1974.

you?'). Ayckbourn wrote to Hall that he would like to be there at some stage, although he stressed the ensemble nature of his work: 'I feel certain that a great deal of the success of *Absurd Person* is due to the fact that Michael Codron and Eric Thompson have managed to create the feeling of a team.'

The Normans also acquired a fine team, another cast of all the talents – Tom Courtenay as Norman, the gigolo trapped inside a haystack, Felicity Kendal as Annie, Michael Gambon (Ayckbourn had seen him in the TV series *The Borderers* and was also keen on a large, heavy man as Tom), Mark Kingston as the seemingly compliant but surprisingly splenetic Reg, Penelope Wilton a myopically caustic Ruth (Bridget Turner in the West End) and Penelope Keith as Sarah: 'Penny was my suggestion – I'd seen her in a play Donald Sinden had directed out at The Intimate, Palmers Green; her appearance, in a small part, was electrifying. And then I'd seen her be very good in a Francis Durbridge thriller, and the others agreed she was perfect for Sarah. When the plays took off at Greenwich and we were setting up the move to the Globe I got a deputation – Mark Kingston tended to be a good intermediary – bargaining hard that all the actors except Tom (on a percentage) should receive the same money. I had to agree, which meant some of them ended up on much better money than their going rate, but they *were* all first among equals.'

The trilogy took off equally successfully at the Globe, eventually run-

313

ning for well over a year, recasting with Ronald Pickup as Norman and, as Ruth, another of Michael's shrewd choices, Julia McKenzie, who had done mostly musical work but in whose performance of Cole Porter's 'Mrs Lowsborough-Goodby' in particular in the Mermaid show *Cole* he had spotted 'something extra'. Later the production moved to the Apollo. Audiences loved the plays' assured command as they swung from side-splitting comedy to quieter scenes of contrastedly relative inaction – Ayckbourn was especially pleased that in a long scene from *Living Together* with his three siblings simply sitting and reflecting on their mother and family life he could hold the house without any technical tricks or invention. Their reviews in the West End were even more fervent than the Greenwich notices, the *Daily Mail*'s Jack Tinker going so far as to claim for the plays 'a place in the history of British light comedy as indelible as 1066 itself'. They catapulted Keith to major stardom. Soon afterwards she, Kendal, Richard Briers and Paul Eddington co-starred in *The Good Life* on television; as Ayckbourn wrote of Keith to his agent: 'TV viewers will assume I've based her character on *The Good Life* series, which will be a little bit galling.'

On Broadway things were less happy. Eric Thompson did his best but could not weld actors such as Paula Prentiss or Richard Benjamin into any suggestion of an ensemble (the common consensus was that Estelle Parsons's Sarah emerged most creditably) and it never built into a solid New York success. Despite the problems the Brits on Broadway – Ayckbourn, Thompson, Michael and David – had an enjoyable, sometimes riotous, time during the pre-opening period.

In London *The Normans* remained unrevived until 2008 when they re-emerged with great success in Matthew Warchus's Old Vic production (the theatre was reconfigured for in-the-round production), transferring to New York in 2009. Michael always retained a soft spot for the trilogy, which Ramsay constantly referred to as 'that plum that fell into your lap'.

The now seemingly fail-safe producer-writer-director team reunited for another success with *Absent Friends* (Garrick, 1974) set in the executive belt and demonstrating the relaxed freedom and confidence Ayckbourn had acquired in the more reflective sections of *The Normans*. With no complex plot – twists or technical innovation but essentially a 'conversation piece' taking place in one set in real time, at its heart lie more of Ayckbourn's troubled marriages. Paul, a hectoring, insensitive adulterer (played with no bids for sympathy by Peter Bowles) and Diana, lonely without her children who have been sent to public school to 'better themselves' against her wishes are hosting a tea party for an old friend, Colin, whose fiancée has recently drowned. Also present are Marge, who covers the aching void of her childless marriage by brightly treating her husband (another potent Ayckbourn offstage presence – forever on the telephone to Marge with the most trivial problem) like a child, Paul's complacent business associate underling John and his bored young wife Evelyn (whose brief fling with Paul in the back of his car she memorably describes as 'like being made love to by a sack of clammy cement'). Nervously expecting a tricky after-noon, they are wrong-footed by Colin who turns out to be the one blissfully happy character present, constantly by recalling his own supposedly idyl-lic past with his dead fiancée reminding the others of their present dissatisfaction. The comedy of embarrassment is often extremely funny but from the outset there is, too, an undertow of pain, of death (and of the death of love) climaxing in Paul's appallingly insensitive treatment of Diana resulting in her near-breakdown. Richard Briers again demonstrated his understanding of *homo Ayckbournensis* with his transparent innocence as the ever cheery Colin and Cheryl Kennedy captured the venomous frustra-tion of a woman shackled to a weakly compliant husband. It was generally well received critically ('If it is the saddest and most moving thing he has written, it is also the most clear-sighted and the funniest' wrote Harold Hobson) and it settled down profitably at the Garrick while both *Absurd Person* and *The Normans* ran on.

And then came *Jeeves*, the musical adaptation of P.G. Wodehouse on which Ayckbourn (book and lyrics) collaborated with Andrew Lloyd Web-ber produced by Michael White, directed by Eric Thompson, a venture which went spectacularly awry (to no little *schadenfreude* from within the theatre world) although the creators successfully reworked and down-scaled it for the opening (as *By Jeeves!*) of the revamped Odeon in Scarborough as the Stephen Joseph Theatre in 1996 (subsequently the show played the West End and Broadway). Friendships on the 1975 version became strained as the problems on an overlong show (neither Ayckbourn nor Thompson knew much about the complex process of staging a major musical while Lloyd Webber had never composed for a 'book' show) became only too evident. After a dishevelled Bristol try-out Thompson was fired in London previews – the dismissal of the director is fairly traditional on troubled musicals at a late stage – with Ayckbourn taking over as director. When the dust had settled after *Jeeves*'s four-week run, with the question of the next London Ayckbourn play in the air, Thompson sug-gested that he needed some 're-trenching time'. Michael agreed, writing to

315

the director 'it will make for the general good and happiness of us all if you do have a breather' (his workload had been heavy and sadly, before his professional relationship with Ayckbourn could be repaired, he died still in his fifties).

In the event I came on board as director of the next two West End Ayckbourns before he finally began to direct the London productions himself. *Confusions* (Apollo, 1975) was an evening of five interconnected short plays – they were billed as 'An Entertainment' – for a company of five, ranging from an uproarious farce to a Beckettian coda of monologues on park benches. Michael took strongly to this venture: 'My background in revue probably made me respond more positively than other producers who shrank from short plays.' It attracted a top-flight and extraordinarily versatile cast – John Alderton, Pauline Collins (revealing the rare actor's talent of an ability apparently to change shape as well as voice) Sheila Gish, James Cossins and Derek Fowlds ('Five stars in a golden constellation' said one review, remarking on the nimble team-playing of this cast). It was a happy but bizarrely jinxed production; on the pre-London tour Alderton broke his ankle and for a time gamely played in a wheelchair and then on crutches (not easy playing a waiter) before full mobility returned, Sheila Gish was hurt in a car crash and missed six weeks of the run, while Collins's later pregnancy (involving constantly adapted costumes) forbade any extension of the run.

Confusions was well received critically although with some – Milton Shulman most vocally – insisting that the penultimate play, the hilarious *Gosforth's Fete* should be the closing play rather than the ruefully downbeat *Talk in the Park*. Audiences seemed not to mind, and indeed it was no bad thing to have something with which to come down to earth after the mayhem of *Gosforth's Fete*. This was a mini-miracle of spiralling invention set in the marquee of a village fete involving the British weather, a pack of marauding Boy Scouts offstage, a malfunctioning PA system unfortunately publicly airing the news of an unwelcome pregnancy, a drunken fiancée and a climactic disastrously stuck tea urn – the sight of Cossins's unctuous vicar trying to staunch the unstoppable boiling flow but getting his finger stuck in the spout remains impaled on the memory. *The Guardian*'s Michael Billington noted that behind an almost copybook illustration of Henri Bergson's theory of laughter in its picture of people stuck in obsessional grooves, *Confusions* was 'sad, sharp and funny, as if A.G. Macdonnell's *England, Their England* had been rewritten by a Chekhovian who knew that conversation is largely a matter of interrupted monologues.'

54. Marital discord with waiter in attendance – Derek Fowlds,
John Alderton and Pauline Collins
in *Confusions*, 1976.

For the first time Ayckbourn, in 1977, had productions in London at both the National Theatre and in the West End. Peter Hall co-directed with him on *Bedroom Farce* on the South Bank while I directed *Just Between Ourselves* for Michael at the Queen's on Shaftesbury Avenue. Michael said wryly of Sir Peter: 'He is a very lucky Knight'; *Bedroom Farce* was the more obviously commercial of the two plays (indeed there was at the time a good deal of press tut-tutting about the subsidised theatre presenting any overtly 'commercial' dramatist like Ayckbourn) and it went on to play a long West End season after the South Bank run while *Just Between Ourselves* emerged as by far Ayckbourn's darkest and most unsettling piece to date and was a decidedly nervous hit. Set mainly in the garage (a section of patio is also seen) of a surburban house – Dennis is selling his car – it takes place over four seasons and four birthdays. Dennis is archetypal Ayckbourn man – affable, absorbed by his bungling DIY efforts tucked away in his garage safe from emotional proximity to his wife Vera, slowly cracking up from lack of committed attention from her husband and the insidiously undermining domestic rivalry of her live-in dragon mother-in-law Marjorie. A potential buyer of the car, Neil, with his edgily frustrated wife Pam become involved in their lives. A birthday party for Dennis turns to disaster when Vera overlooks the family tradition of baking a cake, capped by Marjorie's birthday when, after failing to get through emotionally to her husband (he interprets 'I need help, Dennis' as meaning she wants assistance with the housework) Vera attacks Marjorie with an electric drill, just as Neil enters the garage with the 'surprise' of a cake with lit candles singing 'Happy Birthday'. The final desolating scene, shot through with dark comedy, sees Vera on a crisp January day, huddled in a blanket on the patio with Dennis, Neil and Pam celebrating her birthday with Marjorie, who seems to have taken on rejuvenated vitality as Vera has declined and who has iced a cake – a very small one – to mark the occasion. Vera remains mute throughout the scene except when she is asked if she would like to go inside the house, now Marjorie's domain, to which she whispers, simply, 'No' before silently mouthing the words while the others reprise 'Happy Birthday'.

On its brief pre-London tour *Just Between Ourselves* diverted and amused up to the unfailing communal roar of delight at the climax to the third scene. But the last scene seriously disconcerted audiences; *Absent Friends*, aspects of *Absurd Person* and the opening *Mother Figure* from *Confusions* had given audiences glimpses of the deeper tone in his work but in 1977 Ayckbourn was still identified mainly with what he once called 'the giggle business' and some audiences genuinely resented the close of *Just*

Between Ourselves; during the final scene there was a regular exodus, complete with banging of seats in protest, during the Richmond week. Michael was somewhat shaken: 'I was not prepared for the reaction to the last scene.' He also got a hard time from Peggy Ramsay 'decidedly grumpy that on this occasion her client Alan Tagg did not design.'

The cast was of the highest quality – Rosemary Leach heartrendingly touching as a Vera sliding into despair, not waving but drowning, Michael Gambon's Neil guiltily enjoying his time with Dennis in the garage more than being with an increasingly sardonic Pam. Colin Blakely's Celtic quality – so suited to a later Ayckbourn, *A Chorus of Disapproval* – crucially just missed the sheer suburban ordinariness of Dennis, unable to disguise a complexity which the character simply did not possess although he was wonderfully enjoyable as he botched yet another piece of DIY. The play went – just – into profit and won Ayckbourn his first *Evening Standard* Best Play (rather than Best Comedy) Award but at the time it was not properly valued (Shulman – getting it wrong again – claimed that Ayckbourn was making fun of mental illness).

After returning to the National to co-direct the first of his 'choice' plays (its progress depending on the toss of a coin) in *Sisterly Feelings*, Ayckbourn finally steered one of his own plays, *Ten Times Table* (Globe, 1978) for Michael in London himself. Drawing on endless Scarborough committee meetings for affairs such as the Royal Jubilee and the minutiae of theatre Board meetings, it takes place in a cheerless hotel ballroom where a group are planning a Pageant to celebrate a piece of local history involving Industrial Revolution martyrs, the Pendon Twelve. A cross-section of the local great and not-so-good – befurred Thatcherite socialite and her wet husband (Julia McKenzie and Paul Eddington), rabidly Marxist student, barking crypto-Fascist, pedantic councillor forever raising minor points of order (Benjamin Whitrow) and his deaf, piano-thumping mother – come under scrutiny and the tensions between members climax in the Pageant going on outside while anarchy rages within as the participants try to cope with ill-fitting costumes, increasing drunkenness and a randy Russian student ready to ravish the socialite. Nobody could describe it as Ayckbourn's deepest work and the cast never quite gelled together in a unified style but this genial play proved popular enough at the Globe without breaking box office records.

This period was a high watermark for the Codron management and for Ayckbourn alike. Investors were falling over themselves to join Michael's band of angels; in addition to his long-time regulars he now had senior producer Peter Saunders, John Reid (Elton John's then manager), Pieter Toerien, the South African producer and groups including Vanmark Industrial Finance and British Entertainment Ltd backing him. The heady air of success around this time was crystallised in a stylish Christmas party hosted by Michael and David at the Aldwych Theatre with slap-up food and wine, cabaret (including Michael's favourite of a ventriloquist – Roger de Courcy and Nookie Bear on this occasion) and a band in the foyer – the highlight of the dancing was a jive from a velvet-suited David and Penelope Keith in a long red dress, with moves so inventively athletic that they cleared the floor.

Keith was due to lead the company of Ayckbourn's *Joking Apart* (1978), which followed *Ten Times Table* into the Globe. Michael was keen and Ramsay urged her client, typically trenchantly, to cast her: 'Bear in mind that the middle and upper classes that support your plays like their women to bear a faint resemblance to a horse – that's their idea of total allure. And she must be the most desired actress on the English stage at the moment.' Negotiations were all over bar the shouting, down to such minor details as the shade of telephone in the star dressing room (Michael sent Keith a huge furry red phone when she decided on the colour) before Keith backed off, worried about Ayckbourn directing his own play ('Penny told me "I have to have a jockey on my back", which meant I had to reply, "You're forcing me to choose between Alan and you and I have to choose Alan."'). Ayckbourn was philosophic to Michael: 'She obviously felt strongly about the director, which is sad. I guess she wanted more love than I could give her, said he as Tyrone Power in *The Sun Also Rises*.'

Keith's decision reflected a continuing contentious point about Ayckbourn as director of his own work (he is not unique – Pinter, Gray, Terry Johnson and David Hare also often directed or direct their plays). For many, not just his regular actors, he is an outstanding director of his own and others' work. Some others feel that while he has proved a superb director of Chekhov at Scarborough and of Arthur Miller (his production of *A View From the Bridge* with Gambon's mesmeric Eddie Carbone at the National and then the Aldwych was revelatory) he can be too rigid when in charge of his own plays, so clear in his mind as to the way they work that his method can be too restricting. Ian McKellen found his way of rehearsing tricky and Richard Durden, cast in the Scarborough production of *Communicating Doors*, has trenchantly described how he felt straitjacketed under his author's direction in rehearsal and it is no secret that Ayckbourn is no fan of in-depth discussion, which might disrupt his detailedly plotted schedule of rehearsal progress. But he has worked successfully with actors of all backgrounds and training on both sides of the Atlantic (Judd Hirsch, David Soul and most of the cast of the Broadway *By Jeeves!* included among American actors) although he tends to respond best to those who can work at his own comparatively fleet pace without too much introspection.

In the event Alison Steadman, still glowing in the success of Mike Leigh's *Abigail's Party* on stage and television, played golden girl Anthea in *Joking Apart*. She and husband Richard (Christopher Cazenove), a successful businessman, are a rich and happy couple radiating a charm and beneficence which unwittingly poisons those their generosity touches. Set over twelve years – an acting challenge which this cast mostly dealt with effortlessly – and over four 'occasions' (a fireworks party, a birthday, etc.) the Edenic garden setting (including a section of tennis court) seems to harbour more serpents and longer shadows than most previous Ayckbourn outdoors to date in a play of often muted, Chekhovian poignancy. This is balanced by some ripely comic sequences including a tennis match between Richard and his Swedish-born business partner Sven (Robert Austin, a Scarborough regular, who nearly stole the show), once a junior champion but now with a heart problem, whose envy of Richard deepens when he discovers that he has won only because Richard has played left-handed. The lives of barely cloaked quiet desperation include those of Olive, Sven's ever-anxious wife and the local vicar who is hopelessly in love with Anthea but married to a nervy wife who is by the end of the play a pill-popping wreck.

Joking Apart completely divided metropolitan critics, some levelling the by now shop-worn charge that Ayckbourn patronises his characters, others (fewer of them) finding this self-styled 'winter' work (the first of his plays to be written during the winter had been *Just Between Ourselves*) a successful attempt to darken his comedy and deepen his audience's laughter although *Daily Telegraph* felt strongly that elements of the play's subtlety had evaporated since Scarborough. It ran for barely a hundred performances, the first Ayckbourn produced by Michael to fail to recoup its costs even with royalty cuts (the run-up to a General Election did not help) to reduce a weekly break figure of £8,500. Ayckbourn of course agreed to the cuts, while adding to Ramsay: 'It does seem to suggest perhaps, after all, that however famous the author is – unless the play is wreathed in notoriety or other special distinction – it won't really survive without *either* Ingrid Bergman, Diana Rigg or Penelope Keith, or perhaps all three.'

After the comparative disappointments of *Ten Times Table* and *Joking*

Apart, Michael suggested that on *Taking Steps*, his hommage to Ben Travers and the sole full-length play in his canon which can be genuinely labelled as farce, Ayckbourn should not direct (his availability, given his Scarborough commitments, was in any event limited). He suggested 'The Texan' or 'Rudders' as he called Michael Rudman and Ayckbourn, emerging from a stint at the National and mindful of Rudman's success with early Frayn plays, agreed.

Taking Steps presented more than the usual problems in moving from in-the-round to proscenium staging. It is set on three floors – ground floor sitting room, first floor bedroom and attic of a decaying, reputedly haunted house, supposedly once a brothel, inhabited by Roland, a rich but near-alcoholic bucket manufacturer and his ex-dancer wife Lizzie, forever dithering about leaving him. Other characters include a nervously incoherent solicitor, Lizzie's brother Mark (probably the leading contender for the title of English Drama's Most Boring Man – he puts people literally to sleep once he gets talking) and his dim fiancée Kitty, all whipped up into an accelerating imbroglio of action, enhanced by its taking place in three spaces simultaneously on one floor of the stage, with the marked-out stairs ascended or descended in mime only. The staging demanding split-second timing to avoid collisions between characters spatially close but of course in different rooms and unaware of each other, a discipline even more demanding for director and cast than that of the overlapping rooms in *How the Other Half Loves*.

Somehow the transposition to a West End stage was never happily solved. Not long before rehearsals Michael was writing to Toby Rowland, the play's planned landlord on behalf of Stoll Moss at the Lyric: 'I sense from discussions yesterday afternoon between Rudman and Ayckbourn that they haven't quite hit on an agreement for how the set should look.' Ayckbourn could have drawn the ground plan on the back of an envelope but did not want to appear to be interfering or dictatorial and was also worried about the central casting as Roland of Dinsdale Landen, a favourite Rudman actor (for Michael too) since *Alphabetical Order*. His doubts surfaced in a letter to Michael: 'It struck me – why are we doing it? As always happens the stars will overwhelm it, either deliberately or accidentally … And if it isn't your fault or mine it must be the system. I'm in a genuine quandary, Michael. I don't want *Taking Steps* to go through the machine for just another routine West End offering by AA.'

Nobody connected with the production ended up very happy. The set, even with Alan Tagg's input, never satisfactorily worked – all the business on the stairs, which had reduced close-up Scarborough houses to hysteria, received at best polite titters at the Lyric – and on this occasion Rudman signally failed to rein in Landen. A great comic actor in the Roland Squire or A.E. Matthews tradition potentially capable of a sublime farce performance (as he demonstrated in Travers's *Plunder* at the National), in *Taking Steps* he sailed way over the top, exaggerating Roland's drink problem with gargantuan gulps of huge Scotches and bug-eyed squiffiness, leaving the young Michael Maloney to salvage some genuine laughs as the inarticulate solicitor, Tristram (his night in what he fearfully imagines to be a haunted bedroom has episodes rivalling Travers's *Thark*).

On seeing a late rehearsal Ayckbourn had found proceedings unsettlingly more suited to a broader Ray Cooney farce, all exaggeration and no reality. Michael tried to reassure him that he would counsel Rudman: 'Rudders and I will forswear Cooney for Keats, truth and beauty.' The Richmond try-out saw, for Ayckbourn, no significant improvement and Michael too was disappointed in Landen (once 'MFA') and his embroideries. 'The nadir was the evening there when Alan and Heather came and I gave a dinner afterwards for them with Rudman. And Felicity Kendal (then Mrs Rudman) to help the evening go with a swing. It was really very, very heavy going all the same and Alan made it pretty clear what he thought. And next day he elaborated it to me and I did try to lean on Rudman to subdue Landen.' It was an uneasy Lyric opening, however, and although some critics enjoyed Ayckbourn's return to unadulterated comedy and business was initially strong, before long it began to slide. It did not quite recoup its production costs (£69,000) at the Lyric; Ayckbourn worried also about the projected post-London tour ('I don't think it got the best showing in London and I'm very anxious that it shouldn't have a tour that turns out to be a sub-sub version of the Lyric'). The tour went ahead with Dave King under David Kirk's management; its income for the Codron office pushed *Taking Steps* finally into the black. Ayckbourn's own deliriously funny Orange Tree, Richmond production in 2010 saw the play properly balanced, with a cast of his regulars including Stephen Beckett, Michael Simkins and Matthew Cottle, a wonderfully bemused Stan Laurelish Tristram. In the Orange Tree programme Ayckbourn rightly described it as his '*most round play*', recalling how the West End version never solved the move to the proscenium.

Ayckbourn's career seemed unusually flat as the 1970s ended. And *Season's Greetings*, his Christmas-set play of family tensions with the hall, dining room, sitting room and landing of the house all on stage, looked like disappearing through the net. After his recent less than satisfying West End experiences and with Michael not exactly ecstatic about *Season's Greetings* ('only faint moaning noises are emanating from Regent Street' Ayckbourn wrote to me then) he brought the play with the Scarborough cast to the Round House together with his musical written with Paul Todd, *Suburban Strains*, at the invitation of Thelma Holt, then running the venue. But despite the attempts to create a theatre-in-the-round, the cavernous space, sheathed in black drapes, proved an inhospitable home, especially with the thin houses during a season of disappointing business. As Ayckbourn said himself: 'People were generally assuming I'd finished.' I liked the play and thought the only problem with the Round House production was the Round House and so suggested a new production at Greenwich Theatre of which I was then artistic director. This production used some familiar Scarborough actors – the brilliant Diane Bull as a put-upon pregnant wife included – alongside a terrific line-up including Gareth Hunt, Nigel Havers, Barbara Ferris, Bridget Turner (hilarious as a tipsy aunt grasping a very wrong end of the stick to assume that all train drivers are homosexual) and Marcia Warren. This, too, had some delirious passages of comedy – the first act curtain a particular high point involving the household's wife, Belinda, caught under both Christmas tree and her sister's new boyfriend when the household, triggered by her athletic passion inadvertently setting off a loud mechanical toy wrapped up under the tree, discover them.

Some saw in the contrasted uncles – benign but boring Bernard obsessed with his annual puppet show (Bernard Hepton memorably muddled) and crypto-fascist security guard Harvey (an awesome Peter Vaughan) – a suggested paradigm of the polarities between well meaning but pallid liberalism and ruthless authoritarianism created in the year of Margaret Thatcher's first government, but if audiences took this subliminally on board they also found Ayckbourn's scrutiny of Christmas rituals both gorgeously funny and wincingly accurate.

The Apollo business for Michael on transfer after a sell-out Greenwich run was strong enough for the production to recoup (its capitalisation to move from Greenwich had been a modest £50,000). The cast cheered up when a mid-run slump in business picked up again, and when Michael and David hosted a sumptuous summer lunch party for them and the *Noises Off* company at Frederick's restaurant in Islington. *Season's Greetings* became the National Theatre's first revival of an Ayckbourn play, aptly for Christmas 2010, directed by Marianne Elliott.

With only four collaborations, the 1980s were slightly less occupied than previously with Ayckbourn for the Codron office. This period would see some of his finest work in the commercial sector alongside his National Theatre work (he took two years off from Scarborough in the 1980s to base himself on the South Bank) and the epic two-hander *Intimate Exchanges* sequence (presented at Greenwich before its West End transfer by Ray Cooney's Theatre of Comedy Company). Michael was especially proud of *Woman in Mind* (Vaudeville, 1980). Inspired to a degree by Oliver Sacks's *The Man Who Mistook His Wife for a Hat* in the manner in which it relates its story from within the mind of a vicar's neglected wife and also – as Ayckbourn's biographer Paul Allen suggested – by a 1950s breakdown suffered by Lolly, then trapped in a stalemate marriage, it traces Susan's retreat into the solace of a loving fantasy family and subsequently, in a climactic sequence of increasing surreality, into madness.

Having finished writing the play unusually early ('I feel very uneasy' said an author often in the past spurred on by deadlines) he sent it to Michael, warning: 'It's the one I promised you would see first and here it is. By my own pessimistic calculations, based on the principle that you like every other one of my plays, this should be the one you're least keen on. I'm quite excited about it but don't let that influence your judgement, please.'

In fact Michael was immediately enthused by *Woman in Mind*: 'I thought – and still think – that it's in his very top rank.' They spent longer than usual considering the crucial casting of Susan, one of Ayckbourn's most challenging central roles to date with a lot riding on the choice for a larger-cast play with a demanding set (dreary vicarage garden alternating with seductive *Ideal Home* vistas of lawns, mazes and statuary) budgeted at £100,000. Judi Dench and Penelope Wilton (a great favourite of both men) were touched on before Ayckbourn veered towards Julia McKenzie (he remembered especially her superb Diana, the maltreated wife of *Absent Friends* on TV). He wrote to Michael: 'I do think our thoughts that she might be too lightweight for Susan in *Woman in Mind* should be retracted.'

McKenzie did them proud in the play; hardly ever offstage, she mapped every facet of the woman – sad, sometimes caustically bitter in the real world of uncaring husband (little Christian charity from this vicar, played by Martin Jarvis, a chill figure in rimless glasses) and sister-in-law, glowing in her fantasy of immaculate lawns and white linen in her dream world before her mind begins to give way under the pressures of inhabiting a twin-plane existence. As the fantasy husband turns tempter the stresses of the dream-world become increasingly urgent. Future thesis writers will have field days exploring the Carrollian influence on the final sequence, a nightmare racecourse scene during which Susan's grasp on reality finally slackens, but undeniably few Ayckbourn plays affect audiences as shatteringly as this. Its pace, accelerating almost imperceptibly from its abrupt opening with Susan having struck her head on a garden rake and discovering her solicitous local doctor bending over her, never loses its control.

A cautionary voice from the pre-London Richmond week came from Peggy Ramsay, who wrote to her client admitting that a packed house had adored the evening 'but it was a kind of easy, almost mindless laughter that I found unworthy of what you were trying to do'. She conveyed her reservations to Michael, counselling him to lean on Ayckbourn as director to warn all involved to beware the temptation of easy laughs. Ramsay was aware of Ayckbourn's anxieties after two 'downbeat' plays adding, 'but I don't think they were your very best plays, Alan dear, and I think this is one of the best you've ever written … I think you and Michael care too much about the success of a play and I think you would be amazed to find better notices still if you weren't so nervous. It took them a long time to recognise your true talent, Alan, and it will take them a long time to see you are still developing if you and Michael are frightened.'

Few agents would have bothered with this, happy to take the ten per cent, but Ramsay's relationships with Michael and Ayckbourn were too close for her not to speak out and for them not to listen. Certainly the production was infused with an exhilaratingly high-wire tension between comedy and near-tragedy by the time of its Vaudeville opening (it was the first Codron production to play the Vaudeville under the firm's ownership). The notices were virtually unanimously favourable; McKenzie won the *Evening Standard* Best Actress Award, succeeded by an equally fine Pauline Collins. In New York the play had a strong Manhattan Theatre Club production with Stockard Channing in magnificent form as Susan, while Ayckbourn's 2008 much admired Scarborough revival with Janie Dee came to the West End, returning to the Vaudeville, in 2009.

It was one of the happiest Ayckbourn runs – sometimes the unhappiness of so many of the characters can affect his actors – with Michael's only major concern being the lacklustre Vaudeville staff he had inherited from Peter Saunders. Nobody on the production had been thrilled to overhear a stage crew member, cursing as he moved heavy statuary during the play's technical rehearsal: 'All this fucking effort just for three weeks.' And Julia McKenzie was regularly greeted by a stage doorkeeper of legendary sloth, rarely taking his eye off his TV screen (occasionally even showing her *Fresh*

Fields series) as she came in to the theatre for the show with 'Good evening, Miss Jarvis'. Finally she snapped: 'It's McKenzie – Julia McKenzie. Jarvis is Martin Jarvis. He's got fair hair. I'm Julia McKenzie – the red-haired one from the television!' To which his response was simply, 'It's no use saying that to me. I've only got black and white.'

Henceforward … (Vaudeville, 1987) was similarly successful but markedly less happy. A dystopian and dark futuristic comedy, it is set in the fortress-like flat of a composer, Jerome. More than a few saw elements of a self-portrait in this not altogether flattering portrayal of the inherent solipsism of the creative artist – its production coincided with Margaret Thatcher's third election victory by which time her philosophy of individualism was in the ascendant after a deeply divisive period, often violent, including inner-city riots in London's Brixton and in Toxteth in Liverpool and angry confrontations with unions, the NUM most savagely. Jerome's is a grim world – his flat has steel guards over doors and windows, a rampant female gang, The Daughters of Darkness, roams the streets and he is served by a robot called Nan (who bears a strong resemblance to his estranged wife Corinna). Beadily observed by Nan, Jerome interviews a ditsy young actress, Zoë, to assess her suitability to pose as his girlfriend to convince the Department of Child Wellbeing that he is fit to see his young daughter Geain. Gradually the withdrawn Jerome admits to Zoë his ambition to compose 'in an abstract musical form' a piece to express love and all the emotions involved in a way that anyone, of whatever culture, can recognise. They sleep together but the sweetly trusting Zoë is appalled when she discovers that he has recorded the sounds of their lovemaking to incorporate in his work and she leaves. The second act sees Corinna appear; Nan has been reworked by Jerome to resemble Zoë (now of course played by the actress playing Zoë in Act I) although he has not quite finished her programming, giving rise to some unpredictable behaviour when faced by the Wellbeing official (himself a walking arsenal wired up to various technological devices including an alarm system), who arrives with a spiky Corinna (played by the Nan from the first act). When Geian appears she proves no longer Jerome's innocent child but a tough unisexual member of another gang, the Sons of Bitches, who exposes Jerome's plan by revealing Nan to be a robot. The play ends with Jerome again alone, unmindful of increasingly desperate and violent images on his video and entry-machine screens, working obsessively on the material on his tapes, including Corinna's confession that she still loves him, to realise his ambition to express that feeling in music, manically shuttling between his synthesisers and batteries of speakers as he builds his symphony – one impossible ever to realise because he is incapable of love.

An unpredictable, uncomfortable play for all its riotous robotics *Henceforward ...* received excellent notices, winning the *Evening Standard* Award as Best Comedy and, with a cast change seeing Martin Jarvis as Jerome and the West End debut of Sara Crowe as Zoë (Michael was captivated by her audition), ran for over a year. But the familiar star-casting problem had reared its head with the original cast. Jerome, for most of the first act, is essentially a passive role, often simply observing while Zoë takes centre stage. That, of course, is usually where stars expect to be and there were more than a few difficulties between Ian McKellen and Ayckbourn in rehearsal. Most who saw both casts felt that although Jane Asher had been eerily unsettling as the first Nan alongside Serena Evans's endearingly ditsy Zoë, the ensemble of the second cast put the play into truer perspective.

The run of top-flight Ayckbourn in the commercial sector of the 1980s continued when Michael produced an ambitiously scaled play (the cast is large and the set requires a functioning swimming pool in the grounds of the Spanish villa in which the play is set), *Man of the Moment* (Globe, 1988), with its classic clash of venal self-interest and genuine goodness. Triggered by his regular observation while working at the National Theatre of the Great Train Robbery's Buster Edwards at his Waterloo flower stall (Edwards became a minor celebrity, his story filmed with Phil Collins while the robbers' victim, Jack Mills, was soon forgotten), the play covers the making of a TV programme ('Their Paths Crossed'). The producer/presenter, the ambitious Jill Rillington, brings together Vic Parks (a permatanned Peter Bowles) a former bank robber, now a celebrity chat show host, and Douglas Beechey, the 'forgotten hero' whose charge on Parks during a raid nearly twenty years before foiled the robbery, although a bank teller (now Beechey's wife) was badly facially scarred by gunfire. When Douglas (Michael Gambon) arrives he proves a problem for Jill; he simply has no ill feeling or envy confronted by the symbols of Vic's success (Gambon's penguin-footed entrance, blinking behind thick glasses, dressed in hairy sports jacket and classic British sandals in the Costa del Crime heat, constantly repeating 'Oh!' and 'Isn't this glorious?' as he padded about taking in his surroundings, was a comic tour de force – Michael still recalls it as 'one of the most memorable, sublime moments of all my productions'). Jill, who wants on-camera conflict to energise her programme, is continuously foiled by Douglas's benevolence, even when

55. Reprogramming: Jane Asher as 'Nan' and Ian McKellen as
Jerome in Ayckbourn's *Henceforward*, 1989.

Vic is at his most boorishly sexist, snapping orders at his wife Trudy,
treating the overweight maid who mutely adores him with loutish insults,
or cynically teaching Douglas how to exploit the media. A clue to
Douglas's motives for taking part is his admission that he and his wife still
dream of Vic and that perhaps participation in the programme may 'exor-
cise' him. The chasm between the two men makes for some very funny
scenes, as does the frustration of chic, media-savvy Jill, those passages
fused to more poignant episodes including a muted late-night poolside
conversation between Douglas and Trudy (beautifully finessed by Gambon and Diane Bull). The climax comes with Vic being barged into the pool
by Douglas, roused to action once more when Vic goes finally too far in
insulting Trudy and the suicidal maid, who rears up, *Jaws*-style, in the pool
to drown Vic. The play sharply cuts to a television studio reconstruction
(Vic's death is now an 'accident') with actors as the docudrama's participants (cosmeticized for the screen – the maid for the screen is a sylph, for
instance) as Jill's 'spin' (the word was just coming into usage then) gives

56. Michael Gambon dressed for the Costa del Crime in *Man of the Moment*, 1990.

her at last the 'good television' she wanted. Michael Holt, a regular Scarborough designer and responsible for *Man of the Moment*'s set there, intriguingly posited that the studio reconstruction involves the audience in unusual complicity by the way 'it indicts us all as accomplices in the television scam'.

Written before the explosion of reality television shows, *Man of the Moment* looks at its world of contrivance and clever editing with unblinking candour but that element in the play is conveyed, as usual with Ayckbourn, through an involving human story. Critics mostly admired the play, although by now Ayckbourn's technical skills were so taken for granted that there was barely any mention of the almost Ibsenite way in which the past, crucial to the story, gradually drip-feeds into the narrative. With a cast change after six months – Nigel Planer and Gareth Hunt as Douglas and Vic – *Man of the Moment* was a major success at the Globe.

Stephen Joseph, outwardly an unlikely anarchist, used to assert that theatre buildings should be blown up after seven years to prevent stagnation. Ayckbourn could hardly do a *River Kwai* detonation in Scarborough but his equivalent was every so often to initiate a kind of 'impossible' project to galvanise the entire set-up – the epic *Intimate Exchanges* two-hander sequence, the double-auditorium *House and Garden*, or the twin-play *The Revengers' Comedies* (Strand, 1989).

This saga with its 'Maguffin' resembling that of Hitchcock's movie *Strangers on a Train* (itself adapted from a novel by an Ayckbourn favourite, Patricia Highsmith), its title taken from the Jacobean *Revengers's Tragedy* has over twenty roles and multiple locations ranging from Albert Bridge and a ramshackle country pile to London bars and bistros and, in Part II, a high-tech corporate office world of ruthless power games. Beginning one midnight on Albert Bridge, the conventional Henry Bell, recently made redundant, meets the wacky Karen Knightly, despairing over losing her married lover, both intent on suicide; they then hit on the scheme of each becoming architect of the other's revenge. Karen will deal with the repellent Bruce Tick, Henry's boss, while Henry will avenge Karen's treatment by the arrogant landowner Anthony Staxton-Billing. In the country Henry unfortunately falls for the delectable Imogen Staxton-Billing and becomes dilatory over his revenge (Karen wants her dead), while Karen is soon cutting a swathe through the hierarchy of his old company, beginning as a secretary and then soon, after crushing the odious Tick, in the power-suited ascendant. On the way a crowded cast of characters both urban and rural appear before the play comes full circle returning to Albert Bridge at midnight for a cliff-hanger ending.

In Scarborough the plays were a triumph. I was directing the George S. Kaufman/Ring Lardner Tin Pan Alley comedy *June Moon* for Scarborough that season with several of the *Revengers'* cast and it was a delight to watch the plays come together during their technical and dress rehearsals. Designed by Roger Glossop with minimal realism (Albert Bridge evoked by a section of ironwork and some dry ice) so that scene flowed seamlessly into scene (the play's filmic structure did lead to a film – one almost as bad as Michael Winner's version of *Chorus of Disapproval*. Only Ayckbourn's friend Alain Resnais with three films – *Smoking* and *No Smoking* plus *Private Fears in Public Places* – has cracked Ayckbourn on screen). The Cottesloe stage at the National would have preserved this fleetness but Richard Eyre was not prepared to stage the plays unless Ayckbourn conflated them into one evening. The attitudes of both men – similarly affable but obstinate characters – led to stalemate and eventually Michael, feeling that 'morally I owed Alan a production', mounted them in 1981. It was a major gamble – a large cast, over forty scenes and the necessity of persuading the public to see the plays in the right order (unlike *The Normans*) at a then top price of £35 (a reduction for booking for both plays was offered) at a time of looming recession and the Gulf War. Griff Rhys Jones and Joanna Lumley (prior to her stardom in *Absolutely Fabulous* on television) were headlined with Karen played by the new-to-London Lia Williams, who had worked at Scarborough the previous year. She proved a terrific choice – moving with increasingly exhilarated glee up Karen's various ladders – launching a major career. The main problem was the physical production, a potent illustration of the difficulties sometimes involved in moving from the round to the proscenium arch, with audience expectations at West End ticket prices understandably wanting value for money. So Albert Bridge for the opening spanned the whole stage – spectacular but leaving only two actors looking dwarfed – with house and office sets moving up, down and side stage on trucks or tracks, making for narrative-breaking waits compared with the instant, even overlapping, transitions possible in the round. The London version damagingly missed what had so impressed the *New York Times*'s Frank Rich when he visited the theatre in Scarborough in 1989 and saw beyond a tale of double-revenge and English eccentricities to find 'an immensely disturbing vision of contemporary middle-class England poisoned by the rise of economic ruthlessness and the collapse of ethics … In Part Two the game has become synonymous with the national sport of hostile corporate takeovers, wholesale job 'redundancies' and industrial destruction of the countryside'.

Michael tried hard to boost the venture after rather disappointing reviews overall – a lot of publicity was created around Lia Williams's success and various marketing offers were soon in operation. He was able, when business showed no sign of significantly improving, to renegotiate the Strand's rental terms and so the final loss was less horrific than it might have been, but it was a disappointing venture for those involved, running for less than a hundred performances.

Perhaps too many Ayckbourns had occupied subsidised and commercial stages for a while. Certainly Michael's next outing with his most regular collaborator resulted in another disappointing run and again – this time through no problems with the production – its technical invention and double-pulse comedic strain were undervalued. *Time Of My Life* (Vaudeville, 1992) has a double time scale, moving forwards and backwards; we see some relationships in their first careless rapture and then others lose their innocence, all set in the barely changing Essa de Calvi restaurant over a number of years (the various waiters are all played by the same actor – the versatile Terence Booth – both in Scarborough and London). Lunches, birthdays, anniversaries are all 'celebrated' there with the narratives of the central couple's adulterous son and his unhappy wife and of the younger son and his 'unsuitable' lower-class girlfriend told in different time formats. It may sound confusing or tricksy but in performance the play captures the tensions and unpredictabilities of family life genuinely absorbingly. Its production coincided with the unpopularity of John Major's government as unemployment hit three million with the UK's continuing slide into the recession of the early 1990s (Gerry Stratton, the self-made builder and paterfamilias of the play makes it evident how small businesses are struggling, not just with larger rivals but often simply because their bills are not being paid), a background which charges the personal relationships in the play with an added layer of urgency. Anton Rodgers played Gerry, rather soft-pedalling the character's edge, but Gwen Taylor was a fine, tough Laura, forced by her life to be pragmatic, with the rest of the cast ably coming from Scarborough. The notices were only moderate, the run disappointingly brief; it remains one of the least familiar Ayckbourn plays.

It was six years before Ayckbourn returned to the Codron stable with the double-whammy of *Things We Do for Love* (Gielgud) and *Comic Potential* (Lyric) in 1998. The former was unusual in being one of the very rare

Ayckbourns not originally written for in-the-round production (it was first seen in the smaller end-stage McCarthy auditorium at the Stephen Joseph), allowing the dramatist to realise an ambition of staging a play on three vertical levels of the same house. It is set in the neatly antiseptic sitting room of Barbara (Jane Asher), a sterner Bridget Jones – singleton suspicious of emotional involvement – 'I've had sexual intercourse and it really wasn't worth the time or effort' – while the audience sees also a slice of the basement flat where Barbara's adoring transvestite tenant Gilbert (Barry McCarthy, another Scarborough regular) lives (painting a fresco of his nude landlady on the ceiling) and part of the bedroom in the upstairs flat, up to the actors' knees. Barbara plans to rent upstairs to an old schoolmate Nikki, a dizzy blonde (Serena Evans) and her hunky boyfriend, vegetarian oceanographer Hamish (Steven Pacey).

Initially hostile to each other (Barbara disapproves of vegetarianism on principle) Hamish and Barbara in an hilarious upstairs scene find dislike turning to lust as we see their lower limbs in wildly erotic action against the soundtrack of their gasps and moans ('You've made me an animal' says a shaken post-coital Barbara). But the things they do for love involve pain – Nikki on discovering the pair's involvement, reacts unexpectedly dramatically, cutting up all her lover's clothes. A contrasting later scene sees Hamish and Barbara, after a scratchy argument, coming to shakingly violent blows in a frighteningly realistic fight, although the end of the play – reflecting one description of it as 'a *Private Lives* for the nineties' – sees Barbara and Hamish united, at least tentatively, for the future.

The physical violence took some houses by surprise – mental cruelty of course was nothing new in Ayckbourn – and some emerged from it uneasy, with no final definitive answers from the dramatist. For most critics this shotgun wedding of Feydeau and Strindberg in tracing Barbara's thawing when out of emotional deep freeze, was a return to peak form, a daring mixture of domestic comedy and sexual tragedy (not, in that regard, unlike Patrick Marber's *Closer*, produced the same year).

Ayckbourn's note to Michael when he sent the play just after his knighthood had been announced had said it was 'just to prove that a "K" will not slow me down'. Michael, after reading it, responded quickly ('It's wonderful. It's painful and hilarious'), confirming a personal conviction that 'the more technical expertise and invention Alan displays the more freely, passionately he seems to write', illustrating in this play that love, as the song has it, can hurt.

Back on Shaftesbury Avenue with Ayckbourn, Michael could not but help reflecting on changes. Central London had altered rapidly; with the move to Nine Elms of Covent Garden's market that whole area where now the Codron office was based had been transformed with up-market new hotels and restaurants galore. The area around what was once the heart of the London commercial theatre, dynamic and busy, had begun to follow 1980s Broadway in sliding into squalor, the surrounding streets off Shaftesbury Avenue itself littered with junkies' needles, clip joints and detritus. He wrote to Nica Burns, then working for Andrew Lloyd Webber's Really Useful Group, now owner of what had been the Stoll Moss chain (more recently for a time before the sale to RUG under the Australian tycoon Rupert Holmes à Court) 'If something drastic is not undertaken by the police to clean up the area there is a danger of losing the middle-aged and even not so middle-aged audiences that make up a large proportion of audiences for the kind of plays which I produce', lamenting the contrast between the Gielgud's beautiful interior and the surroundings, 'noticeable all the more to me as a tenant during the eight years since I was here with *Man of the Moment'*. The changes to central London had been often dramatic; at the start of his career Michael would not have been alone in never imagining that nearby Old Compton Street, for instance, would by the 1990s be predominantly a lively gay thoroughfare.

RUG were sympathetic to the complaints about the squalor around the Globe (security guards were hired) and also to Michael's problems when *Things We Do for Love* moved to another RUG house, the Duchess, negotiating a deal whereby RUG bore fifty per cent of transfer costs (for a commensurate share of takings), allowing Michael, with a low rental, to maintain what he called his 'good housekeeping' for the extended West End run. Its subsequent tour, with Belinda Lang succeeding Asher, did well enough to take the production safely into the black.

A decade previously *Things We Do for Love* would have recouped much earlier. Even more surprising was that *Comic Potential* which drew mostly very positive notices (with unanimous bravos for its leading lady, Janie Dee) did not even recoup its production costs.

Initially all seemed set fair for this future-set play. After seeing Dee's Scarborough performance, Michael had no qualms about her repeating it in London. She played Jacie Triplethree (JC333), an 'actoid' in *Hospital Hearts*, a slick TV soap opera inhabited by programmed robots, directed by ex-movie director Chance but ruled over on behalf of the TV company by Carla Pepperbloom, a voraciously ratings-driven executive with a predatory eye on young Adam Trainsmith, a writer and nephew of the studio's boss. Adam writes a script for Jacie and falls for her as she begins, *Pygmalion*-style, to become humanised by love. They escape together, risking Carla's jealous revenge, in a second act set in various locations unfamiliar for Jacie (luxury hotel, restaurant, etc.) after the studio-set first half.

The satirical strain in its picture of the television world has an S.J. Perelman-like slant (the characters' names – including the lesbian lovers Trudi Floote and Prim Spring – echo Perelman), the adventures of Adam and Jacie recall the screwball screen comedies of the 1930s (Jacie dancing like a life-size Barbie doll to ZZ Top) with other scenes reminiscent of Ayckbourn's favourite Keaton-esque slapstick while the narrative takes on an oddly touching strain as Jacie struggles to comprehend emergent human feelings, dimly perceiving what it might mean to be human. Dee was extraordinarily fine – her slightly vacant wide-eyed good spirits and lithe body language evoking a kind of comic-strip android – with Matthew Cottle ideally partnering her as the love-struck Adam.

The 'Star Casting' question arose once more with Michael and Ayckbourn over casting the American over-the-hill director Chance. Larry Hagman and John Mahoney (from *Frasier* – both were keen on that idea) were proposed but failed to work out. Ayckbourn squashed a suggestion of Christopher Plummer, stressing the problem of casting a major name: 'They would immediately and instinctively (that's why they're stars) set about competing with our Miss Dee ... I really don't want my play turned into a battlefield. The fact is that it's *her* play and everyone else is support. He has his moment of Act One glory but in the end *he's* support too.' Finally the part was taken – more than capably – by David Soul, well enough remembered from television's *Starsky and Hutch*.

Within only a week of the Lyric opening, despite the enthusiastic notices, Michael was faxing Nica Burns; 'Last night's figure seriously concerned me ... if things don't substantially improve I will have to come to the sad conclusion that I've miscalculated the play's popular appeal.' The boards outside the theatre were plastered with laudatory quotes from the notices but the advance booking mulishly refused to convert on the week regularly enough. RYG helped by supporting Michael's participation in the Showpairs reduced price ticket scheme and after Christmas revised the rental as part of what he described as 'an emergency package to enable us to weather the bad weeks waiting upon the outcome of the Olivier Awards'. Dee won the Olivier Best Actress Award as well as the *Evening Standard* and Critic's Circle Awards in the same category (an achievement matched by Judi Dench only), and Michael heavily advertised her achievement but still the box office would not significantly build.

The play closed in early June 2000 ('one of the few Ayckbourns which haven't recouped their investment, highly disappointing' wrote Michael to his backers). His personal loss was cushioned by help from RUG, significantly reducing the original high weekly break-even figure (£48,000 at full rent and royalties) and by co-producing with Lee Dean who had taken on a quarter of the production costs.

While the next new Ayckbourn – the double of *House* and *Garden* – went to the National to play the Lyttleton and Olivier stages simultaneously, Michael had approached Tom Erhardt (who had worked with Peggy Ramsay for many years and who took over as Ayckbourn's agent after her death – Ayckbourn had first met the affable Erhardt in America when he worked on the US version of *How the Other Half Loves* before coming to the UK and working for Peter Bridge) suggesting a revival of *Bedroom Farce* (Aldwych, 2002), which he had envied losing to the National back in 1975. Ayckbourn agreed, allowing another director, and Michael picked Loveday Ingram who had recently had a Chichester success with the Gershwin musical *My One and Only* (with Janie Dee). It took time to cast – it was increasingly difficult to find home-grown names prepared to commit to a play for a viable period ('When I started actors used to like run-of-the-play contracts. Or at least nine months. Now the first question they ask is how quickly can they get out of it') but finally some sharp younger actors – Jasper Britton and Suzi Aitchison included – were signed with the bonus of the older couple Ernest and Delia in the hands of Richard Briers ('He said how nice it was that we were going to do something together again before we die') and June Whitfield.

But this one started on the wrong foot and matters never signally improved. Ingram and designer Lez Brotherston made a major error in putting one of the three bedrooms making up the play's set on a much higher level than the other pair; not only did it give that room an unnecessary immediate prominence, it compromised the play's symmetry and the Aldwych sightlines, making some transitions between rooms needlessly clumsy. Ayckbourn was far from happy when he saw a run-through in London but he was busy in Scarborough when the play opened its pre-London tour in Guildford. It was clear that there were problems and he was further exercised, writing to Michael: 'I'm getting confused messages. You tell me all is sunny and everyone is happy and the play is well on course. On the other hand I'm getting messages from one actor's agent at least that his client is unhappy along with other members of the cast. And from other independent sources that it's not just good enough.'

Even had he been available he did not want to come to Guildford ('I suspect that what would happen is I would set about the whole show and leave you with a pile of rather worried actors'). But finally – under pressure from a deeply worried old colleague Briers in particular – he did come to Richmond for two days to try to help pull the production, which he felt Ingram had directed too coarsely, into shape for London. This, too, caused problems – Jasper Britton wrote to Michael that while the actors were grateful to see their author, his brief availability and his 'notes', stressing truth and the need to avoid obvious laughs actually led to a confused production (as Ayckbourn had predicted) now too pause-bound and slow, caught between two approaches with not the time left to right the imbalance.

The Aldwych opening was less sweaty than anticipated. The notices had some strong criticisms of the production ('flaccid and slovenly' was *The Independent*'s verdict) although the play emerged largely unscathed. But again business struggled to build significantly and the revival closed two weeks ahead of its announced 16-week season. The close sadly scarred the long friendship between Michael and Richard Briers, who was never happy in the production. Michael and co-producer Lee Dean hosted a farewell dinner for the company at Sarastro's in nearby Drury Lane after a performance in the final week. Briers arrived both late (he had explained he would have a recently bereaved Geraldine McEwan backstage afterwards) and clearly, Michael sensed, having had a drink or two: 'He became abusive, accusing me of putting the play into the wrong theatre – we'd all agreed that the Aldwych had that useful link with Ben Travers and the Aldwych Farces – and finally I felt I had to leave. I wrote to the company next day to apologise for leaving a supper party of which I was co-host but there are certain rules of good manners, which I think, if one is a guest, should be observed.' After the close and still without any explanation or apology from Briers, Michael wrote to ask 'why he chose to spoil the farewell supper by berating me in an abusive manner in front of half the company', the response to which was 'a rambling phone message accusing me yet again of choosing the wrong theatre'. Richard Briers and Michael have now happily returned to sending each other affectionate Christmas cards.

Bedroom Farce had also briefly slightly frayed the relationship between Michael and Ayckbourn and although it was not long before it was back on its old familiar footing the three-play venture of *Damsels in Distress* (2002) proved more lastingly damaging to their collaboration if not, ultimately, to their mutual regard and very deep friendship.

With a strong and happy 2001 Scarborough company, Ayckbourn originally wrote two plays for his team of seven actors ('The Magnificent Seven' was Michael Billington's description in *The Guardian*), both set in the same Docklands flat with completely different characters. *GamePlan* involves a single mother in tough financial circumstances, having lost a lucrative job and now cleaning offices, whose teenage daughter Sorrel tries to solve their problems by going on the game using the Internet and mobile telephones to liaise with clients and pressing into service as 'maid' her chum Kelly, well intentioned if not the brightest bunny on the block (in one scene she hilariously mistakes condoms for wrapped biscuits). Unfortunately, and leading to spiralling complications, her first lonely widower client drops dead of a heart attack, leaving the girls with an inconvenient body to try to dump in the Thames. His second play was titled *FlatSpin*, a comedy with overtones of the thriller, with a 'resting' actress filling in as janitor of a block of Docklands flats, posing as its owner, only to be stymied when she discovers that the owner's name is a cover for a Secret Service stake-out.

Both plays were immensely popular in Scarborough and Ayckbourn, never one to be idle or miss an opportunity, decided to write another play for the same company in the same conveniently available setting. For many who saw them all, *RolePlay* was the best of the three plays, perhaps because it had fewer uncomfortable moments than the others, being more a comedy of personal relationships. All the plays reflect the way social regeneration of the Docklands area can bring together characters whose very different backgrounds would have prohibited their meeting in an earlier period; *RolePlay* is structured round a formal middle-class dinner party galvanised by a pair of unexpected cockney chancers.

Technology – the Net, Broadband, mobiles – plays a key role too in all three plays (Ayckbourn has always been fascinated by the Digital Revolution) but more than anything else *Damsels in Distress*, with each play involving a young woman amidst a crisis of her own, is a glorious celebration of acting, of what acting involves. Ayckbourn created some gorgeous chances for his seven; it is hard to forget Jacqueline King's *RolePlay* imperious mother-in-law from Godalming (and hell), drunkenly condescending ('I adore your accent – it's like listening to gravy'), Robert Austin's retired dry cleaner client, more keen on talking about his late wife than on sex in *GamePlan* or the extraordinary versatility of Alison Pargeter moving assuredly from the dim Kelly in *GamePlan* to a blithely breezy babe in *FlatSpin* and the gangster's moll, ex-dancer Paige Petite, in *RolePlay*.

Undeniably disenchanted by the current West End, Ayckbourn when Michael expressed a willingness to produce *Damsels in Distress* in London made his conditions clear – the Scarborough cast was to be retained in its entirety and the plays performed in repertoire as they had been seen there (and as *The Normans* had in the West End). The combination of repertoire (even without the costs of changing settings) and a cast without a star made for a major commercial risk, even with the Ayckbourn name attached. Capitalising the venture at £250,000 Michael had co-producers including Andrew Lloyd Webber, the composer's colleague the musicals producer David Ian, Michael Linnit and Lee Dean. At a meeting in Scarborough in September, 2001 over a Sunday breakfast, Ayckbourn, Michael, Nica Burns from Lloyd Webber's RUG and Tom Erhardt all discussed the enterprise and agreed the decisions to use the original cast and repertoire schedule rotating the plays.

The production toured successfully to excellent box office during the summer of 2002 while Burns kept the Duchess Theatre (a RUG house) available for the plays. Predictably with no star attraction the box office advance there was hardly massive, but the openings went well and the reviews overall were predominantly positive. Oddly, although the female characters in the plays emerge (not unusually for Ayckbourn) in a considerably better light than the males, the women critics mostly gave the plays a rough ride ('little more than easy viewing, ploddingly crafted with no ingenious grand design' wrote Kate Bassett of the venture overall in the *Independent on Sunday*) while even those giving the enterprise a clear thumbs-up had reservations about the implausibilities they saw in *FlatSpin*. They contained many attractively positive quotes but overall the question remained whether they were 'selling' notices.

The box office phones remained mostly troublingly silent. The opening period was desperately miserable, the production haemorrhaging money as it lost over £60,000 in its first four weeks and remaining inert at the box office despite press advertising (including a prominent *Evening Standard* display ad – extremely expensive still, even with many producers now beginning to question the value of press advertising). Ayckbourn unfortunately was mostly unavailable having gone on a long-planned barge trip on French rivers soon after the opening and, ironically in light of his plays' clever use of technology, hard to reach except by erratically functioning mobile telephone and fax.

RUG could have given the venture notice to close (contractually a production normally has to dip beneath the agreed weekly break figure for two consecutive weeks after opening week before a landlord can give notice – and *Damsels* had not yet had one week above the break figure). Drastic action was taken by revising the schedule to give the lion's share of performances to *RolePlay*, by far the most popular critically and at the box office (and, one would guess, by word-of-mouth recommendation – at a few performances *FlatSpin*, the least popular of the three, was playing to around 60 people). No proper analysis or discussion had been possible with Ayckbourn, but when word finally got through to him that this course of action was being pursued, he was aghast. *Damsels* for him, it must be remembered, was a special venture with a cast who had been together with him for some time and to all of whom he was very close.

Ayckbourn and Burns had never been easy with each other – they were in any event temperamentally unakin – especially since she had stated at the previous year's Scarborough breakfast meeting that she would have preferred a different play mounted every week. Further, she had in July, 2002 during the regional tour, faxed Michael (with a copy to Ayckbourn) to express 'for the record' her trepidation over the repertory schedule.

Faxing Michael from France Ayckbourn insisted that it was 'far too early for panic measures' adding that he felt strongly that they should not be stampeded by theatre owners, 'especially not *these* theatre-owners, into compromising what we believe in artistically'. He added a key point for him, that any solution '*must* grasp the nettle of these being a trilogy, not one plus two', which of course was what the revised schedule suggested. The management, on its side, had to face a box office that was sending a strong message that *Damsels* was for whatever reasons not being perceived publicly as a trilogy in *The Norman Conquests* sense, possibly lacking that sense of 'event' in tracing the same characters through over seven hours; however strong the feast of acting in the different plays of *Damsels*, seemingly it was not lure enough at a £35 top price ticket (there were, of course, concessions for booking two or three together).

Soon matters became more heated. In the *Daily Telegraph* of 24 October, six weeks after the opening, under the headline: ' "I'll boycott West End" says Angry Ayckbourn', a story reported the dramatist, who had just given an Orange World lecture on the contemporary theatre in London, as 'furious and deeply disappointed' in claiming that the producers (curiously Lloyd Webber alone was named) had 'condemned two plays to the dustbin' and that the West End with its new focus on celebrities – not all adept on stage – such as Madonna, Martine McCutcheon or Denise van Outen was becoming 'ossified, lethargic and incapable of producing new work'. Upset at what he saw as a kick in the teeth, Lloyd Webber at once wrote to Ayckbourn, stressing how he and the co-producers had supported Michael's original agreement to shun 'starring up' the project and that they had only been able to keep *Damsels* running in one of the worst periods ever reported in the West End by revising the playing schedule. Ayckbourn in reply apologised for some *Telegraph* misquotation but he insisted strongly still that he felt Burns had never fully supported the repertoire concept or the need to 'sell' it in advertising: 'Andrew, there was a distinct lack of will all along for this adventure to succeed. The blame is not yours, nor, I suspect, Michael's. It lies largely with Nica who managed to live up to her own determined lack of faith or conviction … I do fear for the West End's future. Believe me, I don't wish it dead; after 25 or so plays I owe it a lot. But surely someone needs to show initiative and originality and take it in hand. And if that someone is not the theatre owners, then who?'

In the event Lloyd Webber sold off part of his theatre chain soon afterwards, leaving that question unanswered (and Burns, with her American business partner and co-producer, Max Weitzenhoffer, bought several of his theatres including the Duchess and the Garrick, now known as Nimax houses).

Ayckbourn remained unhappy at the decision to throw in the towel with its suggestion that repertoire was unworkable in the West End. He wrote to me in mid-October: 'So, the "trilogy" only plays on Saturdays. The rest of the week it's one single play all week. The *same* single play week after week. So unless you get up early on a Saturday, you'll never get to see the other two. Needless to say, I'm *mightily* pissed off.' Michael was as upset as Ayckbourn at the turn of events but tried to preserve calm, faxing him in early November: 'Of course I'm very disturbed that you are angered by the course of action we felt impelled to take during the crucial week when we could have faced notice. Of course I try as your "long-term producer" to present your work as you would have me do.'

When it was clear that even with (or, perhaps, because of) the revised playing schedule *Damsels in Distress* had no encouraging box office future, its early January closure was announced. The whole unhappy experience brought thoughts for the author, who had weathered so many changing times in the West End with Michael as his producer, to a crucial point. Ayckbourn wrote, much more in sorrow than in any anger to his old friend and collaborator that after careful consideration: 'I think that whatever writing future I have left … I will have to pursue it in the way I want and where I feel I'll get a better guarantee of spiritual reward – yes, it's that time of life, I fear! That is to say, with a company of theatre actors who are prepared to commit long term to a repertoire based in, if not confined to, Scarborough. It seems, sadly, that this is not the sort of theatre which interests the West End. At least not the investors, the press, or many of the producers. We've tried the alternative, the Dickie and June show with inadequate supporting cast and that certainly doesn't work. I think it's time to admit defeat, withdraw gracefully and stand aside. For truly the sort of theatre that the West End does seem to want these days is not one that much appeals to me.'

He added a rueful coda: 'What more can I say, Michael? Thank you with all my heart is sadly inadequate. But I guess it will have to do.' In reply Michael echoed the valedictory tone: 'So be it, if be it, it must. I look back on the years of our friendship and collaboration as the very best in my long, some may say too long, stint at this producing lark.' That friendship, at least, survived *Damsels*; Michael, Peter and the Ayckbourns still meet whenever possible and the mutual respect underpinning their long collaboration also remains untarnished.

To date no new Ayckbourn play since *Damsels in Distress* has been seen in the West End, although the several he has written (he recovered remarkably well from his stroke in 2006) have toured extensively with their Scarborough casts, often launched from Guildford's Yvonne Arnaud Theatre, where Ayckbourn has a good relationship with James Barber, for the proscenium arch after Scarborough and have regularly with great success played the 'Brits-off-Broadway' seasons in New York, while he has permitted West End revivals – *Absurd Person Singular*, *Woman in Mind* and *Bedroom Farce* (2010, directed by Peter Hall) – all produced by Bill Kenwright. It would still please many who know and respect them both if – even for one last time only – a top-flight new Ayckbourn could be presented in the West End, advertised with that old familiar billing 'Michael Codron Presents'.

CHAPTER 18

LATE CURTAIN

Any theatrical producer in order to survive to build an enduring career needs not only taste, discrimination, shrewd business sense wedded to an appetite for occasional and sometimes hair-raising risk, tact and charm – but also luck. Michael, who has seen many producers start promisingly only to fade away or go under (one of the more depressing aspects of the commercial theatre in his time has been the scarcity of younger, genuinely lasting producers), is the first to admit that he has had his share of luck, most crucially in that his prime coincided with the active careers of a generation of major dramatists who genuinely wanted to write for the West End. That heyday also saw a remarkable generation of actors, mostly with a solid theatre background rooted in the repertory system, similarly happy to commit to the West End for viable runs. Theatrical agents then, too, many of them with backgrounds as casting directors, stage managers or actors – Michael Anderson, Barry Burnett, Jeremy Conway, Rosalind Chatto, Larry Dalzell and Patricia Marmont included – valued the commercial theatre somewhat more highly than those of a more rapacious modern era, with 'mega agents' now often representing celebrities and models alongside actors. Michael is conscious that producers today have often more hurdles to clear in order to put together a West End enterprise compared with his earlier career. Partly that explains why so many – too many – producers today seem to be more merely shoppers, casting around for the best available product from the subsidised sector, than the individuals, often with major personalities of their own, who look for and nurture their own writers.

As well as being constantly willing to meet and often to advise and help aspirant producers Michael passed down a good deal of his views on production to a whole younger generation during a happy year he spent partly based in his *alma mater* (1993) when occupying the Cameron Mackintosh Chair of Contemporary Theatre; the impresario generously endowed the Chair, at Oxford's St Catherine's College, to allow each year a theatre practitioner – Ian McKellen, Alan Ayckbourn, Michael Frayn and

Thelma Holt have been others – to talk (there is usually an inaugural lecture), hold workshops or otherwise advise undergraduates. Given a small house during term time in Beaumont Street near his old college and the Playhouse Michael held a kind of 'open house' policy whereby students with producing, directing, writing or acting ambitions could come to him for advice.

One talent of real potential emerged when Ben Brown, a law student at Worcester sent 'Professor Codron' a one-act play, *Four-Letter Word*, scheduled for an Edinburgh Festival student production, which Michael liked enough to commission a full-length play. The resulting *All Things Considered*, an Oxbridge comedy based on Albert Camus's proposition that the only true serious philosophical problem is suicide, began with a distinguished philosopher about to take the classic 'No Exit' route out before being interrupted, rather like Simon in *Otherwise Engaged*, by a string of unwelcome visitors. Michael, considerably enthused, sent it to a few possible try-out venues, including Hampstead under Jenny Topper but every theatre turned it down until he approached Alan Ayckbourn who ·programmed it for Scarborough, where I directed it in 1996. With the same cast led by Christopher Godwin it appeared after all at Hampstead Theatre in 1997 where Brown received the kind of notices tyro dramatists dream of ('a dramatist of exceptional promise … who remains loyal to the honourable traditions of boulevard comedy', wrote Charles Spencer for *The Daily Telegraph* while *The Sunday Times*'s John Peter greeted 'an astonishingly mature and accomplished debut') and the play won the Theatrical Managers' Association Most Promising Play Award. For a time, swayed by the capacity Hampstead houses and the reviews Michael contemplated a transfer (budgeted at £80,000 with Cameron Mackintosh and James Nederlander joining in capitalising the venture) but changed his mind when the Marketing supremo at the time, Michael McCabe, reminded him of the number of successes, even some with box office names (including *Marvin's Room* with Alison Steadman) recently transferred from perimeter theatres such as Hampstead only to fail in the West End.

Ayckbourn commissioned another play from Brown, a poignant and funny account of Philip Larkin's surprisingly complex love life ('Don Juan in Hull'), *Larkin With Women* (1999), which I also directed at Scarborough with a remarkable Larkin from Oliver Ford Davies. Later the young producer Richard Jordan, who had been much encouraged by Michael, co-presented it in different productions with West Yorkshire Playhouse and Manchester's Library Theatre but nothing came of these versions.

Subsequently I directed it at Richmond's Orange Tree Theatre (2003), once more with Ford Davies and again to very positive notices. But without a box office star, its commercial future seemed uncertain (like Ayckbourn, Brown tends to write ensemble plays). Michael however continues to keep a benevolent eye on Brown's progress, most recently with the well-received *The Promise* (2010), centred round the Balfour Declaration of 1917 and Britain's part in the creation of what would become Israel, with Ford Davies as Lord Balfour, again at the Orange Tree.

Michael's enthusiasm for Brown's work was matched by his response to Simon Mendes da Costa's *Losing Louis* (2004), an agile and often wildly funny comedy with an Ayckbournian quality (da Costa, like the elder writer, often profitably mined a twin time-scale). First seen at Hampstead, its West End run under the Codron banner, with the cast still headed by Alison Steadman and David Horovitch, would have been much longer, Michael remains convinced, had a lack of available smaller-capacity houses not forced it into the less than hospitable Trafalgar Studios (once the Whitehall Theatre).

Brown's and da Costa's theatrical values seem akin to those of that golden generation – Ayckbourn, Bennett, Frayn, Gray, Stoppard – coinciding in the 1960s into the 80s with Michael's busiest years. More recently it has not been possible to build up such a stable, although he continued to look hard, especially for gifted new writers of farce and comedy. But then the frontiers of farce had shifted with the growth of feminism and the sexual revolution – a piece such as *Look, No Hans!* (Strand, 1985) by the established John Chapman/Michael Pertwee team had a topical theme (industrial espionage in West Berlin) and a performance from David Jason as a keen but inept British agent of dazzling physical inventiveness (his business with a malfunctioning filing cabinet was physical comedy worthy of Buster Keaton) but it essentially harked back to a limbo-world of old farcical conventions with scantily clad kissogram-cuties and naughty-naughty adultery (it opened in a bad week for farce – its reviews were kind when compared to the pasting for Ray Cooney's *Wife Begins at Forty* or Adrian Noble's disastrous Feydeau venture *Women All Over* for Thelma Holt and the Theatre of Comedy Company).

Much more fruitful was Terry Johnson's *Dead Funny* (Vaudeville, 1994) which almost reinvented the genre. A kind of *hommage* to British comedy, most of its characters belong to the Dead Funny Society, obsessives passionate about and occasional impersonators of such dead performers as Frankie Howerd, Jimmy James or Benny Hill (the play is set in 1992 over a weekend that saw the deaths of both Howerd and Hill). Concurrent is the portrait of a troubled marriage with one Society Member, a flagrant adulterer, pretending impotence to his increasingly unhappy wife but whose bluff is finally called. Johnson, who owned to a great admiration for Ayckbourn ('If I had a structural problem I'd think "What would Alan do now?"'), created some delicious and finely-crafted comedy (the end of his first act, with *coitus* rudely interrupted, was a blinder) miraculously without unbalancing the pain in the other strand of a duplicitous marriage. With Zoë Wanamaker's lacerating wit cloaking the character's anguish, David Haig's mendacious husband and Sam Kelly an endearing Benny Hill-freak, under Johnson's own direction *Dead Funny*, following its Hampstead opening, was very popular at the Vaudeville and later transferred with a new cast headed splendidly by Belinda Lang to the Savoy and had a successful tour also. But Johnson's subsequent plays have gone either to the National or The Royal Court.

Although Michael was greatly impressed by Patrick Marber's *Dealer's Choice* (Vaudeville, 1995) – 'one of the best first plays I've ever come across' – a taut, twistingly plotted dark comedy with a poker school setting and an energy comparable to David Mamet, when he moved it from the National although it had a comfortable run it never quite built to repeat its South Bank sold-out success (the PR Lynne Kirwin told Michael she felt it was because women do not warm to plays or movies about gambling, cutting down the potential audience). And the next Marber play, *Closer*, went to Robert Fox for the West End and Broadway after its National run ('again, like with David Hare, it can be tough when they leave, but then Fox is younger than me, probably more akin temperamentally to Marber and he has a higher Broadway producing profile').

Indeed, increasingly often a partnership might be established over one play but then lead no further. *The Rise and Fall of Little Voice* (Aldwych, 1992) took the National Theatre by storm in Sam Mendes's Cottesloe production; Michael had originally commissioned it as a vehicle for Jane Horrocks and secured it early for a commercial transfer which proved equally successful. The performances were richly on target – Alison Steadman's gloriously slatternly Mari, mocking her obese neighbour while swigging any booze going, Pete Postlethwaite's seedily lubricious agent and the revelatory performance from Jane Horrocks as Mari's introverted daughter Little Voice (LV) with her amazing gift for evoking the souls as well as the voices of past stars including Marilyn Monroe, Judy Garland and Billie Holiday. But Cartwright's subsequent *Road* went to The Royal

Court and little stage work has been forthcoming since. *Little Voice* was revived (Vaudeville) in 2009 directed by Terry Johnson with – sign of the times – a winning contestant from a television talent show (*The X Factor*'s Diana Vickers) as LV but its impact was discernibly more muted on this occasion. These television talent shows were cousins of the ventures involving Andrew Lloyd Webber or Cameron Mackintosh using a panel and viewers' votes to cast Maria in *The Sound of Music*, Joseph in *Joseph and the Amazing Technicolour Dreamcoat*, Nancy in *Oliver!* and, most recently, Dorothy (not to mention an occasional Toto) in *The Wizard of Oz*. Not entirely convincingly, Lloyd Webber has attempted to reason that such shows help boost all theatre; the TV format is certainly popular with viewers but cultural commentator Mark Lawson undoubtedly reflected the opinion of many in the theatre world in asserting that the BBC has allowed itself to be used as a glorious casting couch and advertising hoarding for new productions by those most central to the most lucrative form of theatre devised. TV and the theatre have always had a kinship, apart from 'Binkievision' and Jack Hylton's variety shows – in the old days of black and white, the BBC would occasionally show an outside broadcast excerpt from a current West End play – but today the symbiosis seems decidedly unbalanced, leading Lawson to say that although the stage and the small screen may share some DNA, 'commercial and artistic logic suggests that the relatives need to grow apart'.

After its South Bank run Michael moved Joe Penhall's *blue/orange* to the Duchess (2001), still after *Copenhagen* in its redesigned Cottesloe style configuration, co-producing with Lee Dean (an indication of soaring costs – even this small cast, one-set play was capitalised for the West End at £350,000). William Dudley's design carved out a boxing ring of a space for Roger Michell's tense production of Penhall's play of two psychiatrists (Bill Nighy the senior and Andrew Lincoln the younger and more idealistic) arguing over the question of releasing a young patient (Chiwetel Ejiofor) whose delusions include the belief that he is the son of Idi Amin whose favourite fruits, oranges, are in fact blue. Christopher, on the border between neurosis and psychosis, presents an awkward case for two men of an utterly different culture. With something of a Shavian cut and thrust for much of its length (indeed the play echoes *The Doctor's Dilemma* in its picture of the manner in which the medical trade can seem a metaphor for doctors' self-interest), *blue/orange* does become fevered, almost melodramatic, in its final stages as the rival medicos battle for supremacy which for some undercut the wit and tension of the previous scenes but *blue/orange* deserved its *Evening Standard* Best Play Award. It was playing to solid business when the New York events of September 11 shattered the world. Inevitably most theatres' business fell away, *blue/orange*'s more than most, and it closed without quite recouping its costs. But – once again – Penhall's next play went to the subsidised sector (at The Royal Court).

Sometimes promising writers simply moved on to other things. In the early 1980s, Michael had earmarked Anthony Minghella as a rising talent, particularly struck by *Two Planks and a Passion*, his beguiling play set in medieval York visited by Richard II during rehearsals for the Mystery Plays, when (directed by Danny Boyle) it was produced at Greenwich Theatre winning him a Most Promising Playwright Award. He commissioned a play from Minghella – from an Italian family settled in the Isle of Wight, another of Michael's writers with an outsider's perspective – who wrote to him during the writing: 'I'll do my best to shrug off the "promising" with this play. I'm wrestling and punching and struggling with it – but I'll win. Be patient, please.'

Patience was not a Codron virtue but his anxious waiting was to his mind rewarded when he received Minghella's script. Originally titled *The Perks* (which Michael did not care for), *Made in Bangkok* (Aldwych, 1986) involved Brits in the Thai capital, beginning deceptively divertingly with a classic scene of tired travellers waiting at a luggage carousel before subtly shifting into territory often very dark indeed. Felicity Kendal starred as Frances, a woman married to a man (Paul Shelley) whose latent, violent and disturbing desires are triggered by the city's temptations and Peter McEnery played a repressed dentist whose closeted defences slip, humiliating his Thai guide in a shocking scene, which especially reflected the way the play constantly asked who is exploiting whom in its multi-layered view of values Eastern and Western. Michael Blakemore directed against John Gunter designs, aptly simple initially and then using quantities of neon and advertising slogans rather overstating the brashness of Bangkok and too often crucially crushing the actors.

Michael knew that this trenchant piece of Westerners in a supposed Buddhist paradise with a knife slicing regularly into the audience's funny bone was not easy West End fare, even with the insurance of a popular star, but he was totally committed to Minghella's talent and made sure it was strongly cast all down the line (Benjamin Whitrow's businessman was another top-flight performance) and he consulted closely with his trusted PR consultant Lynne Kirwin to get as much press coverage as possible. The reviews were extremely mixed; intriguingly the most perceptive came from overseas including Frank Rich in a *New York Times* survey of London theatre which noted on this visit a lack of 'more provocative theatre voices in London', remarking of Minghella's play: 'Oddly enough it is on the West End stage where one can find a brand new political play that vents its anger at the local audience.' A few others took up its cause; Sheridan Morley in *Punch* wrote: 'A serious strong new play in a commercial London production almost invariably now means one presented by Michael Codron', noting that the appearance of Kendal as one of a group of Anglo-Saxons in a foreign country of which their knowledge is scanty inevitably recalled the world of Frayn's *Clouds* and describing its concerns of trade and sex as underpinning 'the best new English play since Frayn's *Benefactors*'. Some were more blinkered, crowned by the *Evening Standard*'s Milton Shulman, rapidly declining into the ideal audience for plays 'suitable for the tired businessman', who brushed Minghella's work aside as 'a crass, unappetising and basically humourless evening'.

Before long Michael had to request royalty cuts and reducing the costs for a time coincided with an upturn in business; after six weeks of the run he was able to write to investors that 'takings seem to be on the increase' and sign off 'Yours hopefully'. The trend did not last. *Made In Bangkok* closed after seventeen weeks, recouping less than half its investment. Still Michael would gladly have combined again with Minghella, as delightful company as he was a gifted writer but after *Truly, Madly, Deeply* on screen he devoted himself to the cinema and wrote no further stage-play before his sadly early death in 2008.

David Farr was another dramatist of whom Michael had major hopes. After its first Watford run he took on Farr's *Elton John's Glasses* (Queen's, 1998), directed by Terry Johnson, for co-production with Lee Dean which he opened coinciding with the World Cup. Football and rock music – as Farr's play posits, these twin symbols of contemporary success and fame can become surrogate lives inhabited vicariously by dreamers and drifters – combine in a genial, genuinely warm-hearted play. It takes place on the afternoon of Watford Football Club's relegation in May, 1996 with the hero, Bill, a virtual recluse continually replaying a video of key points in Watford's loss to Everton in the FA Cup (he believes because Watford's goalkeeper was blinded by the sun reflected off the huge spectacles worn by Watford's Vice Chairman, Elton John). Bill's confined world, shared only with his girlfriend on secret Saturday afternoon trysts, is invaded by his brother Dan, manager of a failing rock group (Goldilox). The play mostly stayed balanced on the tightrope between farce and pathos, enhanced by the Bill of Brian Conley, recalling something of Tony Hancock's lugubrious, resigned perspective on a dangerous world.

Perhaps because of the World Cup on television Farr's play never began to take off at the box office. Stoll Moss helped by adjusting the rent but as Michael wrote to Conley's agent Sue Latimer 'Our business at the Queen's is a total mystery' (the reviews had been mostly excellent) and *Elton John's Glasses* had to close after only thirty-five performances ('It was, luckily, not a cataclysmic loss because of the initial Watford participation and Stoll Moss's help'). But Farr subsequently chose to concentrate on his directing career and Michael has not collaborated with him again.

Certainly he would have wanted to work with Wendy Wasserstein again – and again. He presented only a few American plays in his career but wanted to produce her New York success *The Sisters Rosensweig* in London if only because – like most people who knew her – he was utterly captivated ('I simply fell in love with her') by her witty, life-enhancing personality. He wrote to her once: 'How pleasurable it was to meet you in my declining years – I hope we will go on meeting and, if you want me to, go on producing'. Although much of the play's background and its riffs on Jewish family life and ties truck chords with him, he was aware that *The Sisters Rosensweig* (which involved epic negotiations with Lincoln Center, the original producers), a family play of three Jewish sisters meeting in the London home of the eldest, Sara, not long after their mother's death had a vein of sentiment which might not necessarily travel well. But he was also keen to work with Maureen Lipman again. She played Gorgeous, a chat show hostess whose effervescent manner masks private tensions, keen to acquire a Chanel outfit to resemble her heroine Catherine Deneuve (Janet Suzman played the eldest sister Sara and Lynda Bellingham the travel writer Pfeni) and, although very different, gave a performance easily matching that of the award-winning Madeline Kahn in New York. With Michael Blakemore directing Michael set up a first production by arrangement with Greenwich Theatre, topping up its budget in order to meet items such as Blakemore's fee – but the Greenwich notices were fairly cool: 'So my worries were compounded by the press. Also my investors, although I didn't totally rely on them, were cautious when they saw it before I decided to take it to the Old Vic where David Mirvish (his father Ed owned the theatre then) was keen to house it'. Two of his favourite investors, the much loved theatre-mad couple Eddie and May Jones – he was a rubicund ex-bookmaker, she a petite and jolly blonde – actually pleaded with him not to bring it in. 'Then Wendy's formidable UK agent, Patricia Mac-Naughton, said that in her opinion we'd opened before we were properly ready with not enough previews at Greenwich and therefore we got iffy notices so at the Vic we did more previews before the press returned. And the reviews were even worse. Still, it did good business and recouped'.

Wasserstein and Michael became fast friends. She stayed with him at times in Kent during the Greenwich run and one enjoyable weekend he took her with Hampstead Theatre's director Jenny Topper to a favourite theatrical attraction, the Ellen Terry Museum in Smallhythe. Unfortunately there would be few more chances to enjoy such happy expeditions; Wendy Wasserstein wrote one more play, *An American Daughter* (which starred Kate Nelligan), too localised for a London showing, but died soon after its production.

Other productions which ended up as one-offs – for whatever reason – included Tracy Letts's *Killer Joe* (Vaudeville, 1995), a piece as controversial as Sarah Kane's contemporaneous *Blasted*, co-produced with the Bush Theatre and American producer Darren Lee Cole, an early play (Letts was then 28) from the author of the later Pulitzer Prize-winning *August: Osage County*. It was a visceral dark comedy of white trailer-trash life on Dallas's outskirts involving venality, projected matricide, hired killers, drug-busts and similar general all-American family values. Its American cast – the aptly named Hired Gun Company from Chicago, backed by Steve Martin – had phenomenal energy in Wilson Milam's production, not flinching from Letts's roller-coaster swerves into some grotesquely unsettling psychic corners; it certainly satisfied Michael's penchant for Websterian drama with its neo-Jacobean attack.

The first night of *Killer Joe* at the Vaudeville following its run at the Bush Theatre, an on-going power house of new writing where Michael went to most productions, gave the Bush's then artistic director Dominic Dromgoole a rare glimpse of Michael caught off-guard. He was finishing his ritual discreet walk-round of the dressing rooms backstage in the half-hour prior to curtain-up when Dromgoole bumped into him: 'He was pale. "Are you all right?" I asked. "Yes. Yes … I just found … er … the actress rogering … er … being rogered by the writer," he said in some alarm. "Oh. Oh dear," I said, "What did you do?" "I said, 'Good Luck'", he replied, a spasm of foolishness crossing his face. He walked away, throwing a light command over his shoulder, "Make sure they're ready, Dominic"'.

Alan Plater's *Peggy For You* with Maureen Lipman (Comedy 2000) could probably have been produced only by Michael. A loving but by no means

57. Peggy Ramsay with her stage incarnation, Maureen Lipman
    – a photograph prepared by advertising agents Dewynter's.

hagiographical portrait of Peggy Ramsay (Lipman once more physically spot-on as she recreated Ramsay's akimbo elegance and going beyond impersonation to convey the woman's moral stature and unquenchable passion for life as well as for plays) it became much more than a picture of an English eccentric. Serena Griffiths as a long-suffering secretary was another plus in an evening inevitably somewhat caviar to the general. It did not quite recoup its costs at the Comedy but a subsequent tour with Lipman still heading the cast took it into the black.

Michael hoped he had found a strong new writer and author/director partnership when he brought Michael Blakemore on board to direct fellow –Australian Hannie Rayson's *Life After George* (Duchess, 2002). An established name in Australia but unknown beyond, it was a risk to put her play directly into the mainstream, even in a small theatre. Rayson's play took a wry look at radicalism's queasy encounters with feminism over thirty years. It opens at George's funeral at which the women in his life display decidedly mixed emotions about this British-born academic, a kind of R.D. Laing-figure understandably popular with students for his credos, which included the assertion that having plentiful sex at university is one of the primary goals of higher education. The gap between his public and private personae – he is hardly a model father or son – is, for all his bravado ('To be magnificent and to fuck' is his slogan for life) extremely wide. Each of the women in his life embodies a different aspect of post-war feminism and Rayson derived some especially sharp comedy from his involvement with the wacky Polly whose website ('Dirt') includes the feature 'Buddy, can you spare a paradigm?'

Its filmic construction in many short scenes was a problem never quite satisfactorily surmounted in production; too few scenes seemed fully developed. Blakemore responded to the play because 'coming from a feminist writer, it's sensitive and forgiving about men', but despite a central performance of some charisma from Stephen Dillane, it was a short-lived failure, running for only four weeks at a considerable loss.

A new stage writer was another actor, Stephen Churchett, whose first play Michael rated highly and opened directly into the West End after a brief run at Guildford which, under its director James Barber, was an excellent and well-run venue from which to launch London-bound productions. *Tom and Clem* (Aldwych, 1997) had a hugely promising set-up taking place at the Potsdam Conference of 1945 after the Tories' defeat in the first post-war election with a contrasted central pairing of newly elected PM Clement Attlee, slightly vinegary, prim, a hard-line pragmatic socialist and a new Labour MP, journalist Tom Driberg, exotic (and fla-grantly gay) individualist and all-round bad boy (before long he is under a table, ostensibly in search of his pen, groping an attractive Russian officer – 'Sir, that is not your Parker'). With the inspired casting of Alec McCowen and Michael Gambon this should have been a cast-iron hit – a decade previously it surely would have been – but it was a disappointing commer-cial failure. It had its faults – rather too many schoolboy jokes (easy plays on words like 'shag') and, more vitally, the Attlee/Driberg personality clash never really advanced the plot after its initial outlining. Some im-plausibilities did not help; under Stalin it is unlikely to say the least that a Soviet intelligence officer would reveal secrets to someone like Driberg, especially on first meeting. But it was an intelligent and often funny play, crisply directed by Richard Wilson and buoyantly acted. Michael shortly afterwards produced Churchett's follow-up, *Heritage* (1998), initially at Hampstead (he remained happily on its Board under Jenny Topper). For this more gently ironic take on the Heritage industry than that of Bennett in *Enjoy*, Mark Rayment had a fine cast headed by George Cole but the play was a desultory affair and the reviews were disappointing mainly; it toured after Hampstead but it did not transfer to the West End and subsequently Churchett has concentrated on television.

There was a happy later reunion with a writer from Michael's past when he produced Ronald Harwood's *Quartet* (Albery 1999). Twenty years pre-viously he had presented *The Dresser* (Queen's 1980) Harwood's play based on his early experiences in Sir Donald Wolfit's company, set in 1941 during a performance of *King Lear* by the ailing actor/manager known in the play as 'Sir' during the Blitz (which punctuates the performance in the play like the storm in *Lear*). The play began at Manchester's Royal Exchange Theatre directed by Michael Elliott who handled the play's progress from compara-tively light comedy to a second act of increasing darkness with masterful control while also capturing all the dusty, greasepaint-and-size aura of provincial touring theatre. Freddie Jones gave the performance of his career as 'Sir', raging as furiously as Lear combating the storm against a war which means, 'I'm reduced to a company of old men, cripples and nancy boys'. He was matched superbly by Tom Courtenay as Norman, his bitchy, prissy dresser-cum-nanny (and, metaphorically, the Fool to his Lear). Backstage plays can often be tricky to succeed but the power of Harwood's writing, Elliott's production and the performances took it to success in London and (with Paul Rogers as 'Sir') New York. Courtenay repeated his Norman in Peter Yates's film opposite Albert Finney's Guinness-fuelled knight. A 2005 revival (Duke of York's) directed by Peter Hall with Julian Glover and Nicholas Lyndhurst fared less well.

Quartet was very different. A mellow play of old age it was set in a gracious Kent country house, now run as a home for retired opera singers, with the ex-wife (Angela Thorne, touchingly dignified) of one resident arriving to stay leading to recollections of old love affairs and rivalries before the foursome of the title (Donald Sinden, Alec McCowen and Stephanie Cole completed a classy quartet) combine in the great number from *Rigoletto* at the close for an annual concert. Verdi claimed that '*Rigoletto* is the best subject that I've ever set to music' but Harwood hardly matched that, substituting character for plot in a somewhat low-wattage and static piece, climaxed inevitably but disappointingly with a mimed 'Bella Figllia dell'amore'. There was enough of a traditional West End audience to give *Quartet* a decent run after a very successful tour.

In more recent years, fighting continuing competition from the subsidised sector and faced with the ever-rising costs of launching new plays – often involving more co-productions or launches in association with regional theatres such as Guildford's Yvonne Arnaud Theatre, West Yorkshire Playhouse or the Theatre Royal, Bath, Michael carried on looking for new work 'in his own voice'. He enjoyed working with another two female dramatists in the same year in 2003 when he produced Geraldine Aron's *My Brilliant Divorce* (Globe), featuring a stand-out Dawn French performance and Moira Buffini's corrosive *Dinner* (Wyndham's), a ferocious black comedy of metropolitan manners with a central glitteringly venomous Harriet Walter. The latter began nervily after its transfer from the National Theatre but soon developed into a solid attraction.

From West Yorkshire Playhouse came Roy Smiles's *Ying Tong* (Ambassador's 2005) subtitled 'A Walk with the Goons'. Smiles – introduced to Michael by Terry Johnson – had been a chat-show scriptwriter in the 1990's and was also an actor. He used a fictional incident of Spike Milligan attacking Peter Sellers with a potato peeler to highlight his main purpose, the scrutiny of the dynamic between the two, both comic geniuses but inevitably bound on a collision course. It is set in 1960 when a clinically depressed Milligan plans to escape from an asylum while his fellow Goons Sellers and Harry Secombe coax him back to prevent him killing off Eccles, the most celebrated *Goon Show* character.

Smiles's play coincided with a revival of interest in classic British com-

58. An actor prepares – Freddie Jones as 'Sir' in
Ronald Harwood's *The Dresser*, 1980.

edy; following *Dead Funny* Johnson had written *Cleo, Camping, Emmanuelle – and Dick* based on the *Carry On* world, three separate editions of *Round The Horne* had been recreated on stage and the Right Size team came up with *The Play What I Wrote*, a long running tribute to Morecambe and Wise.

Johnson had helped Smiles with a workshop production of *Ying Tong* when based at the National Theatre Studio and the portrait of Milligan was spot-on ('You're never alone with a split personality'). Copyright reasons prohibited extracts from *Goon Show* scripts but Smiles's pastiches were

357

uncannily accurate and his device of having Milligan's psychiatrist be a dead ringer for the Goons' Wallace Greenslade was inspired as the play swung between psychiatric ward and a BBC studio.

Budgeted for its London transfer at a tight £150,000 (with a £50,000 overcall) and breaking even at a weekly £37,000 (the capacity take at the Ambassadors was £90,000) Michael co-produced with the Ambassador Theatre Group (the theatre-owning company which also actively produces), National Angels Ltd (a company created partly by agent Michael Linnit) with two associate producers and West Yorkshire Playhouse – the kind of multi-producer billing unprecedented in Michael's earlier career although a Broadway norm for years). *Ying Tong*'s notices were mainly glowing but the play obstinately 'just sat there', playing to dreadful business. Quickly the producers increased advertising and marketing drives by dipping into the overcall beyond the initial capitalisation, while reducing the weekly break figure to £28,000, less than 30% of capacity (the Ambassador Group reduced its rent and royalty waivers were introduced) but still the box office seemed unaccountably paralysed. Michael wrote sadly to Henrietta Duckworth of West Yorkshire Playhouse shortly after the 14th February opening, to tell her that the official closing notice would be posted backstage shortly, meaning a total run of only five weeks: 'We threw all our resources on trying to market the show but there seemed to be a definite resistance to the production – we used up all our capital with the running costs we had, the advertising and the early losses'. *Ying Tong* graphically illustrated how perilous it had become to launch even a modest-sized and tightly budgeted new play without stars in the West End of the 2000's. It did not stop Michael from involvement (with a young producer, Nick Frankfort of CMP Productions, previously the Donmar's General Manager), again at West Yorkshire Playhouse, on Smiles's *Year of the Rat* (Leeds, 2008), a flawed but a boldly imaginative piece on George Orwell set on the Isle of Jura where he was finishing *Nineteen Eighty-Four*. I enjoyed directing this play a great deal – it (fictionally) had Sonia Brownell and the corpulent critic Cyril Connolly joining Orwell in his remote farmhouse, not to mention in the play's more surreal episodes visiting animals including the Rat from *Nineteen Eighty-Four* and *Animal Farm*'s Stalinist pig dropping in on the writer in his imagination. Hugo Speer made a touching, tubercular Orwell heroically chain-smoking his roll-ups and the play was very popular with a predominately younger audience in Leeds. The notices were completely divided however and Michael decided not to risk the venture in London.

With Birmingham Rep. he and Lee Dean co-produced a new play by Peter Quilter, *Glorious!*(2006), an unabashed star vehicle in its portrayal of the eccentric American Florence Foster Jenkins who could not sing ('The First Lady of the Sliding Scale' was one description) but, even to the extent of hiring Carnegie Hall to prove it, was convinced that she was a greater coloratura soprano than Nellie Melba. I directed this one too – Maureen Lipman was cast as Florence and I was keen to work with her again – although I said to Michael at the time that the play, despite being often very funny, was a frail vessel as it stood and would need extensive work in rehearsal and pitch-perfect casting. Michael had written to Quilter before rehearsals: 'Florence as a character chimes with my feelings of life at the moment and the terrifying world we're living in; she's positive, deluded but positive and I hope life-enhancing.'

The reception and business at Birmingham were strong but during its run there and on a seven week tour before opening in London at the Duchess rewrites and re-rehearsals continued, with considerable nudging from Michael, until a genial but somewhat one-joke play developed into something – if not of Ibsenite depth – which touched audiences as well as amused them with its picture of someone almost heroic in her self-belief and her dreams, however unlikely, ending by them having the kind of affection for Florence felt by her original public. Wittily designed by Simon Higlett with artful projection-work by Jon Driscoll – shadowy opera – house background against which sets such as Florence's New York apartment or Carnegie Hall which she hired (and filled) appeared – it framed a Lipman performance (very much, so to speak, on song) again, like her Grenfell or Peggy Ramsay, transcending impersonation to evoke a real original, intrepid and often magnificent ('They may say I can't sing, but nobody can say I *didn't* sing!'), reaching real heights in Quilter's final scene with her faithful accompanist Cosme McMoon. Following her massacre of The Queen of the Night's aria from *The Magic Flute* ('like a coloratura Chihuahua' said one notice), as Cosme describes the ecstatic reception at her last Carnegie Hall concert Jenkins seems to be singing on under his lines but then a glorious soprano voice takes over (I used an early Maria Callas recording of Gounod's 'Je vieux vivre dans le rêve' from *Romeo et Juliette*) the sound of which was of course, what she heard in her imagination, starting faintly underneath Cosme's account of the event and then swelling to fill the whole house against the opera-house's chandeliers lighting up in the background, peaking with a final fade to iris out on Florence.

Glorious! had positive notices in the main – Lipman's performance and a brilliant supporting cast were unanimously praised – but it had a very slow start at the Duchess. Michael's opening night card to me – we had first collaborated thirty years before – hinted at his worries faced with a low box office advance: 'It's all getting rather tempestuous. Perhaps it always was. But we had gumboots to weather the storm then'. Only gradually – word of mouth clearly was important on this production – did the box office begin to climb and *Glorious!* eventually ran for Lipman's contracted six months.

For the first time since *Donkeys' Years* – not for want of trying – Michael was reunited in the West End with one of his favourite actors, Penelope Keith, when he co-produced with Bath's Theatre Royal a revival of *The Importance of Being Earnest* (Vaudeville, 2008). Directed by Peter Gill whose staging sharply highlighted the symmetry of Wilde's construction, this saw Keith eschewing the dragon-empress of convention to give a Lady Bracknell of stylish aplomb, utterly secure in her opinions – so much so that the revelations of Jack Worthing's origins convincingly underpinned her dread of the worst excesses of the French Revolution running through the drawing rooms of Belgravia, rather like Suez through that of Clarissa Eden in Downing Street. A handsome production in William Dudley's airy designs the production did almost capacity business on tour after a sticky technical start in Bath; it settled in, looking good in the Vaudeville, for a healthy London run.

Keith had been central to *Entertaining Angels* by Richard Everett, actor turned dramatist, whose plays had been performed in regional theatres such as Windsor and Worcester and on whom Michael had kept an interested eye. Intrigued by this new play, centred round a recently-bereaved vicar's wife and the problems of women in a riven contemporary Anglican Church, he took it to Chichester where in 2007 with Keith in the leading role it opened new artistic director Jonathan Church's first season, gratifyingly seeing the House Full boards dusted off for the first time in years. I directed this production – I had worked enjoyably with Keith previously – although I said to Michael before rehearsals began that I thought the script needed further work. There were some revisions in rehearsal and it became a popular success with mostly positive press reactions both at Chichester and on a subsequent regional tour, although Michael felt too that there was still unfinished business with the play. Unusually, he commissioned Everett to return to the drawing board; eventually he received a considerably revised version, crucially involving the excision of

one previously significant supporting-role and a subplot along with extensive reshaping elsewhere.

The revised *Entertaining Angels* focused the tension between comedy
and a darker substrain much more surely, the play now subtly deepening
significantly in texture as it proceeded. With most of the same strong
original cast – Polly Adams as a colonial sister, Benjamin Whitrow the
rueful shade of Keith's husband – this toured once more (co-produced with
Bath Theatre Royal) in 2009, again to packed houses. No West End theatre
of a suitable size was available to coincide with the tour's close in November. When it looked likely that it could open in London before Christmas
or in early 2010 the deal fell apart, in no small measure because of Keith's
stipulations, unexpectedly and deeply disappointing Michael, especially in
light of their partnership in earlier years when he had so championed her.
He had hoped very much to be represented – ideally by a new play – in the
West End in his eightieth year. He was discernibly somewhat downcast
for a while that it would not be with Everett's play, on which he had spent
so much time and trouble.

Nonetheless as he approached his ninth decade (SOLT marked his 80th
birthday at the 2010 Olivier Awards with a Special Award at Grosvenor
House, where a capacity audience gave him a standing ovation) although
constantly vowing that retirement is imminent, he seemed to most who
knew him to be happier, certainly more mellow, than in the 1990's. There
had been sadnesses, inevitably more recently including the deaths of
increasing numbers of close colleagues and friends – Simon Gray, John
Mortimer and Harold Pinter among them – and the major shock of David
Sutton's sudden death in 2004.

David had retired from active business partnership with Michael in 1996
and now was contentedly settled in a new relationship with Geert van
Meel, although he still kept up a lively interest in the theatre. He seemed
at sixty still fit and active, retaining his lithe figure – he played tennis
frequently – but he was also a lifelong heavy smoker. David died in the
street of a massive heart attack, almost instantly; he had enjoyed one
favourite pastime, a game of tennis, and was on his way to enjoy another,
a bridge game. The hospital, finding telephone numbers for both Michael
and Geert in David's pocket diary contacted Michael who then had the task
of informing Geert with the news; both raced to the Chelsea and Westminster hospital but David was already dead.

Some months later Michael and his new partner Peter Hulstrom (who
had liked David very much) flew with Geert to scatter David's ashes in the

sea near Beaulieu in the South of France, an area where they had spent relaxed and happy times together on past holidays. They went out into the bay by motor-launch, spread the ashes and then paused for private memories amid the peace of the open sea before thinking of the return journey. At which point the engine stalled leaving them stuck and contemplating a dauntingly long swim to shore. 'This', thought Michael wryly, 'must be David's revenge', before abruptly the engine sparked into life to return them to land.

Personally, after chequered times, he seems contented in what would seem to be a settled 'Last Attachment'. He met Peter Hulstrom outside the Aldwych one day in 1998 not long after he and Mark Rayment had separated after nearly twelve years (for a time subsequently Rayment lived in South Africa with a new career as an actor – he appeared there in *The Lion King* – before relocating to New York). Peter was accoutred with a quantity of what looked to a curious Michael like some strange scientific apparatus; it transpired when he asked that it was some of the equipment for Peter's window-cleaning business. Only gradually did a relationship develop, leading to Peter moving in with Michael in both London and Kent (their mutual love of dogs was another bond). Cockney-born and bred Peter – who continues to run his own business – retains a possibly healthy scepticism towards the sometimes overheated hothouse world of the theatre; while he enjoys musicals, he can find some plays, especially revivals, tough going (still recalled by many is his remark – not possessed of a practised stage whisper, he was widely overheard by the audience – on the opening night of a turgid Haymarket revival of Oscar Wilde's worst play, *A Woman of No Importance*, when he turned to Michael as they returned to their seats after a slow first half of seemingly never-ending tedium with: 'If this act isn't better than the first I'll have your guts for garters!').

Office life still occupies Michael for most of the week, his weekends virtually always spent in Kent with occasional visits to old friends such as Lord Montagu overlooking the Solent and sometimes trips to the sun in Mallorca, Morocco or Antigua. A lifelong connoisseur of lunch – rivalling Keith Waterhouse for whom it was a *Who's Who* recreation – he is a regular patron of most of London's leading watering-holes including the Ivy Club, Christopher's, Orso's, very occasionally the Garrick Club (he tends to use it more for private celebrations such as Peter's birthdays, using one of the private smaller rooms), the Wolseley and, near the office, the Loch Fyne fish restaurant (a favourite meal there is a pair of succulent kippers with Sarson's malt vinegar to hand). He, Andrew Lloyd Webber and Anthony

59. Michael with Peter on Edward Montagu's boat.

Pye-Jeary form a kind of informal dining-club, always seeking out new restaurants. Lunching with him can be on occasion something of a mine-field. Like Michael Winner he is often dissatisfied with the first table offered (likewise with hotel rooms) and he is notoriously unpredictable with waiters; incompetence can swiftly induce a tight-lipped black mood while guests at times might be left briefly to their own devices and a convenient newspaper should a personable new young waiter materialise ('only window-shopping these days' he says in self-defence).

Over the years relaxation has come easier to him (Peggy Ramsay's insistence on the importance of some 'inner life' to balance the theatre's demands was something he always remembered), his various interests joined now by one which became the most absorbing when he discovered in later life the joys of jigsaw puzzles of which he has amassed an enormous collection, stored in his Kent attic. Margaret Drabble when writing her book *The Pattern in the Carpet: A Personal History with Jigsaws* found that Michael disproved her theory that most adults who do jigsaws were introduced to them in childhood, usually by kindly aunts. One Christmas Michael had bought a puzzle of Canterbury Cathedral in a village shop as a stocking filler for David; when it was clear that he was uninterested Michael took pity on it and did it himself and was smitten, catching the habit when already into middle age. After doing all the English Cathe-

363

drals, and by now almost an addict, he embarked on other motifs. There is usually a puzzle in progress on specially-placed tables in London and Kent; Michael after completing one needs somebody (usually Peter) to admire the handiwork before he puts all the pieces back in the box, ready to join what must be the thousands stored up in the attic. Every jigsaw, of course, can always finally work out. Unlike every play. As Drabble wrote: 'He says he likes making order out of chaos, and he likes the solipsism of living inside the world of the jigsaw.'

Although less active in production than before the health of London's commercial theatre continues to exercise him. He remains deeply involved in the affairs of the Peggy Ramsay Foundation and in those of SOLT – he was foremost among those agitating for major changes, including the widening of membership to bring in neighbourhood London 'off-West End' theatres such as the Almeida or Hampstead as the tightly exclusive SWET morphed into a body more genuinely representative of London theatre overall (and one with a more euphonious acronym). In his position as a kind of SOLT Elder Statesman ('venerated and venerable' in Dominic Dromgoole's description) he remains always still ready and available to advise fellow or younger aspirant producers.

At various times he has attempted to galvanise key issues concerning producers both new and established. An especially crucial notion was the suggestion of a collaborative and concerted effort to explore the possibility of establishing a viable 'off-West End' within the mainstream whereby smaller capacity West End houses could become homes for limited seasons of new writing at lower than prevailing top prices, hopefully going some way towards restoring an element of the genuine risk-taking once so vital in keeping the commercial theatre in the capital as varied as it had been previously. Obviously such an ideal – as Michael was well aware – would involve complex and time-consuming negotiations, most crucially with the theatre-owning landlords as well as with the various unions involved (Actors' Equity, the Musicians' Union and the Technicians' Union BECTU) in order to deal with terms, salary scales and working agreements, which could keep production costs realistic enough to satisfy professional person- nel while still holding running costs within bounds possible enough to 'nurse' a play slow to take off at the box office (now becoming almost impossible). It was a major disappointment to him that so many younger producers (sadly, some of whom seem to have no interest in actors, think- ing purely in box office terms) seemed to want to play their own tunes rather than join a united band, however. As it is, two smaller London

60. More of Michael's 'Wall of Shame' in the Aldwych office.

houses – the Ambassador's and the St Martin's – ideal for riskier new work, seem permanently unavailable, housing a cheap-to-run dance show (*Stomp!*) and *The Mousetrap* respectively.

The 2000s so far have seen mostly buoyant financial figures for the West End, always predictably trumpeted by SOLT as proof of a flourishing and hale commercial theatre, even in a year of major recession such as 2009. However these ever-spiralling 'record figures' on closer examination are at base mostly due to the ever-increasing number of long-running musical productions in big houses at progressively higher ticket-prices (most musicals now have a top price of £60 – Lloyd Webber's sequel to *Phantom of the Opera*, the Adelphi's *Love Never Dies*, announced a 2010 top of £67.50 – plus often extra, and always invidious, 'Booking Fees'). Unless previously launched and critically-approved in subsidised houses (*Enron*, *Jerusalem* and *War Horse* most prominently recently) or unless garlanded with a star-name, preferably these days one with a popular press and/or celebrity-magazine profile (Keira Knightley, Anna Friel, Rupert Friend, Matt Lucas, Kim Cattrall) the new play – essential for maintaining at least something of the range of a broad church rather than a narrow pulpit in London's commercial sector – struggles more often than not to survive.

Michael, however, never seems to be a disappointed man. It would not be surprising if the way the West End has gradually become so unadventurous – a seemingly endless string of plays (let alone musicals) adapted from popular screen originals (*Breakfast at Tiffany's*, *Calendar Girls*, *The Shawshank Redemption* – none exactly a milestone dramatically – were all running simultaneously in 2009) when once it was the stage which fed the screen, plus a string of revivals, quite a few of them of plays which came out of his office first time round – were to depress him, so fired always by the discovery and development of a script new and original. Yet he accepts that a younger generation, raised in a different culture more screen and media conscious than his, might be glamorised by adapted screenplays, cast often with film or 'celebrity' personalities rather than actors who have earned their real spurs on stage. That the commercial theatre – West End and Broadway alike – has always tended to be cyclical in its patterns is something which he has always stressed. Booing, for instance, may have vanished along with galleries from the theatre (if not the opera house) but an even more unpleasant hazard has arisen in the internet era with 'bloggers' (the very word makes Michael flash with anger), defying the convention that critical comment be embargoed until press night by reviewing productions in preview with mostly reactionary responses. Often little more than malicious gossip and also often ill-informed these can create a toxic pall around a show (notably the musical *Love Never Dies* from Lloyd Webber). For Michael 'They are the modern equivalent of the lot that used to boo plays in the 50s and 60s. I think they're ghastly.'

Similarly, within the theatre world itself there are occasional flurries of alarm together with whispers of conflicts of interest whenever theatre-owners increase their spheres of influence, particularly when they are also active producers. In 2009 more than a few concerned voices were raised to point out the perils of too much power, even suggesting a possible case for the Monopolies Commission, when the Ambassador Theatre Group, also busy producers and already owners of many London and provincial theatres, acquired the First Leisure Group's theatre holdings. But an old hand like Michael could recall a situation over fifty years before when a mogul such as Prince Littler at the head of The Group consortium controlled more than fifty per cent of West End theatre seats as well as exercising considerable influence in the regions through the Howard and Wyndham chain, with many worried by his pervasive influence just as much as by the H.M. Tennent firm's sway over the West End, to the extent of lobbying MP's and organising the tabling of questions in the House of Commons. Also, although 'celebrities' today appear in predictably larger numbers on London's stages (one of the replacement cast in *Calendar Girls* was a newsreader from TV), one could point out that as far back as the days of the Edwardian theatre a star-attraction such as Lillie Langtry was not selling out theatres on the strength of her acting talent, while American film stars (not just Michael's early goddess Ingrid Bergman, but also Mae West, Tyrone Power, Ginger Rogers, Elizabeth Taylor, Katharine Hepburn, Charlton Heston, James Stewart and Al Pacino) appeared over the years in the West End long before the current wave, the main difference being that yesterday's stars mostly had had real stage grounding.

With Michael, aware of all this, there is little hankering after some prelapsarian Golden Age. He is still an extremely active theatregoer (often at matinees these days), catching most new London productions and well aware of such developments as a powerful wave of contemporary and impressive younger women dramatists (Lucy Prebble, Polly Stenham, Alia Bano, Bola Agbaje, Laura Wade). He has watched over countless trends and changes, even seeing how in the early 2000s, with the proliferation of site-specific work, performance-art and the activities of companies such as Shunt, KneeHigh or Punchdrunk (themselves much influenced by Theatre de Complicite), the essential nature of the theatrical event itself has increasingly come under reappraisal although, once again highlighting the cyclical nature of theatre, he could remind people of similar enterprises back in the brave new world of 1960s and early 1970s euphoria – Liquid Theatre, a sensory exploration underneath the Villiers street arches, or the dynamic Arts Lab created by his old friend Jim Haynes in Drury Lane where the theatre-space (there was also a cinema and a bar area) housed such legendary pioneering companies as Freehold, People Show and Moving Being and was regularly raided by the Metropolitan Police sniffing out drugs and/or nudity. Nevertheless the whole metropolitan theatrical scene – Shaftesbury Avenue and experimental Fringe alike – seemed more innocently enjoyable, while no less committed, at that time.

Michael's single affair away from the theatre when he helped put together the film of Michael Frayn's *Clockwise* as Executive Producer was happy enough (the film was generally well received) and he might well have made other screen excursions had circumstances been right. He spent considerable time working on another venture, keen to collaborate again on the big screen with Frayn on a delightful script centred round an elderly man's decision to walk all round the British coastline (it was titled *First and Last*) in which Alec Guinness was eager to star. However compared to raising the money for *Clockwise* with John Cleese (Michael's 'angel' Nat Cohen was a major player on that film) this time, even with the talent involved, raising the capitalisation developed into a nightmare of frustrations. Discussing his vicissitudes with his friend John Schlesinger, veteran of many a movie battle, the director trenchantly told him: 'Michael, you have to realise that these days, if you want to get films made you have to eat shite.'

First and Last never could raise enough funding and was abandoned, although Frayn later revised it for a television version starring Joss Ackland. Michael had few real regrets. The theatre was, fundamentally, where he belonged, where what Peggy Ramsay described as his good taste allied to genuine modesty most thrived. She had in her time seen quite a few producers go under; as she said: 'This metier is so hard that from time to time people who survive in it do so by a kind of stoical endurance' and in that light Michael emerges as a real survivor, prepared still to endure his profession's not infrequent buffets, its disappointments and occasional crushing instances of ill luck. Although the theatre has provided him with a good lifestyle for most of his time in it he has survived enough financial scares (the major disaster of *The Golden Touch*, which nearly scuppered him, was his financial nadir) throughout his career never to take that for granted. Moreover although the commercial theatre world often can be – increasingly more so recently – both venal and ruthless, the money has never been Michael's primary motive ('I don't see why commercial cannot also be good').

For
Michael
Good luck in
Show Biz
love

John.

61. A star's encouraging words for his Executive Producer –
John Cleese on *Clockwise*.

369

One of his major strengths and a reason for the unusual longevity of his career is a constant acceptance of change together with recognition of the need in any healthy theatre, commercial and subsidised alike, for change to continue. Long after the theatre has undergone further seismic sea-changes much of the extraordinary body of work which Michael Codron Ltd has put on will surely serve still for future generations as a unique index to the shifts alongside the constants of human behaviour, to the foibles and follies, the fads and frenzies, the aspirations and illusions, the failures as well as the fun of giddily changing times, a roller-coaster era.

BIBLIOGRAPHY

The texts of many of the plays produced by Michael Codron are readily accessible. Most of the output of his major dramatists – Ayckbourn, Bennett, Frayn, Gray, Hampton, Hare, Orton, Pinter, Stoppard included – is in print, much of it in various collected editions. Other scripts, including a good deal of those of his earlier productions, are harder to track down. Some were published in Samuel French Acting Editions but many are out of print; these and the scripts of plays unpublished prior to the abolition of the Lord Chamberlain's control of the British theatre can be found in the British Library.

Of books consulted in writing this book, the following were particularly useful:

ALLEN Paul
Alan Ayckbourn: Grinning at the Edge (Methuen, 2001)

BECKETT Andy
When the Lights Went Out: Britain in the Seventies (Faber & Faber, 2009)

BENNETT Alan
Writing Home (Faber & Faber, 1994)

BILLINGTON Michael
Harold Pinter (Faber & Faber, revised ed. 2007)

State of the Nation: British Theatre Since 1945 (Faber & Faber, 2007)

BLACK Kitty
Upper Circle (Methuen, 1984)

BLACKER Terence
You Cannot Live as I Have Lived and Not End Up Like This: The Thoroughly Disgraceful Life and Times of Willie Donaldson (Ebury Press, 2007)

BROWNE Terry
Playwrights' Theatre: The English Stage Company at the Royal Court
(Pitman, 1978)

CHAMBERS Colin
Peggy: The Life of Margaret Ramsay (Nick Hern Books, 1987)

COVENEY Michael
Maggie Smith (Gollancz, 1992)

CRAIG Sandy (ed.)
Dreams and Deconstructions: Alternative Theatre in Britain (Amber Lane, 1980)

CROALL Jonathan
John Gielgud (Methuen, 2000)

DE JONGH Nicholas
Politics, Prudery and Perversions: The Censoring of the English Stage, 1901-68 (Methuen, 2000)

DROMGOOLE Dominic
The Full Room: An A-Z of Contemporary Playwriting (Methuen, 2000)

DUFF Charles
The Lost Summer (Nick Hern Books, 1995)

ELSOM John
Post-War British Theatre (Routledge, 1978)

FEUER Cy
I Got the Show Right Here (Applause Books, 2005)

FINDLATER Richard (ed.)
At the Royal Court: 25 Years of the English Stage Company (Amber Lane, 1981)

FRAYN Michael
Stage Directions: Writing on Theatre, 1970-2008 (Faber & Faber, 2008)

FRISBY Terence
Outrageous Fortune (First Thing Publications, 1998)

GRAY Simon
An Unnatural Pursuit (Faber & Faber, 1985)

GROVE Valerie
A Voyage Round John Mortimer (Viking, 2007)

HEWISON Robert
In Anger: Culture in the Cold War, 1945-60 (Methuen 1988)

HOBSON Harold
Theatre in Britain: A Personal View (Oxford: Phaidon, 1984)

INVERNE James
The Impresarios (Oberon Books, 2000)

JOHNSTON John
The Lord Chamberlain's Blue Pencil (Hodder and Stoughton, 1990)

KYNASTON David
Austerity Britain (Bloomsbury, 2007)

LAHR John
Prick Up Your Ears: The Life of Joe Orton (Allen Lane, 1978)

LOGAN Pamela
Jack Hylton Presents (BFI Publishing, 1995)

MARWICK Arthur
British Society since 1945 (Pelican, 1982)

MILES Barry
London Calling: A Countercultural History of London since 1945 (Atlantic Books, 2010)

MURRAY Braham
The Worst It Can Be is a Disaster (Methuen, 2007)

ORTON Joe (ed. John Lahr)
  Diaries (Allen Lane, 1980)

READ Piers Paul
  Alec Guinness (Simon & Schuster, 2005)

REBELLATO Dan
  1956 And All That: The Making of Modern British Drama (Routledge, 1999)

RICH Frank
  Hot Seat (Random House, NY, 1998)

SHELLARD Dominic
  Kenneth Tynan (Yale University Press, 2003)

SHEREK Henry
  Not in Front of the Children (Heinemann, 1959)

SPOTO Donald
  Otherwise Engaged: The Life of Alan Bates (Arrow, 2008)

THOMPSON Harry
  Peter Cook (Sceptre, 1997)

TREWIN J.C.
  A Play Tonight (Elek Books, 1952)

TYNAN Kenneth
  Curtains (Longmans, Green, 1961)
  Tynan Right and Left (Longmans, Green, 1967)

VINEN Richard
  Thatcher's Britain: The Politics and Social Upheaval of the 1980s (Simon & Schuster, 2009)

WEXLER Paul
  The Non-Jewish Origins of the Sephardic Jews (SUNY, 1966)

WHEEN Francis
  Strange Days Indeed (Fourth Estate, 2009)

WILDEBLOOD Peter
  Against the Law (Penguin, 1957)

WILLIAMS Kenneth
  Diaries (Harper Collins, 1993) (ed. Russell Davies)

The authors are grateful to the following for assistance or for permission to quote from copyright material: Sir Alan Ayckbourn, Alan Bennett, the staff of the British Library, Dominic Dromgoole, Michael Frayn, Samuel French Ltd., the Garrick Club Library, Jacki Harding, John Haynes, the staff of Heywood Hill Bookshop, the staff of the London Library, Basil Moss, Sir Tom Stoppard, Ion Trewin, the staff of the Victoria and Albert Museum. Special thanks are due to Andrew Hewson, most loyally tenacious of literary agents and his colleague Ed Wilson at Johnson & Alcock Ltd., and also to our original gifted editor Mary Morris (now at British Museum Publications), ably succeeded by Tracy Carns, and the staff at Duckworth headed by Peter Mayer.

MICHAEL CODRON
THEATRE PRODUCTIONS

Title	Author	Theatre
1956		
Ring For Catty	Patrick Cargill & Jack Beale	Lyric/Lyric Hammersmith
1957		
A Month Of Sundays	Gerald Savory	Cambridge
The Wit To Woo	Mervyn Peake	Arts
Share My Lettuce	Revue	Lyric Hammersmith/ Comedy/Garrick
Breath Of Spring	Peter Coke	Cambridge/Duke of York's
1958		
Little Eyolf	Henrik Ibsen	Lyric Hammersmith
The Dock Brief and What Shall We Tell Caroline?	John Mortimer	Lyric Hammersmith/ Garrick
The Birthday Party	Harold Pinter	Lyric Hammersmith
Honour Bright	Donald Ogden Stuart	Lyric Hammersmith
Valmouth	Sandy Wilson	Lyric Hammersmith/ Saville
1959		
Fool's Paradise	Peter Coke	Apollo
How Say You?	Kay Bannerman/ Harold Brooke	Aldwych
Why The Chicken?	John McGrath	Tour
Pieces Of Eight	Revue	Apollo
1960		
The Wrong Side Of The Park	John Mortimer	Cambridge/St. Martin's
The Caretaker	Harold Pinter	Arts/Duchess
The Golden Touch	Julian More & James Gilbert	Piccadilly
1961		
Three	Harold Pinter/John Mortimer & N.F. Simpson	Arts/Criterion
Stop It Whoever You Are	Henry Livings	Arts
One Over The Eight	Revue	Duke Of York's
The Tenth Man	Paddy Chayefsky	Comedy
Under Milkwood	Dylan Thomas	Lyric Hammersmith
Ducks And Lovers	Murray Schisgal	Arts
Big Soft Nellie	Henry Livings	Stratford East/Arts

377

1962

Two Stars For Comfort	John Mortimer	Garrick
Everything In The Garden	Giles Cooper	Arts/Duke Of York's
Infanticide In The House Of Fred Ginger	Fred Watson	Arts
Rattle Of A Simple Man	Charles Dyer	Garrick
Doctors Of Philosophy	Muriel Spark	Arts
End Of Day	Samuel Beckett	Arts
A Cheap Bunch Of Nice Flowers	Edna O'Brien	Arts
Three At Nine	Revue	Arts
Cindy Ella	Ned Sherrin & Caryl Brahms	Arts/Garrick

1963

An Evening of British Rubbish	Revue	Comedy
Next Time I'll Sing To You	James Saunders	Arts/Criterion
Licence To Murder	Elaine Morgan	Vaudeville
Kelly's Eye	Henry Livings	Royal Court
Private Lives	Noël Coward	Duke of York's
The Lover and The Dwarfs	Harold Pinter	Arts
Cockade	Charles Wood	Arts
Cider With Rosie	Laurie Lee	Garrick
Out Of The Crocodile	Giles Cooper	Phoenix

1964

Poor Bitos	Jean Anouilh	Arts/Duke of York's
The Brontes	Margaret Webster	Arts
Hedda Gabler	Henrik Ibsen	Arts/St Martin's
Hang Down Your Head and Die	Revue	Comedy
The Formation Dancers	Frank Marcus	Arts/Globe
Entertaining Mr Sloane	Joe Orton	Arts/Wyndham's/Queen's
See How They Run	Philip King	Vaudeville
A Scent Of Flowers	James Saunders	Duke of York's
Busybody	Jack Popplewell	Duke of York's

1965

Loot	Joe Orton	Tour
Travelling Light	Leonard Kingston	Prince of Wales
Killing of Sister George	Frank Marcus	Duke of York's
Ride a Cock Horse	David Mercer	Piccadilly
Anyone For England	Revue	Lyric Hammersmith

1966

A Lily in Little India	Donald Howarth	St Martin's
Little Malcolm and his Struggle Against the Eunuchs	David Halliwell	Garrick
The Anniversary	Bill MacIlwraith	Duke of York's
There's a Girl in My Soup	Terence Frisby	Globe/Comedy
When Did You Last See My Mother?	Christopher Hampton	Comedy
Public And Confidential	Ben Levy	Duke of York's
A Present For the Past	John Stone	Edinburgh Festival
Big Bad Mouse	Philip King & Falkland Cary	Shaftesbury
Four Degrees Over	Revue	Fortune

1967

The Judge	John Mortimer	Cambridge
The Flip Side	Hugh & Margaret Williams	Apollo
Country Dance	James Kennaway	Edinburgh Festival
Fill the Stage with Happy Hours	Charles Wood	Vaudeville
Wise Child	Simon Gray	Wyndham's
The Boy Friend	Sandy Wilson	Comedy
Fanghorn	David Pinner	Fortune

1968

Not Now Darling!	Ray Cooney & John Chapman	Strand
Mrs Mouse Are You Within?	Frank Marcus	Duke of York's
The Real Inspector Hound	Tom Stoppard	Criterion
They Don't Grow on Trees	Ronald Millar	Prince of Wales
The Servant of Two Masters	Goldoni	Queen's

1969

The Death and Resurrection of Mr Roche	Tom Kilroy	Edinburgh Festival
There'll Be Some Changes Made	Alun Owen	Fortune
The Bandwagon	Terence Frisby	Mermaid

1970

It's a Two Foot Six Inches Above the Ground World	Kevin Laffan	Wyndham's
Girlfriend	David Percival	Apollo
The Contractor	David Storey	Royal Court/ Fortune
The Two Of Us	Michael Frayn	Garrick
The Philanthropist	Christopher Hampton	Royal Court/ Mayfair

1971

A Game Called Arthur	David Snodin	Royal Court Upstairs
The Foursome	E.A. Whitehead	Royal Court/ Fortune
Butley	Simon Gray	Criterion
Voyage Round My Father	John Mortimer	Haymarket
Slag	David Hare	Hampstead/Royal Court
The Changing Room	David Storey	Royal Court/ Globe

1972

Siege	David Ambrose	Cambridge
Veterans	Charles Wood	Royal Court
Me Times Me	Alan Ayckbourn	Tour
Time And Time Again	Alan Ayckbourn	Comedy
Crown Matrimonial	Royce Ryton	Haymarket
Owners	Caryl Churchill	Royal Court Upstairs
My Fat Friend	Charles Laurence	Globe

1973

Collaborators	John Mortimer	Duchess
Savages	Christopher Hampton	Royal Court/ Comedy
Habeas Corpus	Alan Bennett	Lyric
The Sea	Edward Bond	Royal Court
Absurd Person Singular	Alan Ayckbourn	Criterion/ Vaudeville

1974

Knuckle	David Hare	Comedy
Flowers	Lindsey Kemp	Regent
Golden Pathway Annual	John Burrows & John Harding	Mayfair
The Norman Conquests	Alan Ayckbourn	Globe/Apollo
John Paul George Ringo		
...& Bert	Willy Russell	Lyric

1975

A Family And a Fortune	Julian Mitchell	Apollo
Alphabetical Order	Michael Frayn	Mayfair
A Far Better Husband	Donald Churchill &	
	Peter Yelland	Tour
Ashes	David Rudkin	Young Vic
Absent Friends	Alan Ayckbourn	Garrick
Otherwise Engaged	Simon Gray	Queen's/Comedy
Stripwell	Howard Barker	Royal Court

1976

Funny Peculiar	Mike Stott	Mermaid/Garrick
Treats	Christopher Hampton	Royal Court/Mayfair
Donkey's Years	Michael Frayn	Globe
Confusions	Alan Ayckbourn	Apollo
Teeth 'N' Smiles	David Hare	Royal Court/
		Wyndham's
Yahoo	Alan Strachan/Alec Guinness	Queen's

1977

Dusa, Stas, Fish & Vi	Pam Gems	Hampstead/Mayfair
Just Between Ourselves	Alan Ayckbourn	Queen's
Oh Mr Porter	Revue	Mermaid
The Bells of Hell	John Mortimer	Garrick
Breezeblock Park	Willy Russell	Mermaid/Whitehall
The Old Country	Alan Bennett	Queen's

1978

The Rear Column	Simon Gray	Globe
Ten Times Table	Alan Ayckbourn	Globe
The Homecoming	Harold Pinter	Garrick
Alice's Boys	Jonathan Hales &	
	Felicity Browne	Savoy
The Unvarnished Truth	Royce Ryton	Phoenix
Night and Day	Tom Stoppard	Phoenix

1979

Joking Apart	Alan Ayckbourn	Globe
Tishoo	Brian Thompson	Wyndham's
Stage Struck	Simon Gray	Vaudeville

1980

Balmoral	Michael Frayn	Guildford
Dr Faustus	Christopher Marlowe	Lyric Hammersmith/
		Fortune
Make And Break	Michael Frayn	Lyric Hammersmith/
		Haymarket

380

The Dresser	Ronald Harwood	Queen's
Taking Steps	Alan Ayckbourn	Lyric
Enjoy	Alan Bennett	Vaudeville
Hinge & Bracket at the Globe	Revue	Globe

1981

Rowan Atkinson In Revue	Revue	Globe
House Guest	Francis Durbridge	Savoy
Quartermaine's Terms	Simon Gray	Queen's
Smash!	Jack Rosenthal	Tour

1982

Noises Off	Michael Frayn	Lyric Hammersmith/ Savoy
Season's Greetings	Alan Ayckbourn	Apollo
Funny Turns	Victoria Wood & Geoff Durham	Duchess
The Real Thing	Tom Stoppard	Strand

1983

The Hard Shoulder	Stephen Fagan	Aldwych

1984

Benefactors	Michael Frayn	Vaudeville

1985

Why Me?	Stanley Price	Strand
Jumpers	Tom Stoppard	Aldwych
Look, No Hans!	Michael Pertwee & John Chapman	Strand
Who Plays Wins	Revue	Vaudeville

1986

Made In Bangkok	Anthony Minghella	Aldwych
Woman in Mind	Alan Ayckbourn	Vaudeville
Kafka's Dick	Alan Bennett	Royal Court

1988

Hapgood	Tom Stoppard	Aldwych
Uncle Vanya	Chekhov/Michael Frayn	Vaudeville
Re:Joyce!	Revue	Fortune
The Sneeze	Chekhov/Michael Frayn	Aldwych
Henceforward ...	Alan Ayckbourn	Vaudeville

1989

Re:Joyce!	Revue	Vaudeville
The Cherry Orchard	Chekhov/Michael Frayn	Aldwych

1990

Man Of The Moment	Alan Ayckbourn	Globe
Look Look	Michael Frayn	Aldwych
Hidden Laughter	Simon Gray	Vaudeville
Private Lives	Noël Coward	Aldwych

Ladies Night	Stephen Sinclair & Anthony McCarten	Wimbledon

1991

Re:Joyce!	Revue	Vaudeville
What the Butler Saw	Joe Orton	Wyndham's (Hampstead 1990)
70 Girls 70	Kander & Ebb	Vaudeville (Chichester 1990)
The Revengers' Comedies I & II	Alan Ayckbourn	Strand
Ladies Night	Stephen Sinclair & Anthony McCarten	Tour
Hidden Laughter	Simon Gray	Tour

1992

The Rise and Fall of Little Voice	Jin Cartwright	R.N.T. & Aldwych
Ladies Night	Stephen Sinclair & Anthony McCarten	Tour

1993

Re:Joyce!	Revue	Tour
Time of My Life	Alan Ayckbourn	Tour & Vaudeville
Jamais Vu	Ken Campbell	Cottesloe & Vaudeville

1994

Kit And The Widow's January Sale		Kit & The Widow Vaudeville
Dead Funny	Terry Johnson	Hampstead/ Vaudeville/Savoy
Arcadia	Tom Stoppard	Theatre Royal Haymarket (RNT 1993)
The Sisters Rosensweig	Wendy Wasserstein	Greenwich & The Old Vic

1995

Indian Ink	Tom Stoppard	Aldwych
The Killing of Sister George	Frank Marcus	Guildford/Tour & Ambassadors
Killer Joe	Tracy Letts	Bush & Vaudeville
Dealer's Choice	Patrick Marber	Cottesloe & Vaudeville
The Shakespeare Revue	Revue	The Pit & Vaudeville

1996

A Talent To Amuse	Peter Greenwell (Noël Coward)	Vaudeville

1997

Tom & Clem	Stephen Churchett	Aldwych
Silhouette	Simon Brett	Guildford & Tour
Heritage	Stephen Churchett	Hampstead & Tour

1998

Things We Do For Love	Alan Ayckbourn	Guildford/Gielgud/ Duchess

Elton John's Glasses	David Farr	Watford/Tour/ Queens
Alarms & Excursions	Michael Frayn	Guildford/Tour/ Gielgud
The Invention Of Love	Tom Stoppard	Haymarket

1999

Copenhagen	Michael Frayn	Cottesloe & Duchess
Quartet	Ronald Harwood	Guildford/Tour/ Albery
Comic Potential	Alan Ayckbourn	Guildford & Lyric

2000

| Peggy For You | Alan Plater | Hampstead & Comedy |

2001

| blue/orange | Joe Penhall | Cottesloe & Duchess |

2002

Life After George	Hannie Rayson	Guildford & Duchess
Bedroom Farce	Alan Ayckbourn	Guildford & Aldwych
Damsels in Distress	Alan Ayckbourn	Tour & Duchess

2003

| My Brilliant Divorce | Geraldine Aron | Apollo |
| Dinner | Moira Buffini | Wyndham's |

2004

| Democracy | Michael Frayn | Wyndham's |

2005

Ying Tong	Roy Smiles	New Ambassadors
Losing Louis	Simon Mendes Da Costa	Hampstead/ Trafalgar
Glorious!	Peter Quilter	Tour/Duchess

2006

| Losing Louis | Simon Mendes Da Costa | Tour |
| Entertaining Angels | Richard Everett | Chichester & Tour |

2007

| The Bargain | Ian Curteis | Tour |
| The Importance of Being Ernest | Oscar Wilde | Bath/Tour/Vaudeville |

2009

| Entertaining Angels | Richard Everett | Bath/Tour |

INDEX

(References in *italic* indicate an illustration in the text,
bold indicates whole chapter references)

385